VOLUME ONE
LEVIATHAN'S
RUSE

THE COMPREHENSIVE GUIDE TO THE BATTLE

...BETWEEN GOOD & EVIL

Alexander Lawrence

Published by Watchman Alexander Publications
107 Axis Deer Trail, Unit A
Hutto, TX 78634

www.WatchmanAlexander.com

Cover and interior design by the author. Back cover headshot by Dawit H. Tariku.

Paperback ISBN: 978-0-9972578-0-9
ePub ISBN: 978-0-9972578-1-6

First printing: April 2016

Printed in the United States of America

———————————————————————□

All references to chapters and verses in the Book of Enoch adhere to the numbering scheme of the eth-Cepher version® of the book.

For Amanda, my lovely and gracious bride, and my biggest supporter.
Thank you for helping me answer my calling.

CONTENTS

FOREWORD

L ike myself, you have decided to pick up *Leviathan's Ruse* by Alexander Lawrence. I would say *mazel tov*, and a job well done, but that might be overdoing it, because James 1:22 challenges us not to be just hearers of the Word, but doers. So after aligning Alexander's warnings with Scripture, as I have done, and being convinced that we are living in a time of great deception, the question is, will we or will we not take action on what we read? Before you begin this journey, I am going to tell you a little bit about Alexander. I will also help alleviate any trepidation about digging into eschatological (end-time) studies. Finally, I will wrap up with why I believe this book is relevant.

Some of you have already realized that our world is spiraling downward (2 Timothy 3:13). Once-in-a-lifetime events are happening frequently. The truth is, sooner or later this roller coaster ride will stop—but no exact dates will be set in this book (Mathew 24:36), and you will not be left feeling fearful (Jeremiah 10:2). Instead, you will become aware of the deception and prepared to win the battle. So if you want to be part of the Elect, who prevail, then let's get to it.

Although Alexander lived less than an hour's drive from our house in the Washington, DC, suburbs, I did not have the pleasure of meeting him on the East Coast. He was serving in his church and designing 3-D graphics for a living while I was serving in mine and pushing snacks for Frito Lay. Yet God works in mysterious ways, and he communicated to both of us that it was time to move on. I went first, taking a job with Michelin, travelling the country, and eventually landing in Austin, Texas, where God had me plant a Messianic (Jewish and Christian) congregation. Alexander felt the push second, and after making his way down south, he began to search for a church that believes in salvation through our Messiah (Romans 10:9-10), that values biblical study (2 Timothy 2:15), and that honors the "Old" Testament equally with the "New" (2 Timothy 3:16). Not that we as a congregation are perfect or have it all figured out, but Alexander and his wife, Amanda, immediately felt right about the church I've planted, and it was as if God predestined the friendship that our families now share. So I pray you, too, enjoy your time with Alexander, as he truly is a genuine, practical, scripturally-minded guy with a lot of wisdom.

Warm fuzzies aside, which we all know guys struggle with anyway, this book is about eschatology, and end-time prophecies. If you are like me, Revelation contains the least-used pages in your bible, and those seminary classes that talked about the scary stuff… yeah, just speed-read the materials and be done with it. I implore you not to do the same with this text. It will not be as difficult as you may presume, and you will come to enjoy the peace and empowerment of knowing what to expect in the final days. As previously stated, this book is not about setting dates but equipping the reader with a map in one hand and a compass in the other. (The Book of Daniel does this as well, but those pages in my Bible are also unusually white). Alexander helped even me, a teacher, to become more interested in what we all know is already underway. It is not a question of *if*; rather, we need to be prepared for *when* the universe becomes fully unhinged, like a door off its frame. And when that time comes, it will not be as simple as running to the hardware store for tools or a new door.

This book is relevant because we live in a time of intense spiritual warfare (Ephesians 6:12), yet some people do not even know where the enemy is hiding. The biggest ruse, or trick, of the adversary is entrenching himself in many areas of our society, then deceiving us by saying that he's not there. Many of us walk right by his strongholds on a daily basis, yet fail to realize that he has our morals, ideals, and doctrines squarely in his sights. Alexander points out that one tactic of the enemy is to hide behind misleading titles, including *Lord*. "In fact, the Semitic word for Lord, *Adon*, was used in some pagan nations to refer to a variety of male gods" (page 11), and Satan would love for us to mistakenly give them homage with such. No thank you. Another, more sinister strategy Alexander identifies is the lie that "man can be God's equal and that Adam's disobedience was in fact a blessing because it set him on a path of spiritual upliftment" (pg. 145). Since Genesis, Satan has baited us with being like God, and we keep getting hooked by it! When will we learn? God is more, and knows more, than us humans. One final example is how Satan hides within modern groups, fraternities even, including the seemingly innocent Free Masons who "trace the origin of their fraternity back to Nimrod" (pg. 301). Wow, Satan sure is an effective strategist, but Alexander will help you to counter his moves.

If, after reading this book, you are moved to learn more about things to come, I encourage you to take advantage of the additional resources that Alexander will be providing. And one of the most important resources you can leverage is fellowship with like-minded believers. If you are in Central Texas, whether South of Austin, North of Killeen, West of Burnet, or East of Rockdale, I pray you visit Messiah Echad Messianic Congregation in Georgetown. At the printing of this book, M.E. is a positive, two-years-old testimony to being doers of the Word. Globally, we have touched the lives of people in over 137 countries, and locally, we are a rapidly growing community of over 100 people who serve their neighbors! We affirm that God reveals himself throughout the scriptures, from Genesis to Revelation. There are Jewish believers in our midst, who can tell you all about biblical customs, Christian types who intensely study church history, and the rest, who like to get into deep, spirit-led discussions. We are all echad, one, just as the image of God is echad.

May Adonai (the Lord) bless you and give you his Shalom (Peace).

Jonathan L. Dade
Senior Pastor (Rabbi)
Messiah Echad .org

INTRODUCTION

And what I say unto you, I say unto all: Watch. (Mark 13:37)
–Jesus of Nazareth

Something is changing, and it's not just the climate. Wherever one goes, there's a tension in the air like the foreboding that people share as they watch a fearsome storm roll in. It feels as though the whole world is on the brink of systemic failure, and no one knows what to do about it. People are nervous that the house of cards has grown far too large, and the next card will be the last. Are we headed for a collapse of unprecedented proportions, or will mankind as a whole merely stumble and carry on as always?

Every generation has had its Chicken Littles crying out that the sky is falling, but it seems as though our generation has had more than it's fair share of false alarms—think Y2K, December 2012, or *88 Reasons Why the Rapture Could be in 1988*. The public has grown weary of these needlessly upsetting predictions. People may agree that it's theoretically possible for a global cataclysm to ensue at any time, but after the umpteenth "fire drill" in a row, the folks in the building eventually stop filing out at the sound of the alarm. Today, even though we have more disturbing signs than ever, and more heralds sounding their horns, fewer and fewer people are actually listening. They've become numb to the noise and perhaps even resigned to what may come. In fact, so many supposed experts have said for so many years that the end is just around the corner, that many people now shy away completely from any discussion of Armageddon. Yet this book is about just that: the End. Not the end of time, mind you, but the end of the age. Don't worry, I won't be setting any dates. The value of this book is to expose the devil's schemes, not to place timestamps. However, we can estimate our general position on the timeline by surveying the landscape.

Our culture looks upon so-called Doomsday Prophets with a mix of pity and contempt, and that makes writing a book like this one an act of sheer folly if what it presents is founded on anything less than immutable truth. If it were not for the staunch assurance of the Holy Bible that the world will *not* continue on as it has until now, I would scarcely believe in a near-future doomsday. I might brace myself for another World War or significant loss of life from natural disasters, but not the end of the world as we know it.

However, the Bible clearly teaches that our current world is destined for an overhaul, and that the transition will not be a pleasant one. According to the word of God, the sins of this world are heaping up to heaven, tainting and destroying everything here below, and just when it seems that things can't get any worse, the creator of the universe will intervene. There must be a reckoning for the unrighteous before the kingdom of God can come in its fullness.

Even non-Christians believe that some type of widespread chaos is soon to descend on us. Though they are not expecting biblical plagues and the subsequent return of Messiah, they do expect the birth of a new world, and they realize that the delivery will be painful. As a result, an inordinate amount of books, blogs, and documentaries concerned with global catastrophe have come forth in recent history. Is there something to all the fuss? When we look around us, what do we see?

Perhaps the best barometer is the state of the Middle East, and Israel in particular. The United Nations spends nearly a third of its time focusing on Israeli relations and policies, which is a humorously disproportionate amount. Israel is tiny! Who would have thought that such a seemingly insignificant place would occupy the spotlight on the global stage?

God thought it, in fact. He foretold through the prophet Ezekiel that Israel would be reborn as a nation in the latter days and that she would be a "cup of trembling" and a "burdensome stone" for the nations (Zech. 12:2-6). Israel may be small, but she is the rightful tenant on God's land—even though she is temporarily apostate—and the world will be continually frustrated in its efforts to deal with her.

U.S. Secretary of State John Kerry worked long and hard during President Barak Obama's second term to mediate an agreement between the Israelis and Palestinians. He had believed that a deal would be reached by April 2014, but talks failed after the PLO and Hamas made an agreement with one another to form a new, united government.[1] But the Obama administration is not giving up, and the President is contemplating asking the United Nations to force a two-state solution.[2] This is terrible news for America, and here's why:

I will gather all nations and bring them down to the Valley of Jehoshaphat. There **I will put them on trial** for what they did to my inheritance, my people Israel, because they scattered my people among the nations and **divided up my land**... (Joel 3:2, emphasis added)

God considers Israel to be his inheritance and the land of Israel to be his land, and he will bring judgment on anyone who divides up for men what belongs to God. When God called the Jewish patriarch Abraham into an everlasting covenant, God promised to bless those who bless the family of Abraham and curse those who curse them (Gen. 12:3; cf. Gen. 27:29). This promise was reiterated through the prophecy of Balaam when the spirit of God came upon him (Num. 24:1–9). Until recently, America has been on the blessing end of that deal because of our support of the Jews. Unfortunately, that began to change in the early nineties when the first Bush administration proposed that Israel give up land for peace. Since then, America has been hit with a severe natural disaster on the heels of every official move to divide Israel. This has happened at least ten times since 1991![3] The last instance was April 19, 2010, when the Obama administration announced that they would no longer automatically stand with Israel in the U.N. Security Council. It was the first time that America had refused to back its long-standing, Mid-East ally. The very next day, BP's Deepwater Horizon oil rig exploded, flooding the Gulf of Mexico with crude in one of the worst man-made environmental disasters of all time. What will happen when we finally force Israel into giving up large portions of Jerusalem and its western territory to the enemies of God? True, many of the Jews living in Israel are presently enemies of God, but not all of them are. Some are still interested in knowing and obeying Adonai, although these faithful are, as the apostle Paul said, temporarily blinded regarding the Messiah.

Meanwhile, in happier news, a growing number of Israelis are becoming open to the Way. This shift is due in part to evangelistic efforts and in part to the proclamation of the late Rabbi Yitzhak Kaduri. Kaduri was for many years the most venerated ultra-orthodox rabbi in Israel. In 2004, he claimed to have seen the face of the Messiah in a vision, and he wrote the name of the man in a letter which was sealed until a year after Kaduri's death. The note was read in 2007; it stated that the Messiah was named Yeshua (Jesus). One can imagine the shockwave that resulted from that announcement. Just a few months before his death at the age of 108, Kaduri prophesied that the Messiah would come shortly after the death of Ariel Sharon.[4] At the time, Prime Minister Sharon did not exhibit signs of ill health, yet he inexplicably fell into a coma only two months later.[a] Sharon remianed in a vegetative state until his death in January 2014. If the vision which the elderly Kaduri received was a true one, then we are close indeed to the return of the Messiah.

One of the most prophetically significant things going on in Israel is related to the Jewish temple; the citizens of Jerusalem are all abuzz with the possibility of the rebuilding of the Holy Temple, which has been lost to them for centuries.[b] In Jerusalem there exists an organization, the Temple Institute, which is dedicated to every aspect of the Biblical commandments regarding the Holy Temple on Mount Moriah. Towards that end, the Institute has created the altar and all of the sacred vessels and priestly garments to the exact specifications found in the Torah. They've even procured a rare red heifer without blemish, the ashes of which are essential to the operation of the Temple. If the third Temple were to be built tomorrow, the priests could begin service immediately. Why is that important? Because the third Temple plays a key role in end-times prophecy; the Antichrist will at some point stop the daily sacrifices and set up an abominable idol inside the Temple.

Additionally, we are approaching both the 70th anniversary of Israel's rebirth and the 70th Jubilee since the Israelites entered the Promised Land. Seventy is a critical number in Bible prophecy. For example, the prophet Daniel was told that seventy *sevens* were decreed for his people to atone for wickedness, to put an end to sin, and to bring in everlasting righteousness. Some scholars interpret that oracle (like many in the Bible) as having dual fulfillment—seventy sabbatical cycles (490 years) and seventy jubilee[c] cycles (3,430 years). An angel told Daniel that the sabbatical cycles would begin at the moment of the royal decree to rebuild the city of Jerusalem, and that sixty-nine of the seventy "weeks" of years would pass before the arrival of the Messiah (Dan. 9:25). The angel also explained that after sixty-nine weeks, the Anointed One would be executed, "but not for himself" (Dan. 9:26). Then there would be a

---

[a] Sharon's lapse into coma occurred less than a year after he gave away the West Bank to the Palestinians. Many have chalked it up to divine displeasure.

[b] The Holy Temple of YHVH built by Solomon was destroyed by the Babylonians in ca. 587 BC, and the Second Temple was destroyed by the Romans in ca. AD 70.

[c] A Jubilee is the year following 7×7 years. It is the 50th year, but also the first year of the new cycle.

hiatus, and the last seven years would occur at a far future time when a contemptible ruler would enter into a treaty with Israel.

We know from ancient documents that Artaxerxes issued the decree to rebuild Jerusalem on March 14, 445 BC. Incredibly, if we add sixty-nine *sevens*[a] to that date, we find ourselves in the spring of AD 32, the very time of Jesus' triumphal entry into Jerusalem, when he was first publicly declared to be the Messiah.[5] Jesus the Messiah is indeed the King of the Jews, and it was declared hundreds of years in advance.

The secondary fulfillment of Daniel's prophecy may very well occur within the next decade or two because our current position in history is approximately seventy jubilees after the Jews entered Canaan. Scholars are divided as to what event marked the beginning of Israel's first Jubilee—was it when the priests first stepped foot into the Jordan, or forty-nine years after the Exodus? Even if we did know the initiating event, we might not be able to pinpoint the date associated with it. In short, we can only make an estimate, but many would argue that we're about to enter the ballpark of the 70th Jubilee.

Also, there are signs in the heavens. Pastor Mark Biltz has brought attention to a phenomenon known as a blood moon tetrad—four consecutive total lunar eclipses without any partial eclipses in-between. The tetrads which fascinate Pastor Blitz are those in which the eclipses fall precisely on the biblical holy days of Passover and Sukkot, two years in a row.[b] That kind of suspiciously well-synchronized tetrad occurred around the time of Israel's national rebirth, and again around the time when Jerusalem was recaptured. A third blood moon tetrad has recently concluded, having run from April 2014 through September 2015. Interestingly, the fourth and last lunar eclipse of the 2014–15 tetrad was the only one that was visible from Jerusalem, and it was a super moon (meaning that the moon was at its perigee). Never mind the odds of having four eclipses

---

[a] 173,880 days. Bible prophecies conform to a 360-day year because God's reckoning of a year is 360 days plus four extracalary days that are not counted. The books of Jubilees and 1 Enoch confirm this.

[b] Pastor Blitz may be right to assign significance to sets of eclipses falling on God's feast days, but I disagree with his assertion that these lunar eclipses are the fulfillment of Joel's prophecy that the moon will turn to blood before the day of the Lord (Joel 2:31). Joel's prediction that the sun will be blotted out and the moon bloodied corresponds to Jesus' description of his Second Coming (Matt. 24:29–30) and also to the 6th seal of Revelation, which falls at the end of the Great Tribulation. The sun will not be blocked from view, as in an eclipse, but will actually cease to shine; and the moon will not be tinted red, as we perceive during an eclipse, but will literally become coated in crimson fluid.

on pairs of particular holy days; the statistical probability of having a full moon at perigee at eclipse position on Sukkot and visible from Jerusalem is way beyond random chance.[a] Furthermore, the last tetrad was the only one to be flanked by symmetrically-spaced lunar eclipse triads, and it will be the last tetrad to synchronize with the biblical holy days until the years 2582–83. Some of the watchmen of the Christian world take these tetrads as signs that we are entering the lead-in to Daniel's 70th week, the last seven years of the age. The Torah states that every matter must be established by two or three witnesses, and we have now had three of the same type of stellar witness within seventy years.

The Gentile world also sees a significant transition at our current point in history. Many New Age practitioners believe that we are moving out of the Age of Pisces and into the Age of Aquarius, a humanitarian era of group consciousness, high technology, and global solidarity amid a so-called spiritual awakening. The Mayan Long Count calendar has completed its thirteenth *b'ak'tun*[b], meaning that we have moved into the *Fifth World*, a new era of harmony and cosmic awareness. The Maya believed that the transition into the Fifth World would be marked by a spike in immoral behavior, the fall of existing world powers, widespread war, a more active sun, and dramatic earth-changes. That list is amazing and more than a little disconcerting considering the very similar signs which Jesus described during his Olivet Discourse (Matthew 24/Mark 13/ Luke 21), as well as those found elsewhere in the Bible.

Bible prophecies indicate that earthquakes, diseases, and famines will mark the end of the age. "These," Jesus said, "are the beginning of birth pains" (Matt. 24:8). Birth pains are contractions, and they come in waves of increasing intensity. Therefore, when we see an upsurge of quakes, famines, and epidemics gradually growing more and more extreme, we will know that the delivery of the kingdom of God is very soon.

Jesus said that great earthquakes would occur in diverse places (Luke 21:11). Until recently, earthquake activity had not increased significantly over the last century, but 2014 saw a doubling in the number of major quakes[6] (not to mention the recent series of giant sinkholes opening up without warning or explanation), and activity hasn't slowed in 2015. As

---

[a] Another thing to take into consideration is that the last blood moon fell within three weeks of the end of the Shemitah (or the beginning, depending on who you ask). The Shemitah is the year of release which YHVH commanded to be observed at the end of each cycle of seven years.

[b] 144,000 days, or 400 prophetic years of 360 days each.

I write this, massive earthquakes just devastated Nepal, and many places across the U.S. that are unaccustomed to earthquakes are suddenly experiencing clusters of them. The recent uptick in quake activity could be a fluke, but even if that is the case, we cannot escape the fact that the effects of quakes have been felt more in recent decades due to the increase in population, urbanization, and globalized news coverage. Did Jesus take into account our increased ability to perceive quakes when he indicated that seismic activity would mark the last days? After all, at the time that Jesus was foretelling earthquakes in "diverse places," there was no way for men to monitor diverse places. The Lord did not mention other types of natural disasters, but those are, in fact, trending upward. According to both the United Nations Environment Programme and CRED's EM-DAT (International Disaster Database), the occurrence of natural disasters worldwide has increased almost exponentially since the 1940s (right around the time of Israel's rebirth).[7]

Weather patterns are more erratic and storms are more devastating than ever before. Hurricanes, tsunamis, and floods are extracting a heavy toll on creatures and crops, especially in densely populated coastal regions. Not only are human casualties high, but we are witnessing mass animal deaths on a frequent basis and often without explanation.[8] In August 2014 alone, there were nearly four dozen die-off reports globally—over forty-five events in one month! The prophet Hosea linked mass animal deaths to the wickedness of people, saying, "Because of this [rampant sin] the land mourns, and all who live in it waste away; the beasts of the field and the birds of the air and the fish of the sea are dying" (Hos. 4:3, NIV). That's exactly what we are seeing today.

Famines have killed over seventy million people since 1900, with the highest number of casualties occurring between the late 1920s and early 1960s.[9] Since then, we've had a bit of a reprieve, but it seems as though severe and widespread famine is just around the bend. According to a 2013 report by World Resources Institute, exponential population growth, climate change, and soil depletion will soon leave us unable to grow enough food to sustain ourselves.[10] Another reason to be expecting famine is the death of our bees due to a phenomenon called Colony Collapse Disorder. The North American Pollinator Protection Campaign estimates the loss of fifty to ninety percent of managed colonies over the last ten years.[11] The cause of CCD is uncertain (pesticides/herbicides are likely to blame), but the consequences are very certain—all that needs to be said is that a third of our food supply relies on pollination by honey bees. If not prevented, honeybee extinction will be one of the biggest catastrophes of all time. Increasing weather irregularities and natural disasters are already driving up food prices, and could very well exacerbate CCD-caused food shortages in the near future. The worst scenario would be the addition of wide-spread war to the equation, especially war of the nuclear variety.

What about epidemics that directly affect humans? Are we experiencing an increase in those? Ebola has been in the spotlight lately, but we are also contending with bubonic plague, HIV, antibiotic-resistant bacteria, increasingly virulent strains of the flu, the reemergence of measles, and more. Tuberculosis, malaria, and cholera are running rampant in Asia and the Pacific. Meanwhile, the infectious diseases known as hepatitis B and C are particular problems in Europe and North Africa. The U.S. Center for Disease Control recently reminded Americans that sexually transmitted diseases are an ongoing epidemic, with 110 million infected at any given time.[12]

In addition, there are mysterious booms and sustained noises being heard around the globe, sometimes by entire towns.[13] These haunting *skyquakes* have been compared to fog horns, brass instruments, and bending or sliding sheets of metal. They are sometimes painfully loud for minutes on end and have no discernible source.[14] My own mother recently experienced one of these skyquakes at my parents' remote mountaintop homestead. The sound she heard was a deep, very load rumbling which lasted for about four minutes. It was unlike anything she had heard before, and it understandably scared her quite a bit. Something very unusual must be happening within the earth to cause such sounds.

Our social climate is as stressed as our biological climate, with the family structure disintegrating, crime skyrocketing, and dangerously rebellious and antisocial behaviors becoming the new norm. People are progressively more selfish, and what used to be known as *evil* has been repackaged and sold to us as *good*. We in the western world are contending with terrorist acts both from foreign enemies and from within our own ranks, increasingly from our own children. Skepticism and distrust are at all-time highs. Cancer, obesity, addictions, and mental disorders are ravaging the western world, and our response is to mask the worsening symptoms with an endless variety of pharmaceuticals. To top it all off, the combination of global economic insecurity and friction in the Middle East has put us on the precipice of World War III.

Those who have not studied the Bible seriously will be surprised to learn that almost all of the above were predicted in the Holy Scriptures. God has not left us ignorant of what is to come so that we must grope through the halls of time as blind men. Rather, he has provided us with prophetic landmarks by which to navigate the otherwise unknowable future. Careful examination of the signs given in the scriptures indicates that we are entering the final years before the return of Jesus. Elohei Mishpat (the God of Justice) will not let sin reign in his creation forever, but will come soon to put an end to all wickedness and decay, as promised in his unchangeable Word.

Yet we must prepare ourselves for tribulation because a different messiah returns first, a false savior, a substitute christ who exalts himself above the Law and everything that is considered sacred. He will come in the name of Peace but will wield great power and conquer many. The Book of Revelation describes him as a beast that comes up out of the Abyss. As he rises, a great delusion will descend such as men have never seen. Regarding the last days, the apostle Paul said, "[The unrepentant] perish because they refused to love the truth and so be saved. For this reason God sends them a powerful delusion so that they will believe the lie and so that all will be condemned who have not believed the truth but have delighted in wickedness" (2 Thess. 2:10–12, NIV).

To make matters worse, the Beast will have miraculous powers that he will use to reinforce the deception that he teaches. "The coming of the lawless one will be in accordance with how Satan works. He will use all sorts of displays of power through signs and wonders that serve the lie" (2 Thess. 2:9, NIV). Were it not for the revelation of God illuminating our way, we would all suffer the effects of Satan's system of deception: it's that powerful and pervasive.

When Jesus spoke to his disciples about the end of the age, he started by saying, "Watch out that no one deceives you" (Matt. 24:4). Isn't it telling that when asked about the signs of the End, our Lord immediately zeroed in on the issue of deception? He knew that the greatest problem of that time period would be the widespread acceptance of a replacement Truth. Our quest, therefore, is to anticipate the delusion and to be ready to stand against it. As we do so, our defense lies in taking the Word of God seriously, studying it assiduously, praying passionately, and putting on the whole armor of God (Eph. 6:10–18). Part of that armor is the belt of truth, and part is the sword of the Spirit, which is the Word of God. We need both knowledge and discernment in order to cinch ourselves with truth.

There's a famous quote by John MacArthur about learning to identify counterfeits by first becoming intimately familiar with the real deal:

> Federal agents don't learn to spot counterfeit money by studying the counterfeits. They study genuine bills until they master the look of the real thing. Then when they see the bogus money they recognize it.[15]

The quote is famous because of its veracity. Wisdom instructs us to become experts at the things of God; then, when we encounter false teachings and ungodly practices, we will easily see them for what they are. This book aims to expose the works of Satan by holding them up against the teaching of Scripture. Although our journey will be guided by the Bible, we will not fail to utilize our God-given powers of deduction, nor the accumulated knowledge of hundreds of talented researchers (to whom we are greatly indebted). Anything that will help us shed light on the mystery is a good thing. Not only do we need to be able to identify who the Beast is at his coming, but we need to understand the exact nature of the lie that he will wield if we are to escape the powerful deception of the last days, and especially if we hope to open the eyes of those who are perishing so they may come to know the real Savior.

As knowledge of ancient history and pagan cults increases, and as the internet facilitates the rapid dissemination of that knowledge, we Christians are finding ourselves increasingly confronted with claims that the Bible is nothing more than a repackaged version of older myths and religious traditions, and that the exclusivity of Christian doctrine is almost criminal in light of its pagan origins. Some—but certainly not all—of these claims come from *ancient astronaut* theorists, who propose that mankind was seeded on this planet by extraterrestrials, and that religious myths are primarily the result of primitive humans viewing aliens as gods and misinterpreting advanced technology as magic (the *History* channel has become notorious for giving these theorists a platform). When hit with such accusations, most Christians are woefully unprepared to combat it. We may have strength of resolve, but many of us lack knowledge. It's absolutely critical that we vaccinate ourselves against this plague now, before the silver-tongued Antichrist arrives and infects the whole world with it simultaneously through mass media.

My fervent hope is that through my written words the people of God may be equipped to weather the coming storm, propelled out of lukewarm lifestyles, and emboldened to rescue many sheep from slaughter.

We are nearing the final scene; Jesus approaches the stage. Now is not the time to be complacent, but to get right with God and fellows, to live in light of eternity, and to store up treasures in heaven. May the Holy Spirit usher every reader into a richer, stronger relationship with the redeeming Son of God and an unshakable confidence in him. May we all stand strong until the end.

A quick note about the Hebrew names found herein: for the remainder of this book you will see Jesus the Christ referred to as *Yeshua ha-Mashiach,* and the Godhead as *YHVH.* I prefer to use the original Hebrew names as a sign of respect to the one who has revealed them, and because they hold special meaning not found in the English.

Yeshua literally means "YHVH saves." It is the Aramaic version of the name Yehoshua, and since Yeshua's family spoke Aramaic, it is the name by which our Savior would have been known during his lifetime. The Old Testament character known to us as Joshua actually had the same Hebrew name as Jesus—Yehoshua—and that truly solidifies the prophetic tie between the two men. There is, of course, nothing wrong with calling the Messiah *Jesus* if that is your preference.

Occasionally you will see *Elohiym* (pronounced "el-oh-HEEM") as a reference to God within these pages. This is a Hebrew title for deity, and not a proper name. It signifies power and justice.

English Bibles usually translate the name of God as Lord (in small capitals), but this is quite misleading, as *lord* is a title that could be applied to any ruler. In fact, the Semitic word for lord, *adon,* was used in some pagan nations to refer a variety of male gods. YHVH is God's personal name in the Old Testament, and it was used over 6,800 times. Unfortunately, the exact pronunciation of this name has been lost to time, but we do know that it does not begin with a *J* sound, as in Jehovah.

The four letters that comprise God's name can be used to form the phrase *hayah hoveh yi'yeh,* "He was, He is, He will be," which parallels the answer given to Moses when he asked for God's name at the burning bush: "I AM THAT I AM."

More amazingly, the proto-Hebrew form of the letters reveal the very identity of Messiah. *Yod* means "hand," *Hey* means "behold," and *Vav* means "nail." So Yod-Hey-Vav-Hey translates as "behold the hand, behold the nail." Who is the right hand of God, and whose hands were pierced by nails? The Bible really is all about Yeshua!

ONE

A Clearer View

When a well-packaged web of lies has been sold gradually to the masses over generations, the truth will seem utterly preposterous and its speaker a raving lunatic.
    –ATTRIBUTED TO DONALD JAMES WHEAL (1931–2008)

Most ignorance is vincible ignorance. We don't know because we don't want to know.[16]
    –ALDOUS HUXLEY (1894–1963)

The Christian world hardly needs another book on eschatology[a]. Many and diverse tomes have been written concerning the interpretation of the biblical prophecies that deal with Earth's last days, and this author has been blessed by many of them. What's largely absent from existing offerings, however, is a broader survey of history that connects the first days to the last and that purposes to reconcile the whole Bible—even obscure portions such as descriptions of Leviathan and the Abyss—with discoveries made by the secular world. When we take a systematic approach, it is even possible to fit within our biblical worldview the odd but persistent mysteries of life that Christian teachers usually shy away from. There is so much concerning our history and destiny that is hidden just out of sight, and it is well worth our time to search for that hidden treasure. Wise King Solomon said it this way: "It is the glory of God to conceal a thing, but the honor of kings to search it out" (Prov. 25:2).

What's needed now is a Grand Unified Theory of human history and the unseen forces that propel it, but only such a theory as is founded on traditional biblical doctrine. It must decipher the riddles of mankind's story and wrangle the outlying phenomena of human experience that

---

[a] Eschatology is the branch of theology concerned with the end-times.

defy integration with our current philosophy, all while remaining true to the teaching of the Word of God. And it must help us to understand where we as a race are going by telling the tale of our collectively forgotten past. As it is said, those who forget the past are doomed to repeat it. And God has spoken: "My people are destroyed for lack of knowledge [of the truth]" (Hos. 4:6).

God wants us to have the Big Picture. He has provided all of the pieces of the puzzle, but we have to put them together. This book is your guide to that process.

What if it were revealed that the greatest mysteries of all ages are not disconnected, but interrelated? What if megalithic structures, unexplained artifacts, astronomy and astrology, magic, UFOs and abduction reports, crop circles, ancient cave paintings, secret societies, numerology, mythology, demonology, sacred geometry, hauntings, the netherworld, eugenics, Atlantis, and Bible prophecy could all be woven together to form a tapestry that tells a story so earth-shaking that it has the power to rewrite our worldview? Would you, reader, be willing to expand your horizons in the light of such a revelation?

In fact, all of the topics listed above and more do fit together, and upon seeing the whole, one wonders how the significance of the individual pieces could have been missed. Why are more people not aware of the connections? The problem is five-fold: (1) The behind-the-scenes elements of our world seem irrelevant or impenetrable; (2) Critical information is withheld from us, often purposefully; (3) We are socially programmed to disregard anything that smacks of conspiracy theory; (4) We think we already know it all; (5) We are afraid.

Issue Number One: Filtering

Humans are masters at ignoring things. We have to be. For the most part, filtering inputs is highly beneficial to our ability to operate in a manner that maximizes survival. Our environment throws a gargantuan amount of data at us in a plethora of formats every day; without the power to downplay less relevant information, we would all drown in a sea of neuro-clutter (say thank you to your pre-frontal cortex). The situation has only become more extreme in the last century as we've come into the information age, where our access to a wide spectrum of data is unprecedented. Thanks to the internet, modern media, electronic publications, and easier access to higher levels of academia, we are inundated with knowledge. But what are we to do with it all? Our brains must continually assign relevance to incoming data in order to catalog each item for storage. Such cataloging is more automated than purposeful, and its method is based on a framework of values which we construct over the years of our lives. That framework is literally the network of neural pathways which grow into a certain pattern as we experience situations and associate them with feelings and emotions. If our brain labels a given item as having little relevance within the established neural network, no matter how interesting or curious that item may be in and of itself, then we will not be motivated to expend time and energy integrating it into our system. So, while content filtering keeps us sane, it can also work against us. It's too much effort, our brains tell us, to deal with issues that seem far removed from our daily experience. Why exert ourselves solving the great mysteries of this world when we could more easily ignore them and continue on with our lives, unaffected? After all, ignorance is bliss. This is the reason that many otherwise responsible people pay little attention to politics. Despite the fact that the more advanced parts of their brains understand that they should be concerned about the operation of the political system on which they depend, the primitive parts of their brains convince them that there are more important things to worry about. People do become more interested in politics when the decisions of the bureaucracy begin to greatly alter their lifestyle at a noticeable rate. When that happens, citizens suddenly want to be involved—of course, by that time it could be too late to turn the ship around. Thankfully, we have a choice. We can choose from day to day not to take the path of least resistance, but to search diligently for the truth because we realize that there is more going on in this world than meets the eye. We can choose to educate ourselves.

Issue Number Two: Ignorance

We're being kept in the dark. For evidence of that, we need look no further than news reports from 2013 which exposed that the NSA has been spying on both US citizens and foreign dignitaries without permission.[17] We were lied to about Benghazi, we were lied to about IRS practices, we were lied to about weapons of mass destruction in Iraq, we were lied to about Iran-Contra, and on and on and on. Even the agency whose sole duty it is to protect Americans' collective health, the Food and Drug Administration, is guilty on multiple counts of malpractice.[18] One must wonder: if bureaucrats will cover up activities that threaten not only our constitutional rights, but our physical well-being...then what *won't* they hide? When they want to take an ethically questionable course of action and they can't hide what they are doing, they will instead twist the facts, re-frame the story, and appeal to our emotions while assuring us that their actions are for the collective good. Don't get me wrong, there are some genuinely honorable folks in the U.S. government, but there aren't enough of them to outweigh the crooks. Following the release of the Pentagon Papers in 1971, former White House chief of staff H. R. Haldeman commented, "You can't trust the government, you can't believe what they say, and you can't rely on their judgment."[19]

Even within academia, not all knowledge is brought into the open. Despite the fact that the rules of science demand the re-evaluation of theories in light of new evidence, not everyone is happy to have prior assumptions challenged. It has become common practice in certain circles to dismiss out-of-hand any evidence that lies outside the accepted paradigm. Experts in many fields will scoff at the suggestion that some academics are suppressing knowledge, yet the fact is that clandestine efforts to misrepresent history, discredit unpopular research, or hide challenging evidence have been exposed on multiple occasions. Case in point: Piltdown Man. A fossilized male skull was paraded for decades as important evidence supporting evolution, yet was revealed in 1953 to be a forgery produced by combining human and orangutan bones.[20] Similarly, the celebrated dino-bird *Archaeoraptor liaoningensis*, a supposed transitional fossil, was revealed to be a hoax.[21] Another example of academic dishonesty involved one of Japan's most accomplished archaeologists, Shinichi Fujimura, who was caught on tape planting stoneware pieces in the Kamitakamori ruins.[22] More recently, the University of Frankfort's Professor Reiner Protsch von Zieten falsified the dating of

Neanderthal skulls.[23] Or how about this one: Dozens of historical sites around New Zealand testify that the island was settled before the arrival of the indigenous Maori—who were greeted upon arrival by a race of red-haired, fair-skinned people, according to their own oral histories— yet the government has slapped embargoes on the scientific findings, and historians have flippantly dismissed all speculation of pre-Maori civilization.[24] Given these kinds of scenarios, we can hardly be expected to put our full faith in the scientific community.

And let us not forget: Science once believed that the body contains four humors, that saturated fats are unhealthy, and that the continents are im- movable. Whether due to honest mistakes, false assumptions, treachery, or blind adherence to an agenda, experts are bound to get things wrong from time to time. This should motivate us to question our ideology, to wonder what we don't know, and to keep an open mind.

Speaking of keeping an open mind, it should be said that some of the subject matter contained within these pages will seem outlandish. It may be so far removed from normal experience that one's gut reaction will be premature dismissal. Rest assured that this author is not interested in telling tall tales, but sometimes truth really is stranger than fiction. Pains have been taken to ensure that all research contained herein is accurate and trustworthy; nonetheless, the ultimate responsibility for verifying these things falls upon the reader. Don't be afraid to do some sleuthing of your own. As the apostle Paul instructed: "Test all things; hold fast that which is true" (1 Thess. 5:21).

Issue Number Three: Social Programming

Most folks don't want to be lumped in with the crazies, so we distance ourselves from ideas that come with a social stigma attached. Without a doubt, there are some individuals who will believe anything and who seem unable to listen to reason, but not all theorists are sensationalists, and the wise among them will not give heed to every wild idea that comes along. Experience teaches us to treat everything with a healthy dose of skepticism. We want to avoid falling prey to the tendency to grasp at unsubstantiated explanations for events, which we do because possess- ing special knowledge makes us feel less helpless in the midst of an often frightening world. Nonetheless, after examining all claims with a critical eye, there are some incidents which can only be classified as conspiratorial in nature. Consider the Dreyfus Affair, or Enron, or Watergate, or the asbestos coverup, or the burning of the Circus Maximus by Emperor Nero... the list of uncovered scandals and conspiracies is extensive.

Writers Christopher Knight and Alan Butler have this to say about conspiracies:

> There is nothing remotely odd about conspiracy. It is merely two or more people acting together in an undeclared way to bring benefit to themselves—and perhaps others.... The key component is simply secrecy. Did Bernard Madoff act alone in his Ponzi scheme that lifted billions of dollars from the wallets of the wealthy? If he was not acting alone, then it was obviously a conspiracy of embezzlement. We feel sure that Madoff would have been a keen denier of conspiracies.[25]

Unfortunately, after we've seen enough well-educated people shaking their heads at supposed conspiracies (many of which really are loony), we become shy about searching beneath the surface because we don't want to be labeled as gullible or, worse, as unstable. "No tin-foil hats needed here," we assure the world. The solution? We stop worrying so much about what other people think, and worry about what is true.

The truth is, not only are small-scale conspiracies hatched from time to time, but an all-encompassing conspiracy against God and his creatures has been carefully and diligently implemented in shadow down through the generations. Human beings are not the masterminds, but the puppets. Yeshua told the Jews who stubbornly opposed him: "You are of your father the devil, and your will is to do your father's desires" (John 8:44). We only directly perceive the human element, thus we tend to believe that human desires alone are to blame when plots are exposed. But is that always the case? Concerning the plot of the disciple Judas to deliver Yeshua to the Sanhedrin, John wrote, "As soon as Judas took the bread, Satan entered into him. So the Lord told him, 'What you are about to do, do quickly'" (John 13:37). Similarly, we see in 1 Chronicles 21 that "Satan stood up against Israel and incited David to number [the populace]" (v. 1). In this instance the word Satan, meaning "adversary," is preceded by an indefinite article, so the proper rendering is "an adversary stood up against Israel." It could have been Satan, or it could have been another devil. Had the prophet not exposed the adversarial spirit as the driving force behind the king's action, we would not suspect that it was anything other than a foolish act[a] of human will.

If, like Dorothy and her gang, we want to see what is happening behind the curtain, we must first acknowledge that there are dark spiritual forces at work in the world. They are real, powerful, and insidious, and they manipulate spiritually defenseless people to accomplish their goals. "Be self-controlled and alert. Your adversary, the devil, prowls around like a roaring lion, seeking whom he may devour" (1 Pet. 5:8). *Devour* in this instance does not mean to eliminate, but to dominate. Peter wants us to realize that if we leave an opening through sin or disbelief, devils can influence us, twisting our thinking until we are subservient to their desires. Paul's instruction to Timothy was in accordance with Peter's warning, for he wrote that some Christians would be drawn away from proper behavior, yet "God may perhaps grant that they will repent and come to know the truth, and they may escape from the snare of the devil after being captured by him to do his will" (2 Tim. 2:26). There is no shortage of Christians in the modern world who have been captured by the devil as a result of indulging in secular activities and ways of thinking. That being the case, how much more easily are devils able to manipulate unbelievers into carrying out satanic designs?

Also, Satan has done a superb job of guiding many people in the West into either a naturalist philosophy which denies the supernatural altogether or a candy-coated spirituality which focuses solely on positive aspects like love and peace while ignoring the fact that we are in a spiritual war. As of September 2013, only slightly more than half of Americans believed that Satan exists.[26] Such denial is good for the devil, since people can't oppose what they don't acknowledge.

If you, reader, have been blind to the reality of spiritual warfare, it's time to take off the blindfold. There is no reason to believe that fallen angels are any less active today than they were during ancient history. One could argue that their tactics have shifted since the spread of Christianity, and especially since the Age of Reason. Regardless, we need to realize that evil entities and their followers are working hard just out of sight, and they will continue to carry out their plan to enslave humanity through a system of lies for as long as God allows.

---

[a] This does not imply that David was not accountable for his action. Devils play on the impure motives that already exist in human hearts, and humans remain responsible for the condition of their hearts and their failure to seek help from YHVH.

Issue Number Four: Pride

Some of us think we know it all, and pride won't let us consider otherwise. In order to accept the premise that most of the world is deceived, we first have to admit that we've been outwitted for our entire lives. That leads to self-accusation on charges of gullibility, naïveté, and obliviousness, and the courtroom of the mind is a loathsome station.

Some of us see more clearly than others, but none of us are immune to deception. It's okay to admit that we don't know it all and that we aren't smarter than our spiritual adversaries. The only shame lies in not changing direction once we know that we're off course.

As astronomer Carl Sagan observes, "One of the saddest lessons of history is this: If we've been bamboozled long enough, we tend to reject any evidence of the bamboozle."[27] We lose the motivation to try thinking any other way. The effect is akin to walking a well-trodden path, which is the path of least resistance. Almost no one is willing to expend the effort to leave the established path, even if that path leads nowhere good.

King Solomon said, "The way of a fool is right in his own eyes: but he that hearkeneth unto counsel is wise" (Prov. 12:15). While the pain of admitting that we've been credulous may be great, the pain of being foolish is eventually much greater. As wise children of the Lord, we should take heed of good counsel and reorder our steps accordingly.

Issue Number Five: Fear

We human beings are very scared.

We fear the unknown; the new things we encounter may be more than we can handle.

We fear change; our situation could get worse rather that better.

We fear increased responsibility; it isn't easy to be entrusted with valuable information because "to whom much has been given, much shall be required" (Luke 12:48).

We fear being mistaken; our pride could be hurt if we espouse something unpopular or untrue.

The list of things we fear is practically endless, and it's a wonder that we aren't all in a perpetual state of paralysis. Maybe we're able to keep moving because we've put on blinders. Denial can be an effective tool of defense against the frightening and overwhelming parts of life. Unfortunately, it keeps us from addressing problems that need addressing. Humans are masters at keeping our heads in the sand, and for proof of that, look at the standard American diet and lack of exercise. Obesity has become an epidemic in America because many among us deny the importance of maintaining a proper diet and engaging in strenuous activity. Likewise, some Christians deny the importance of being well-informed, worldly-wise (but innocent), and culturally relevant, and of actively combating the increasing intolerance of all things Judeo-Christian. That kind of denial is destructive, and it can be hard to identify because the degeneration is gradual. Nevertheless, we must confront our problems or else slowly perish.

This book is intended to get us to a better state by exposing lies, fallacies, and conspiracies, and equipping us with little-known but useful information. Doing so will involve confronting a few harsh realities. If you wish to remain (temporarily) blissfully ignorant, feel free to put the book down now, but a better choice is to trust in the fact that Christians needn't be afraid of hard truths.

Listen, loved ones: Our God is bigger than all the fearful things out there, combined!

Throughout the many books of the Bible, God instructs his people again and again not to fear: What's that? Pharaoh's army is encroaching like a swarm of locusts? Have no fear—I am the Lord of Hosts. The residents of the Promised Land are mighty giants? Don't sweat it—they are but gnats in my eyes. The Babylonians are plotting to exterminate the Jews? No cause for worry—I am more crafty than man.

When all variations of the command to not be afraid are added together, they total 365—one for every day of the year. Someone should make a daily devotional book of those verses, because fear is our most relentless internal enemy.

Satan understands how much we can accomplish in Christ when we are properly equipped and motivated, and he will strive to keep us mired in fear so that we don't act. But when we become fully aware of God's faithfulness, power, and love, and our identity as members of his family, we will not be afraid. God is Love, and "perfect love casts out fear" (1 John 4:18).

Our ultimate goal during this journey in ink is to understand the ungodly, mysterious, and multifaceted system of Babylon—its origins, its evolution, and its final incarnation. By the time we are finished, the forked tongue of Babylon's mastermind will have lost its power to confuse and intimidate us. But in order to get to that point, we will have to lay down a lot of track, and it may at times seem that we are headed nowhere. Have faith; persistence will pay off in spades.

Honestly, the book you hold in your hands does not make for quick or easy reading. We have a lot of ground to cover, and the sheer volume of information may at times be overwhelming. But stick with it, and don't give up! You owe it to yourself to be informed, because information is power.

Remember what Yeshua told his disciples: "Behold, I send you forth as sheep in the midst of wolves: be ye therefore wise as serpents, and harmless as doves" (Matt. 10:16).

Before going any further, we need to talk about the Rapture. Some Christian readers are no doubt wondering why we should concern ourselves with learning about the ancient installment and final outworking of Satan's agenda when we won't be present for the climax. If, as put forth in the preface, we are on the cusp of the Great Tribulation, won't we be raptured soon? (In that case, this book might have worth to anyone who becomes a believer after the Rapture, but disciples of Messiah living before that event would have less motivation to study it.) The argument is valid, but what if the premise is flawed?

What if the idea of a pre-Tribulation removal of the saints is plain rubbish?

Does the Bible actually teach a gathering up of the saints[a] before all of the apocalyptic events of the last days? The numerous adherents of popular premillennialism would assure us that it does, but eighteen hundred years worth of Christian scholars would beg to differ. Dissecting the issue will require a chapter unto itself.

---

[a] Despite Roman Catholic convention, saints are not just Christians who have led particularly holy lives. The New Testament labels as saints all those who are redeemed. All true disciples of Messiah Yeshua are saints (Acts 9:32; Eph. 4:12, 5:3; Phil. 4:21).

Wishful Thinking

Come now, and let us reason together. (Isa. 1:18)
–YHVH

The doctrine of a pre-Tribulation Rapture is held dear by many good and learned Christians, and so it is with appropriate humility that I challenge its validity. Nevertheless, my duty is not to please men, but to please Adonai, and he would not be pleased if I taught anything other than what I see in his Word. What I see is not a secret snatching away of Christians seven years before the Millennium, but a late-Tribulation, pre-Wrath resurrection at the time our Lord's return, 1,290 days after the Abomination of Desolation is set up in the Holy Temple. I have great concern that the Church has been mistakenly led to embrace an escapist fantasy that contradicts emphatic New Testament instructions to prepare ourselves for at least seven years of suffering.

Soft Saints

In 1974, Holocaust survivor Corrie Ten Boom wrote a letter to Christendom warning against the false teaching of a pre-Tribulation Rapture. In that letter she lamented over the many Chinese Christians who were unprepared when Mao Tse Tung leveled great persecution upon them. She heard a Bishop from China say,

> We have failed. We should have made the people strong for persecution, rather than telling them Jesus would come first. Tell the people how to be strong in times of persecution, how to stand when the tribulation comes, to stand and not faint.[28]

How many young Christians who have been taught that they will escape the hard days ahead might fall away from the faith when they find themselves in the midst of severe tribulation instead of having been yanked out of it? Most Western Christians have never undergone any kind of physical persecution for their faith, so imagine how shocking it will be when they are suddenly thrust into the worst tribulation in history.

The Book of Revelation tells us that the Dragon will wage war against those who hold to the testimony of Yeshua and also that the Beast will be given authority to overcome the saints. How many first-world Christians are spiritually equipped to deal with that reality? Yeshua warned us that some believers are like seeds which are sown on hard soil and receive the Gospel with joy but do not put down good roots, "and when tribulation or persecution arises on account of the word, immediately he falls away" (Matt. 13:21).

Sadly, worldly-wise Christians in the pampered West have shallow roots and are thus spiritually emaciated. We have been groomed to operate in a system of materialism which drives us mercilessly into a life-long pursuit of happiness (read: comfort, abundant possessions, and immediate gratification), displacing the pursuit of God. In accordance with this anti-Christian system of Mammon, many prominent religious leaders—more *positivity peddlers* than Gospel preachers—have become wealthy by spreading a happy-go-lucky Christianity. The pre-Trib view helps such teachers draw crowds because it comforts congregants with the idea that they can altogether escape suffering.

This version of eschatology has strong synchronicity with the currently favored salvation formula, which asserts that anyone who asks Jesus into their heart by praying a prayer will receive permanent salvation. Supposedly, if the person who prayed was genuine in that moment, they are set for life. No matter what they do after that point, they are going to heaven, even if they are apathetic towards God and bear no fruit. This is very disconcerting for any intellectually honest student of the Bible because the scriptures clearly teach (when taken as a whole and in context) that believers can walk away from the Faith and give up their salvation (Matt. 13:3–23, 24:13; Rom. 11:20–22; 1 Tim. 4:1; Heb. 6:4:–6, 10:26–31; 2 Pet. 2:20–22). Just because we received a free gift from God at one point in our lives doesn't mean that we can't give it back[a]. When we look at it that

---

[a] Is there such a thing as election? Yes, but it helps us to understand how God works, not how man works. We will keep our discussion in the exoteric realm.

way, we understand why the command to stand firm is reiterated dozens of times throughout the Bible. Let us not forget that many unrepentant sinners who professed Christianity will hear Yeshua say to them on the Day of Judgment, "I never knew you; depart from me, you workers of lawlessness" (Matt. 7:19–23).

This is not to say that the *sinner's prayer* has never gotten anyone saved by starting them on a walk of discipleship. Many genuine Christians will testify otherwise. But there is also no shortage of false converts as a result of people being led in such a prayer only to discover later that they didn't really want to change. When Yeshua called people into the Kingdom, he called for more than words—he demanded action and obedience. Doesn't the New Testament tell us to work out our salvation with fear and trembling (Phil. 2:12)? Salvation does not come by saying words as in a magic spell, but rather in full repentance, public confession, and abiding faith. The fruit of that faith, consequently, is the process of making amends for our sins and proceeding to do good works.

Ask yourself: is the Gospel of the kingdom of God proceeding forth with power from our congregations in a manner that brings holistic change? For most of us, the answer is no. Why not? Because the combination of teaching easy salvation and easy escape makes for shallow soil where little can grow. Most of us just can't be bothered to pour ourselves fully into the kind of discipleship that produces good growth, because we're too busy making comfy lives for ourselves.

Yeshua didn't take on flesh and suffer horribly so that we all could have a real nice time 'til kingdom come. Mashiach Adonai did not redeem us to live high on the hog, but to hang high on a cross (Gal. 2:20). Much suffering will be required of us if we are genuinely walking as disciples.

In the world **you will have tribulation**, but be of good cheer—I have overcome the world. (John 16:33)

Join with me in suffering, like a good soldier of Christ Jesus. (2 Tim. 2:3)

We must **through much tribulation** enter into the kingdom of God. (Acts 14:22)

Dear friends, **do not be surprised at the fiery ordeal** that has come on you to test you, as though something strange were happening to you. But rejoice inasmuch as you participate in the sufferings of Christ, so that you may be overjoyed when His glory is revealed. (1 Pet. 4:13)

[He] comforts us **in all our tribulation**, that we may be able to comfort those who are in any trouble. (2 Cor. 1:4)

I, John, your brother and **companion in the suffering** and kingdom and patient endurance that are ours in Jesus... (Rev. 1:9)

As these verses make clear, the Christian life is not supposed to be a walk in the park. Don't get me wrong: true and abiding joy is the great gift of discipleship in Christ and is not to be traded for any worldly treasures, but the joy and peace that Yeshua promised us often comes in the midst of trials (Matt. 5:10). When we are mocked, reviled, and killed for the sake of Yeshua, we become living models of the loving sacrifice of God's son, and that is the greatest testimony to unbelievers. For that reason, the Church grows most rapidly when it is under distress.

A consequence of the pre-Trib stance is that it minimizes our incentive to engage with secular culture. Daniel's 70th week and the years immediately preceding it will be the very time when the names of Yeshua and YHVH will be the most maligned. That's when the world will sincerely need us here to speak out against false Christs and demonstrate the goodness of the Nazarene. Why would we want to be hidden in heaven during a time of such great need? When Yeshua appears from the sky to tread the wine-press of God's wrath, no more souls can be saved, but until that time there is still work to be done. Upon careful consideration of the character of God, we might conclude that he has many great deeds prepared for his people to accomplish during the last days.

Another concerning aspect of the pre-Trib view is its late date of acceptance. No one taught it until the 1830s, meaning that every one of the scores of bishops, theologians, and scholars who lived during the nineteen centuries after Christ's resurrection managed to overlook a major eschatological doctrine. It's possible, but not likely.

Rapture and Resurrection

To ensure that we're on the same page before delving into the details, let's take a brief look at the biblical passages that describe the Rapture.

The term *Rapture* is never used in the Bible. It comes from the Latin word *rapturo*, which is a translation of the Greek verb *harpazō*, meaning "caught up." This verb appears in Paul's first letter to the Thessalonians.

> And the dead in Christ will rise first. Then we who are alive, who are left [lit., *survive*], will be caught up [*harpazō*] together with them in the clouds to meet the Lord in the air, and so we will always be with the Lord. (4:16–17)

This supernatural translation of both living and dead children of YHVH is spoken of elsewhere as the *First Resurrection.*

> Then I saw thrones, and seated on them were those to whom judgment was committed.... They came to life, and reigned with Christ a thousand years. (The rest of the dead did not come to life until the thousand years were ended.) **This is the first resurrection.** Blessed and holy is he who shares in the first resurrection! Over such the second death has no power, but they shall be priests of God and of Christ, and they shall reign with him a thousand years. (Rev. 20:1–6, RSV)

While the preceding passage does not specifically mention the raising of any but dead Christians, we remember that Paul said that those who have survived until Yeshua's return will experience harpazō immediately after the dead rise. We may therefore assume that the First Resurrection involves *all* of the elect, both living and dead.

The resurrection of God's elect as an event distinct from the resurrection of the wicked was demonstrated also when Yeshua said, "You will be repaid [for your kindness] at the **resurrection of the just**" (Luke 14:14, RSV). And again in the Book of John we read,

> All who are in the tombs will hear his voice and come out, those who have done good to the resurrection of life, and those who have done evil to the resurrection of judgment. (5:25–29)

The Book of Revelation simply expounds on this teaching by indicating that the resurrection of the wicked will occur one thousand years after the resurrection of the just.

An important segment of Scripture linking the Resurrection and the Rapture is found in 1 Cor. 15:35–58, wherein Paul discusses the resurrected body. He begins by affirming Yeshua's own resurrection and continues by describing the bodily restoration of his disciples. Paul writes, "Behold! I tell you a mystery. We shall not all sleep [a euphemism for being deceased], but we shall all be changed, in a moment, in the twinkling of an eye, at the last trumpet. For the trumpet will sound, and **the dead will be raised imperishable, and we [who remain] shall be changed**" (1 Cor. 15:51–52). The mystery of which Paul speaks is not the fact that there will be a resurrection, for even the Old Testament teaches that the dead will rise bodily (Dan. 12:2); rather, it is the mystery that some will not be dead when they experience resurrection. Take note that he did not say how many Christians would be alive at the time of the Rapture—it could be a very small number.

Another applicable verse is Phil. 3:20–21, which states, "But our citizenship is in heaven, and from it we await a Savior, the Lord Jesus Christ, **who will transform our lowly body** to be like his glorious body."

The promise of this transformation is one of the great hopes of the Christian life. Our spirits are exceedingly strengthened by the knowledge that we will attain eternal, incorruptible bodies as a result of lives well lived in submission to Christ.

A Dark and Terrible Day

In addition to the promise of resurrection, part of the hope to which Christians hold is the understanding that the saints will be saved from a period of horrendous calamity which will be poured out in the last days. Sadly, the unrepentant inhabitants of the world will not be spared and must pass through nearly unspeakable judgments during the dark and terrible day of the God's wrath. The *Day of the Lord*, or *Yom Adonai* has great significance to our study of the Rapture and will inform our entire vision of the end-times. What exactly does it entail?

The prophet Isaiah summed it up well when he wrote, "Yes, the LORD of hosts has a day against all that is proud and lofty, against all that is lifted up—and it shall be brought low" (Isa. 2:12), and also, "Behold, the day of the LORD comes, cruel, with wrath and fierce anger, to make the land a desolation and to destroy its sinners from it" (Isa. 13:9).

The return of Yeshua to punish the nations, which scholars often refer to as the *Parousia* (Greek: παρουσία, meaning "presence" or "arrival"), is triggered by the convening of Gentile armies at the place called Armageddon (the valley of Megiddo). Their purpose is to wipe Israel off the map, for they understand that Abraham and his descendants are the only ethnic group with which YHVH has made an unconditional covenant. By eliminating all Jews, they hope that God will no longer have any stock in the world and will cease all involvement with humanity. King David prophesied,

> The kings of the earth set themselves, and the rulers take counsel together, against the LORD and against his Anointed, saying, "Let us burst their bonds apart and cast away their cords from us." He who sits in the heavens laughs; the LORD holds them in derision. Then he will speak to them in his wrath, and terrify them in his fury, saying, "As for me, I have set my King on Zion, my holy hill." (Psa. 2:2–6)

The Messiah first came as the Lamb of God to be slaughtered so that the mercy of YHVH could be extended to all men, but the Messiah will come a second time as the Lion of Judah to obliterate the system of Satan and crush the Grapes of Wrath, which are those who persist in rejecting their maker.

> I have trodden the **winepress** alone, and from the peoples no one was with me; I trod them in my anger and **trampled them in my wrath**; their lifeblood spattered on my garments, and stained all my apparel. For the day of vengeance was in my heart, and my year of redemption had come. (Isa. 63:3–4)

What a striking and fearful picture of the coming judgment! This life is not a game, but a deadly serious battle of good and evil. To fight against God is ludicrous, and yet people are so delusional that they continue to rebel even though they are weak and he is omnipotent. It's impossible not to feel deep anguish for those who set themselves against the Lamb of God.

At his return, Christ will appear in the firmament and descend to the earth in a reversal of his post-Resurrection method of departure (Acts 1:9–11). Unlike during his Ascension, however, major astronomical and geological changes will take place when Yeshua makes his dramatic re-entry onto the world stage.

And **I will show wonders in the heavens and on the earth**, blood and fire and columns of smoke. The sun shall be turned to darkness, and the moon to blood, **before the great and awesome day of the LORD comes.** (Joel 2:30–31)

When he opened the sixth seal, I looked, and behold, there was a great earthquake, and the sun became black as sackcloth, the full moon became like blood, and **the stars of the sky fell to the earth** as the fig tree sheds its winter fruit when shaken by a gale. **The sky vanished like a scroll that is being rolled up, and every mountain and island was removed from its place.** Then the kings of the earth and the great ones and the generals and the rich and the powerful, and everyone, slave and free, hid themselves in the caves and among the rocks of the mountains, calling to the mountains and rocks, "Fall on us and hide us from the face of him who is seated on the throne, and from the wrath of the Lamb, for the great day of their wrath has come, and who can stand?" (Rev. 6:12–17)

No disaster flick coming out of Hollywood could portray the extremes of desolation and terror that will be seen on the Day of the Lord.

The Day of the Lord is not all gloom and doom, however. It will also be a time of salvation as the remnant of Israel will see the Son of Man, who is the Righteous Branch of David, appear in the sky, and repent of their stubborn unbelief. On that day, God promises,

I will pour out on the house of David and the inhabitants of Jerusalem a spirit of grace and pleas for mercy, so that, when they look on me, on him whom they have pierced, they shall mourn for him, as one mourns for an only child, and weep bitterly over him, as one weeps over a first-born. (Zech. 12:10–11)

It is that very moment which Paul has in mind when he says,

Israel has experienced a hardening in part until the full number of the Gentiles has come in, and in this way all Israel will be saved. As it is written: "The deliverer will come from Zion; he will turn godlessness away from Jacob. And this is my covenant with them when I take away their sins." (Rom. 11:25–27, NIV)

What remains of the Jews in that late hour, having finally softened and acknowledged Yeshua as their Messiah, will enter into the Millennium and serve our Lord Yeshua at his tabernacle in the City of Peace. The last chapters of the book of Ezekiel describe in great detail the millennial Temple and the beauty of the surrounding landscape, including the healing trees of life which will grow on the banks of a perfect river.

At the risk of losing our train of thought, let me quickly share my opinion that the entire millennial reign of Christ constitutes the Day of the Lord. The apostle Peter urges us not to forget Moses' declaration that "with the Lord one day is as a thousand years, and a thousand years as one day" (2 Pet. 3:8). His statement makes sense when we realize that the whole history of mankind encompasses seven thousand years,[a] with the seventh millennium belonging to the Messiah, for we are told that Satan will be locked away for exactly one thousand years while Christ and his saints reign on earth. While the inauguration of that day involves much travail in the same way that the birth of a child is accomplished with great pain, the remainder of the Day of the Lord will be marked by peace, harmony, and sustainable growth. After the thousand years, Satan is released to lead a final revolt, then all souls are judged and heaven and earth are recreated and combined (Rev. 20).

What should we think of the many Old Testament verses pertaining to the Day of the Lord which speak of it being near or at hand (Isa. 13:6; Ezek. 30:3; Joel 2:1, et al.)? It is likely that the prophets usually saw future events without the benefit of parallax, in what might be called *prophetic foreshortening*. Theologian Anthony Hoekema said of this phenomenon that "events far removed in time and events in the near future are spoken of as if they were very close together."[29] He offers the analogy of looking at mountain peaks from a distance; the peaks of several different mountains may appear to be close together when they are in fact miles apart. For an example of this phenomenon we can turn to the Gospel of Luke, where we find Yeshua standing before the congregation in the synagogue at Nazareth.

The scroll of the prophet Isaiah was handed to him. Unrolling it, he found the place where it is written: "The Spirit of the Lord is on me, because he has anointed me to proclaim good news to the poor. He has sent me to proclaim freedom for the prisoners and recovery of sight for the blind, to set the oppressed free, to proclaim the year of the Lord's

---

[a] For information to support this claim, see the blog entry titled "The 7,000-year Plan of God" at http://www.WatchmanAlexander.com.

favor." Then he rolled up the scroll, gave it back to the attendant and sat down. The eyes of everyone in the synagogue were fastened on him. He began by saying to them, "Today this scripture is fulfilled in your hearing." (4:17–21, NIV)

Yeshua stopped reading the scroll in mid-sentence, at exactly the point where Isaiah's prophecy transitions from speaking of the Messiah's first coming to speaking of the Messiah's second coming. The remainder of the oracle is thus: "And the day of vengeance of our God to comfort all who mourn" (Isa. 61:2). More than two thousand years were omitted in the middle of the oracle. Therefore we needn't be concerned with the fact that Old Testament prophets were unaware of the extent of the gap between their own day and the Day of the Lord.

Besides, it hasn't even been two "days" (of millennia) since Yeshua's first advent. Anything within the span of a couple of days is indeed near at hand.

Like a Thief in the Night

Even after we take prophetic foreshortening into account, the area of strongest evidence in favor of the pre-Trib interpretation is the doctrine of immanency. The word imminent is not found in the Bible but is used to express the concept that the Parousia of Christ could occur at any moment without prerequisite. Verses that contribute to that idea are scattered throughout the New Testament, with some notable ones found in James, First Thessalonians, and Luke. Let's take a look at those three instances as a sampling:

You also, be patient. Establish your hearts, for the coming of the Lord is at hand. Do not grumble against one another, brothers, so that you may not be judged; behold, the Judge is standing at the door. (Jam. 5:8–9)

"You also must be ready, because the Son of Man will come at an hour when you do not expect him." (Luke 12:40)

For you know very well that the day of the Lord will come like a thief in the night. (1 Thess. 5:2)

If there weren't any verses in the Bible describing signs which must precede Christ's return, we would likely conclude from these verses that Yeshua could show up at any second. However, there are many signs given which must be fulfilled first, and our interpretation must take that into account. None of the texts just quoted absolutely require us to conclude that his coming will be without prerequisites. The instruction to be ready does not imply that our wait will be abruptly interrupted, nor does the fact that he comes as a thief imply that no one will see him approaching. Pre-Tribbers often focus on 1 Thess. 5:2 (quoted above), but ignore 5:4, which says that the saints "are **not** in darkness so that this day should surprise you like a thief."

In Yeshua's letter to the church at Sardis, he warned them that if they would not watch, then he would come upon them as a thief, and they would not know what hour he would come (Rev. 3:3). That being the case, the opposite must be true, as well, that if we watch carefully, then Yeshua will not surprise us like a thief, and we will know the hour.

In the parable of the watchful porter (Mark 13:32–37), the owner of an estate takes a trip and puts his servants in charge of various tasks, one being put at the door to keep watch. If Yeshua's return was without portend, why watch at all? We would never see it coming.

The prophet Daniel was told that there would be seven "times" (360-day years) between the Antichrist's covenant with many and the end of the age. When we witness a host of nations making a pact with the Antichrist, we will know almost exactly how much time is left!

Noah was told the exact day on which the Flood would come, but he didn't receive that information until a week before it started to rain. At that point, YHVH revealed that the purge would occur seven 24-hour days hence (Gen. 7:4). Likewise, we saints of the End-times will know when the seven-year countdown begins.

Besides the powerful signs in the heavens that immediately precede the Day of the Lord, what events must be accomplished before Christ can return?

- The preaching of the gospel to all nations (Matt. 24:14; Mark 13:10)
- False Christs and false prophets working wonders (Matt. 24:23–24; Mark 13:22)
- Exaltation of the son of perdition (2 Thess. 2:1–10)

- The successful installment of a global government (Rev. 17:1–2, 12–18)
- The Great Tribulation (Matt. 24: 29–31; Mark 13:19–20; cf. Rev. 7:14)

The last sign in that list is of particular importance when debunking the theory of immanency. During the Olivet Discourse, Yeshua gave us a clear chronology which places the Parousia and the Rapture back-to-back. He prophesied,

> **Immediately after the tribulation** of those days the sun will be darkened, and the moon will not give its light, and the stars will fall from heaven, and the powers of the heavens will be shaken. Then will appear in heaven the sign of the Son of Man, and then all the tribes of the earth will mourn, and they will see the Son of Man coming on the clouds of heaven with power and great glory. And he will send out his angels with a loud trumpet call, and they will gather his elect from the four winds, from one end of heaven to the other. (Matt. 24:29–31)

When Yeshua used the phrase, "immediately after the tribulation," to what exactly was he referring? If we scroll back several verses in the narrative we discover Yeshua warning believers in Jerusalem to flee when they see

> the abomination of desolation spoken of by the prophet Daniel, standing in the holy place (let the reader understand), then let those who are in Judea flee…. **For then there will be great tribulation**, such as has not been from the beginning of the world until now, no, and never will be. (Matt. 24:15–21)

The sequence of events becomes clear when we take the discourse as a whole: first the Gospel is spread throughout the world (v. 14), then the Abomination of Desolation is erected in the holy place (v. 15), then the 3½-year Great Tribulation occurs, then the sun and moon will be darkened and the stars will fall (v. 29), then the Son of Man will appear in the sky and the elect will be gathered from the whole earth (vv. 30–31). If there had been a separate, unannounced coming of the Son of Man and harpazō of the elect between verses fourteen and fifteen, wouldn't Yeshua have included it in his teaching? Why would our Lord be careful to mention the harvesting of believers who survived the Great Tribulation, whilst completely ignoring the much more extensive harvest of all the elect who ever lived[a] from Eden until the Tribulation? He wouldn't! Yeshua would by no means fail to mention such a monumental part of the story.

The apostle Paul reiterated the timeline established by Yeshua during the Olivet Discourse and, in so doing, gave us a very clear refutation of immanency. In his second letter to Thessalonica he wrote,

> Concerning the coming of our Lord Jesus Christ and our being gathered to him, we ask you, brothers and sisters, not to become easily unsettled or alarmed by the teaching allegedly from us—whether by a prophecy or by word of mouth or by letter—asserting that the day of the Lord has already come. Don't let anyone deceive you in any way, **for that day will not come until the rebellion [apostasy] occurs and the man of lawlessness is revealed**, the man doomed to destruction. He will oppose and will exalt himself over everything that is called God or is worshiped, so that he sets himself up in God's temple, proclaiming himself to be God. (2:1–4, NIV)

First, note that Paul links the coming of Adonai and our gathering unto him. This is a strong clue that the Apostle saw the Parousia and the Rapture as two sides of the same coin. Next, don't miss the emphasis that Paul places on his command that we deny other teachings about that day, meaning the day of Yeshua's return. He said, "Don't let anyone deceive you in any way." If our interpretations of other letters or prophecies don't line up with the clear teaching that Paul is giving here, we're required to disregard them. This is not a suggestion, but a direct command, and since Paul is not contradicting anything already established in the scriptures, we need to obey his command. Finally, notice how Paul describes the events that reveal the man of lawlessness for what he really is. This son of perdition, as other translations call him, will exalt himself as God, and although the world will already have known him for some time, it is not until he breaks his covenant with the Jews and enters the Holy Temple that his true colors are shown.

The beast of the Abyss, here called the man of lawlessness, won't set his image up to be worshiped in the Holy Temple at Jerusalem until the

---

[a] Minus Yeshua and the dead saints buried in Jerusalem, who became the firstfruits of the Resurrection (Matt. 27:52-53). Think of the firstfruits as being like the foreword to the first chapter of a book.

mid-point of Daniel's 70ᵗʰ week. How do we know? The angel Gabriel explained the timing, saying,

> [The Beast] will confirm a covenant with many for one "seven." **In the middle of the "seven"** he will put an end to sacrifice and offering. And on a wing of the temple he will set up an **abomination that causes desolation**, until the end that is decreed is poured out on him. (Dan. 9:27, NIV)

Therefore we can deduce that the Parousia will not happen until some time after the midpoint of Daniel's last seven, when the Abomination of Desolation is put into place. Consequently, the Apostle could not have believed, as some suggest, that the Lord might return during his lifetime.

Pre-Tribbers will quickly object that Paul was not speaking of the visible Second Coming of Christ, but of a secret, intermediate visit of Christ. The problem is that they have absolutely no scriptural evidence of such a thing. Not a single verse so much as hints that Yeshua will swoop down in stealth mode to nab his bride. On the contrary, as detailed earlier, every reference we have to his coming associates it with supernatural signs and wonders visible in every part of the earth.

The Bibles' insistence that Yeshua will come like a thief in the night (Matt. 24:36; 1 Thess. 5:1; 2 Pet. 3:10) is more literal than most have understood. The exact phrase "like a thief" is found in Rev. 16:15, shoehorned between the sixth and seventh bowls, when the armies of the nations are being gathered to the valley of Meggido in preparation for the complete extermination of the Jews. Looking back at the fifth bowl plague, we see that the beast's entire kingdom has been plunged into darkness. That should cause us to recall the words of Old Testament prophets such as Zephaniah, who said, "The great day of the Lord is near... a day of darkness and gloom, a day of clouds and thick darkness"[a] (1:14–15). In other words, when Yeshua descends from heaven to the Mount of Olives, he will do so during the darkest night the world has ever experienced—and what better time for a thief to arrive? The glory of his appearing in the midst of total darkness will be incredible to see!

---

[a] The gathering of Antichrist's armies will have to be accomplished using electrical lights and/or fires.

As It Was in the Days of Noah

I have to admit that when I first began to accept the evidence of a late-Trib Rapture, one passage—and one only—gave me fits because of the trouble that I had trying to fit it into my new paradigm. The passage clearly teaches that people will be carrying on with the basic functions of civilized life when Yeshua appears. During the Olivet Discourse, Yeshua explained that no one except God knows the day or the hour of the Son's return. He then proceeds,

> As it was in the days of Noah, so it will be at the coming of the Son of Man. For in the days before the flood, people were eating and drinking, marrying and giving in marriage, up to the day Noah entered the ark; and they knew nothing about what would happen until the flood came and took them all away. That is how it will be at the coming of the Son of Man. Two men will be in the field; one will be taken and the other left. Two women will be grinding with a hand mill; one will be taken and the other left. (Matt. 24:37–41, NIV)

We should be careful not to read into this passage that everything will be fine and dandy when the Parousia occurs. Obstinate, foolish human beings have always excelled at covering up their pain with vanities. Social studies reveal that people purchase more alcohol, recreational drugs, and cosmetics as times grow more difficult, which is why those industries are largely recession-proof. It could be that when Yeshua crashes the party, the world will still be in a sore state following the seal and trumpet judgments, but people will be stubbornly self-medicating and even growing more optimistic about the future under the reign of the Anti-Christ. It is my opinion that the first six trumpets will have been completed by the mid-point of the 70th week (I do not subscribe to the idea that Revelation is chronological). Whatever the case may be, the condition of the world at the time of the Parousia cannot be so bad as to prevent day-to-day functions. That poses a problem for the late-Trib view. How in God's green earth, I wondered, could people be continuing to work their jobs and throw parties all the way through the seven horrific bowl judgments, when all the seas and springs of water have become blood, the sun is scorching people with severe heat, and painful sores have covered the Beast's worshipers? That doesn't seem even remotely plausible.

The solution lies in realizing that all seven bowl judgments are poured out back-to-back over a very short span of forty days. In other words, the Parousia will be a late-Trib, pre-Wrath event, not a post-Trib event. The seven last plagues are specifically denoted as "the seven bowls of God's wrath" in Rev. 16:1, making it easy to link them to the Day of the Lord. Recall that both Old and New Testament prophecies described the Day of the Lord as a time of wrath and great fury. This short period of the Bowls of Wrath concludes with what the Bible symbolically describes as the gathering and trampling of the Grapes of Wrath.

> Still another angel… called in a loud voice to [the angel] who had the sharp sickle, "Take your sharp sickle and gather the clusters of grapes from the earth's vine, because its grapes are ripe." **The angel swung his sickle on the earth, gathered its grapes and threw them into the great winepress of God's wrath.** They were trampled in the winepress outside the city, and blood flowed out of the press, rising as high as the horses' bridles for a distance of 1,600 stadia. (Rev. 14:18–20, NIV)

Some people are confused by the fact that the gathering of the grapes—which we know from later verses is speaking of the movement of troops to Armageddon—is found earlier in the text than the seven bowls. It makes no sense as long as we assume that Revelation is chronological, but as we will see again and again throughout our study, the Book of Revelation is _not_ chronological. Certain sections of it are sequential, but John's visions as a whole unfold more like an *exploded view* drawing than a linear slideshow. Deciphering the prophecies requires us to make thematic associations; we will drown in chaos if we attempt to build our model entirely upon a perceived progression of events. The eastern mind was never so linear as we try to make it.

Wrath vs. Tribulation

Moving forward, we need to understand that the wrath of God is not the same as tribulation. In order to support the theory of the early removal of the Church, pre-Tribbers always bring up the fact that the people of God are not destined for wrath. This argument is based on a faulty understanding of the terms *wrath* and *tribulation*.

God's wrath is the natural expression of the holiness of the Creator against the willful iniquity of the created. God is slow to anger, is not easily provoked, and does not desire that anyone should perish; the unleashing of his fury is a means of leading men to repentance. Even during the final judgments which God brings upon the earth, people have a chance to repent and escape wrath, for we are told, "[Men] were scorched by the fierce heat, and they cursed the name of God who had power over these plagues. They did not repent and give him glory." (Rev. 16:9). When aroused, God's wrath is always regarded in Scripture as proper and just. The sinner who continually rejects God's mercy and sovereignty is "storing up wrath against [himself] for the day of God's wrath, when his righteous judgment will be revealed" (Rom 2:5, NIV). Paul also taught that we should be afraid if we commit a crime, "for rulers do not bear the sword for no reason. They are God's servants, agents of wrath to bring punishment on the wrongdoer" (Rom. 13:4, NIV). Elsewhere, he wrote of certain hostile Jews, saying "The wrath of God has come upon them at last" (1 Thess. 2:15–16, NIV).

We see from these verses that God's wrath accumulates against individual sinners and is released over the course of their lives via any number of calamities, yet wrath will also be meted out after death, on the Day of Judgment. Meanwhile, other scriptures reveal that God's wrath also accumulates against sinful mankind *as a whole*. Such was the case during Noah's day.

The global flood was an expression of God's wrath against a whole population, as was the destruction of Sodom and Gomorrah. Likewise, the ten plagues poured out on Egypt, the destruction of the pharaoh's army, and the obliteration of 185,000 Assyrian soldiers who were coming against Israel, were all manifestations of wrath which foreshadow the judgments to come during the climactic Day of the Lord. In all those instances, the righteous people involved were spared from the wrath. Noah's family was sheltered from the storm, and the Jews living as Pharaoh's slaves were not affected by the plagues that struck Egypt. Therefore it is erroneous to believe that the saints must be removed from the earth in order to be spared from all of the plagues during Daniel's 70th week.

Let me reiterate: God's elect will not be harmed by the plagues even while they reside upon the earth.

The wrath of God leading up to and during the Day of the Lord is distinct from the natural disorders inherent to living in a broken world, and is expressed through potent, even supernatural, plagues. This culminates at the end of the age in the supernatural slaughter of the Anti-Christ's armies.

Unlike God's wrath, which is God's actions against sinners, the Tribulation as described by Yeshua during the Olivet Discourse is the result of the actions of devils and men against saints, including gross deception and merciless war against the saints. The wrath of Satan is not the same as the wrath of God. The war against the saints is detailed in Revelation 13, which says,

> [The beast] was given power to wage war against God's holy people and to conquer them. And it was given authority over every tribe, people, language and nation. All inhabitants of the earth will worship the beast—all whose names have not been written in the Lamb's book of life, the Lamb who was slain from the creation of the world. Whoever has ears, let them hear. "If anyone is to go into captivity, into captivity they will go. If anyone is to be killed with the sword, with the sword they will be killed." This calls for patient endurance and faithfulness on the part of God's people. (vv. 7–10, NIV)

We also see in Revelation 13 that the Tribulation will involve the denial of purchasing power to anyone who does not take the Mark of the Beast (vv. 16–17).

The combination of deadly persecution and inability to procure goods will make life during the Tribulation absolutely horrific for Christians. Things are so bad that God must shorten the reign of the beast. "If those days had not been cut short, no one would survive," said Yeshua, "but for the sake of the elect those days will be shortened" (Matt. 24:22, NIV).

The Word is clear that the elect will be present during the Great Tribulation—otherwise, who are the holy people that the beast will be hunting down and executing, and why would the days be shortened? Yet YHVH has promised Christ's Church that she will *not* be subject to the wrath of God (John 3:36; 1 Thess. 1:10, 5:9; Rom. 5:9). Yeshua already paid the penalty to satisfy God's wrath when He died in our place, and all who accept that free gift are held guiltless in the heavenly court and may not legally be harmed by any expression of God's wrath. Praise Yah!

Although believers may still be living on the planet during most of the seal and trumpet plagues, they are removed before the Bowls of Wrath, "which are the last, for with them the wrath of God is finished" (Rev. 15:1). These plagues are the same ones that the Old Testament prophets foresaw initiating the Day of the Lord. Continuing onto the next verse,

John sees a choir of worshipers "who had conquered the beast and its image and the number of its name" (v. 2). These Tribulation saints are already in heaven before the seven last plagues begin. Pre-Tribbers will claim that these worshipers are the *spirits* of martyred saints and not the resurrected individuals, but that view is a hard sell considering that the passage directly preceding this one is about the angelic harvesting of the earth.

Unbeknownst to many, a very concise account of the last days can be found in Isa. 26:16–21. The events as Isaiah describes them unfold in this order: 1) The unbelieving Jews are in travail and recognize that they've misplaced their faith; 2) Isaiah and the other elect ones who have died arise to new life; 3) God invites his people into his chambers to hide for a short time, "until the **fury** has passed by"; 4) Messiah leaves heaven to punish the inhabitants of the earth. *Fury* is another word for *wrath*, so this passage reveals that the Jews must first be in great pain under the boot of the Antichrist, whom they will believe is their Messiah, and only then will the saints be raptured and hidden away while God's wrath is poured out on the earth.

If this theory is correct, and the Rapture takes place immediately before the seven bowls, where will the saints be during the days of wrath? And how long will those days last? Let's now answer those questions.

Spirited Away

As we just touched upon, the harvest of the Grapes of Wrath is not the only harvest taking place immediately before the seven bowls of wrath. There is also a harvest of good crops, which is the Resurrection/Rapture of the saints (Rev. 14:14–16).

How do we know that the aforementioned passage is describing the accrual of human beings, since such a thing is not explicitly stated? One reason is that no other interpretation makes sense. A literal reading of the passage would be ludicrous[a]. More importantly, the Bible frequently speaks of humanity in agricultural terms. Yeshua compared the righteous to wheat and the unrighteous to tares, likened new believers to seed sown by a farmer, and used the imagery of a vine and branches to explain his relationship with his disciples.

---

[a] Biblical literalism does not require denial of figures of speech within the narrative (e.g., parable, allegory, simile, or metaphor).

An oracle given by John the baptist will be particularly helpful to us at this point. Speaking of the coming Messiah, he said, "He will baptize you with the Holy Spirit and fire. His winnowing fork is in his hand, and he will clear his threshing floor and gather his wheat into the barn, but the chaff he will burn with unquenchable fire" (Matt. 3:11–12).

A threshing floor is where sheaves of wheat are unbound and placed upon a hard surface to be beaten with a flail or crushed under a wooden sled until the valuable kernels are separated from the worthless chaff. A harvest worker uses a winnowing fork to throw the wheat into the air so that the breeze can blow the chaff away. Once separated, the wheat grains are collected and placed in a garner for safekeeping while the chaff is gathered and burned.

The wheat in John's parable represents believers; the chaff represents both unrepentant men and the worldliness which makes believers unsuitable for the kingdom of heaven. We might be tempted to view this parable as pertaining only to the lifetimes of individuals and not to the whole of humanity in the latter days, but such an interpretation falls short because it does not take into account other eschatological prophecies. Micah 4:12 speaks of the time when YHVH will gather the nations "as **sheaves** to the threshing floor," and Isa. 17:13 says that "the nations roar like the roaring of many waters, but he will rebuke them, and they will flee far away, chased like **chaff** on the mountains before the wind and whirling dust before the storm."

Several verses teach that believers are also afflicted and put through a refining fire:

> [The remnant] I will put into the fire; I will refine them like silver and test them like gold. (Zech. 13:9, NIV)

> Behold, I have refined you, but not as silver; I have tried you in the furnace of affliction. (Isa. 48:10)

> Each one's work will become manifest, for the Day will disclose it, because it will be revealed by fire.... If the work that anyone has built on the foundation survives, he will receive a reward. If anyone's work is burned up, he will suffer loss, though he himself will be saved, but only as through fire. (1 Cor. 3:13–15)

It is not until after the threshing-floor affliction that the good grain is picked up and put in its right place (the garner). In other words, we will not escape tribulation, but will be refined by it. Our worldliness is then burned up at the judgment seat of Messiah, and shortly thereafter the unrepentant nations are also burned up by the glory of his coming (Isa. 30:27–28).

John the Baptist's brief but amazing prophecy leaves little question as to the order in which our destiny unfolds, but it does not tell us how long the grain will be in the garner. With more study, we can develop a hypothesis about that. Evidence points to *forty-five* as the number of days that the saints will be safely sequestered. To understand why, we must consider three things: the final prophecy given to Daniel, the timing of the God's holy days, and biblical precedent.

Daniel's Timetable

Daniel was told that the period which we know as the Great Tribulation would last for a "time, times, and half a time," meaning 3½ prophetic years of 360 days each. Three hundred sixty multiplied by 3½ equals 1,260. The angel told Daniel that after 1,260 days, "when the power of the holy people has been finally broken, all these things will be completed" (Dan 12:7, NIV). The Antichrist will bring the saints under complete subjection over the course of 1,260 days. We are told about the coming persecution in Rev. 13:7–10, wherein the saints are implored to endure faithfully as the Beast is given power to capture and execute them.

The final nugget given to Daniel is as follows: "From the time that the daily sacrifice is abolished and the abomination that causes desolation is set up, there will be 1,290 days. Blessed is the one who waits for and reaches the end of the 1,335 days" (Dan. 12:11–12). From this declaration we see that there will be a gap of thirty days between the final breaking of the holy people and the occurrence of some critical but unnamed event, followed by an additional forty-five days to the ultimate consummation of the age. Twelve-hundred sixty, 1,290, and 1,335 are our milestones.

What happens during the thirty-day period is a mystery, but we find in Revelation 10 that something unexplained occurs in the days preceding the seventh and last trumpet: "But in the days when the seventh angel is **about to** sound his trumpet, the mystery of God will be accomplished, just as he announced to his servants the prophets" (v. 7, NIV). Now, the New Testament teaches that the mystery of God is Christ in us, but the

final unveiling of that mystery to the whole world is the undeniable arrival of Yeshua to meet his bride in the sky at the last trumpet. Paul also
included as part of the mystery of God the hardening of Israel until the
Day of Atonement, when they shall see the sign of the Son of Man in
the sky and mourn. The point to ponder is that something within those
thirty days at the end of the Tribulation sets the stage for the Rapture and
Day of Atonement.

In any case, something pivotal will happen 1,290 days into the Great
Tribulation; the angel does not tell Daniel what it entails, but we will
show that the last trumpet and Rapture/Resurrection occur on that day.
The angel also reveals that something wonderful will happen forty-five
days later, at the 1,335-day mark. Everyone who waits expectantly for
it, the angel says, will be made joyous. And indeed we can have that joy
right now by meditating on the glory of that day, which will kick off the
Lord's Millennium. It can be nothing other than the Parousia, the return
of Christ and his bride to establish the kingdom of God on the earth.

This will all make more sense when approached with an understanding
of the prophetic holy days of God.

The Feasts of Israel

God gave his people seven special days (popularly called "feasts") to
keep every year without fail—these were the divine appointments (Hebrew: *mo'ediym*) that God instituted at the time of Creation (Gen. 1:14).
They are divided into two groups: the feasts of the Former Rain, which
occur in Spring; and the feasts of the Latter Rain, which occur in Fall.
The former include Passover (*Pesach*), Unleavened Bread (*Chag ha-
Matzot*), Firstfruits (*Reishit Katzir*), and Pentecost (*Shavuot*). The latter
include Trumpets (*Yom Teru'ah*), the Day of Atonement (*Yom Kippur*),
and Tabernacles (*Sukkot*).

Amazingly, all of the spring mo'ediym were fulfilled between the cruci-
fiction of Yeshua and the giving of the Spirit on Pentecost, fifty days later.
The mo'ediym were assigned to particular days because God intended
for redemptive milestones to take place on those days during one particular year in history—the year of Messiah's death and resurrection. If
you haven't studied that subject in depth, you are encouraged to do so
because it will grow your appreciation of our Lord and his Word. Realize
this: In the same way that Yeshua completed the former-rain feasts at his

first Parousia, he will complete the latter-rain feasts at his second Parousia. Therefore, if we hope to fully understand the events surrounding Messiah's return, we must investigate the fall feasts.

We begin with the Feast of Trumpets: Yom Teru'ah falls on the first day of the seventh month of the Jewish year (*Tishri*) and is also known as the Day of Judgment and Rosh ha-Shanah. The day itself is sweet and hopeful but marks the beginning of a ten-day period of somber self-examination and repentance, and it culminates in a fast. The *shofar* (ram's horn trumpet) is blown throughout the day to jolt the people into awareness and remembrance that Adonai is king. For nine days following Yom Teru'ah, the people mourn and prepare to be judged; this time is know as the Days of Awe (*Yamin noraim*). In the last year of this age, beginning on Yom Teru'ah, something unknown but dramatic will happen to the Jews, and it will prepare them to receive the savior that God will unveil on Yom Kippur.

On exactly the tenth day of the seventh month is Yom Kippur, the Day of Atonement. It is the holiest day of God's sacred year. The term Yom Kippur is pluralized in the Torah, so it actually reads *Yom ha-Kippurim* (Day of Atonements).[30]

During the years when the Tabernacle or Holy Temple was standing in Israel, the Aaronic high priest would enter the Holy of Holies on the Day of Atonement, as instructed by Lev. 16:11–34. It was the one day of the year when the high priest could stand before the Ark of the Covenant in the Most Holy Place. He would sprinkle the blood of the sacrificial animal on the atonement cover above the Testimony and by so doing make atonement for the whole community of Israel.

Of course, Yeshua's blood is the only blood that makes final and eternal atonement, because only a human life can substitute for another human life. The ceremony of Yom Kippur is a demonstration of the eternally acceptable work of Christ, the Lamb of God who took our place and became a rebellious goat slaughtered on account of sin. When Messiah appears in the sky, the Jews will understand what they've been doing all these years.

Is it possible that Yeshua could return on the Day of Atonement? It's not only possible, it's incredibly likely. Most scholars suspect that the Rapture will occur on Yom Teru'ah, when trumpets are blown all day long, but if that were the case, then the day of Israel's national salvation would be Yom Teru'ah, not Yom Kippur. But the Feast of Trumpets is neither the holiest day of the year nor the climax of the High Holy

Days—Yom Kippur is. What most people miss is the fact that **the last shofar blast of the fall holy days is sounded on Yom Kippur once every fifty years**. It's blown ten days *after* the Feast of Trumpets! Referring to the Jubilee year, God instructed Israel: "Then you shall sound the loud trumpet on the tenth day of the seventh month. **On the Day of Atonement you shall sound the trumpet** throughout all your land" (Lev. 25:9). That is the final trumpet of which Paul speaks.

In fact, the very word *Jubilee* (Hebrew: *Yovel*) means "trumpet!"

Support for a Jubilee Rapture can be found in an obscure verse in 2 Kings.

> And this shall be the sign for you: this year eat what grows of itself, and in the second year what springs of the same. Then in the third year sow and reap and plant vineyards, and eat their fruit. And the surviving remnant of the house of Judah shall again take root downward and bear fruit upward. For out of Jerusalem shall go a remnant, and out of Mount Zion a band of survivors. The zeal of the LORD will do this. (19:29–31)

This was spoken by the prophet Isaiah after he assured King Hezekiah that Jerusalem would not be overcome by the king of Assyria, whose armies were set against the city. This scenario was a foreshadowing of the end-times siege of Jerusalem by the armies of the Antichrist, whom Isaiah elsewhere calls "the Assyrian." In Hezekiah's time, "the angel of the LORD went out" and decimated the Assyrian encampment, but on the Day of Lord, Yeshua himself will fight for Jerusalem and decimate the innumerable host of the Antichrist. Isaiah says in v. 29 that the sign of this prophecy was related to the gathering of crops. The people of Judah were not to farm their land for two consecutive years, but they could do so on the third year. The only times when farming was not allowed in Israel for two years in a row was at the turn of the Jubilee. (The 49th year of the cycle was a Sabbath year, and the first year of the new cycle—called the Jubilee year—was also a Sabbath.) Therefore the Second Coming of Messiah and the simultaneous resurrection of the saints during the siege of Jerusalem must occur on a Jubilee year.

So it will be: Just before the shofar sounds on Yom Kippur of the last Jubilee, the arch-angel will shout and the sixth seal will be opened. The earth will reel like a drunkard, the sign of the Son of Man will appear in the sky, and "all the nations of the earth will mourn" (Matt. 24:30). They will hide "in caves and among the rocks of the mountains" and wail because they see that the Lamb of God is crowned king, and his day is come. They will shout, "Fall on us and hide us from him who sits on the throne and from the wrath of the Lamb! For the great day of their wrath has come, and who can stand?" (Rev. 6:16–17).

The earthly shofar will never be blown in Jerusalem on the last Jubilee, but one will be blown in heaven instead. When the seventh and last trumpet issues its proclamation from above, the saints will be raised incorruptible (1 Cor. 15:51–52). The appearance of the Son of Man to meet the Redeemed in the sky will occur on the very day when Israel's national repentance is scheduled. How incredible! The divine reconciliation which Israelites have been rehearsing for centuries will reach astounding fulfillment on the last Yom Kippur of this age, when every man and woman in Israel will realize that Yeshua has made atonement for sins by his own blood. They will acknowledge that he is the Way, and thereby "all Israel will be saved" (Rom. 11:26).

Five days after Yom Kippur is *Sukkot,* the seven-day Feast of Tabernacles (Lev. 23:34; Deut. 16:13). Sukkot runs from the fifteenth to the twenty-first of *Tishri* (the seventh month). God instructed the Israelites to observe the Feast of Tabernacles by building booths and living in them for a week so that they would remember how they dwelt—and how God dwelt among them—after he brought them out of Egypt. The feast is celebrated with much dancing, singing, and imbibing, and is known as the *season of our joy.* At the end of the week of Tabernacles is an additional holy day of assembly, when all of Israel is expected to come together at one place for joyous feasting and worship.

What is the significance of a five-day pause between the Rapture and the seven-day celebration of Sukkot? The number five in the Bible represents redemption, salvation, and purity:

- Five animals were killed when YHVH made an unconditional covenant with Abraham, whose seed he promised to use to bring forth the Redeemer (Gen. 15:9–10).
- Nearly every measurement in the Tabernacle of YHVH was a multiple of five.
- The holy anointing oil was composed of five liquids, each of which

was measured out in amounts that were multiples of five (Exo. 30:23–25).

- The Israelites came out of Egypt in ranks of five.
- The fifth book of the Bible recounts all of YHVH's instructions on how to live pure lives.
- Jesus bled from five wounds before his death on the cross.
- Daniel's prophecies establish the fifth kingdom of the world as the righteous kingdom of the Prince of Peace.

Five also represents bounteous provision/recompense:

- On the fifth day of creation, God filled the seas and the firmament with animals and commanded them to be fruitful.
- Joseph gifted Benjamin five times more food than his brothers (Gen. 43:34) and five sets of clothes (Gen. 45:22)
- Jesus fed five thousand people with five loaves.
- Thieves in Israel were expected to repay five times that which they had stolen (Exo. 22:1).
- God told the Israelites that five of them would chase a hundred enemies and fell them (Lev. 26:7).

And, lastly, it represents preparation:

- In Jesus' parable, the five wise virgins were prepared for the bridegroom.
- The Pentateuch of Moses (first five books of the Old Testament) prepares us to understand God and live holy lives.
- David took up five stones in preparation to fight Goliath (1 Sam. 17:40).
- Paul was lashed for Christ on five occasions (2 Cor. 11:24).
- Jesus appointed a five-fold ministry of workers—apostles, prophets, evangelists, pastors, and teachers (Eph. 4:11–12)—to prepare the saints for heaven.

It follows, then, that the raptured bride of Christ will be cleaned, rewarded, and prepared during the five days after Yom Kippur. In a moment we will take a closer look at what that process entails.

One of the aspects of Sukkot is that it is only to be celebrated "after you have gathered the crops of the land" (Lev. 23:39). Israelites are commanded to rejoice before YHVH for seven days *after* gathering the produce of the threshing floor and wine-press (Deut. 16:13). It is striking that God would link the joy of Sukkot to the harvest. Suddenly the Revelation 14 harvest of the crops gains more meaning. For the thousands of years that God's people have observed Sukkot, they have been demonstrating how the Lord will gather the peoples of earth into appropriate groups before retreating with his bride for the Season of Joy.

The period of a week for celebration is important for another reason: When an ancient Israelite married, his parents would throw a wedding feast lasting seven days (Judg. 14:12; Gen. 29:27).

The Hebraic Wedding

Ancient Hebraic wedding customs are directly and astoundingly relevant to the Rapture. Let's take a few minutes to learn about them.

In biblical times, a man or his advocate would go to the house of the virgin girl that he loved and negotiate a covenant (contract) with the girl's father (Gen. 21:21, 24:2–4, 38:6). He brought with him a *bride-price* of either money or valuables for the father (Gen. 34:12; Josh. 15:16–17; 1 Sam. 18:25; Hos. 3:3), and gifts for the daughter (John 14:16–17, 27; Rom. 11:29; 2 Cor. 1:21–22).[31]

Glasses were filled with wine, and the daughter was formally asked if she would agree to marry her suitor. (This was not always practiced, as asking for the daughter's consent was customary but not essential; the best fathers would give their daughters a choice.) If her answer was affirmative, she drank the wine.[32] That wine was a prophetic type of the blood of God's son. God made a promise through the prophet Jeremiah that he would "make a new covenant with the house of Israel and the house of Judah" (Jer. 31:31), and Yeshua fulfilled that promise at the Last Supper when he took the cup of wine and gave it to his disciples, saying "Drink from it, all of you, for this is my blood of the covenant that is poured out for many for the forgiveness of sins" (Matt. 26:27–28). The bride of Yeshua was bought with a price.

As soon as the virgin and her suitor drank wine together, they were considered husband and wife, bound by covenant. However, the consummation of the marriage would not happen for a year or more. Both bride and groom used the intervening time for preparation and introspection.[33]

After the wine was drunk, the groom withdrew and began work on a place for he and his wife to live. Most often this meant building a new room onto the existing structure of his father's house.[34] Once the living quarters were erected and the time of waiting was completed, the father would give his son permission to go collect his bride and bring her back to the house. This may sound familiar, for Yeshua said,

> In my Father's house there are many dwelling places; if that were not the
> case, would I have told you that I am going there to prepare a place for
> you? And if I go and prepare a place for you, I will come again and take
> you to be with me, so that where I am, there you may be also. (John
> 14:2–3)

While the groom was away, the bride's unmarried friends would wait
with her; among other things, these bridesmaids were tasked with providing light from lanterns on the night of the groom's arrival (recall the
Parable of the Ten Virgins). On some undetermined evening, maybe
years later—some men had to save up or work off the bride-price, as in
the case of Jacob—the bridegroom would show up at the bride's house in
order to claim her as his own. Typically, the abduction of the bride would
occur in the middle of the night, which ensured that the lucky lady would
be home, and also enhanced the thrill of the event (Matt. 25:5–6).[36] The
groom brought with him two or more close friends as well as family and
servants, all of whom wore white robes (cf. Matt. 22:11–12).

Completely surprising the bride and her family by bursting through
the front door unannounced was not in good manners, so the groom's
entourage would announce his arrival as soon as they were within shouting distance of the bride's home. Thus, those who slumbered would be
roused to the loud shout of the attendant, the noise of joyful music, and
possibly by the sound of a shofar (1 Macc. 9:39; Jer. 7:34).[37] There was
much dancing and hollering, as there will be when Yeshua comes for his
people: "As the bridegroom rejoices over the bride, so shall your God
rejoice over you" (Isa. 62:5). Hearing the commotion, the bride would
leave her home and proceed with her attendants to meet the approaching
groom. The man then took his wife to his father's house where she put
on a white robe called a *kittel* and presented herself to her groom in the
bridal chamber. There they experienced union under a covering called
a *huppah*. Regarding this special place, Jewish author Hayyim Schneid
writes,

> It is evident from the Bible itself that the huppah was a tent or a room be-
> longing to the bridegroom. Psalms 19.6 speaks of "the bridegroom com-
> ing forth from his huppah," and so too in Joel 2.16: "Let the bridegroom
> come forth from his chamber and the bride from her huppah." The room

or huppah had to be his (and then theirs) because until she came under his protection or into his premises, she was still *arusah*, betrothed, and not yet *nesuah*, the very word meaning "taken by him".... Generally, the conclusion is that not until they are in the huppah in privacy, so that sexual relationship may be possible, is she actually "acquired" to him as wife.[38]

While the acquisition was taking place, the wedding party waited elsewhere until the best man (acting as witness) heard the groom announce that the marriage had been consummated. That is why John the Baptist said, "The friend who attends the bridegroom waits and listens for him, and is full of joy when he hears the bridegroom's voice" (John 3:29). Once the groom's friend was informed that the union was complete, the wedding festival could proceed.[39] All of the guests would occupy themselves with festivities for a week while the bride and groom stayed sequestered inside the huppah.

The climax of the wedding celebration was the eighth day, when the newly betrothed couple would emerge from the huppah and feast with all of their friends and family. This corresponds to the eighth day of Sukkot and the joyous assembly that ends the Hebrew sacred year. Beginning on the eighth day, the Israelites cease living in tabernacles and return to permanent homes to celebrate, and without any corresponding rituals.[40] This communicates to us that the redemptive plan of God is completed when Yeshua emerges with his bride from the heavenly huppah. All that remains is to rejoice, rest, and fellowship with all of the Holy Ones.

There is yet one more instance of a seven-day period which has prophetic significance. Noah and his family were shut up in the Ark for seven days before the Flood began (Gen. 7:9–10). This is critical to our timeline: The outpouring of wrath only began on the eighth day, *after* the completion of one week wherein God's people were concealed in a special chamber.

Moreover, Noah was exactly six hundred years old when he and his family entered the ark. Those six centuries of his lifespan preceding the Flood correspond beautifully to the six millennia of human history which precede the seventh and final millennium, the Day of the Lord. After the seven days of waiting, "rain fell on the earth for forty days and forty nights" (Gen. 7:12).

Isn't it amazing? The seven days Noah's family spent in the Ark are the equivalent of the seven-day honeymoon of ancient Hebraic custom. The account of Noah and the Ark is a perfect parallel of the bride and her rapture. It makes one want to break into praise for the elegant manner in which God has foreshadowed the return of his Messiah.

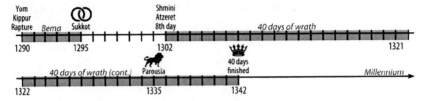

The Function of Forty

We started with forty-five days to account for between the Rapture and the Parousia; five of those make up the gap between Yom Kippur and Sukkot, leaving forty (of which the first seven will be the honeymoon of the Lamb). And as most readers will know, forty is an important number in the Bible, as it represents dramatic transformation or transition into a new paradigm.

Noah and his family were safely tucked away in the Ark for forty days while the wrath of God decimated the inhabitants of the earth with a flood (Gen. 7:12, 17).

For forty days Moses communed with God in the clouds at the peak of Mt. Sinai (Exo. 24:18).

The twelve Israelite spies roamed the Promised Land for forty days before returning to the wilderness (Num. 13:25).

The disciples were transformed as they spent every waking moment with the resurrected Yeshua for forty days before his ascension (Acts 1:3).

And lest we forget, Yeshua sequestered Himself in the desert and fasted for forty days before starting his ministry (Matt. 4:2).

The Weighing of Deeds

After the Rapture but before our final and eternal union with Yeshua, all of us who comprise the Bride must give an account before the judgment seat of Christ (2 Cor. 5:10; Rom. 14:10). The Greek word which

Paul used to describe that seat is *bemā*. In Greece and Rome, the *bemā* was a platform used by orators and judges (Matt. 27:19), and also the place where Olympians stood to receive their awards.[41]

At the seventh and last trumpet, the twenty-four elders[a] around the throne of God fall down and cry out,

> The time has come for judging the dead, and for rewarding your servants the prophets and your people who revere your name, both great and small—and for destroying those who destroy the earth. (Rev. 11:18, NIV)

Notice the conjunction: the time for judging/rewarding saints and the time for destroying the earth are combined. The judgment spoken of must be for resurrected believers only, because the wicked dead do not come to life until after the Millennium. This judgment will evidently occur while the seven last plagues are beginning. We can deduce that the judgment happens immediately after the Rapture but before the wedding banquet because a bride always cleans up and gets dressed *before* the ceremonies. "'For the wedding of the Lamb has come, and his bride has made herself ready. Fine linen, bright and clean, was given her to wear.' (Fine linen stands for the righteous acts of God's holy people.)" (Rev. 19:7–8).

The saints must be given proper raiment for the wedding, but each individual will receive a different outfit based on the quality of their Christian walk. The judgment of the saints will not involve punishment, for Yeshua has paid the price for sins; instead, it will be an evaluation of positive deeds. Here are several categories by which God may measure Christians: how consistently we placed God first in our lives; how well we loved our neighbor; how gracious we were towards others, even our enemies; how seriously we treated his Word; our fulfillment of the Great Commission; the adequacy of our stewardship over all that was entrusted to us; our level of charity; and our motives.

Paul compared our works to precious metals and organic materials: when exposed to the refining fire, only the metals survive. He said, "Every man's work shall be made manifest: for the day shall declare it, because it shall be revealed by fire; and the fire shall try every man's work of what sort it is" (1 Cor. 3:13, KJV). It is not faith that is judged, but actions.

---

[a] Possibly chief angels, or possibly the "first fruits," those deceased saints who were resurrected at the same time as Yeshua (Matt. 27:52-53)

Our good works are the *evidence* of the quality of our faith. However, works without faith are like "filthy rags" (Isa. 64:6). Therefore let us be full of faith *and* works for the kingdom of God.

The Marriage of the Lamb

God loves a good wedding—as well he should, since he created marriage. Yeshua's first miracle was turning water into wine for a wedding feast, and he told parables about weddings during his ministry. He even referred to himself directly as a bridegroom on one occasion (Matt. 9:15). John the baptist called himself the attendant of the bridegroom and identified Yeshua as the one on whom he waited (John 3:28–30). So it should not surprise us that a marriage will take place in heaven. Just as Adam was wed to Eve in the earthly Eden, so will Yeshua, the "last Adam" (1 Cor. 15:45), be wed to the Church in the heavenly Eden.

After this I heard what sounded like the roar of a great multitude in heaven shouting: "Hallelujah! For the Lord our God the Almighty reigns. Let us rejoice and exult and give him the glory, for the marriage of the Lamb has come, and his bride has made herself ready. (Rev. 19:1,6–7)

Without a doubt, this glorious wedding is an event to be eagerly anticipated. Not even the grandest wedding receptions, hosted by the wealthiest families on earth, will hold a candle to the heavenly extravaganza that YHVH will throw for his son. Unfortunately, not everyone who is acquainted with the bridegroom will be known *by* him and brought into his joy (Matt. 7:22–23). Only those disciples who have an intimate and obedient relationship with their master will be invited. Praise God, many such disciples will be created during Daniel's 70th week (Dan. 11:35, 12:10). Out of the crucible of the Great Tribulation a spotless congregation will emerge. Our Redeemer will have "a radiant church, without stain or wrinkle or any other blemish, but holy and blameless" (Eph. 5:27, NIV).

The Last Seven Days

This is where thing get a bit complicated. As we established earlier, Daniel gave us forty-five days to account for in his prophecy. We've seen that the first week of the marriage is the honeymoon, during which the couple spends much time in the wedding chamber, and five days are spent before that in preparation. That leaves thirty-three days in order to reach the 1,335-day mark. However, we've also seen that the honeymoon of the Lamb and the Church corresponds to Noah's time waiting in the Ark, and that the flood-waters started pouring immediately after that week and did not stop for forty days. We have a discrepancy of seven days to account for.

Since Daniel's prophecy stated that the destruction of the Antichrist and his forces will be "poured out" (Dan. 9:27), and since the Bowls of Wrath will be poured from heaven unto earth in the last days just like "the floodgates of the heavens were opened and rain fell on the earth for forty days and nights" (Gen. 7:12) in Noah's day, it is not wild to imagine that the seven Bowls of Wrath will cover a span of forty days.If the forty-day "flood" starts after the honeymoon of the Lamb, and his wedding banquet spans thirty-three days, that would leave us with seven days *after* the 1,335-day mark. What could fill that week?

We feel confident that Yeshua will descend as the conquering Lion of Judah, with the armies of heaven following him, on the 1,335-day mark, but the Bible doesn't stipulate that Yeshua will complete his victory on the same day as he rides forth. It seems likely that Yeshua's military campaign to eradicate all of Antichrist's forces will last for a week. That notion is based on passages (e.g. Hab. 3) which speak of the Redeemer moving with plague and sword through multiple theaters before destroying the Lawless One at Jerusalem.

Additionally, the place where the armies of the world gather to destroy Israel is the valley around Mount Megiddo, but the place where the majority of the forces are actually slain turns out to be the Valley of Jehosaphat. In Rev. 14:20 we discover that the Grapes of Wrath are trampled outside of the city, meaning *near Jerusalem*. Though it's a heart-breaking image, it's a good clue, because it informs us that troop movements will be taking place for some period of time before the final and decisive battle at Jerusalem. Megiddo will only be the staging area for the war.

Alternatively, it could be that the defeat of Antichrist's armies attacking Jerusalem will be accomplished in less than a week, but Christ's armies will take several days to make a clean sweep of the middle east before returning to Jerusalem.

When we put it all together, we see that Yeshua will appear for his bride on the cusp of Yom Kippur—the 10th day of Tishri, 1,290 days after the Abomination of Desolation is erected—and all of the unbelieving Jews will be spiritually awakened to their plight. They will mourn on account of the one whom they have pierced, and they will repent and accept Yeshua as Mashiach. Both the quick and the dead who are in Messiah will be taken to heaven, where for five days they will be evaluated at the bemā and clothed in the rewards of their righteous deeds. Beginning on the 15th day of Tishri, which is the Feast of Tabernacles, Yeshua will *tabernacle* with his bride for seven days; the 8th day marks the beginning of the Lamb's marriage banquet, which will last for twenty-six days; it also marks the first day of the flood of God's wrath upon the earth, initiated by the pouring of the first bowl judgment. On the 1,335th day, Yeshua (now the Lion of Judah) and his heavenly armies will mount white horses[a] and descend to earth to tread the Grapes of Wrath underfoot for seven days. Then the King of Kings will be enthroned forever on David's mountain in the City of Peace. Amen.

It all sounds almost too wild to believe, doesn't it? Yet this heavenly marriage is indeed foretold in the Word of God. As strange as it may at first seem, the entire story of divine redemption is really the story of the king's marriage. That is why Paul could say, "'For this reason a man will leave his father and mother and be united to his wife, and the two will become one flesh.' This is a profound mystery—**but I am talking about Christ and the church**" (Eph. 5:31–32).

Additional Concerns

In addition to the concerns already raised, pre-Tribulationists should ask themselves the following questions:

In Rev. 20:4–6, we find that the first Resurrection[b] involves saints who did not worship the Beast or his image, and were beheaded as a result. How could the Resurrection/Rapture happen before the Tribulation if it includes those who die during the Tribulation?

---

[a] Rev. 19:11-14. It is unclear whether the horses are actual heavenly creatures or merely representative of some form of otherworldly transport.

[b] The first resurrection takes place before or on the cusp of the Millennium, while the second resurrection takes place after the Millennium, on the day of the Great White Throne Judgment. (Rev. 20:5)

Paul said that Yeshua will come down from heaven to gather his people (1 Thess. 4:15). How can that event occur before the Tribulation, considering that Acts 3:21 states that Yeshua must remain in heaven until the Millennium?

Why did Yeshua and Martha talk about the Resurrection being "on the last day" (the 7th Millennium/Day of the Lord) if we are raptured before that day? (John 6:39–40,11:24)

Why did Yeshua say that the wheat and the tares grow together until the end, if we are going to be raptured years before the harvest of the wicked? (Matt. 13:24–30)

Messiah's bride does not receive her white garments until Rev. 19:7–8, which most agree is the end of the Tribulation. If the Bride was raptured seven years earlier, why is she only now receiving her wedding attire?

Conclusion

The pre-Tribulation Rapture doctrine is jeopardizing the mission of the Elect and the faith of young believers. Peter warned us that in the last days there would be many scoffers asking, "Where is the promise of his coming? For ever since the fathers fell asleep, all things are continuing as they were from the beginning of creation" (2 Pet. 3:4). The pre-Trib doctrine leaves the door wide open for such scoffers.

Before Y2K arrived, numerous Christian ministries were sucked in by the hype and began to cry that the sky was falling, despite the utter lack of biblical prophecies forecasting the failure of digital systems in the developed world. Their intentions were mostly good, no doubt, but it didn't matter. After Y2K, ministries which had preached a coming disaster died off in droves as followers withdrew their monetary support. That should give us an inkling as to the consequences of unfulfilled pre-Trib predictions. When the Four Horsemen of the Apocalypse hit the earth and Christians must pass through the fire like everyone else, or when the beast from the Abyss establishes a covenant with Israel and Christians are left behind to watch it happen, there will be a major falling away from the Faith (just as occurred during World War II). Unless, that is, we prepare the flock for trouble.

In the King James version of the Bible, the word *tribulation* is found twenty-five times. Not one of those instances mentions the harpazō occurring before said tribulation. In fact, the last reference is contained in

Rev. 7:14, where we are told that the saints John sees in heaven "are the ones coming out of [Greek: *erchomai ek*] the great tribulation. They have washed their robes and made them white in the blood of the Lamb." They did not *avoid* great tribulation but are *coming out* from the midst of it.

When taken together, everything that can be found in the Bible pertaining to the resurrection of the saints indicates that the harpazō is a one-time event that occurs after a period of great tribulation for the Church. The Rapture—or "first resurrection" as John the Revelator called it—will be anything but secret, for the sun and moon will be darkened, the stars will fall from the sky, and the sign of the Son of Man will be visible from all points on the globe. The harvest of the saints will be carried out after the "tribulation of those days," yet before the Day of the Lord brings the "flood," which is the full measure of the supernatural wrath of God on unrepentant humanity. With those things in mind, the best eschatological rendition is one in which the Rapture takes place at the very end of Daniel's 70th week, immediately after the sixth seal, in conjunction with the last trumpet, and before the first bowl of wrath. The wedding of the Lamb then takes place in heaven while the first six bowls are poured out on earth. After forty days, Christ returns to the earth, and the seventh and final bowl judgment is executed.

I believe that I have presented a solid case for a late-Tribulation, pre-Wrath Rapture. Still, I know that some Christians will not accept my conclusions, and that's okay. We remain brothers and sisters who are trying our best to take God's Word seriously and interpret it respectfully.

Interpretation of prophecy is a complex venture. Because there are so many variables, none of us can say with one hundred percent certainty the sequence in which events will unfold. Christians will continue to disagree on the chronology of future events because the Word of God does not give us an unmistakably clear timeline detailing every event to come. I used to get mildly aggravated with our heavenly Father for not making the order of events more apparent, but I've since come to know better. Abba always has good reasons for keeping things from us.

One day as I was praying about this topic, God was gracious enough to explain to me one of the main reasons that prophecies are (usually) initially indistinct and gradually resolve in clarity as the prophesied event approaches.

Before expounding, let me provide an example of gradual revelation. The Messiah was first introduced to Adam and Eve merely as the seed of the woman. Hundreds of years later, God revealed that the Messiah would be a descendant of Abraham. Additional hundreds of years passed before God further revealed that the Messiah would be of the tribe of Judah. Eventually the lineage of the coming Redeemer was narrowed down to King David's family.

Why not provide all of the details from the get-go? Because there exists a powerful adversary, Satan, who is plotting against God's people. Ever since the Garden of Eden, when God revealed that the Messiah would be human, Satan has been desperately trying to cut off or corrupt the seed of the woman (Eve) and prevent the incarnation. As made evident when Satan tempted Yeshua in the wilderness, the Adversary has excellent knowledge of the Word of God. Anything which God revealed to the prophets would be seen by Satan and used to his advantage, therefore God had to conceal many of the details of his plan while simultaneously revealing to us—his saints throughout the ages—just enough information to fulfill our needs and firmly establish God's omniscience. Understanding that, I no longer gripe about the vagueness of parts of the prophetic timetable. I am encouraged to know that more and more pieces of the prophetic puzzle will fall into place as we approach the last days, and that we have the honor of witnessing God's Word being fulfilled.

For most of us, it is not easy to come to grips with the idea that we who make it through the times of the Four Horsemen must then suffer under the insane regime of the Antichrist. Nevertheless, it would be wrong to interpret biblical prophecies based on our emotions. We must put our feelings aside and refuse to introduce foreign ideas into what is already a complex set of prophecies. The doctrine of a secret rapture which happens years before the sign of the Son of Man appears, is not native to the Bible.

Yet we need not fear the coming tribulation. As long as we remain pure and meek and walk in the Holy Spirit, we will not be overcome, but will share in the victory of Yeshua, for we are his beloved!

> Who shall separate us from the love of Christ? Shall tribulation, or distress, or persecution, or famine, or nakedness, or danger, or sword? As it is written, for thy sake we are being killed all the day long; we are regarded as sheep to be slaughtered. No, in all these things we are more than conquerors through him who loved us. (Rom. 8:35–37)

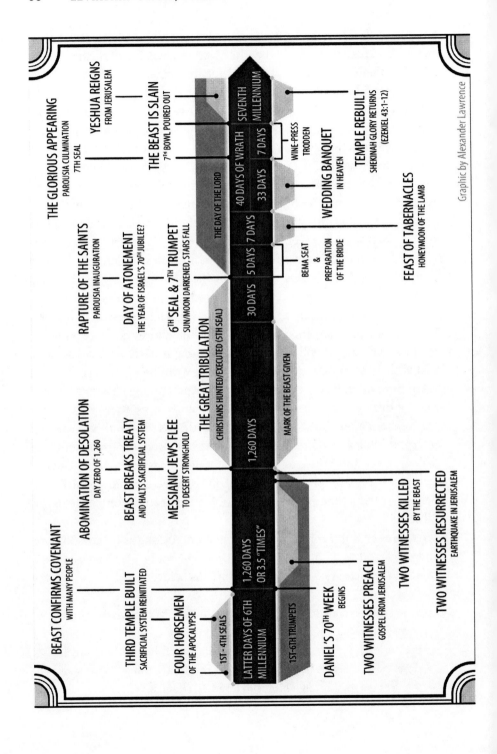

Graphic by Alexander Lawrence

THREE
The Sons of God

> Let us think of the whole host of angels, how they stand by
> and serve his will, for Scriptures say: "Ten thousand times
> ten thousand were doing service to him, and they cried out:
> Holy, holy, holy, Lord Sabaoth; the whole of creation is full
> of His glory."[41]
>
> —CLEMENT OF ROME (c. AD 96)

I t is time we turn our magnifying glass on the past. In the next volume we will conduct a more elaborate study of the chronology of the last days, but for now we will make due with our current understanding of the main events of the Apocalypse. Now follow me back in time... way, way back, to the creation of the universe. We will find that it was filled with life long before the planets were habitable.

Best Supporting Actors

At the beginning of most plays, just after the title page, is a cast page which lists all of the characters we can expect to meet during the play. The Bible, called the Greatest Story Ever Told, does not have a cast page, but if it did, then it would certainly include the hosts of celestial beings which we commonly call *angels*. We need to gain a basic understanding of angels before we can effectively study three of the major antagonists in the battle between good and evil: the Divine Council, Satan, and Satan's Seed. (Most of the topics covered in this book cannot be grasped without first building a foundation of relevant knowledge. Each sub-topic, even if it seems extraneous at the time, is a brick that will eventually form a fully realized structure.)

Scripture tells us about four classifications of heavenly beings, named Malakiym, Cherubiym, Seraphiym, and Watchers. We'll take them in that order.

Malakiym

Malakiym are always depicted in the Bible as human-like, masculine entities who are mature but youthful. They are observed in Scripture carrying out various roles. They make pronouncements on behalf of God (Luke 1:11-19; Acts 10:3-6; Rev. 14:6-9), mete out punishment (2 Sam. 24:16-17; 2 Kings 19:35-36), engage in battle (2 Kings 6:15-17; Rev. 12:7-9), patrol the earth (Zech. 6:1-8), transport the spirits of the Elect when they die (Luke 16:22), and guard and deliver the Elect (Acts 12:7-11; Dan. 3:19-27). Although they sometimes fly (Dan. 9:21; Rev. 14:6), this class of angels is not explicitly said to have wings.

Cherubiym

Unlike Malakiym, Cherubiym could not be mistaken for men, and a Cherub does not look anything like a baby, as popularly depicted. They are fearsome creatures which God set alongside a flaming sword at the entrance of Eden to guard the way to the tree of life (Gen. 3:24). They are also found in the heavenly temple of God. The prophet Ezekiel had a vision involving four Cherubiym with four faces each, moving about under the throne of YHVH. The first face was like a Cherub (whatever that is), the second like a man, the third like a lion, and the fourth like an eagle. Their appearance was likened to burning coals or torches (Ezek. 1:13). They were covered with eyes over their entire bodies, even their extremities (10:12-14)—if the Cherubiym are babies, those are some *ugly* babies! Unlike the Malakiym, the creatures Ezekiel saw did have wings, and the sound of their wings moving was like the booming voice of El Shaddai when he speaks, and they could be heard for a great distance (10:5).

Ezekiel used the term *living creatures* more than once in reference to the Cherubiym, and the apostle John also described seeing four living creatures with six wings each, encircling the throne of God (Rev. 4:6-8).

Seraphiym

Seraphiym are the other type of angel which have wings. In fact, the Seraphiym that Isaiah saw had six wings like the Living Creatures in John's vision.

With two wings they covered their faces, with two they covered their feet, and with two they were flying. And they were calling to one another: "Holy, holy, holy is the Lord Almighty; the whole earth is full of his glory." At the sound of their voices the doorposts and thresholds shook and the temple was filled with smoke. (Isa. 6:2–4, NIV).

Humans quake at the roar of a lion; imagine how Isaiah must have felt when the cry of the mighty Seraphiym shook the entire Temple! These creatures are not to be taken lightly.

There are so many similarities between the descriptions of the Seraphiym, Cherubiym, and Living Creatures, it would be justifiable to suppose that Cherubiym and Seraphiym are different races of the same type of Living Creatures which fly around the throne of God.

Watchers

The last category of angels are those tasked to vigilantly survey Creation, though how and to what degree is completely unknown. There is precious little information about them in the Bible, as only the Book of Daniel gives any mention. After a prophetic dream, King Nebuchadnezzar reported seeing "a watcher, a holy one come down from heaven" (4:13). This messenger decreed a sentence on Nebuchadnezzar and said, "The decision is announced by watchers, the holy ones declare the verdict, so that the living may know that the Most High is sovereign over the kingdoms of men" (v. 17, NIV).

Much more is said about the Watchers in the Book of Enoch, which tells of the judgments against two hundred rebellious Watchers who permanently inhabited physical bodies and took wives. Although the Book of Enoch (properly: 1 Enoch) is not part of the biblical canon, there are reasons to trust that the original text was God-breathed in the same fashion as biblical books, and we will cover those reasons later.

The Book of Jubilees also speaks of these angels: "[In the days of Jared] the angels of the Lord descended on the earth, those who are named the Watchers, that they should instruct the children of men, and that they should do judgment and uprightness on the earth" (Jub. 4:15). It sounds as if mankind's proto-society was experiencing growing pains. As the population exploded, disputes became frequent, so God sent some of the Watchers to teach men how to establish a legal system and order a society.

Several verses later, Jubilees records the rebellion of some of the Watchers: "And [Enoch] testified to the Watchers, who had sinned with the daughters of men; for these had begun to unite themselves, so as to be defiled, with the daughters of men, and Enoch testified against them all" (Jub. 4:22).

We will return later to the subject of the Watchers and their sins.

The Nature of Angels

Angelology (the study of angels) has not been given much treatment by theologians. In relation to other doctrines, the amount of material discussing angels is paltry. This apparent neglect has mainly to do with the lack of explicit descriptions of celestial beings.[42] Nonetheless, angels play indispensable roles in the story of this universe, either as servants of the Creator or as adversaries seeking to win a conviction of malpractice and force God to hand over his creation. The dramas of these spirits in heaven play out on the stage of the material world.

We know that angels are spirits, but that begs the question, What exactly is *spirit*? It is a difficult thing to define. Job said of it, "All the while my breath [is] in me, and the spirit of God [is] in my nostrils" (Job 27:3). The Hebrew word for spirit is *ruach* and means "breath" and "wind," because the animating principle of a living creature is made apparent by its breathing. Also, breath and wind cannot be seen. But that is only partially helpful because it defines a spirit by its effects.

According to Eccl. 12:7, the spirit of a man returns to God after physical death. How can that be, since the scriptures repeatedly teach that souls are confined to Sheol[a] after the death of the material body? Some verses even state that spirits are connected to souls (1 Eno. 22:3; Heb. 4:12). The Sumerians, whose civilization was the oldest in postdiluvian history, used the word *gidim* to communicate the idea of an immaterial power distinct from the soul, and they believed that the *gidim* was

---

[a] The New Testament may indicate that the half of Sheol called Paradise was emptied of souls at the time of the resurrection of Yeshua (see Eph. 4:8–10).

released from a human being at the time of death.[43] Either Ecclesiastes 12:7 is wrong, or we each have two spirits (or two parts to our spirit): one that animates the biological self and another that animates the eternal soul. The former returns to God upon the death of the body, as Solomon indicated, while the other eternally animates our soul. That leads us to conclude that a spirit must be something like *energized intention*, or *exerted will* which derives its power from YHVH.

Isaiah 11:1–10 lists the seven spirits which rest on the Messiah: kingship, wisdom, understanding, counsel, might, knowledge, and humility (cf. Rev. 3:1). From this we realize that spirit is the essence of a thing; it is an archetype proceeding from the divine mind. The New Testament instructs believers to be unified in spirit and to take on the spirit of Christ, which tells us that a spirit can be an organizing formula or axiom, and a disposition. The New Testament also teaches that Christians receive a new spirit from God when they repent and trust in Yeshua as Messiah (John 3:5–7). The spirit which they receive is of God, not of Adam, as was their original, deadened spirit.

In technological terms, we could say that *spirit* is like the mind and will of a computer programmer. *Soul* is like software code which is made from the programmer's thoughts and intents. A soul is a set of instructions programmed by God to define the characteristics and dispositions of a creature. However, this programming isn't unchangeable. Since created minds exert their own will, over time they can greatly affect the makeup of their respective souls—they can reprogram themselves. This is why Peter could say to the saints, "Ye have purified your souls in obeying the truth through the Spirit" (1 Pet. 1:22, KJV). By actively practicing obedience to the Word, which is Truth, the saints had developed clean souls.

Understand that while souls are energized by spirits, not all spirits conduct souls. Plants have a spirit that gives them life, but they do not have souls; they are only spirit and matter.

Star Lords

Before moving on, it would be beneficial to understand that angels possess a mysterious link to stars and planets (a.k.a wandering stars). In Scripture we find both celestial bodies and angels referred to as *the host of heaven*, and angels are pointedly called *stars* in multiple verses (e.g.,

Job 38:7; Dan. 8:10; Rev. 1:20, 9:1, 12:4).

Ancient Hebrew tradition has it that "there are seven archangels, each of whom is associated with a planet."[44] This is not quite right, as Yeshua is both Jupiter in his role as king and Venus in his role as servant and bridegroom, but the concept is accurate.

The Book of Enoch provides numerous examples of angels appearing in the form of stars, and even tells us that they change form when desired. The prophet says, "They raised me up into a certain place, where they [the angels] were like the appearance of a burning fire; and when they pleased they assumed the likeness of men" (17:1). Consider also the following passage, wherein an angel has taken Enoch to a void in the South:

> And there I beheld **seven stars**, like great blazing mountains, and **like spirits entreating me**. Then the angel said, This place, until the consummation of heaven and earth, will be the prison of the stars, and **the host of heaven**. The stars which roll over fire are those which transgressed the commandment of Elohiym before their time arrived; for they came not in their proper season. Therefore he was offended with them, and bound them, until the period of the consummation of their crimes in the secret year. (1 Eno. 18:14–16)

Are these seven stars the famous Pleiades of the constellation Taurus? It seems likely when we compare Enoch's experience with these two verses in Job:

> ...who made the Bear and Orion, the Pleiades and the **chambers of the south**... (9:9)

> Can you bind the **chains of the Pleiades** or loose the cords of Orion? (38:31)

Why would a star cluster be bound in chains? According to Enoch, it's because that portion of space is a prison. The Pleiades is actually a group of over a thousand stars, but only seven are visible with the naked eye. We will discover later in this volume why there are cords around Orion.

Enoch also had an allegorical dream-vision in which he beheld stars falling to earth and pasturing among the descendants of Seth and Cain. These stars began acting like horses and mating with the earth-born

(84:1-85:6). The stars which Enoch saw can only be those sons of God mentioned in Gen. 6:1-2.

This dichotomy of angels as simultaneously humanoid and stellar is admittedly difficult for us to comprehend, but we shouldn't let it overly concern us; after the resurrection we'll come into a full understanding of the spiritual realm. For now we can be content knowing that God's creation is wonderfully and incomprehensibly complex.

The Sons of God

Not only do angels dwell on a higher plane than humans, but they were created first. As we all know, God made the heavens and the earth on the first day of creation. Although it is not specified, God evidently populated the heavens with angels at some point during that first day, yet before creating our planetary habitat. We come to that conclusion from a verse in the Book of Job. Starting in ch. 38, God launches into a divine monologue which details his amazing feats of creation. Regarding the fashioning of the world, God asks, "On what were its bases sunk, or who laid its cornerstone when the morning stars sang together and all the heavenly beings shouted for joy?" (vv. 6-7) The phrase translated here as *heavenly beings* is *b'nai Elohiym*, literally *sons of God*.

We encounter these sons also at the beginning of Job: "Now there was a day when the sons of God came to present themselves before the LORD, and Satan came also among them" (Job 1:6). And shortly thereafter we read, "Again there was a day when the sons of God came to present themselves before the LORD..." (Job 2:1). From these verses, it would seem that the sons of God, of whom Satan is one, hold regular meetings with the Most High. Since humans did not rejoice at the creation of the earth and do not since that time gather before God in heaven, the sons of God as exhibited in the Book of Job are clearly angels.

After Shadrach, Meshach, and Abednego were thrown into the fiery furnace and did not burn, the Babylonian king Nebuchadnezzar looked in and saw four men, one of whom he said looked like "a son of the gods" (Dan. 3:25), meaning a divine creature.

The b'nai Elohiym first show up in the Book of Genesis, where they claim human women as mates.

When man began to multiply on the face of the land and daughters were born to them, the sons of God saw that the daughters of men were attractive. And they took as their wives any they chose. (Gen. 6:1-2)

These sons of God are the same as the lustful Watchers of the books of Enoch and Jubilees.

Some confusion may arise when we remember that the New Testament in several instances calls Christians *sons of God*. We are said to be b'nai Elohiym (Greek: *hyios theos*) through faith in Yeshua. We have to wonder why New Testament believers are labeled differently from Old Testament believers, who were never called sons or daughters of God. Both Ezekiel and Daniel, for instance, were called *son of man* (Hebrew: *b'nai Adam*), which is what Yeshua was referencing when he called himself the Son of Man. We know that Yeshua was also frequently called the Son of God. On the one hand, he was descended from a human being, but on the other hand, he was uniquely begotten of YHVH. It is the same with anyone who has repented and been identified with Christ through baptism; we are descendants of Adam, but we are later "born from above" (John 3:3) by the Holy Spirit and thereafter considered to have divine parentage. Only those beings who are formed as a direct result of the creative hand of God are considered sons, which is why Yeshua, angels, and Adam are all called sons of God. In support of that interpretation, we find in Luke's messianic genealogy that Adam is the only man labeled a son of God (Luke 3:38).

While humans who become b'nai Elohiym do not remain in rebellion to the Father, the same is not true of all the angles. Having heeded the prideful plan of Satan, a third of the heavenly sons of God became adversaries of the Maker. From that point forward there have been two camps: holy b'nai Elohiym and fallen b'nai Elohiym.

The Divine Council

We sometimes subconsciously operate under the premise that when YHVH affects people or events on earth, he does so by direct intervention, but the Bible does not support that idea. God nearly always acts via subordinate spirits, and he even deliberates with angels before issuing orders (1 Kings 22:19-13). This is not because Elohiym needs help making up his mind, but because he is charitable, and it pleases him to involve his creatures in governance and grant them some measure of authority.

One of the clearest passages regarding the Divine Council is found in Psalm 82, which begins by showing us a heavenly scene: "God has taken his place in the divine council; in the midst of the gods he holds judgment" (v. 1). In this short psalm, YHVH accuses the members of the council of ineptitude, of neglecting justice, and of showing partiality. He reminds them that they will not get away with it forever, saying, "**You are gods**, sons of the Most High, all of you; nevertheless, like men **you shall die**, and fall like any prince" (vv. 6-7).

Who are these sons of the Most High that will perish like mortals? They are the rulers of the pagan nations spoken of by Paul when he wrote, "For we do not wrestle against flesh and blood, but against the **rulers**, against the **authorities**, against **the cosmic powers** over this present darkness, against the spiritual forces of evil in the heavenly places" (Eph. 6:12). The Greeks called them *Kosmokraters*. These are angels who agreed with Satan that they could outperform YHVH at running the world. The Kosmokraters did not receive permission to rule until after the dispersion from Babel, so simple logic would suggest that these angels did not bring accusation against the Most High until after witnessing the travesty of the global flood and the rapid postdiluvian decline into apostasy.

Yet guiding the destinies of billions of selfish and willful human beings and keeping them from destroying themselves is no easy task, as YHVH points out. He states in Psa. 82:5 that these gods "know not, neither will they [ever] understand." In the Hebrew, there is emphasis on the first verb, *yada*, which means "to have a full grasp on a subject." These angelic rulers didn't fully appreciate how difficult it would be to govern the earth, but in their pride they thought they could handle it; yet they are failing miserably. I don't know about you, reader, but I'm thrilled to be a member of the kingdom of God and not under the authority of the Kosmokraters! My great Elohiym has everything under control.

These Kosmokraters have not always possessed the authority to rule over the earth, but they gained it at the Dispersion from Babel, when God said "Go to, let **us** go down, and there confound their language" (Gen. 11:7, CEPH). The last book of the Torah explains that "when the Most High divided the nations, when he separated the sons of Adam, he set the bounds of the nations **according to the number of the angels of God**" (Deut. 32:8, LXX). This division occurred in both the tongues of men and in their geographical location, for God first confused their language and then scattered them abroad (Gen. 11:7-8). Exactly **seventy**

people-groups were created at Babel, and a Kosmokrater was assigned to each group. In Canaanite mythology, the god El had seventy children by Asherah.[45]

Genesis 10 sets the number of the nations that came from Noah at exactly seventy. Even though this *Table of Nations* precedes the story of Babel in the text, the last verse of the account sets the chronological context by noting, "These are the families of the sons of Noah, after their generations, in their nations: and **by these were the nations [Goyim] divided** in the earth after the flood" (10:32). The proper number of families may have already been in place, but the division of those families didn't actually occur until after Babel.

Noah and his sons are not included among the seventy Goyim because they already belonged to God's kingdom[a]. When God called Abram out of Babylon and into the Promised Land to begin a new nation, Abram's tribe also was not counted among the seventy goyim, for they had become members of God's kingdom through faith in YHVH. Abraham and his descendants were the seventy-first nation, which YHVH calls "my inheritance" (Deut. 32:8-9; Isa. 19:25; Jer. 16:18). Jubilees states that "there are many nations and many peoples, and all are his [God's], and over all has he placed spirits in authority to lead them astray from him. **But over Yisra'el he did not appoint any angel or spirit**, for he alone is their ruler" (15:31-32).

Bringing in more extra-biblical evidence, we find that both the Book of Jasher and the Targum Pseudo-Johnathan[b] state that there are seventy angels who stand foremost before God. While these books are not authoritative, it is interesting that their testimony matches Scripture. The portion of the Book of Enoch called *the Second Dream-Vision* also speaks of seventy angels described as shepherds to whom God hands over the apostate Israelites at the time of the Assyrian and Babylonian invasions and the destruction of Solomon's Temple. Rather than Abraham's descendants being handed over to a single Kosmokrater, as is the case with the other nations, all of the members of the Divine Council take turns overseeing the sheep of Israel. By this we learn that the Israelites became Goyim through unbelief and disobedience and had to be given over to the Kosmokraters (all except a remnant of the faithful, that is).

---

[a] Notice that Ham, when he sinned against Noah, was not cursed; but his son received the curse. Despite his failings, Ham did trust YHVH.

[b] A western, medieval, Aramaic translation of the Torah, with commentary.

At this point we run into a discrepancy, for the number seventy-two, not seventy, is found repeatedly in nature, in the Bible, and in occult teachings. Some researchers have suggested that occultists purposefully changed the number for the sake of mathematical eloquence, but such an explanation isn't necessary for the simple reason that there *are* in total seventy-two rulers of the cosmos: YHVH's seed, Satan's seed, and seventy Kosmokraters. This will make more sense as we continue our study, but the linchpin of this interpretation is Ezekiel 31, where it is revealed that Satan's seed was not under the authority of any god, and indeed made the Kosmokraters jealous, which led to the Divine Council demanding the removal of that great leader.

Think about this: three days of twenty-four hours each equals seventy-two hours. Scripture teaches that Yeshua was in the grave for three full days and three full nights, which is to say *seventy-two hours*. Our Savior spent an hour in Sheol for each and every nation descended from Noah. That's an amazing way of illustrating that the Messiah perished for the sake of *all* of the people on the face of the earth—all seventy-two groups of them. I wish that they would all accept his sacrifice and be saved.

It's worth noting a handful of the other places where the number seventy-two pops up:

- Seventy-two is the sum of four consecutive primes (13 + 17 + 19 + 23), and the sum of six consecutive primes (5 + 7 + 11 + 13 + 17 + 19).
- Three hundred sixty—the number of degrees in a circle—divided by twelve (the number of months in the year, signs in the Zodiac, tribes of Israel, apostles of Messiah, etc.) equals 72.
- The 70 elders chosen in Num. 11:14-17, plus Moses and Aaron, makes for 72 men with permission to speak for God.
- Yeshua sent 72 disciples on a missionary trip in Luke 10 (70 according to some manuscripts).
- The Greek Septuagint (LXX) version of the Old Testament was translated by 72 scholars in 72 days.
- The Temple Institute, which is currently manufacturing items for the third Temple, has decided to place 72 bells on the garment of the High Priest.
- Jewish mystics teach that seventy-two names for God can be made from the letters of three verses in Exodus (14:19-21), and each verse contains 72 letters.
- The cornerstone of the occult obelisk called the Washington Mon-

ument was laid by Freemasons exactly 72 years after America's declaration of independence in July 1776.

- The unfinished pyramid on the Great Seal of the United States consists of 72 stones.
- There are 72 major temples of Angkor, Cambodia.
- There are 72 stupas around the central dome of the temple of Barabador, the largest Buddhist monument in the world.
- The mass of the moon is 1/72nd that of Earth, while Saturn's mass is 72 times greater than Earth's.
- The precession of the equinoxes occurs at a rate of one degree every 72 years.
- In a regular pentagram, each of the exterior angles measures 72 degrees.

On that note: the pentagram is an extremely important shape in sacred geometry, and one finds it nearly everywhere in occult architecture and illustrations. In fact, the underside of the dome of America's capitol building—allegorically the womb of the goddess Isis—houses a mural of Greco-Roman gods and goddesses arrayed around the central figure of a deified George Washington. The whole mural is encompassed by a circle of seventy-two pentagrams intended to magically bind the powers of all the nations. That is only the tip of the iceberg of occult symbolism found in Washington, DC.

The seventy Kosmokraters and the Seed of Satan will all be punished for their rebellion on the day of the Glorious Appearing of Messiah. The prophet Isaiah saw this and said, "On that Day the Lord will **punish the host of heaven**, in heaven, and the kings of the earth, on the earth" (Isa. 24:21). The Orthodox Jewish Bible translates *host of heaven* in this verse as *pagan deities*, and some other translations use *gods*. Just as the Antichrist and his armies will be destroyed upon the earth on the day of the Lord, the spirit rulers of the nations will be ruined in the heavens on that day. During the Millennium, the whole earth will be at rest under Yeshua and will worship YHVH alone, while Satan and his Kosmokraters are bound in the Abyss.

The obvious question is, why would God allow rebellious, subordinate beings to take over control of our planet until the Millennium? This is his way of demonstrating beyond the shadow of a doubt that he knows best and that no created thing will ever be able to displace the Eternal and Holy One. Technically, he could take advantage of his omnipotence and kick the offending angels to the curb, but YHVH will not do that because he is the God of Justice, and Justice demands that guilt must be absolutely proven before punishment can be inflicted. So the Kosmokraters have their day in court, so to speak, and are given plenty of time to try a variety of methods by which to construct an earthly utopia apart from YHVH.

FOUR

The Paradise War

Rebellion cannot exist without the feeling that somewhere,
in some way, you are justified.[46]

–ALBERT CAMUS (1913–1960)

Try to imagine it: You are the first and greatest being created by the hand of the Everlasting Father. Only the uniquely begotten Son of God preexisted you. You are perfect in both form and function, glorious to behold, full of understanding, and exalted above the heavenly host. The unfathomable treasures of the universe are yours to inspect; almost nothing is hidden from you. You sit in the Divine Council made up of the elder sons of God, deliberating with the King of Kings about how to execute his plans and policies. As the preeminent cherub anointed to oversee important aspects of God's creation, and dwelling in absolute paradise, why would you even think to misbehave? Yet the Bible teaches that Satan did just that and rebelled against the Holy One.

This insurrection must have taken place after the formation of man from clay, but before Adam and Eve were tempted by the serpent, for at the end of the sixth day of creation the Lord saw "all that he had made" and declared it "very good" (Gen. 1:31). Consequently, the so-called *Gap Theory* is untenable. Satan was among those created things which God called *very good*, implying that sin and rebellion had not yet entered Creation at that point. So what changed?

The most significant change was that God began to walk with Adam. Satan saw that Adam had a unique relationship with YHVH, and that God intended the angels to function as mankind's helpers. Even now, they serve us. "Are they not all ministering spirits sent forth to serve, for the sake of those who are to obtain salvation?" (Heb. 1:14).

For these reasons, it has been suggested that Satan[a] was blameless until

---

[a] Satan means *adversary*, a description which was not applicable until after his rebellion. The Bible does not tell us what name the great cherub wore before sinning. For the sake of

the arrival of Adam and rebelled because he refused to accept the plan of God for mankind. It was bad enough that he had to share the affection of God with lower beings, but it was madness to think that he would ever actually serve creatures made of dirt! After all, Satan was given glory greater than any but God himself. Why would he denigrate himself by catering to another created thing, especially one as inferior as Adam? Satan didn't understand that in the economy of God, the least of all is the greatest (Luke 9:48). Unlike Satan, Yeshua humbled himself and became lowly in service to the very creatures which he had crafted (Phil. 2:5–9).

Satan's high opinion of himself led him to distrust God's designs for life on earth. His right thinking was ruined because of pride. "Your heart was proud because of your beauty; you corrupted your wisdom for the sake of your splendor" (Ezek. 28:17). The wisdom of living in unity with God's purposes was replaced by the folly of divining a new and unauthorized program. Satan wanted things done differently, and he brazenly said so, conducting a campaign of slander in order to sway the other angels to his way of thinking. By the time that men were reaching for heaven via the Tower of Babel, a third of the heavenly host had come into agreement with Satan that a new approach was needed (Rev. 12:4). But before that point, he had already accused mankind before the heavenly court and so earned his new title: the Adversary (Psa. 74:10; 1 Pet. 5:8). Perhaps Satan intended to force God's hand, to pressure him into changing his program.

Filled with bitterness, Satan decided to make a clear demonstration to the Divine Council that mankind was not worthy of being served, only lorded over. Since he could not hurt God, he would hurt God's children. He went straightaway to the garden where God had placed Adam and Eve.

The Fall

Everyone knows the story of the Garden of Eden and man's fall from grace, but let us refresh our memories. God placed Adam and Eve in the garden of Eden and told them that they could partake of all the fruits of the garden except for the fruit of the Tree of the Knowledge of Good and Evil. A crafty serpent (Hebrew: *nachash*) appeared and posed a ques-

simplicity, we will retain the moniker Satan when referencing his state prior to rebellion.

tion to Eve: Did God really say that you may not eat of every tree of the garden? When Eve responded that she and Adam would die if they ate of the Tree of Knowledge, the serpent contradicted God's warning by telling her that she would not die, but rather become like God.

Who was this serpent that led Eve astray? The last book of the Bible gives us the answer. Satan is described in the Book of Revelation as a crimson dragon and an "ancient serpent" (20:2). This is a good example of the fact that when we take the Bible as a whole, it interprets itself—and it strikes one as poetic that the last book of the canon fills in the missing details of the first book. The Dragon is not just symbolism—Satan is literally a flying, reptilian humanoid. Originally he was beautiful and full of light, but one can only guess at his appearance after being cursed.

While the Israelites were in the wilderness, God instructed Moses to hang a bronze serpent on a pole to undo the curse of fiery serpents (Hebrew: *nachashim saraphim*) that were killing them (Num. 21:9). Any Jew who stared at the gleaming, uplifted serpent would be cured from the effects of snake venom. That event was a foreshadow of Christ's work on the cross. The endeavor of Satan was undone when Yeshua was nailed to the cross, and those who gaze at it with grateful hearts are freed from the effects of Satan's deception; the New Testament says that Yeshua appeared in order "that he might destroy the works of the devil" (1 John 3:8). The importance of Moses' serpent sculpture being made of bronze is only understood by associating the nachash with the glorious and shining Cherub. Many times throughout the Bible, heavenly creatures are described as having the appearance of bronze (Ezek. 40:3; Dan. 10:6; Rev. 1:15).

Let's do a quick word study. *Nachash*, like other Hebrew words, is derived from a three-letter root. In this case the letters are Nun, Chet, and Shin. From those three, several words may be rendered which are similar in nature but have distinct connotations. Some of the meanings of nachash-derived words include *shining/glistening*, *diviner/enchanter*, *descend/press down*, and *hiss/whisper* (especially as in casting a spell). Interestingly, *ha-Nachash* (The Shining One) read backward is Shekinah, which is the shining and settled glory of God. All this to say, we can view the serpentine tempter who came down to Eden as a shining enchanter who had glory like God's but was backward in his nature.

Interestingly, one of the Old Testament synonyms for *serpent*—the one used in Numbers 21, as mentioned above—is *saraph* (also transliterated *seraph*). It means *burning one* and is used in close association with other words for snakes (e.g., nachash and *epheh*). This puts a whole new spin on the Seraphiym as described by Isaiah. Seraphiym and Cherubiym are very similar creatures, and the prideful Cherub called Satan is a dragon who shines brightly (Ezek. 28:17; Rev. 12:3–7). The Book of Enoch mentions Seraphiym and Cherubiym several times and even associates them with serpents and fire.

> [Gabriel], one of the holy angels, who is over the serpents, over paradise, and over the Keruviym [Cherubiym]. (20:7)

> Its roof had the appearance of agitated stars and flashes of lightning; and among them were Keruviym of fire and their heaven was water. (14:12)

> My spirit saw around the circle of this flaming habitation, on one of its extremities, rivers full of living fire, which encompassed it. Then the Seraphiym, the Keruviym, and Ophaniyn [the "wheels" of Ezekiel] surrounded it: these are those who never sleep, but watch the throne of his glory. (70:8–9)

There is even an Egyptian hieroglyph for *seref* that is associated with both *snake* and *enchanter*. The following hymn, found in the pyramid texts, is used at the coronation of the pharaoh:

> He comes to thee, O Red Crown; he comes to thee, O Fiery One [seref]. He comes to thee, O Great One; he comes to thee, O Magician.... O Red Crown, O Inu, O Great One, O Magician, O Fiery Snake! Let there be terror of me like the terror of thee.[47]

Numerous other Egyptian records connect the pharaohs with the fiery, spell-casting serpent spirit. The Bible is not silent on this topic, either, for Ezekiel was given a prophecy concerning the Pharaoh.

> Speak, and say, Thus says the Lord God: "Behold, I am against you, Pharaoh king of Egypt, the great dragon that lies in the midst of his streams, that says, 'My Nile is my own; I made it for myself.'" (Ezek. 29:3)

We have already learned that the preeminent fallen Cherub of the Bible is the Dragon, so we must conclude that the government of Egypt was employed by Satan. Pharaoh in particular could be identified with Satan because his priests performed coronation rituals whose purpose was to cause the spirit of the sun god to indwell every Egyptian king. As we will discover, the sun god is the representative of the Supreme Being of the pagan religions, which they themselves name as Lucifer, the Light-bearer, and worship as the source of spiritual and intellectual illumination.

These things are a trail of breadcrumbs leading us to the conclusion that the highest ranks of angels are serpentine in some aspect. Some expositors have taken a very strong position on the dragon-like identification of the Seraphiym and Cherubiym.[48] Perhaps the *seraphiym nachashim* that attacked the Israelites were not snakes at all, but flying, fiery, reptilian creatures. Believe it or not, there exists ample evidence that at least one type of flying dinosaur remained extant during the time of the Exodus and beyond.[49] There is a verse in Isaiah that speaks of such creatures and distinguishes them from regular earth-bound serpents. It reads, "Through a land of trouble and anguish, from where comes the lioness and the lion, the adder and the flying fiery serpent..." (Isa. 30:6).

Returning to the Garden, we find God pronouncing a curse upon both man and serpent. Snakes ended up being cursed because the Cherub is the spiritual archetype for earthly serpents. We cannot usually see the spirit realm, so it was necessary for us to have a souvenir of God's judgment in the physical realm. God made the material nachash a symbol of the spiritual one and a constant reminder of the degradation of the adversary.

As the narrative continues, we sense a dual meaning within God's prophetic decree regarding the relationship between man and nachash. God said, "I will put enmity between you and the woman, and between your offspring [lit.: seed] and her offspring; he shall bruise your head, and you shall bruise his heel" (Gen. 3:15). This decree could easily be applied to the mutual hostility between snakes and humans, but if that is the entirety of the meaning, then the proclamation was rather worthless, since it is equally true that hostility exists between men and other types of creatures. Since we already made a link between the nachash and Satan, we can assume that God was speaking not only of enmity between Eve and snakes, but between Satan and all of Eve's offspring. The decree was about more than just man's tendency to kill snakes; someone who would come out of Eve would destroy our spiritual adversary, the ancient serpent. God was providing us with hope of a future redemption that would come through the woman's offspring. That is why theologians refer to God's words in Gen. 3:15 as the *proto-evangelium*, or *first gospel*.

When God spoke of the Serpent's Seed, to whom was he referring? Angels don't procreate, so the reference can't be to Satan's progeny. Once again, the Bible will interpret itself if we search it cover-to-cover, in this case for any mention of spiritual seed. In Galatians we find it written, "So in Christ Jesus you are all children of God through faith…. If you belong to Christ, then you are Abraham's seed, and heirs according to the promise" (3:26–29, NIV). What Paul was saying is that even gentiles, who are not physically descended from Abraham, can be part of his spiritual family by sharing his faith in the One True God and God's saving Messiah. Also, Peter wrote, "For you have been born again, not of perishable seed, but of imperishable, through the living and enduring word of God" (1 Pet. 1:23). So through faith in the Word, who is Christ, we are spiritually birthed into the family of God. Whose family were we part of prior to that? The answer: Satan's family.

Listen to what Yeshua said to a crowd of unbelieving Jews who claimed that Abraham was their father: "You belong to your father, the devil, and you want to carry out your father's desires" (John 8:44). Ouch! Yeshua didn't bother being diplomatic. We are all spirit children of Earth's current king, Satan, until King Yeshua redeems us (and yet we have hostility towards our father, the nachash, as God declared in the proto-evangelium). Because we are children of rebellion, we are seeds of the devil—whether we like it or not—until born of the Holy Spirit.

However, note that in the Gen. 3:15 prophecy, the word *seed* is singular, not plural. Returning to Galatians, we can extract another clue about the Seed. "The promises were spoken to Abraham and to his seed. Scripture does not say 'and to seeds,' meaning many people, but 'and to your seed,' meaning one person, who is Christ" (3:16). The Seed which God said would crush the head of the nachash, being singular, was the Christ. All of us who are in Christ are seeds of Abraham, but we are not *the* Seed that would defeat the enemy. Knowing this, who would be the Serpent's Seed? The Antichrist is our best option—the worldly king who will come pretending to be Messiah but will "destroy many and take his stand against the Prince of Princes. Yet he will be destroyed, but not by human power" (Dan. 8:25).

Throughout this book we will work to identify Satan's Seed and how Satan is using human beings to raise his chosen son (briefly) to a position of ultimate glory and authority upon the earth.

Banishment

Eve's sin was disregarding God's word, but Satan's sin was rejecting God's kingship. By casting doubt on God's word and replacing it with his own declaration, Satan had usurped God's authority. The King of Kings cannot make himself any less than what he is, nor can he suffer mutiny, because God is the very standard of righteousness and perfection. Anything out of alignment with YHVH's character and purposes is, by definition, wrong. Evil cannot subsist in God's holy presence, so God—deeply grieved—banished the angelic rebel.

"Your heart was lifted up because of your beauty; You corrupted your wisdom for the sake of your splendor; I cast you to the ground [lit.: earth], I laid you before kings, That they might gaze at you." (Ezek. 28:17, NKJV).

Satan and all who gave him allegiance were removed from the highest heaven[a] and from the presence of the glory of God Almighty. The kings gazing upon Satan are not earthly kings, but angelic rulers, for what mortal king has ever seen Satan laid low? The Hebrew words for king and angel are *melek* and *malak*, respectively, and both come from the same triad of consonants, *m-l-k*.

While the fallen angels still inhabit higher dimensions and are therefore unseen, their range of travel is now confined to the lower heavens (Hebrew: *shamayim*, meaning "heights" or "elevations"). Satan can no longer freely visit the heavenly Zion because he sinned and was cast "as a profane thing from the mountain of God" (Ezek. 28:16). We can only assume that Satan must be escorted into the third heaven by holy angels for assemblies such as those mentioned in the Book of Job. Or, as amusing as the idea may be, perhaps Satan can only remotely access the divine council through some kind of heavenly teleconferencing.

In the future, at the mid-point of Daniel's 70th week, the fallen angels will be cast down further and will become like men, restricted to the surface of the earth. A battle in the spirit realm is described in Revelation.

Now war arose in heaven, Michael and his angels fighting against the

---

[a] "The heavens, even the highest heaven, cannot contain you" (Psa. 2:4). According the Talmud, a collection of Rabbinic instructions and traditions, there are seven heavens. The protestant Bible mentions three.

dragon. And the dragon and his angels fought back, but he was defeated, and there was no longer any place for them in heaven. And the great dragon was thrown down, that ancient serpent, who is called the devil and Satan, the deceiver of the whole world—he was thrown down to the earth, and his angels were thrown down with him.... "But woe to you, O earth and sea, for the devil has come down to you in great wrath, because he knows that his time is short!" And when the dragon saw that he had been thrown down to the earth, he pursued the [Messianic Jews] (Rev. 12:7–13)

How do we know that this event is a future one and does not refer to Satan's original banishment? The war in heaven occurs in conjunction with a group of believing Israelites fleeing into the desert to be protected for "a time, times, and half a time" or 1,260 days, which we know is a reference to half of Daniel's 70th week. Also, the voice in heaven that speaks about the angelic war says, "The accuser of our brothers, who accuses them before our God day and night, has been hurled down. **They triumphed over him by the blood of the Lamb** and by the word of their testimony" (vv. 10–11). This war cannot be the one that occurred before the Fall of Man because Satan is hurled down *after* the saints overcome him by Yeshua's blood.

Chapter 14 begins in the distant past, at the time of Satan's rebellion, then jumps forward in v. 4 to the time of Yeshua's birth, then jumps forward yet again to a time still future, when believing Israelites, represented by the constellation Virgo (i.e., Mary), take refuge in the desert for 3½ years. These refugees must be ethnically Jewish and not Gentile because v. 17 tells us that Satan will give up on trying to destroy the woman in the desert and instead "make war against the rest of her offspring—those who obey God's commandments and hold to the testimony of Jesus" (NIV). The rest of the virgin's offspring are all people of non-Jewish ethnicity who have become spiritual Israelites through faith and obedience. At no time in the last two thousand years has Satan sent a flood (literal or figurative) to eradicate a group of Messianic Jews hiding in the desert and then proceeded to make war against Gentile Christians, therefore we can be sure that the Revelation 12 war in heaven is yet to come. The fallen angels will soon be cast out of the firmament altogether, thus losing their ability to travel through Earth's atmosphere and observe us from above. Whether they will then be visible to us is a frightening but legitimate question.

FIVE

The Ouroboros and the Leviathan

My end is my beginning.

–Unattributed

A female monster, whose name is Leviathan, dwelling in the depths of the sea, above the springs of water…

–1 Enoch 58:7

No study of the Serpent would be complete without exploring his connection to the symbol called *ouroboros*, which dates back to furthest antiquity.

An ouroboros is any depiction of a serpent curled into a circle, with its tail in its mouth. This has a number of meanings, perhaps the most obvious of which is that time and nature run in cycles. It can also represent death and rebirth, which we find illustrated in the animal kingdom by the snake that emerges from its own shed skin. The ouroboros may also convey the concept of either a self-existent deity or a self-existent universe, having no beginning and no end. However, none of these explanations are ultimately satisfying from a biblical perspective. In light of what we already know, we find that we can extract a greater meaning from the ouroboros: it is that old serpent, Satan, the first created being, who encircled the heavens.

In the Bible are found four references to a creature called Leviathan. It is a serpent of the sea and the fiercest of all earthly creatures. During a monologue addressing the genius and power that went into the design of all kinds of animals, God proudly draws attention to the Leviathan, saying,

I will not keep silence concerning his limbs, or his mighty strength, or his goodly frame. Who can strip off his outer garment? Who would come near him with a bridle? Who can open the doors of his face? Around his teeth is terror. His back is made of rows of shields, shut up closely as with a seal. One is so near to another that no air can come between them. They are joined one to another; they clasp each other and cannot be separated. His sneezings flash forth light, and his eyes are like the eyelids of the dawn. Out of his mouth go flaming torches; sparks of fire leap forth. Out of his nostrils comes forth smoke, as from a boiling pot and burning rushes. His breath kindles coals, and a flame comes forth from his mouth... He makes the deep boil like a pot; he makes the sea like a pot of ointment. Behind him he leaves a shining wake; one would think the deep to be white-haired. On earth there is not his like, a creature without fear. He sees everything that is high; he is king over all the sons of pride. (Job 41:12–34)

This passage does not read as allegory, and the fact that it falls within a larger discussion of real animals precludes the notion that Leviathan is imaginary. This was not a mythological creature, but a real dragon (what modern men would call a dinosaur) that was either aquatic or amphibian and produced fire from its mouth. Nearly every ancient civilization told tales of terrible, fiery lizards and made pictures of beasts just like the one described in Job. It would be a mistake to discount all those testimonies for no better reason than modern skepticism.

Figure 5–1. "The Destruction of Leviathan" by Gustave Doré, from *The Holy Bible with Illustrations*, 1866.

Take note, however, of the last verse in the above passage; it says that the sea serpent perceives everything "that is high" and rules over the "sons of pride," which we know are the rebellious sons of god, or fallen angels. How can that possibly apply to an aquatic dinosaur? The Book of Revelation identifies Satan as a dragon in heaven, whose constellation is Draco (that is the sign of the dragon spoken of in Revelation 12). He is the one who sees everything from above and issues commands to the fallen ones.

The physical sea-dragon called leviathan is a stand-in for the archetypal spiritual dragon, which goes to show that the ancients were not naïve in their belief that what exists on earth is a reflection of what exists in heaven.

All that is in heaven has its shadow (or *type*) on earth, and Satan's shadow is the man of perdition, nicknamed Antichrist. Satan and his prideful champion rule a kingdom called Babylon, and it is represented in Revelation 13 as a terrible, seven-headed, ten-horned beast that comes out of the sea. The waters of the sea represent the masses—all the people of the world, excluding Israel (Rev. 17:15). The prophet Daniel had a vision of the same ten-horned beast arising from a churning sea, and the violence of the waters speaks of a time of global chaos that will precede the emergence of the Beast Kingdom, a.k.a. the New World Order[a]. Indeed, the world has never been at peace while under the rule of the fallen angels, and the arrival of each new kingdom must be prefaced by upheaval and the disintegration of existing social structures.

An angel told Daniel that the beast is a kingdom, and its ten horns are ten kings. Many Christians only identify the Beast as the Antichrist and fail to understand that it is primarily a kingdom. Even so, the greatest horn of that kingdom (which starts out as a little horn) is represented by the same beastly symbol as the kingdom itself. In other words, the king and his kingdom are of a similar nature.

Even though the Antichrist is a beast of the same variety as Satan's kingdom, there is a slight difference between the two. Daniel's *little horn* who grows mighty and boastful (i.e., the Antichrist) arises from the Abyss (Rev. 17:8), which is distinct from the sea. The Abyss is the place of deep subterranean fresh water in the physical realm, and in the spiritual realm it is the entrance to Sheol and a prison for angels. In the land where Babylon began, there was an entrance to the Abyss in the waterfront city of Eridu.[50] To the people of ancient Mesopotamia, the Abyss (Sumerian: *Abzu*) was both a cosmic feature and the deep subterranean storehouse of fresh waters.[51] This information will become much more meaningful later, but for now understand that the beast from the Abyss has a different identity than the beast from the sea.

To simplify, Leviathan is the mascot of the Devil and his kingdom. The

---

[a] Both sides of the Great Seal of the United States are represented on the back of the American one-dollar bill. One of the Latin phrases on that seal translates as "New Order of the Ages," and the Freemasons who designed and approved of the Great Seal have as the motto of their 33rd Degree Rite the phrase "ordo ab chao", meaning "order from chaos."

Antichrist is part of Leviathan—a fractal image of the larger beast. Lest we forget, John also saw a beast who came up out of the earth and was a false prophet working lying miracles. If the ocean represents the Gentile masses, then the earth stands for Israel, therefore we should expect the False Prophet to be a Jew.

All of this is certainly difficult to grasp, which is why an angel told the apostle John that understanding the Beast system calls for a mind with wisdom (Rev. 17:9). But don't despair: if we pray diligently for wisdom we will receive it (James 1:5).

In the Book of Isaiah we find an end-times oracle about the day in which the Messiah will slay Leviathan. It reads,

> In that day the LORD with his sore and great and strong sword shall pun-
> ish leviathan the piercing serpent, even leviathan that crooked serpent;
> and he shall slay the dragon that is in the sea (Isa. 27:1, KJV).

Isaiah is revealing the same thing that John foresaw, which is that God will destroy the beastly system represented by the animal called *leviathan*, and punish both Satan and the False Messiah in the Lake of Fire (Rev. 19:19, 20:10). Satan, his Seed, and the idolatrous world order known as Babylon are all leviathans. They are all beasts of the same ilk.

Figure 5–2. Coin produced by Pope Gregory XII. The reverse side features an encircling dragon consuming itself.

It would behoove us as we study our enemy to keep in mind that he *loses*, and badly. After the Seed of Eve crushes Leviathan's head, we will all stand far off to watch the smoke of his burning and praise God with shouts of victory.

In the Beginning

The Hebrew word *leviathan* is composed of two parts: *levi*, meaning "joining," and *tan* (plural: *tannin*), meaning "long serpent" or "dragon." The very name of the creature links it to the ouroboros. This connection is affirmed in the apocryphal *Acts of Kyriakos and Julitta*, where the hero passes through the waters of the Abyss and encounters the king of the worms of the earth, **whose tail lies in his mouth**. This is the serpent that led astray through passions the angels from on high; **this is the serpent that led astray the first Adam** and expelled him from Paradise."[52]

The deep water where the leviathan dwells is the physical representation of the primordial womb of chaos.

The sea of chaos is a common thread in the creation stories of ancient religions and describes the void that existed before the creation of all that we know. *Chaos* is a Greek word which means "space, chasm, or abyss," but not a place that is devoid of substance, as we may think of it today. The Greeks envisioned chaos as a body of fluid where myriads of forms fought.[53] The Sumerians likened it to a swamp; the Babylonians called it an infinite chaos-ocean; and the Egyptian god Nun was a personification of the primordial waters of chaos. The cosmic womb was depicted in early mythologies as the Great Mother of the primary gods.[54]

The concept of a primordial sea of chaos squares with the Genesis account, which states that the spirit of God vibrated over the *theum*, which translates as *abyss*—but the word's root, *theu*, actually means *chaos*. We find in the Book of Job that God "stretches out the north over the deep [*theum*] and hangs the earth on nothing" (26:7). The Hebrew actually says "stretching out north," not *the* north. How does one stretch out a direction over chaos? One doesn't. The word here translated *north* is *zaphon*, which is also the name of a mountain located in northern Syria. Ugaritic texts name it as the home of the storm god Ba'al and gathering place of the gods in like manner to Mount Olympus.[55] However, Psa. 48:2 specifies that Mount Zion is at the heights of Zaphon, making use of Canaanite terminology to speak of the divine mountain in heaven, atop which sits the cosmic temple containing God's throne. Knowing that, we can translate Job 26:7 thusly: "He stretches out the highest heaven above Chaos and hangs the earth in space."

Genesis 1:2 also states that the earth, or lower realm[a], was *tohu* and *bohu*. *Chaotic* and *formless* are both valid and frequently-used English translations of *tohu*, but the common translation of *void* for *bohu* may

---

[a] The fact that the earth was created before it had any kind of form hints that we may not, in this instance, need to take the Hebrew word *artz* to mean the literal planet. Instead, it could be translated as *realm*. The Hebrews had no word to describe dimensions of space-time, so the phrase "the heavens and the earth" could well have been a primitive way of communicating the idea of the higher dimensions of spirit and the lower three dimensions of matter.

not be the best. As physicist Dr. Gerald Schroeder points out, "Both the Talmud and Nahmanides state that bohu means filled with the building blocks of matter."[56] This account is confirmed in modern secular cosmogony, which teaches that the universe began as an expansion of mega-hot radiant energy which then precipitated into matter. Science has revealed that material substance is in fact energy condensed to slow vibrations; or, as Einstein so eloquently expressed it, $E=mc^2$. Modern physicists are behind the curve because mystics have taught for thousands of years that matter was formed out of spirit in a way similar to how gas changes state into liquid and then solid. There was a consensus between ancient mystics of many bents that what existed first was a pool of energy, and light was concealed within it.

Science has in fact determined that light didn't break free from matter until a significant period of time had elapsed after the Big Bang[a].[57] Another way of approaching this is to ask what we get if we continuously divide the molecules that comprise elements. First we get atoms, then subatomic particles, then quantum fields—and what generates those? So-called quantum foam, which is to say *chaos*.

In the Genesis account, it is only after God sees the light, that it is good, that he separates it from the darkness. This, Moses writes, was the first day: it began with evening, and then came morning. Yet there was no sun, moon, or stars to mark days and nights, so how could there be an evening and a morning? By way of answer, know that the roots of the Hebrew words for evening and morning indicate chaos and order, respectively. Moses was telling us in an accurate but poetic way that chaos came first, then God brought order out of it. Order in the material plane was not introduced *ex nihilo*, but chaos was.[b]

The ouroboros is the creature responsible for encompassing the fluids of chaos, much like the walls of a uterus hold in the water where new life begins. Pagan alchemists often illustrated serpents wrapped around the cosmic egg, and an egg is simply a womb external to the parent's body. Water is like the primordial chaos, for it has no structure, but instead

---

[a] I don't necessarily subscribe to the idea that the universe expanded from a singularity, but it did have a sudden beginning.

[b] This does not imply that God is the author of chaos. He made the primordial cosmic soup, but he continually crafts ordered vessels from it. A human author does the same thing, reaching into the chaotic jumble of words and concepts contained within his mind, plucking out those that fit his purposes, and organizing them into a form that has meaning. Through the spiritual power of thought, information arises from meaningless noise.

takes on the form of whatever surrounds it. The womb of chaos, or Abyss, contained only potential—a place wherein differentiation could occur—and had to await the introduction of order from an external organizing force.

The mythological serpent associated with the primordial chaos was know in Mesopotamian lore as Nammu; in Egyptian lore as Apep; in Canaanite lore as Yam; in Hittite lore as Illuyanka; in Vedic lore as Vritra; in Norse lore as Jörmungandr. In most of these myths, it is the god of light who pushes back the ouroboros, and as we know from Scripture, Yeshua is the light of the world.

We must ask ourselves why ancient man would choose a serpent to represent the boundary of the cosmos. Why not pick a pouched or shelled animal, or a round plant?

The Archetype of Created Perfection

In Ezek. 28:14, YHVH speaks directly to the Adversary and calls him a *sâkak* Cherub. *Sâkak* is translated in most Bibles as "covering," but it can also mean "encompass" or "fence in" (also: entwine as a screen, defend, join together, or shut up). This was no ordinary angel, but the very chief of wisdom and beauty, and of him is said something unique in all of Scripture, that he seals up the outline/sum (Ezek. 28:12). Something that seals up is a container, and the sphere is the perfect container; all measurements are equal in a sphere. In two dimensions, the 3-D sphere becomes a circle. The circle is the most beautiful and perfect of all shapes and is the principle element of sacred geometry because every geometric shape can be constructed from the intersection of two or more circles. If Satan was the first created being, as the scriptures seem to suggest, then it stands to reason that he was patron of that most perfect form, the circle. Thus the blueprint of all geometry was integrated within him. This could be why Ezekiel said that Satan fell on account of his beauty.

The ratio of a circle's diameter to its circumference is the transcendental number represented by the Greek letter π (Pi, which equals 3.14159...). As far as we can ascertain, the digits after the decimal point of Pi continue indefinitely with no discernible pattern. The number three not only speaks of the triune nature of intelligent life (mind, body, and spirit), but it gives us the triangle, that most stable of all forms and most basic component of all other polygonal shapes. The triangle is the very symbol of structure. The digits of Pi that fall on the opposite side of the decimal point from 3 are random, a never-ending and never-repeating chaos. Given that, we see how the orb of primordial chaos and the perfection of the Cherub relate.[a]

Knowing that cherubs are serpentine and that the covering Cherub is lord of the circle, it is impossible not to make the connection between the Devil and the ouroboros. It would seem that Satan presided over the primordial waters of chaos in much the same way as other angels preside over stars and natural forces.

Have you ever wondered why stewardship of the world defaulted to Satan after Adam forfeited his charge? Is it not because the entire universe was constructed under the covering of Satan? It was Yeshua who sang all things into being, but he did so in cooperation with the covering Cherub, even as today it is Yeshua who woos sinners into his assembly, but he does so in cooperation with humans.

The ouroboros is actually built into the stars around us. From our vantage point on the outer rim of the galaxy, the Milky Way appears as a serpent encircling us—the edge of the flattened spiral makes up the body,

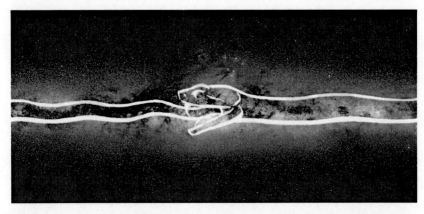

Figure 5–3. Our own Milky Way galaxy, seen from earth's location on the edge, resembles a serpent consuming itself. The head is represented by the galactic core

while the head is defined by the galactic core. By putting a serpent of light in the sky, YHVH was glorifying his preeminent creation in a way that we would see night after night. It is a great tragedy that such an

---

[a] Author Mark Flynn points out that God's pronouncement against the Nachash is given in Genesis 3:14, which seems a strange coincidence. Also, the numerical values of the Hebrew letters comprising the word *leviathan* add up to 1,146, which is equal to 365 x π.

elevated entity chose to break fellowship with the Maker.

Reinterpreting Lucifer

Perceptive readers may have noticed that this author hasn't used the name *Lucifer* to refer to Satan, as is commonly done. There's a good reason for that: Lucifer as a name for Satan is based on a misinterpretation of Isa. 14:1–23. Join me in a little historical revisionism as we snatch this title away from the Devil and give it to one equally despicable.

In the singular occurrence of its use in the Bible, Lucifer is a title given to an *earthly* king. Satan is not directly in view in Isaiah 14, where Lucifer's end is foretold. Let's take a few minutes to read this long but fascinating passage:

> But the Lord will have mercy on the descendants of Jacob. He will choose Israel as his special people once again. He will bring them back to settle once again in their own land. And people from many different nations will come and join them there and unite with the people of Israel. The nations of the world will help YHVH's people to return, and those who come to live in their land will serve them. Those who captured Israel will themselves be captured, and Israel will rule over its enemies. In that wonderful day when YHVH gives his people rest from sorrow and fear, from slavery and chains, you will taunt the king of Babylon. You will say,

> "The mighty man has been destroyed.
> Yes, your insolence is ended.[a]
> For YHVH has crushed your wicked power
> and broken your evil rule.
> You struck the people with endless blows of rage
> and held the nations in your angry grip
> with unrelenting tyranny.
> But finally the whole earth is at rest and quiet.
> Now it can sing again!
> Even the trees of the forest—
> the cypress trees and the cedars of Lebanon—

---

[a] Alternative translation: "How hath the oppressor [masculine] ceased! the golden city [feminine] ceased!"

sing out this joyous song:
    'Since you have been cut down,
        no one will come now to cut us down!'
In Sheol there is excitement
        over your arrival.
The spirits of world leaders and mighty kings long dead
        stand up to see you.
With one voice they all cry out,
        'Now you are as weak as we are!
Your might and power were buried with you.
        The sound of the harp in your palace has ceased.
Now maggots are your sheet,
        and worms your blanket.'
How you are fallen from heaven,
        O shining star, son of the morning!
You have been thrown down to the earth,
        you who destroyed the nations of the world.
For you said to yourself,
        'I will ascend to heaven and set my throne above God's stars.
I will preside on the mount of assembly
        on the heights of Zaphon.
I will climb to the highest heavens
        and be like the Most High.'
Instead, you will be brought down to the place of the dead,
        down to its lowest depths.
Everyone there will stare at you and ask,
        'Can this be the one who shook the earth
        and made the kingdoms of the world tremble?
Is this the one who destroyed the world
        and made it into a wasteland?
Is this the king who demolished the world's greatest cities
        and had no mercy on his prisoners?'
The kings of the nations lie in stately glory,
        each in his own tomb,
but you will be thrown out of your grave
        like a worthless branch.
Like a corpse trampled underfoot,
        you will be dumped into a mass grave
        with those killed in battle.

You will descend to the pit.
>   You will not be given a proper burial,
for you have destroyed your nation
>   and slaughtered your people.
The descendants of such an evil person
>   will never again receive honor.
Kill this man's children!
>   Let them die because of their father's sins!
They must not rise and conquer the earth,
>   filling the world with their cities.
This is what the Lord of Heaven's Armies says:
>   'I, myself, have risen against Babylon! I will destroy its children
and its children's children,'
>   says the Lord.
'I will make Babylon a desolate place of owls,
>   filled with swamps and marshes.
I will sweep the land with the broom of destruction.
>   I, the Lord of Heaven's Armies, have spoken!'" (Isa. 14:1–13)

That was a lot to take in, but there are only a few crucial lessons with which we need to concern ourselves for the time being. First, the entire passage is about a king of Babylon. It has often been assumed that the man in question was King Belshazzar, son of Nebuchadnezzar and last king of Babylon during Israel's seventy years of captivity, but the context of the passage excludes that conjecture. Isaiah set up the context by establishing a few unique parameters: (1) Israel will possess the promised land in peace; (2) Foreigners who had successfully invaded Israel will become Israel's prisoners of war; (3) Israel will rule over its adversaries; (4) The Jews will taunt the king of Babylon only after God has rescued them from oppression and given them utter peace; (5) The whole earth will be at rest and then break into celebration. Even the fir trees will rejoice because no feller comes against them any more (presumably in December). The fact is that none of these prerequisites have been fulfilled, thus we can be sure that the events of the chapter are yet to come.

Verse 4 of the taunt says, literally, that "the male oppressor ceased; she ceased gold-making." The *he* is the king of Babylon and the *she* is his consort. According to Revelation, Mystery Babylon is both a global theocracy and a great city, and is described in feminine terms—she is a harlot and a queen who is exceedingly wealthy. She is also said to ride the Beast (Rev. 17:7), for she "rules over the kings of the earth" until they turn against her (vv. 16–18). God will judge Babylon the Great by letting the Beast destroy her during the second half of Daniel's 70th week, and the merchants of the world will mourn her, crying, "Woe! Woe, O great city, dressed in fine linen, purple and scarlet, and glittering with gold, precious stones and pearls! In one hour such great wealth has been brought to ruin!" (Rev. 18:16). If the *she* of verse four is the rich whore who rides the Beast, then the male counterpart must be the Beast itself, which stands for both the Babylonian empire and its emperor.

The taunt continues on to describe the puzzlement of the throngs of souls in the grave who will not understand how this one king could have mercilessly destroyed the mightiest cities, took many prisoners, and brought the whole world, trembling, to its knees. Will Satan demolish the cities of the world or take prisoners? No, but his emissary will. As Daniel was told, the contemptible king "will cause astounding devastation and will succeed in whatever he does," attacking "the mightiest fortresses with the help of a foreign god."

The conclusion is that the Isaiah 14 oracle concerns the final and future king of Babylon, who is the beast from the Abyss, popularly known as the Antichrist. The oracle is not about Satan, but Satan's Seed.

In v. 12 of the King James translation, the king of Babylon is given the moniker Lucifer. The word *lucifer* was used by the Romans to refer to the planet Venus when it rises in the west, before the sunrise. It is a contraction of the Latin *lucem ferre*, which means "light-bearer," one who carries a source of illumination. Those Latin words were inserted by Catholic translators, but the original Hebrew is *heylel ben-shachar*. Scholars argue over the proper translation of this phrase. *Heylel* (Strong's #H1966) probably derives from *halal*, which can mean "to shine," "to be foolish," "to boast," or "to praise." *Ben-shachar* literally means "son of Dawn." According to Barne's commentary, *Heylel* is used elsewhere in Ezekiel "as a verb in the imperative mood of *Hiphil*, and is translated 'howl' from the verb *yālal* [Strong's #H3213], 'to howl' or 'cry.'"[58] If *heylel* is rendered as a verb, it is unclear whether the son or the parent is the one doing the wailing. Thus, the phrase can be translated "shining son of Dawn," or "boastful son of Dawn," or "howling son of Dawn," or "wailed-for son of the Dawn." Which is preferable? Ancient myths provide the answer.

In Babylon, the fertility goddess, Ishtar, was known as the *Star of Lamentation*.[59] Her insignia was the eight-pointed star, a symbol for the planet Venus with its eight-year cycle. Hymns about the Mesopotamian fertility goddess associate her with that celestial body, which has both a morning and an evening phase. Many of the ancient goddesses which stemmed from Ishtar incorporated bitter mourning as a central theme in their myths. Anat, Isis, Freya, Cybele, Itzpapalotl and others all wandered about with disheveled hair, howling at the loss of their lovers.

A better translation of Isa. 14:12 might be, "How you have fallen from the heights, O son of wailing Venus!" Isaiah was linking the King of Babylon to our neighboring planet, whose unmistakable pre-dawn appearance heralds daylight.[60] Even if the rendering of *heylel* as "wailing" is not correct, it is still the son of Venus which is in view here.

The questions we must now ask are these: How exactly did people of the ancient world regard the planet Venus, and how could a planet be the mother of the king of Babylon?

SIX

Venus and the Hero, Part I

August is the queen, the evening star, Inanna, unto the borders of heaven![61]

–Hymn to Inanna

After the Flood, when enough time had passed that the lowlands were no longer filled with mud and brackish lakes, a large portion of Noah's family moved away from their initial dwellings in the mountains. Both their point of origin and the direction in which they migrated are subjects of debate because the language of Gen. 11:2 is not plain to us, but they eventually ended up in modern-day Iraq, planting settlements along the Tigris and Euphrates rivers. They are known to secular historians as the *Ubaid* or *Proto-Euphratean* people.

The land centered around the two great rivers is known as Mesopotamia, and while the evolution of civilization in that region was nuanced, for simplicity's sake we can say that the primarily Semitic groups (i.e., descendants of Shem) who settled central Mesopotamia became the Akkadians and the primarily non-Semitic groups who settled southern Mesopotamia became the Sumerians.[62] Both groups came out of the Ubaidians and eventually spawned the Assyrians and Babylonians. In these civilizations, the planet Venus was venerated and categorized in a primary triad with sun and moon.[63] By tracking the movements of those three bodies, ancient man was able to precisely apportion cycles of time, predict stellar events, and establish important units of measurement—especially by incorporating Mercury and the very bright star named Sirius.[64]

The people of Mesopotamia believed that the stellar bodies were not simply objects, but gods, and the active members among them (i.e., the sun, moon, and planets) received highest honors. The stellar activities of those gods were sometimes turned into stories to assist in teaching and memorization.

However, there has to be more to ancient myth than a fanciful presentation of celestial mechanics. Some of the mythological attributes and actions of the gods are too unusual to have been derived from the uniform appearance and predictable motion of the planets. For instance, Cronus (Saturn) castrated his father and consumed his own children, and Inanna/Venus was uncovered and raped by a gardener while she slumbered.[65] Although several scholars have tried their hand at linking the gods' mythical traits with planetary appearance and conduct, the results have been less than convincing. We will find that the stories of the gods make much more sense when viewed primarily as embellishments of events that changed the landscape of human life in the early days of our history.

The Original Queen of Heaven

Beginning in Sumer, the planet Venus was personified by the most important goddess of the Mesopotamian pantheon[66]: Inanna, Queen of Heaven, known to the Akkadians as Ishtar. The Sumerians recognized her as both the morning star and evening star,[67] and both titles can be found within the text of a single hymn.[68]

Inanna/Ishtar was the goddess of erotic love, fertility, and war. Always depicted as a bold young woman who unabashedly wielded her feminine power, Inanna was called "The Great-Hearted Mistress" but also the "Queen of All Given Powers."[69] Some representations of her warring aspect show her armored and holding a bow; others show her riding a lion or lions.[70]

Inanna's cult center was in the city of Uruk (Sumerian: *Unug*), the biblical Erech,[71] and her temple there was called E-Anna, "House of Anna". Uruk/Unug/Erech was called "the town of the sacred courtesans" in reference to Inanna's temple prostitutes. Inanna herself was called "courtesan of the gods."[72] In the Babylonian *Epic of Gilgamesh*, the author describes the goddess Ishtar (the Akkadian name for Inanna) as being both generous and cruel to her many lovers, and Gilgamesh pities all those who would fall under her spell. He accuses her of breaking the gods as one would a steed. After the gigantic god-king, Gilgamesh, refuses Ishtar's advances, she complains to the chief god, Anu, and he gives her the mystical bull of heaven with which to avenge herself. Unfortunately for Ishtar, Gilgamesh kills the beast. Despite Ishtar's attempted homicide, she and the giant hero still end up mating at the end of the tale.

Like many other Mesopotamian gods, Inanna was often depicted with wings and a egg-shaped or conical helmet encompassed by horns. The wings indicated deity; the horns, authority and power; and the conical helmet, connection to the spirit world. The same sort of conical head-piece was used by priests and magicians in diverse cultures, which may be why we still depict wizards and witches wearing tall, pointed hats. For instance, the Salii, who were the priests of Mars, donned egg-shaped, spiked headdresses during their religious service.[73] In religious art, coni-cal headpieces encompassed by horns were reserved for the gods, but generally the junior classes of gods, who were corporeal, and not the higher, ethereal gods.

Figure 6–1. Four examples of conical hats worn by deities or priests. From left to right: (1) The Berlin Golden Hat, a Late Bronze Age artifact (one of four such conical hats found in Europe thus far), currently residing in the Neues Museum, Berlin. Photo © Xenon 77, Wikimedia Commons, CC-by-3.0; (2) *Head of a Priest*, c. A.D. 150-250. Limestone. Dallas Museum of Art, gift of David T. Owsley via the Alvin and Lucy Owsley Foundation. Image courtesy Dallas Museum of Art; (3) Lamassu from the citadel of Sargon II, now housed in the Louvre, Paris. Image unattributed; (4) Statue of Osiris sitting, a Late Period Egyptian bronze carving with gold incrustations. Photo © Rama, Wikimedia Commons, CC-by-sa 2.0-fr.

Could this adornment have become popular because it was a real device in use by those with sacred knowledge? Did it, as some claim, increase spiritual sensitivity? Their theory is buoyed by the similarity of conical helmets to cone-shaped *omphalos* stones that were placed on top of pillars in important temples throughout the world. *Omphalos* means "navel," and when used in a religious sense the word signifies a point of connection between the physical and spiritual planes. In addition, many cultures practiced head-binding, a shocking method of cranial constric-tion which elongated the skulls of children into a shape similar to the headdresses of the gods. Some tribes in Australia still maintain the belief that elongated heads are associated with wisdom, higher status, and closeness to the world of the spirits.[74]

The Skidi American Indians of Nebraska were astronomically oriented and had special reverence for Venus. It is taught among the Skidi that the "second god [that] Tirawahat placed in the heavens was Evening Star, known to the white people as Venus.... She was a beautiful woman. By speaking and waving her hands she could perform wonders."[75] Why would these Native Americans describe Venus as a woman performing magical incantations? Is it because the planet behaves in a way that resembles a female magician, or because a famous female magician of antiquity became associated with the planet?

Stronger evidence comes from an Egyptian story, *The Legend of Ra and Isis,* written in the hieratic character upon a papyrus preserved in Turin. In setting the stage for the tale, the narrator reveals that the goddess Isis lived the life of a mortal woman.

> Behold, the goddess Isis lived in the form of a woman, who had the knowledge of words [of power].... Was it not possible to become even as was Ra in heaven and upon earth, and to make [herself] mistress of the earth, and a [mighty] goddess...?[76]

The story goes on to describe how Isis got her wish and obtained the sun god's power through trickery and incantations. Most scholars are agreed that Isis was the Egyptian version of Inanna, so at least one Egyptian lore-master believed that Inanna was a human sorceress who grasped divinity by way of intellect and magic.

Let us embrace the possibility that Inanna was not only a deity traversing the celestial sphere, but also a human priestess upon the earth. She may have been one of the first pagan[a] priestesses in history, teaching men to worship the heavenly host as gods. On account of her spiritual trendsetting, her relationships with fearsome men, and her accomplish-

---

[a] Polytheism and paganism are one and the same. The Bible reveals that the gods who are worshiped throughout Gentile nations are actually Satan and his fallen angels under a variety of guises (2 Kings 17:15, Jer. 19:13, 1 Cor. 10:20). In Scripture, angels are equated with celestial bodies; in the heathen world, gods are almost always associated with celestial bodies. Furthermore, when God dispersed the people at Babel, fallen angels were allotted to them, and God said that the people would be drawn away from him and end up worshiping those angels as gods (Deut. 4:19).

ments in war, sorcery, and urban development, she was elevated to divine status. The legends of Inanna attribute her with many superhuman deeds, and we can safely assume that most of them are myths intended to teach lessons about astronomy or astrology, but they may not all be entirely fanciful. Did the tales of the fertility and war goddess have their origins in an exceptionally well-loved yet feared woman in ancient Mesopotamia? If we heed Euhemerus, a philosopher at the Macedonian court in the 4th century BC, the question is a fair one, for he argued that the gods were originally men who had achieved great success and "after their death received divine honours from a grateful people."[77]

The Anthropomorphic Strategy

If Inanna derived from a historical priestess-queen, which queen was it and precisely why was she deified? Answering those questions will require us to lay some groundwork, and it may seem that our study is diverging from its rightful trajectory, but bear with it because we will return to the issue at hand before long.

Early on, the beauty of the heavenly bodies must have captured the affections of men more than any other aspect of nature, especially since there was no air pollution or light pollution to obscure their radiance. The sun in particular must have made a great impression on the early farmers and nomads who depended on it completely for every aspect of life, from food, to time-keeping, to safe travel. Even in the modern age, that great star seems to draw our thoughts inexorably towards the Great Spirit. In the words of hymn-writer Joseph Addison,

> Th' unwearied sun, from day to day,
>   Does his Creator's pow'r display,
> And publishes to every land
>   The work of an Almighty hand.[78]

The glorious orb of day belongs to no man, but gives life to all without favoritism, and even the earliest men rightly recognized it as the most appropriate symbol of the perpetual power and provision of the Creator. Modern man is guilty of depicting our earliest ancestors as primitive brutes who worshiped an inanimate ball of gas out of sheer ignorance, but that portrayal is naïve. They did not believe the sun itself to be God, but they did revere it as an expression of divine glory and benevolence, and especially steadfastness.

Sovereign Grand Commander of the Scottish Rite of Freemasonry, General Albert Pike (1809–1891), a man with rare knowledge of ancient occult teachings, emphasized the centrality of *immutability* in man's veneration of the sun.

> Originally they looked beyond the orb to the invisible God, of whom the Sun's light, seemingly identical with generation and life, was the manifestation and outflowing…. [I]t came up regularly, as it now does, in the morning, like a god, and again sank, like a king retiring…. We worship immutability…. His light-giving and life-giving powers were secondary attributes.[79]

The sun was—and for some still is—the symbol of an unchanging deity who should be worshiped.

Within relatively little time after the Flood, many of Noah's descendants had lost their understanding of God as a personal creator who desires to be reconciled to his creatures, and had come to see God as an impersonal and distant spirit who had delegated to powerful but lesser spirits (gods) the task of running the world and overseeing the affairs of men. It was thought that the spirits responsible for running the various aspects of nature, including the sun and moon, did their jobs voluntarily. It followed that men should petition the spirits to do their jobs faithfully. The sun and moon, being the most necessary and affecting powers of nature, should be addressed most fervently. At least, that is how the priests of the pagan, *mystery* religions instructed their followers, but the religious leaders themselves had a more complex belief which will be understood as we progress in our study.

Incidentally, the *mystery* aspect of the pagan religions refers to secret teachings learned through a combination of observation, reason, and communion with spirits, and circulated solely amongst initiates of the priesthood. The secret knowledge of cosmic patterns and principles, and the technologies afforded by their application, gave those in sacred office great power over the masses.

According to the Book of Jubilees, man was herded towards polytheism by spirit beings. Secular scholars would have us believe that the Book of Jubilees is one of the pseudepigrapha—texts whose real author(s) attributed it to a famous person of the past—and that it has a 2nd-century origin,[80] but there is no way of proving that claim. All we can know for sure is that the earliest extant copies of Jubilees were made in the 2nd century BC.[a] It could have been originally penned on Mount Sinai, as the book's introduction asserts, or it could have been a scribe's masterful attempt to fill in the gaps of the biblical narrative by drawing on other Hebraic literature and oral traditions. Either way, we should pay heed to the Book of Jubilees because it is referenced and honored often in the writings of the early Christian church. The text presents itself as a divine revelation narrated to Moses by the Angel of the Presence, and when the narrator refers to *us*, it should be understood to mean angels. In the following excerpt, the angel tells Moses that a problem arose soon after the Flood:

> Unclean demons began to lead astray the children of the sons of Noah, and to make to err, and [to] destroy them. And the sons of Noah came to Noah their father, and they told him concerning the demons which were leading astray and blinding and slaying his sons' sons. And he prayed before the Lord his God, and said, "God of the spirits of all flesh.... let thy grace be lift up upon my sons, and let not wicked spirits rule over them lest they should destroy them from the earth.... Thou knowest how thy Watchers, the fathers of these spirits, acted in my day: and as for these spirits which are living, imprison them and hold them fast in the place of condemnation, and let them not bring destruction on the sons of thy servant, my God; for these are malignant, and created in order to destroy.... And let them not have power over the sons of the righteous from henceforth and for evermore." And the chief of the spirits, Mastema, came and said: "Lord, Creator, let some of them remain before me, and let them harken to my voice, and do all that I shall say unto them; for if some of them are not left to me, I shall not be able to execute the power of my will on the sons of men; for these are for corruption and leading astray before my judgment, for great is the wickedness of the sons of men.' And He [God] said: Let the tenth part of them remain before him, and let nine parts descend into the place of condemnation." And one of us [angels] He commanded that we should teach Noah all their medicines; for He knew that they would not walk in uprightness, nor strive in

SATAN

---

[a] Some additions and modifications may have been made to Jubilees between the time of its composition and the time of its use at Qumran. For instance, the second half of the last chapter seems tacked-on and introduces some Sabbath-keeping instructions which have no parallel in the Torah.

righteousness. And we did according to all His words: all the malignant evil ones we bound in the place of condemnation and a tenth part of them we left that they might be subject before Satan on the earth. And we explained to Noah all the medicines of their diseases, together with their seductions, how he might heal them with herbs of the earth. And Noah wrote down all things in a book as we instructed him concerning every kind of medicine. Thus the evil spirits were precluded from (hurting) the sons of Noah. (Jub. 10:1–14)[81]

If this text is to be believed, demons were plaguing the first antediluvian families. Noah asked God for help, and God was willing, but Satan, here called Mastema, objected. He felt it necessary that some of the demons be left on the earth. These spirit creatures were evidently not Satan's peers, but children of the Watchers who had become subject to Satan after death. Nevertheless, Satan worked out a deal wherein a tenth of the demons would serve him while the rest were confined to "the place of condemnation," which is known in the New Testament as the Abyss. Before their numbers were diminished, these demons were leading men astray, and we can imagine that the remnant continued engaging in similar activity afterward, under the direction of Satan. Exactly what *leading astray* entailed is not elucidated in the text, but the Bible uses similar language many times to indicate spiritual rebellion that culminates in idol worship, sexual depravity, and human sacrifice.

In the next chapter of Jubilees, after the narrative passes the Tower of Babel incident, the angel tells Moses that malignant spirits deceived men into worshiping idols.

And they made for themselves molten images, and they worshipped each the idol, the molten image which they had made for themselves, and they began to make graven images and unclean simulacra, and malignant spirits assisted and seduced [people] into committing transgression and uncleanness. And the prince Mastema [Satan] exerted himself to do all this, and he sent forth other spirits, those which were put under his hand, to do all manner of wrong and sin, and all manner of transgression, to corrupt and destroy, and to shed blood upon the earth. (11:4–6)[82]

Here we see a distinction between the angels of Satan who seduced men into worshiping gods, and another class of spirits who were put under Satan's control, who seem to have incited unjust killing and other immoral deeds. The latter must be the remnant of the same sons of the Watchers as were tormenting Noah's grandchildren previously. These two groups encouraged idolatry, vice, and barbarism, thus bringing about the feuding polytheistic kingdoms of Sumeria and Akkad.

By deceiving the children of Noah into worshiping the sun and moon, Satan succeeded in diverting the gratitude that should have been directed to the infinite Creator and aiming it instead at finite natural bodies. Thenceforth it was Sol who gifted the world with the heat that powered the engines of life, and also the illumination by which we learn, do work, and are psychologically energized. It was Luna who presided over water and darkness and, by extension, germination of seed in moist, dark places. Continuous provision from the Lord of Spirits was no longer sought after. This became all the more true because Satan convinced men that the heavenly bodies held the key to knowing the future.[83]

On one level, this belief about the stars was not incorrect. The Bible reveals that YHVH created the celestial bodies not only as time-keeping devices, but also as signs and markers of events that are especially important to God. However, these markers are the milestones of transgressive and redemptive history, not devices by which individuals at any given time may know and alter their destinies. When we engage in astrology, not only are we misapplying the celestial signs, we are trying to rewrite the story that God has already composed—an action which is futile as well as foolish.

A clock shows what time it is but does not make time progress. In the same way, the planets and constellations are indicators of what will occur at important points in history, but they do not determine the course of history. Astrology has it backwards.

To complete our line of thought, we need to understand why the worship of planets and stars became the worship of human beings. The goal of the fallen angels under Satan's leadership is to redirect loyalty and obedience away from God and towards themselves, and success in that venture doesn't come effortlessly. Even though God became distant from the fallen world after sin entered it, men still hunger for him. Rooted deep in the human psyche is a desire to honor and seek out the person who created us; we want to know our Maker. Unfortunately, as long as a man has an unregenerate heart, his model of life is centered on self and he finds it difficult to relate to an unseen spirit who truly is the center of all life. It is perhaps less difficult, but still awkward, for a spiritually lost man to worship the celestial bodies, which are beautiful but distant and foreign. Satan's solution was to link the stars with humanoid characters, real or imagined.[84] In other words, the fallen angels used the technique of anthropomorphism to procure worship by proxy.

Unfortunately, we lack any direct evidence tying a historical woman to the goddess of Venus, but we can find what we need indirectly by examining Inanna's divine family.

The First Ancestor Worship

The Mesopotamian supreme god was Anu (Heaven), the sky-father, and his consort was Ki (Earth). Together they bore Enlil, god of the air, and Enki, god of water and the Abyss. (In Greek mythology, Uranus was equivalent to Anu and Gaia to Ki.) The preeminence of Anu was recognized by the Ubaidians[a] but diminished over time so that he became a rather distant and unconcerned deity. (Likewise, the Greek sky father, Uranus, was not highly regarded and went mostly unworshiped.)

As Anu faded from the limelight, the Sumerians concentrated their worship on the god Enlil. They called him Shepherd, Lord of the Land, and Rightful King. Enlil was the firstborn son of Anu, a faceless deity who could be equated to God-the-Father of Christian theology. Enlil was the Lord of the Wind and the First Breath of the universe, and also god of destruction. He fathered and ruled over the first generation of gods, ordered the creation of mankind, and gifted man with agriculture. Of course, in the Bible, YHVH directs the Four Winds and generates the Breath of Life, and he created both man and the angels whom men call gods. YHVH taught Adam to farm, so immediately we see a parallel between Enlil and YHVH, especially YHVH in the form of God-the-Son, through whom all things were created (1 Col. 1:16; cf. John 1:3).

Enlil's only equal was his brother, Enki, who disputed the birthright. Known as the lord of the waters of the Abyss, it was he who presided over the netherworld, whose watery gate was at a place called Eridu. Enki was the patron of all magic, knowledge, arts, and civilization, and although he was incredibly inventive, he never created anything from scratch. Most telling, an assembly of gods prohibited Enki from communicating with humans, but the clever deity found a way to circumvent that

---

[a] Flood survivors and their early descendants

edict and whisper his instructions to earthlings anyway. That all sounds strangely akin to the biblical Satan.

In the Sumerian creation myth, Enlil created the Garden of Eden and gave the decree to fashion the first man and woman, but Enki acted as lead designer. And in the Sumerian flood myth, it was Enlil who sent the Deluge because of his frustration with mankind, but Enki provided the boat plans with which some humans saved themselves. These stories are very close to Biblical accounts with the exception that a secondary deity is assigned a prime role as mankind's helper.

Tucked within a Sumerian epic poem entitled *Enmerkar and the Lord of Aratta* lies a speech about the division of tongues in early Mesopotamian history. Enmerkar, the king giving the speech, points out that in the beginning everyone spoke to Enlil in one language. The land was at peace, yet Enki saw fit for some unspecified reason to bring confusion into the tongues of men. Renowned Assyriologist Samuel Noah Kramer translates the text as follows:

> Once upon a time there was no snake, there was no scorpion,
> There was no hyena, there was no lion,
> There was no wild dog, no wolf,
> There was no fear, no terror,
> Man had no rival.[a]
> In those days, the lands of Subur (and) Hamazi,
> Harmony-tongued Sumer, the great land of the decrees of princeship,
> Uri, the land having all that is appropriate,
> The land Martu, resting in security,
> The whole universe, the people in unison
> **To Enlil in one tongue [spoke]**…
> (Then) Enki, the lord of abundance (whose) commands are trustworthy,
> The lord of wisdom, who understands the land,
> The leader of the gods,
> Endowed with wisdom, the lord of Eridu
> **Changed the speech in their mouths, [brought] contention into it,**
> Into the speech of man **that (until then) had been one.**[85]

Notice the distinct lack of praise for Enlil and the abundant praise for

---

[a] For many decades after the Flood, the animal population was meager and lacked diversity. It likely took hundreds of years for the surface of the earth to once again teem with life.

Enki even though he was responsible for disharmony among the Sumerians. Something is amiss.

Sumerian records are replete with accounts of Enki's defiance of Enlil. Often, Enlil is portrayed as cruel and abusive, whereas Enki is cast in a favorable light. In *The Anunnaki Chronicles,* popular author Zecharia Sitchin compared the biblical God to the Sumerian gods and made this observation:

> As far as personal characters were concerned, Enki, the fashioner of Mankind, was more forebearing, less stringent with both gods and mortals. Enlil was stricter, a "law and order" type, uncompromising, unhesitant to mete out punishments when punishment was due.[86]

The strictness of Enlil is presented as a bad thing instead of a wonderful thing, as it really is. If God, like Enki, was willing to wink at sin, then he would be a hypocrite, double-minded, and thus flawed. In that case, there would be no absolute standard for goodness and justice, leaving those terms without meaning. Enki may appeal to the sensibilities of fallen, sinful human beings who wish to get away with wickedness, but being appealing is not the same as being good.

In other words, Enlil as Lord of the Firmament and ruler of the gods is the good guy, and is equivalent to the pre-incarnate Yeshua (although a distorted and imperfect version of him that at one point engaged in sexual deviance).[a] And Enki is none other than Satan, the first and most powerful heavenly creature, who in his hubris bills himself as the brother of Yeshua.

After the first branch of the family tree, the Sumerian pantheon becomes increasingly convoluted, with different cuneiform texts providing conflicting reports about who sired who, and who favored who. Fortunately, extant texts do agree on the fact that Inanna had a brother who was the sun god. His name was Utu (Akkadian: *Shamash*), Prince of Justice, and he was favored by Enki.

And who was this Utu? Perhaps a deified version of Shem or Ham (Hebrew: *Cham*), because Utu's Akkadian name was *Shamash*, and Hebrew and Akkadian are both Semitic languages. The name *Ham* means "burnt"

---

[a] It must be stressed that the stories about Enlil and his father, Anu, do not accurately reflect the moral perfection of their real-life counterparts. The Sumerians may have had a decent grasp on the hierarchy of heaven, but over time they twisted the personalities of the holy ones and sullied their reputations.

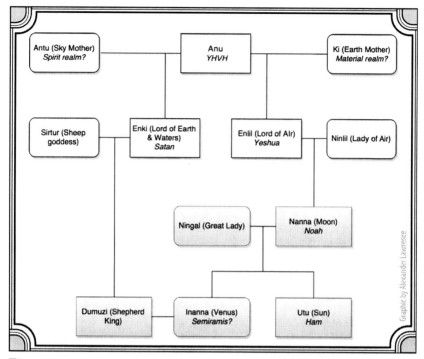

Figure 6–2. Sumerian genealogical tree (simplified for ease of comprehension).

or "hot," which certainly makes it tempting to associate him with Utu. If true, that would make Noah the father of Utu.

Utu's father in the Sumerian pantheon was the moon god, Nanna, who is listed immediately after the preeminent gods Anu, Enlil, Inanna, and Enki in Early Dynastic god registers.[87] Nanna is depicted on cylinder seals as an old man with a flowing beard and a crescent symbol. Both features would be applicable to Noah, but the crescent is particularly telling. It is natural that Noah would be linked with the moon because YHVH's sacred calendar is based on lunar cycles, and old man Noah would have made sure that his family was worshiping Anu (i.e., YHVH) in accordance with that calendar. The Book of Jubilees states that Noah went forth from the Ark on the New Moon of the third month and constructed an altar on which he made atonement for the earth. It states also that Noah held celebrations on the New Moons of the first, fourth, seventh, and tenth months of each year, which became an ordinance for Israel forever.[a]

---

[a] This is why we find reference to New Moon festivals in both Old and New Testaments,

In a text entitled *Nanna-Suen's Journey to Nippur*, Nanna brings first-fruit offerings to Enlil,[88] which is interesting because the Torah establishes first-fruit offerings as a critical component of the worship of YHVH. Like his ancestors, Noah was well versed in the festivals of YHVH (including First Fruits) and the sacrifices that were required in conjunction with those festivals. The fact that Nanna offered such a sacrifice to Enlil and not Enki is suggestive that Nanna was indeed the patriarch, Noah.

If Nanna was simply a pagan god and not a deified version of Noah, we would expect him to be the one granting power and high status to his son, but such was not the case. It was Enki, not Nanna, who exalted Utu/Shamash: "Enki placed in charge of the whole of heaven and earth the hero... the youth Utu."[89] We've seen how Enki parallels Satan, so it would seem that Satan was responsible for turning the wise, long-lived patriarchs into gods.

Identifying Nanna as Noah implies that Noah begat a daughter after the Flood, for Utu was Inanna's brother. Unlike Noah and his sons, however, Inanna did not respect and obey Anu (YHVH). Inanna was described in some Sumerian stories as the beloved of Anu, but she did not favor the sky-father as he did her, for she appropriated his worshipers in one myth and in another defied his instructions not to destroy Mount Ebih, whose crime was failure to acknowledge Inanna's superiority.[90]

In the fragmentary text entitled *Inanna and An[u]*, the goddess and her brother Utu lament the fact that the temple E-Anna is not under their domain, so Inanna journeys to see Anu and convince him to relinquish his authority to her. He is shocked but eventually concedes, and power shifts from the priests of Anu to the priests of Inanna.[91] This story likely illustrates from the pagan perspective the Ubaidians' widespread realignment away from the faith of Noah.

What a Girl Wants

Inanna's quest for power doesn't stop there. In a myth called *Inanna and the Mes* we find the goddess tricking Enki into giving her the divine blueprints of civilization and taking off in his heavenly boat while he lies about in a drunken stupor. Most of the stories about Inanna demonstrate that she gets what she wants, one way or another.

---

even though the Torah contains no explicit instructions about how to celebrate new moons.

One of those things that Inanna fancied was a powerful king, the first postdiluvian world-conqueror, a man described as partially divine and perfect in appearance. Not only was he a mighty warrior and brilliant tactician, but he possessed secrets by which he spread an advanced civilization. Inanna didn't fail to gain his affections.

The world's oldest civilizations held the common belief that demigods with special knowledge from above walked the earth in the early days. References to such men may be found in the Ramayana, Mahabharata, Vedas, Shastras, Edda, Zend Avesta, Codex Chimalpopoca, Popul Vuh, Triads, Visuddhi Maga, Ipuwer, Ermitage Papyri, and other ancient accounts. Chief among the male demigods was a mighty warrior, hunter, and builder who was associated with the solar deity. He went by many names; one of the more familiar is *Gilgamesh*. Through a combination of military power and industriousness, he brought a large degree of unification and urbanization to the early tribes. Towering over other men, his presence was awesome in their eyes. Even his beard was glorious, and most accounts make mention of it. *Who is like him?* is a phrase commonly found in the stories of this archetypal hero. Take, for example, this passage about Ninurta:

> Lord Ninurta, king of the Anuna gods, holding a cudgel (mace) in his right hand, bearded, you fall as a torrent on all enemies; who can rival your great works? Hero, deluge, without equal... who pillages the cities, who subjugates the mountains, son of Enlil, who will rise up against you? Ninurta, lord, son of Enlil, hero, **who is like you?**[92]

Or this passage about the giant Gilgamesh, who regularly petitioned the sun god for favor and assistance:

> Supreme over other kings, lordly in appearance, he is the hero, born of Uruk, the goring wild bull.... Mighty net, protector of his people, raging flood-wave who destroys even walls of stone!.... It was he who opened the mountain passes, who dug wells on the flank of the mountain. It was he who crossed the ocean, the vast seas, to the rising sun, who explored the world regions, seeking life.... **Who can compare with him** in kingliness?.... Two-thirds of him is god, one-third of him is human. The Great Goddesss [Aruru] designed(?) the model for his body, she prepared his form... beautiful, handsomest of men.... "**There is no rival who can raise a weapon against him.**"[93]

This same phrase is used to speak of the Antichrist when he comes on the scene at the end of the age: "And they worshiped the beast, saying, **'Who is like the beast, and who can fight against it?'**" (Rev. 13:4).

In the tales of various ancient cultures, this primeval hero had a wife or consort of legendary femininity who in some fashion gained access to the underworld; Inanna, Isis, Sita, Anat, and others fall into this category. Inanna actually gave her first husband over to the demons of the netherworld in a fit of rage after barely being rescued from it herself.[94] Often the wife of the hero was also his sister and hunting partner. The relationship of the demigod and his sibling-wife was portrayed as a passionate, exotic, and tumultuous one—the epitome of the kind of celebrity marriage that sells tabloids—and they were lucky that the paparazzi weren't around at that time.

Sumerian poems recorded on cuneiform tablets will help us understand more about this power couple.

Figure 6–3. Clay tablet inscribed in Akkadian cuneiform with a fragment of the *Epic of Etana*. (Photo credit: The Pierpont Morgan Library, New York. MLC 1363.)

SEVEN

Venus and the Hero, Part II

As indicated by her title *Urania* ["*Celestial One*"], Aphrodite is to be identified with the planet Venus, known throughout the ancient Near East as the "Queen of Heaven." In this celestial identification the Greek goddess conforms to what amounts to a universal rule. Thus, a systematic analysis of the various mother goddesses will reveal an indissoluble connection with the planet Venus.[95]

–Ev Cochrane

In the epic poem called *Enmerkar and the Lord of Aratta*, Inanna is loved by the lord of a region named Aratta, but she is also loved by the lord of Kulaba. The latter happens to be her brother (or perhaps nephew, depending on translation), a radiant youth named Enmerkar, who is one of the most prominent figures of Sumerian epics. He built a city called Unug Kulaba with mud-bricks—there were no stone quarries available in southern Mesopotamia—and was determined to build ziggurats in both Unug and Eridu. As mentioned previously, Unug is the same as Uruk/Erech, a city near the mouth of the Euphrates river, and it probably lent its name to the modern country of Iraq, in which it is located.[96]

The King's Yoke

Evidently Inanna was very impressed with Enmerkar because she spurned the lord of Aratta, who did not plan to build a house of brick for her.

The lord of Aratta placed on his head the golden crown for Inanna. **But he did not please her like the lord of Kulaba** [i.e., Uruk]. Aratta did not

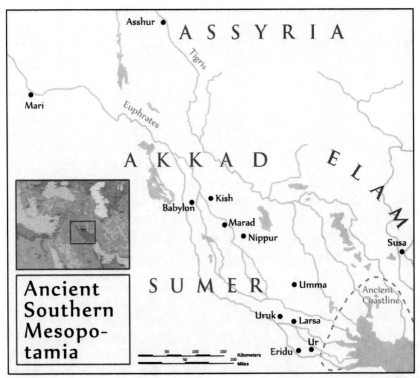

Figure 7-1. Map of major population centers in Southern Mesopotamia only a few centuries after the Flood.

build for holy Inanna—unlike the Shrine E-ana, the ĝipar, the holy place, unlike brick-built Kulaba. At that time, the lord chosen by Inanna in her heart, chosen by Inanna in her holy heart from the bright mountain, Enmerkar, the son of Utu, made a plea to his sister, the lady who grants desires, holy Inanna: "My sister, let Aratta fashion gold and silver skilfully on my behalf for Unug. Let them… build a holy mountain [i.e., a ziggurat] in Unug. **Let Aratta build a temple brought down from heaven—your place of worship,** the Shrine E-ana; let Aratta skilfully fashion the interior of the holy ĝipar, your abode; may I, the radiant youth, may I be embraced there by you. **Let Aratta submit beneath the yoke for Unug on my behalf.**"[97]

This story can be read in two ways as it pertains to Inanna: she can be seen as either a goddess in the heavens or a human priestess on Earth who is simultaneously seated in the heavens as Venus. Most historians subscribe to the former interpretation, but that presents difficulties. A goddess would not be the sister of a human lord. The text tells us that

Inanna's brother intended to embrace her in the house he would build for her, and he appealed to his youthful vigor when stating that intention.[a] Ennmerkar's age and health would hardly be pertinent if he was addressing a spirit being, but would be very pertinent if his goal was to woo a beautiful and influential woman. If Inanna was an exalted priestess before her deification by the Sumerians, we can understand why Enmerkar would want to show his affections by building her a place of worship at Unug Kulaba.

As it turned out, the lord of Aratta was not keen on providing resources for Enmerkar's building project, likely because the young man was a rival for Inanna's affections. Enmerkar eventually laid siege to Aratta, as described in the story *Lugalbanda and the Anzu Bird*.

All in the Family

These stories attest to the reality of Enmerkar as a historical personage, and that fact is reinforced by an ancient manuscript[b] know as the *Sumerian King List*. The relevant entry reads,

> En-me(r)-kar, son of Mes-kiag-gasher, king of Uruk, the one who built Uruk, became king and reigned 420 years.[98]

Of course, the accuracy of such a large number of years is highly suspect. The King List claims reigns of up to fifteen hundred years for some of the antediluvian (i.e., pre-Flood) rulers, which is significantly older than Methuselah, the oldest man ever to live. Either the figures on the King List were exaggerated, or, as suggested by Raúl Erlando López, whatever Sumerian scribe first wrote the King List had a document or oral tradition "containing [decimal] numerical information on the ages of... the patriarchs... and that he mistakenly interpreted it as being written in the

---

[a] The fact that Inanna would desire her close relative should not shock us, because incest would have been common for many years following the Flood. There wasn't yet a risk of genetic mutations occurring as a result of inbreeding. As far as we know, God did not outlaw marriages between siblings until after the Exodus (Lev. 18).

[b] Several ancient sources contain the list in full or in part.

sexagesimal[a] system."[99] Regardless, we shouldn't imagine, due to these fantastical numbers, that the King List is utter fiction. Many of the names and dates of later entries on the list are verifiable through other sources.

The Sumerian King List tells us that Enmerkar built Uruk, yet the book of Genesis tells us that builder of Uruk was Nimrod, the son of Cush.

> Cush begot Nimrod: he began to be a mighty one on the earth. He was a mighty hunter before the LORD: therefore it is said, "Like Nimrod the mighty hunter before the LORD." And the beginning of his kingdom was Babel, Erech [Uruk], Accad, and Calneh, in the land of Shinar. (Genesis 10:8–10, NKJV)

This Nimrod must be of some importance for Moses to have zeroed in on him out of the many descendants of Noah. The reason Moses did so is that Nimrod was the first pagan empire-builder and the prototype for the most powerful monarchs throughout history who have ruled over various incarnations of the Babylonian Empire. The Book of Revelation specifies that there have been seven such kings (17:10).

Nimrod was a rebel whose very name, in verb form, means "let us revolt." As the ruler of several major cities in Mesopotamia, he held sway over many people, and could have led them (further?) away from the faith of Noah. Many people believe that Nimrod built the Tower of Babel, which is a possibility, but Genesis doesn't state that Nimrod directed or even participated in the building of the Tower. Extrabiblical writings such as Josephus' Antiquities and the apocryphal Book of Jasher do specifically name Nimrod as the builder of the Tower and the primary instigator of the rebellion that took place in those days. Then again, Antiquities contains several verifiable errors, and the Jasher that we have today was edited by the Jamnia Council (ca. 100 AD) to conform to traditions which would enforce rabbinical authority.[b] Jasher contradicts the Bible on numerous accounts, which disqualifies it as a trustworthy source. Beyond that, Jasher makes the ludicrous claim that it took three days to walk the circumference of the tower of Babel. That would make for a

---

[a] A base sixty numerical system, as opposed to the base ten (decimal) system that we use in the modern world.

[b] Many Old Testament prophecies concerning the Messiah were also modified by decree of the council of Jamnia, making it harder to correlate the prophecies with the historical Yeshua of Nazareth. This is why the Masoretic version of the Old Testament (found in most Bibles) should be used with caution.

tower approximately twenty-four miles in diameter! Jasher does contain a lot of valid history, but we have to take whatever the book offers with a grain of salt.

There are legitimate reasons to suspect that Cush had more of a hand in the building of Babel than did his son. That's not to say that Nimrod wasn't involved, for many ancient accounts suggest otherwise, but his role may not have been as primary as tradition would claim. If nothing else, it's very suspicious that Genesis doesn't mention Nimrod at all in connection with the Tower. The narrative instead stresses that the decision to build the tower was made collectively, and that work was carried out in a spirit of more-or-less voluntary cooperation between realms. Nimrod may only have gained authority over Shinar after the Dispersion and after his father departed from Mesopotamia. Whatever the case may have been, Nimrod was probably a builder of cities, for Genesis tells us plainly that Babel and the other cities in southern Mesopotamia were only the beginning of his kingdom. The testimony of Moses that Nimrod ruled Uruk and the testimony of the SKL that Enmerkar built Uruk is grounds for correlating the two kings.

Some clarification may be needed here. The SKL states that Enmerkar built Uruk, but how could that be the case if his father was already ruling there as king? When Enmerkar's father, Meskiaggasher, brought kingship to Uruk, the settlement consisted primarily of a sacred complex called Kullab, within which stood a temple dedicated to Anu. It wasn't until the reign of Enmerkar that a temple district for Inanna was built near Kullab and a rightful city sprang up around it.

If Nimrod/Enmerkar inherited Kullab from his father, couldn't he have also inherited Babel, which Gen. 10:10 suggests is at least as old as Uruk? He needn't have been the founder of Babel in order to integrate what was left of it into his kingdom.

A Rebel by Any Other Name

Nimrod may have become venerated as the heroic Ninurta, the Assyrian god of war and agricultural cultivation, who subjugated the mountains and hunted both beasts and monsters. Ninurta had a temple dedicated to him in the city of Marad, which is located very near Kish and Babylon, and the tutelary deity of Marad was Lugal-Marada (lugal means "big man"). Ninurta was a prototype of a later god named Marduk, top dog of the Babylonian pantheon.[100] The first syllable of Marduk's name comes from the Chaldean word *mar*, or *mavor*, a noun meaning "rebel." Enmerkar, Ninurta, and Marduk all have ties to the Abzu/Abyss of Eridu, which is where Enmerkar built the temple of E-Abzu. Ninurta is not said to have built temples, but he did built mighty city walls and canals.

Adding to these shared traits is an etymological connection between the names of Nimrod and Enmerkar. Hebrew and other ancient Semitic languages had no vowels, so the name of Nimrod is represented by the letter *nun* plus the consonants m-r-d. *Nun* happens to be the Sumerian word for *monarch*[a], while the Hebrew *marad* signifies rebellion. Thus, *nmrd* means "Lord of Rebellion" or "Rebellious King." The name *Enmerkar* is comprised of four symbols transliterated as *en-me-er-kar2*. The exact meaning of at least one of these symbols is uncertain, but *en* signifies a divine ruler, and *kar2* is thought to indicate boasting or slandering and inciting. Enmerkar, who was a monarch, could therefore be called "King Enmer the Boastful" or "King Enmer the Slanderer," and both options are a good fit with Nimrod.

If Enmerkar was the real, Bible-attested king known as Nimrod, then Inanna would have been a real queen.

Now Noah and his sons, all of whom lived before the Flood and were saved from it because Noah feared YHVH, would not have easily abandoned his ways, so the practice of assigning godhood to natural bodies and forces most likely arose with Noah's grandchildren or more remote descendants. This is exactly what the Book of Jubilees indicates when it says, "And the sons of Noah came to Noah their father, and they told him concerning the **demons which were leading astray**... his sons' sons" (10:2). Considering the great antiquity of the oldest representations of stellar bodies as gods,[101] we can be comfortable in agreeing with Jubilees that surprisingly little time had passed before the appearance of paganism.

Speaking of early-onset paganism, archaeologists have discovered statues of humanoid lizards at Ur, Eridu, and Al Ubaid, and are at a loss to explain them.[102] These reptile-headed figurines (idols?) are slender overall but have unnaturally wide shoulders covered in bumps, and they have upon their heads cones like those worn by Sumerian gods, sans horns. Some of the figurines have breasts, and one is even breastfeeding a reptilian baby. It's well-known that reptiles were associated with many of

---

[a] Alternatively, the *nun* may stand for the Sumerian NIN, which means *lord*.

the pagan gods of the ancient world, and that serpents stood for wisdom and knowledge. Could it be that some of the families that were led astray by demons began to represent themselves with an appearance like that of the fallen angels? (A Sumerian story called *The Myth of Etana* seems to present one tribe of people as eagles and another as serpents.) We will perhaps never know the true meaning of these Ubaid figurines, but we can be sure that they weren't crafted by men of Noah's faith.

The Priest-King of Uruk

Nimrod is a popular candidate for the role of First Pagan—and that makes good sense considering that his name means "rebellion"—but we shouldn't knock Cush out of the running, because the Sumerians may have recognized Cush as a priestly king.

Author Peter Goodgame makes a good point when he writes in his book *The Second Coming of the Antichrist* that in order for Cush to be "recognized as a priest and king on the Sumerian King List, he had to have been a servant of the god Enki, their favorite god and 'king-maker.'"[103] Technically, Enlil was the god primarily responsible for bestowing royal authority, not Enki, but many of Enlil's roles were purloined by Enki, so the point remains valid. Enki was lord of the earth and water, and god of magic and intelligence. Some Sumerian texts portray him as the brother of the sun, Utu, but others portray him as Utu's grandfather or uncle. We can ignore the conflicting reports and simply acknowledge that Enki and Utu were of the same heavenly family. And as we saw earlier in a quote from *Enki and the World Order*, it was Enki, not Enlil, who glorified the sun.

If the Sumerians wrote about Cush, it was by a different name. Egyptologist David Rohl asserts that Cush can be found in the Sumerian King List as Meskiaggasher (alt. spelling: *Mec-ki-aj-gacer*), Enmerkar's father. The SKL notes that he was a priestly lord and king who vanished into the sea.

Then Kiš [Kish] was defeated and the kingship was taken to E-ana. In E-ana, **Meš-ki-aĝ-gašer, the son of Utu, became lord and king**; he ruled for 324 years.[104]

The ideogram translated here as *lord* means both "master" and "priest."

Kish, the first settlement to have a king after the Flood, was located about a hundred miles northwest of Uruk. There is little doubt that it was named after Cush. Instruments of war were used to conquer the people of Kish, and they became subjects of the priest-king of E-Anna, which is a temple complex in Uruk. Incidentally, the first cuneiform sign of the name *Enmerkar* is the same sign used in the quote above about Meskiaggasher, which indicates that Enmerkar was a chip off the old block.

It is my contention that Cush/Meskiaggasher, not Nimrod/Enmerkar, provided the impetus for the building project at Babel. Allow me to explain.

Babel, Eridu, and the Abyss

Author Peter Goodgame has endorsed David Rohl's theory identifying Eridu as Babel, and he has assumed that Nimrod built the Tower there.[105] However, as previously shown, the division of languages at Babel had already occurred by the time that Enmerkar, king of Uruk, started pressuring Aratta to provide him with materials to build Enki's temple in Eridu. If Enmerkar is Nimrod then we are forced to conclude that he intended to construct a new shrine right over the top of the fallen Tower (if indeed it was toppled, as Josephus, Jasher, and Jubilees suggest). Why would Nimrod have turned around and built a ziggurat to a pagan god at the exact location where YHVH had very recently destroyed the rebel's first venture? And if that was the case, why was the result different? The shrine of E-Abzu at Eridu was completed and utilized extensively, as attested by numerous Sumerian records; yet Heaven never intervened.

The Greeks left us numerous accounts of a character called Belus who was influential in early Mesopotamia. Belus is the Latin version of *Bel* (or *Ba'al*), a title signifying "lord" or "master." Several gods of the Mesopotamian religions were given this title, but it originated with the first king of Sumer. Greek historian Diodorus Siculus claims that Belus founded a town on the river Euphrates[a] and there appointed men to be astrologer-priests (the Babylonians called them *Chaldeans*).[106] Diodorus' report, if accurate, affirms that Cush was the first notable pagan ruler of the area of Mesopotamia that the Bible calls *the Chaldees*. He, as much as Nimrod, was a rebel. Notice that the name *Bel* survives even in modern English

---

[a] The cities of Babel and Eridu were both built on the Euphrates.

within the word *rebel*. (As the rabbis say, coincidence is not kosher.)
The prologue of *The Code of Hammurabi* states,

> When Anu the Sublime, King of the Anunnaki, and Bel, the lord of
> Heaven and earth, who decreed the fate of the land, assigned to Mar-
> duk, the over-ruling son of Ea [Enki]... dominion over earthly man, and
> made him great among the Igigi, they called Babylon by his illustrious
> name, made it great on earth, and founded an everlasting kingdom in
> it.[107]

Hammurabi's words here make it clear that he considered Bel to be separate from Marduk and Enki. If Marduk is associated with Nimrod, then
Bel must have been one of Nimrod's ancestors —either Cush or Ham.

Works cited in Eusebius' *Praeparatio Evangelica* state that Belus established Babylon and lived there in a structure called the "Tower of Belus"
(9.18), and that Babylon's wall was built by Belus (9.41). Eusebius also
quotes Abydenus from *Concerning the Assyrians*, where the author recounts that Babylon "was originally water, called a sea," but Belus "put
an end to this, and assigned a district to each, and surrounded Babylon
with a wall; and at the appointed time he disappeared" (9.41). Don't miss
this bit: Belus and Meskiaggasher both disappeared. Many people wish
to equate Bel to Nimrod—and that is possible because Bel simply means
"lord," and Nimrod undoubtedly did receive that title—but ancient lore
tells us that Nimrod was killed, and his wife mourned over his corpse.
Lord Nimrod did not simply disappear.

To determine whether these accounts about Belus are reliable, we turn
to archaeological and linguistic evidence. We must begin by realizing
that multiple cities may have been called *Babel*. In her contribution to
the *Proceedings of the 51ˢᵗ Rencontre Assyriologique Internationale*, Stephanie Dalley of the University of Oxford shows that Babylon and Eridu
were interchangeable in ancient texts, and she hypothesizes that Eridu
was not the only Mesopotamian city to take up the name *Babylon*.[108] If
common belief is true and pagans changed the name *Babel*, meaning
"confusion," to the Akkadian *Bab-ilim*, meaning "gate of the gods," then
it would be reasonable for any great city with a ziggurat to be labeled
Babylon because the function of the ziggurat was to connect men with
the spirits. When ancient historians referred to Babel, they may not have
even known which Babel they were writing about.

The Book of Jubilees states that God "sent a mighty wind against the tower and overthrew it upon the earth, and behold it was **between As-syria and Babel** in the land of Shin'ar..." (10:26, CEPH). If the Tower was situated between northern Mesopotamia and Babel, then it could not have been *at* Babel. Jubilees also states that the whole land of Shinar is called *Babel* (10:25), which would suggest that the Babel of Gen. 10:10 was not a city at all, but a region. Perhaps the settlement that acted as home and headquarters for the tower-builders was the city of Kish, near modern-day Babylon. The SKL says that Kish was the first city after the Flood to have a king. If the cities listed in Gen. 10:10 are given in order of their founding, then Babel was the first place ruled by Nimrod, which would make Babel and Kish synonymous because Enmerkar began his rule at Kish.

On the other hand, perhaps the name *Babel* was carried to Eridu, being that the ziggurat which Enmerkar built there became the seat of Satan. The Sumerians considered Eridu to be the abode of Enki, the god of wis-dom and magical incantations who we have already associated with Sa-tan. The theory that Eridu can be called *Babel* works in concert with the fact that Saint Peter addressed the church of Rome as the "church that is at Babylon" (1 Pet. 5:13). Biblically speaking, Babel/Babylon seems to be located wherever Satan has stationed himself in order to direct the affairs of the foremost government. Moreover, modern archaeologists consider Eridu, not Babylon, to be the oldest city in Mesopotamia[109]—although it must be said that this is subject to revision. The dating of Babylon is not conclusive because the water table at the site of modern Babylon is too high to allow for further vertical archaeological excavations.[110]

Yet the fact that Eridu is the oldest city that we know of does not rule out the possibility that the Tower was built at an even older site. Arche-ologists would not claim that every Ubaidian settlement has been dis-covered, and since no one can agree on exactly where Shinar was located, it's entirely possible that the remains of the Tower are still buried beneath the sands of Iraq.

Some researchers identify the ziggurat of Enki at Eridu as the bibli-cal Tower, noting that construction of one version of this sizable temple was never completed. It is true that the *Temple 1* structure at Eridu was abandoned midway through its erection, coinciding with the end of the Uruk period of ancient Sumer,[111] but the halt in construction could be attributed to war, climate change, or natural disaster instead of linguistic confusion. According to the SKL, the city-state of Kish fought against Elam, and Uruk warred against both Kish and Ur before being brought to ruin. But Genesis paints a different picture—one in which the spread of civilization into separate, warring city-states did not occur until after the fall of Babel. Before that time, Genesis indicates that Noah's descendants traveled together into Mesopotamia and cooperated to build the infamous Tower; they were not warring with one another during this process. Jubilees confirms this fact in ch. 11, the content of which takes place chronologically after the fall of Babel. It says,

> And the sons[a] of Noach **began** to war on each other, to take captive and to slay each other, and to shed the blood of men on the earth, and to eat blood, and to build strong cities, and walls, and towers, and individuals began to exalt themselves above the nation, and to found the beginnings of kingdoms (11:2–3, CEPH)

Any theory about Babel that places warfare or kingdom-building chronologically ahead of the Dispersion should therefore be viewed with suspicion.

It comes down to this: no one knows where the Tower of Babel was built or which region was considered to be Shinar.

Even though the Tower may have been built elsewhere, Eridu was a city of great importance. To the Sumerian mind, Eridu was sacred for a couple of reasons. First, the preamble to the Sumerian King List has it as the city where kingship first descended from heaven. This was long before "the flood swept over," and I tend to agree with Peter Goodgame's reasons for concluding that Eridu was the world's first city, the one built on the east of Eden by Adam and Eve's murderous son, Cain (Gen. 4:16–17). The Ubaidians somehow found the site of Cain's city and built a new settlement on top of it; perhaps they were led to it by the spirits that were leading astray Noah's grandsons.

Second, Eridu was holy because it sat atop the mouth of the Abzu, which in Greek is called the Abyss. Sumerian-language scholars define *abzu* as "(cosmic) underground water" which was typified by the ritual water container inside temples.[112] The Bible has no shortage of things to say about this water which is both underground and hyper-dimensional.

---

[a] The term *sons* here does not indicate Noah's immediate sons. In Hebrew, descendents many generations removed from their forefather are still considered his children.

The Abyss

As a **geological** feature, the Abzu is the source of water beneath the earth which comes up through the crust and becomes desalinated in the process. In the Hebrew scriptures it is known as *theum*, "the deep." In Job we find a distinction made between the abyss and the sea: "The deep says, 'It is not in me,' and the sea says, "It is not with me'" (28:14). The psalmist praises the mighty God who "set the earth on its foundations, so that it should never be moved. You covered it with the deep as with a garment; the waters stood above the mountains" (104:5–6). Here we see the word *theum* being applied to the primordial ocean which completely covered the new earth, but we know that when God flooded the world he did so by raining down water from heaven and rending the fountains of the deep (Gen. 7:11), so we are forced to conclude that part of the *theum* drained into pockets beneath the crust. This is verified in Ezekiel 31, where a mighty king is represented as a great cedar tree, and of him it is said, "The waters nourished it; the deep made it grow tall, making its rivers flow around the place of its planting" (v. 4). And again, further along, we read, "On the day the cedar went down to Sheol I caused mourning; I closed the deep over it, and restrained its rivers, and many waters were stopped. I clothed Lebanon in gloom for it, and all the trees of the field fainted because of it" (v. 15). These verses reveal that fresh water comes up from the *theum* to feed the plants of the earth, and when the waters of the deep are blocked, vegetation withers. Verse 15 also tells us that the Abyss covers Sheol, the prison of souls.

As a **supernatural** feature, the Abyss is the netherworld; the Bible calls it a pit and combines it as a single unit with Sheol: "O LORD, you have brought up my soul from Sheol; you restored me to life from among those who go down to the pit" (Psa. 30:3). And again: "…like Sheol let us swallow them alive, and whole, like those who go down to the pit" (Pro. 1:12). Moreover, the Abyss curls in on itself like a black hole, for John writes, "I saw a star fallen from heaven to earth, and he was given the key to the shaft of the **bottomless** pit" (Rev. 9:1). The bottomless pit occupies a higher dimension and is superimposed over the physical deep (theum): "Let not the flood sweep over me, or the deep swallow me up, or the pit close its mouth over me" (Psa. 69:15). Upon death, souls[a] are confined

---

[a] Even the soul of Messiah Yeshua was confined to the sides of the pit for three days before the Resurrection: "Now this, 'He ascended'—what does it mean but that He also first descended into the lower parts of the earth?" (Eph. 4:9, NKJV). This was as David

to desolate dwellings in the recesses of the pit, for the prophet says, "Yet you shall be brought down to Sheol, to the **lowest depths** of the Pit" (Isa. 14:15, NKJV). And elsewhere we read, "Graves are set in the uttermost parts of the pit" (Ezek. 32:23).

Yeshua told a story about a righteous man named Lazarus and an unrighteous, rich man who were both deceased; in the story they are on opposite sides of a great chasm—Lazarus in a lovely place but the rich man in torment—and they are able to perceive each other but are unable to leave their respective dwellings and cross over. That chasm which separates their souls is the Abyss, and it is the prison of many unclean spirits and of the Watchers who transgressed. The original Aramaic version of Jude's letter reads, "And the angels who did not guard their head, except left their abode, He keeps under guard in the netherworld, in the dark abyss until the great Day of Judgment" (1:6, ANT). In the last days, the gates of this Abyss will be opened and terrifying spirits will be released from it (Rev. 9:2–11).

The Sumerians were fascinated with the netherworld, and their stories make it clear that the way to enter the region of the dead was through the swirling waters at Eridu. Likewise, Job says that the dead "are **under** the waters" (26:5). The Sumerians described the Abzu as incomprehensible and unfathomable, and they recognized it as a type of the primordial abyss personified as the goddess Nammu. God-lists and other texts call Nammu the *mother of everything, womb of abundance,* and *primal matter.*[113] The Babylonians later clarified the Sumerian conception by splitting Nammu in two: the masculine *Apsû* and the feminine *Tiāmat,* representing the subterranean abyss and the cosmic abyss, respectively.

We will learn more about the significance of the Abzu as we continue our study, but what we need to understand for now is that the Abzu was the secret place of wisdom. Its name is composed of *ab,* meaning "sea," and *zu,* meaning "gnosis/wisdom." *Šurpu* tablet II, line 149, gives an epithet for *abzu* which is translated "home of wisdom." Finnish archaeologist Simo Parpola explains that "the chief synonym of *abzu, engur,* was from the earliest times written with an infixed *hal,* 'secret,' and thus must likewise have been associated with esoteric 'wisdom.'"[114]

The Hebrew name *Sheol* means "unseen," which is another way of describing secrecy. Sheol is unseen because it exists in another dimension, and the Abyss is unseen because it exists beneath the surface of the earth,

had prophesied: "For You will not leave my soul in Sheol, Nor will You allow Your Holy One to see corruption [i.e., decay]" (Psa. 16:10, NKJV).

but both of them are places of great mystery. The Babylonian religion installed by Cush's family is known as the *mystery religion,* and the occult (hidden) institutions which preserve and relay the esoteric wisdom of Babylon are called *mystery schools,* precisely because they revolve around the secret knowledge which was given by the gods now locked within the Abyss. This helps us to understand why Enmerkar/Nimrod was so intent on building a glorious temple (E-Abzu, "House of the Abyss") at Eridu, that he was ready to attack Aratta to obtain the necessary building materials. Not only was Eridu the first city ever built, but it was purportedly the location of an entrance into the Abyss.

The Hammer of the Whole Earth

After YHVH thwarted man's efforts at Babel, we can imagine that a significant portion of the populace blamed Cush for the judgment that befell them, and so he temporarily retreated from Shinar, perhaps to Uruk or Eridu. There he determined to restore order through force, and forged weapons with which to realize his goal.

Bows and slings were probably already being used for hunting before the time of the Dispersion, and these would have become primary weapons of warfare; but some of the first hand-to-hand weapons crafted were simple but brutal clubs with stone or metal heads shaped like pears. The battleaxe was another a weapon favored by the Sumerians and was likely developed in parallel with maces.

The world's oldest known historical document is the Stele of Vultures. A Sumerian record of the military triumph of the king of Lagash, it commemorates in text and image the king's conclusive victory over the city of Umma.[115] One side of the stele depicts the king's patron god, Ningirsu, bludgeoning the soldiers of Umma with a mace. We find the mace also in the story titled *Gilgamesh and Aga,* when the demigod Gilgamesh says to Enkidu, "On this account let the weaponry and arms of battle be made ready. Let the battle mace return to your side."[116]

Sumerian war-making tools were taken into Egypt not long after the Dispersion. Narmer, the first king of Egypt, is displayed on the famous Narmer Palette holding a pear-shaped mace in his raised right hand while grasping the hair of a kneeling enemy in his left hand. Such a mace can be found in the Ashmolean Museum, which houses a mace-head of King Scorpion, dating from the end of the Predynastic Period of Egypt.

Maces were also used early in Indian history, as described in the ancient Indian epics *Ramayana* and *Mahabarata*. Accordingly, it is very likely that maces were wielded when Cush and his followers crippled Kish and took the spoils to his son's city, Uruk. From there, says the SKL, Cush reigned as king for a number of years. As we're about to see, there is a connection between Belus and the mace or hammer.

Figure 7-2. The King Scorpion macehead in the Ashmolean Museum, University of Oxford

The Greek rhetorician named Castor of Rhodes wrote that Belus was deified after his death, but he doesn't specify which god he became.[117] However, the Roman poet Ovid identifies Cush with Janus and has a fictionalized version of the god say of himself, "the ancients called me **Chaos**."[118] In *The Two Babylons*, Reverend Alexander Hislop equated Janus to Bel and noted that in Chaldee, a West Semitic language used in southern Mesopotamia, Cush is pronounced *kaos* and comes that way into the English language.[119] So Belus, Janus, and Chaos are different names for the same character. In Greek mythology, Chaos was the fluid of the cosmic womb, the first thing created. Obviously, Ovid was not equating the son of Ham to the primeval void but rather comparing Chaos to the situation that Cush had wrought. On this topic Hislop writes,

> He who caused the confusion of tongues was he who "broke" the previously united earth (Gen 11:1) "in pieces," and "scattered" the fragments abroad. How significant, then, as a symbol, is the club, as commemorating the work of Cush, as Bel, the "Confounder"? And that significance will be all the more apparent when the reader turns to the Hebrew of Genesis 11:9, and finds that the very word from which a club derives its name is that which is employed when it is said, that in consequence of the confusion of tongues, the children of men were "scattered abroad on the face of all the earth." The word there used for scattering abroad is Hephaitz, which in the Greek form becomes Hephaizt, and hence the origin of the well known but little understood name of Hephaistos, as applied to Vulcan, "The father of the gods."…. Here, then, the reader may see the real origin of Vulcan's Hammer, which is just another name for the club of Janus or Chaos.[120]

Intriguingly, the Egyptian God Thoth, who is accredited with the invention of writing, mathematics, astronomy, and civilization in general, is also called "the cleaver of the earth."[121]

Nimrod—who is most likely identical with Narmer, the mace-wielding king who united Egypt—must have shared his father's appreciation of the mace as a means of subjugation. The mighty heroes Ninurta, Hercules, and Thor can be traced from Nimrod, and all likewise favored the club or war-hammer.

There are two verses in Jeremiah which cannot be well understood apart from the information just covered. Both are part of an oracle about the Day of the Lord. The first says, "Babylon [lit.: *Babel*] is taken, Bel is

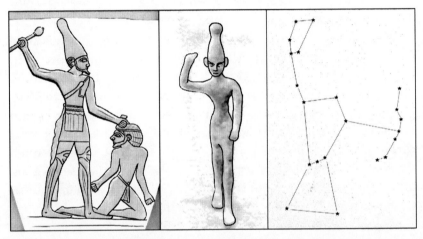

Figure 7-3. Left: (From the famous Narmer Palette) The Egyptian warlord, King Narmer, holds aloft a war club with which to strike the head of a conquered adversary. Middle: A statuette of the Canaanite god Ba'al strikes the same pose found on the Narmer Palette. Right: The constellation Orion represents a giant hunter who raises a club in preparation to strike a foe sometimes depicted as a lion.

confounded, **Merodach is broken in pieces**" (50:2, KJV). King Hammurabi's understanding is verified here by Jeremiah, who assigns Bel and Merodach different identities. The mention of Bel's confusion is a clever jab at the man whose leadership led to the confusion of tongues. The god who developed out of Cush will be impotent against the son of God at his coming. Merodach is the biblical name for Marduk, the Babylonian god who developed out of Nimrod, and it is fitting that he should be broken to pieces not only due to his use of the mace, but because he was already broken in pieces once before[a] (see Ezek. 31).

The second verse in Jeremiah reads, "How is the **hammer of the whole**

---

[a] This will come to make more sense as we continue our study of Nimrod.

earth cut asunder and broken! how is Babylon become a desolation among the nations!" (50:23, KJV). The hammer spoken of here is *phtish* in Hebrew, and can refer to any type of sledge, including a war club or mace. Through Jeremiah, YHVH was giving his people hope, for the kingdom of the mace-wielders will no longer be feared after Yeshua ha-Mashiach crushes the final king of Babylon.

The mess created at Babel was a cauldron of potential in which a new system could form. With his mace and his wits, Nimrod was the one to take advantage of the instability and construct a new world—the first empire, with tendrils touching every distant land unto which men had scattered. This gives new meaning to the beloved occult phrase *ordo ab chao*, "order from chaos," which is a motto that remains powerfully present on the Great Seal of the United States.

Many researchers have wondered what became of Cush as his son rose to power, but no one has yet provided a definitive answer. David Rohl proposes that he set sail into the Persian Gulf and followed the coast of the Arabian peninsula to the horn of Africa, where he and his tribe settled the area now called Ethiopia.[122] The people of that region have long been know as Cushites, but whether they are so named because the patriarch settled in the horn of Africa is up for debate. Personally, I suspect that Cush's disappearance was of a more mysterious nature, which is why the Sumerians felt compelled to mention it in the very concise King List. Whatever the case, we can say confidently that Cush either abnegated or lost the throne to Nimrod, and then bowed out. The title *Bel*, or *Lord*, was thereafter laid upon Nimrod's shoulders, which is why Nimrod is sometimes called Bel Marduk and Bel Jupiter in Greco-Roman writings.

Semiramis and Ninus

The priestess sister of Enmerkar/Nimrod may have been known to the Greeks by the name Semiramis. She was a great queen of famed beauty and wisdom who conquered many strongholds from Ethiopia to Chaldea before being successfully resisted by the Indians. Her majestic image notwithstanding, Semiramis showed little regard for virtue, and historians ascribed to her much of the extravagant and unrestrained character of the heathen religions.

Semiramis was known in Assyria as Shammuramat, meaning "gift of the sea." That brings to recollection the fact that Inanna was considered to be the daughter of the sea goddess. Readers familiar with Roman mythology will recall that Venus, the embodiment of beauty, sexuality, and fertility, was born of sea foam. The Hebrews borrowed the name *Shammuramat* and molded it into the more comfortable form of *Shemiramoth*, which, says Robert Bedrosian, appears in Chronicles "as the name of a Levite, but according to all analogy was originally a place-name and meant 'images of Shemiram,' just as Anathoth means 'images of Anath.'"[123]

The very name of the land where Semiramis ruled, Sumer (known to the Akkadians as *Shumeru*), is likely derived from Shammur-amat. We know of Semiramis through the writings of Greek historians such as Diodorus Siculus, Junianus Justinus, and Ctesias of Cnidus, as well as Roman historian Eusebius, the Bishop of Caesarea. The various accounts disagree with each other on many points, but they all agree that Semiramis was the wife of Ninus (*nin* means "lord" or "lady"), and Ninus was the first great king, a man worthy of renown. They also agree that the couple had a male child, Ninyas, and that Semiramis and her son both held the scepter after the death of the king.

According to both Castor of Rhodes and a Roman historian named Cephalion, Ninus' father was Belus (*Chronicle* g81, g90). Several Greek historians presented Ninus as a mighty conqueror who united Mesopotamia, and Pompeius Trogus, a 1st-century BC Roman historian, wrote,

> The first of all princes, who, from an extravagant desire of ruling, changed this old and, as it were, hereditary custom, was Ninus, king of the Assyrians. **It was he who first made war upon his neighbours, and subdued the nations**, as yet too barbarous to resist him, as far as the frontiers of Libya.[124]

That report harmonizes well with the biblical account of Nimrod, who was the first mighty one (Hebrew: *gibbor*) on the earth after the Flood. According to Ctesias' *Persica* as preserved in the *Library of History* by Diodorus Siculus, Ninus rose to power in southern Mesopotamia and, after initial military successes, proceeded into Assyria to build Nineveh[125]—an exact match to Moses' testimony that Nimrod began his reign at Babel but eventually took his forces north to establish Assyria. Some scholars posit that the Assyrian city of Nineveh got its name from Ninus/Ninurta, which means "abode of Nin." Ctesias of Cnidus (ca. 400

BC) certainly believed this to be the case, for he stated that

> no one in later times built such a large city in terms of the size of the en-
> closure and the magnificence of the fortification wall.... [Ninus] settled
> in the city the most of the Assyrians, especially the most powerful of
> them along with whoever was willing from other nations. **He named the
> city Ninus, after himself** and he attached much of the neighboring land
> into the settlement.[126]

Genesis 10:12 lists Nineveh as the first major city built in northern
Mesopotamia and implies that it was a part of Nimrod's kingdom; thus
the Bible presents no barrier to the idea that Nineveh was named after
Nimrod.

Finally, Pseudo-Apollodorus (2nd cent. AD) declared in no uncertain
terms that "Ninus is Nimrod."[127] If Nimrod is equivalent to Enmerkar,
and Enmerkar wed Inanna, then Semiramis must be Inanna (or the high
priestess that embodied her).

Diodorus Siculus, Castor of Rhodes, and Cephalion all claimed that
Ninus' authority passed to Semiramis upon his death. According to Ctesias, Herodotus, and others, Semiramis continued Ninus' military conquests and building projects. It was she who founded the city known
as Babylon, along with artificial banks to confine the Euphrates. Most
significantly, Roman historian Ammianus Marcellinus credited to her
the dubious honor of being the first to castrate male youths for royal service.[128] This is a clear parallel to Inanna, who almost certainly employed
eunuchs in her service.[129]

The main roadblock in linking Semiramis to Enmerkar is the testimony of Herodotus (484–425 BC), who ascribed to Ninus and Semiramis a much later date than Ctesias gave us. However, Herodotus may
have gotten the original Semiramis confused with another famous queen
named Semiramis: the Assyrian queen of Shamshi-Adad V, who ruled
during the 9th century BC. The name Semiramis is still given to girls in
the Near East and was probably a very popular name in antiquity due
to the glories of the first Semiramis. It's entirely possible that another
renowned monarch later in history shared the name. Scottish scholar W.
Robertson Smith discounted Herodotus' dating in his 1887 essay for *The
English Historical Review*.

Apart from the legends recounted by Greek historians, the main thing known about Semiramis is that she was celebrated in tradition as the author of marvelous works of building and engineering (especially earthworks), and that towns were called after her name far beyond the limits of the Semitic lands.... Ultimately every stupendous work by the Euphrates or in Iran seems to have been ascribed to her.... That Herodotus supposes her to have been an historical queen, of comparatively modern date, is a small matter when set against this substantial evidence that his Semiramis has the same reputation as the Semiramis of [earlier] legend.[130]

Babylonian writer Berossus attempted to refute Ctesias's assertion that Semiramis of the Assyrians founded Babylon, but he was largely unsuccessful.[131] Genesis 10 tells us that the original cities of Sumer and Akkad were constructed in quick succession—certainly within the lifespan of a long-lived descendant of Noah—therefore we shouldn't be surprised to find both the Babylonians and the Assyrians claiming Shammuramat/Semiramis as their own.

In Ctesias's day, a relief on a ruined wall near the famed hanging gardens of Babylon depicted a hunting scene in which Semiramis and Ninus jointly attack a leopard and a lion.[132] In the same city, the ancient Ishtar gate bears evidence which can be seen even today: the title of the mother goddess, *Queen of Heaven*. The proximity of these memorials is suggestive when considered alongside the other evidence linking Semiramis to Inanna/Ishtar.

Outside of Sumer, Semiramis/Inanna became Anat/Ashtoreth/Astarte (Easter), Isis, Freyja/Frigg, Sif, Cybele, Tanit, Libertas (Liberty), and of course Aphrodite/Venus. Although not all of these goddesses were expressly linked to the planet Venus, there are many other similarities that tie them together, and often, ancient records make clear statements that associate two goddesses of separate cultures.[133]

Rama and Sita

As far as I can ascertain, the seventh avatar of the Hindu god Vishnu is based on Nimrod, and his wife, Sita, on Semiramis. The Indians remember Rama as the ideal man, very handsome with piercing eyes and muscles like a lion. Sita was considered to be the perfect woman and beautiful beyond description. Rama was a nomadic king who fought monsters, founded cities, and went on long adventures to distant lands. His favored weapon was the bow, and his skill as a hunter was unsurpassed. His name can mean "trembling," "thunder," and "greatness" or "loftiness," which hints at a connection to the storm aspect of Ninurta/Marduk, and the mightiness of Nimrod.

In Genesis 10 we see that one of the sons of Cush was named Ra'mah. Ra'mah is the only son of Cush whose own two sons, Sheba and Dedan, are listed in the Genesis 10 genealogy. Similarly, Hindu legend assigns twin sons to Rama and Sita. I think it highly likely that the title *Nimrod* was given to Cush's son, Ra'mah, and that Sheba and Dedan became known in the West as the twins Romulus and Remus. Adding support to this is the testimony of a 13th-century AD Hungarian manuscript called *Gesta Hungarorum*, which claims that the twin princes Hunor and Magor were sons of Nimrod the Giant.[134]

Bearer of the Light

We've established the identity of Venus as the deified queen of Babylon, possibly named Semiramis, but we are left with a discrepancy, for the prophet Isaiah linked the morning star to the *male* ruler of Babylon. Isaiah wrote of the king's capitol city as a feminine entity, but Lucifer himself was decidedly masculine.

Not all cultures see Venus as female. The natives of Central America equated Venus (known to them as *Dawn Star*) with the god Quetzalcoatl, the feathered serpent-man, called "Lord of the Dawn."[135] They believed he came to earth and lived as a man and that the evening star represented his life. The winged serpent symbol of Quetzlcoatl and the lore surrounding him demonstrate that he is the Mesoamerican version of Lucifer. In Chinese lore, the morning star is described as an exceedingly handsome young man,[136] while on the other side of the world, the Blackfoot Indians of North America called the morning star "the handsomest person" to walk the earth, and a virile young man.[137]

Throughout the world, different people-groups have assigned different genders to the same celestial bodies. Even within a culture, both genders are sometimes applied to a single luminary. This may have to do with the kinds of stories that are popularly recited about a given luminary. In common speech, objects that are powerful or tough are generally made out to be masculine, while objects that are lovely or delicate are viewed as feminine. Inanna/Ishtar was a goddess of both love and war, so it would have been natural for her worshipers to assign both genders to her planet.

Here is what humanities author Rivkah Harris has to say about the androgyny of the goddess:

> Inanna-Ishtar is both female and male. Over and over again the texts juxtapose the masculine and feminine traits and behavior of the goddess. She can be at one and the same time compassionate, supportive, and nurturing as well as assertive, aggressive, and strong-willed. In short, she breaks the boundaries between the sexes by embodying both femaleness and maleness.[138]

The split personality of the planet Venus may have played into this androgyny. In Sumer, during the early Uruk period, there appear to have been separate cults for Inanna's morning and evening aspects, with a different gender focus for each.[139] To the ancient stargazers, Venus as the morning star heralded the striking, masculine sun, while Venus as the evening star initiated the hours of darkness which belonged to the spirit of fertility (seed germinates in darkness) and passivity (slumber). Each morning star to evening star transition takes approximately the same amount of time as human gestation,[140] further explaining Venus' association with female fertility. However, since Inanna/Ishtar was inextricably linked to her demigod lover, she was also associated with his sun-god aspects and more masculine characteristics like war-making, city-building, farming, and hunting (not to mention that Semiramis herself was said to have been a great builder and commander after Nimrod's death).

In short, Inanna came to represent the bipolarity of yin and yang, incorporating the extremes of the aggressive male and passive female forces into a single heavenly body. Those forces simultaneously oppose and complement each other. Thus, when we speak of Babylon, we speak simultaneously of the overwhelming power of a disciplined war-god and the illicit indulgences of a permissive goddess.

Accept No Substitutes

Concerning Venus in its morning phase, there's a very important relation not to be overlooked: Yeshua calls himself "the bright morning star" (Rev. 22:16), and Peter called Yeshua "the morning star [which] shines in your hearts" (2 Pet. 1:19). Here we have a hint of the quest of the Antichrist to usurp the symbols and functions of the Anointed One. The real light-bearer is the only begotten Son of God whom John called "the light of the world" (John 8:12; cf. 3:19, 9:5). And just as Venus by the pagan reckoning is the combination of the fertility goddess and her demigod husband, Venus from a biblical perspective represents the spiritual union of the Messiah with his bride, the church[a]. The incarnated Son of God is the genuine light-bearer, or lucifer—and his bride also reflects that same light from her heavenly father—but when we use the word *lucifer* as a name we will of course always think of the imposter, Satan's Seed.

If Yeshua finds representation in Venus as the morning star, which reflects the light of the sun with zeal and thus stands as the most bold among all the starry host, then God must be rightly portrayed by the sun, which illuminates all. "God is light" (1 John 1:5), wrote the apostle John, and Moses called the Lord "a consuming fire" (Deut. 4:24). The sun is an all-consuming ball of burning gas, a massive cauldron of super-excited particles undergoing continual nuclear fusion and radiating waves of photons that illuminate all those living under heaven. It is a fitting reminder of the power and ceaseless function of God. We are never to worship the sun, for it is a created thing, and we worship only the Creator. Nevertheless, we can appreciate the boundless energy of God represented in the lesser but still phenomenal energy of the sun.

The rising Venus, which precedes the dawn, gives shining testimony to the greatness of the sun at a time when men cannot see it. Likewise, Yeshua, though God in nature, made himself small for our sake and appeared in our dark world to shower us with God's light during this epoch when we cannot directly see the Father. The priest-king of Babylon has attempted to appropriate that role for himself, replacing Yeshua as the anointed representative of divine illumination. Or course, the source of illumination which Lucifer represents is not YHVH, but that ancient serpent, the Dragon. It is the serpent who promised Eve that by eating the forbidden fruit of the Tree of Knowledge, she would be enlightened and

---

[a] More specifically, the *ekklesia*, or assembly of redeemed believers.

become like God—a promise which Satan has been repeating to mankind in various forms ever since.

In addition to being one who reflects the light of the sun, we see in Isa. 14:12–14 that Lucifer intends to ascend to heaven and sit where Yeshua sits. Taking those verses in isolation, it would seem that Lucifer is an angel, for what man could ascend to God's throne except God call him up? However, the subsequent verses of ch. 14 strongly indicate that Lucifer is a king of earthly nations who will go down to Sheol, to the recesses of the pit (v. 15), yet his body will not go into a tomb (vv. 19–20). Angels do not have physical bodies that die and are buried, thus Lucifer cannot be an angel. According to Rev. 19:20, the king of Babylon will be thrown *bodily* into the fiery lake[a].

In the Isaiah 14 oracle we find that upon Lucifer's entrance into Sheol, other men will point and stare in wonder that the great leader who subjugated the world and attempted to supersede Yeshua has instead become weak and helpless (Isa. 14:9–11). This puts the final nail in the coffin—pun intended—of the popular idea that Lucifer is the fallen Cherub. While it is true that Satan will be made helpless for a thousand years, he will not be kept in Sheol with human beings; instead, he will be imprisoned in the Abyss (Rev. 20:1–3). Satan may be the spiritual power behind the Antichrist, but he is not the Lucifer of Isaiah 14. It is Satan's Seed who is called Lucifer and who intends to replace the true Light of the World.

There was one man in history who fits the profile of Lucifer: Nimrod, the widely-adored husband of the fertility goddess. He was a sower of civilization, a bearer of secret knowledge, an engineer of magnificent structures, and a strong-armed, silver-tongued peace-maker who initially reigned over the empire that would become Babylon. He was the archetype of all the deified shepherd-kings of ancient mythology.

This leaves us, however, with a bit of a conundrum, for we see in Isaiah 14 that Lucifer is the son of Venus, not her husband. But let's not throw up our hands in frustration just yet. Over the course of the next few chapters, we will discover that Nimrod was not only the husband of the fertility goddess, but also symbolically her son, and we will come to the shocking realization that this same Nimrod of ages past will reprise his role in the years leading up to the Messiah's return.

---

[a] The body being thrown into hell may be a resurrected body, since the scriptures indicate that Yeshua will slay the king of Babylon when he returns. John the Revelator saw that everyone, both sinners and redeemed, will receive a resurrected body, but not all at the same time (Rev. 20:5, 12–15).

EIGHT

The Lesser and Greater Occult Mysteries

[T]here exists in the world today, and has existed for thousands of years, a body of enlightened humans united in what might be termed, an Order of the Quest. It is composed of those whose intellectual and spiritual perceptions have revealed to them that civilization has a Secret Destiny—secret, I say, because this high purpose is not realized by the many; the great masses of peoples still live along without any knowledge whatsoever that they are part of a Universal Motion in time and space.[141]

–MANLY P. HALL, 33° FREEMASON (1901–1990)

As tempting as it is to dive into a study of Nimrod, king of Babylon, we must first understand the religious beliefs which developed around him and his family. This is crucial because the lies that Satan has sold us to draw us away from a relationship with the True and Living God are the same today as they were in the beginning. The West is witnessing a resurgence of the particular brand of religious philosophy which ensnared and then empowered the priestly classes of the ancient world. Many of history's greatest minds have fallen prey to this deception, and it will feast upon many more souls as we approach the end of the age.

In this chapter we will start by understanding the pagan conception of God and our cosmic origins, then proceed to explore the characteristics of the mysterious religion installed by Satan through Cush, Nimrod, and Semiramis.

Before getting started, it's necessary to issue a quick disclaimer. We will be discussing the disconcerting beliefs and activities of high-ranking members of secret fraternities (notably Freemasonry), and this may be upsetting to those who have good relationships with men who participate in such fraternities. My purpose is not to imply that all

Masons/Shriners/Rosicruscians are automatically evil, because the truth is that most of them are completely unaware of the true purposes of their societies. Due to the pyramidal nature of these societies, only a select few at the very highest levels possess a full understanding of the world-views and goals of the organizations. If we are wise we will ask ourselves, Why all the secrecy in these groups? Why require initiates to swear oaths in which they agree to undergo brutal, torturous deaths if they reveal the fraternity's secrets? What does a supposedly harmless fraternity and charitable organization have to hide, especially in countries which offer freedom of assembly and freedom of religion? By way of contrast, the creeds of Christianity have been publicly announced and circulated since its inception.

Henry L. Haywood, a Masonic historian from Iowa, writes in *The Great Teachings of Masonry* that "the Fraternity itself exists in order to keep fixed in a man a certain set of influences... its secrecy is a means to that end."[142]

In the ceremonies of Freemasonry, the Fraternity does no more than indicate the pathway to Masonic knowledge. Initiated brothers are encouraged to complete their journey by seeking out the Secret Doctrine behind the symbolism of the ceremonies. This secret can be mined from the writings of advanced and revered Masons.

We will soon discover for ourselves the exact nature of this secret and how it relates to Bible prophecy.

How did we get here? What came before us, and what happens to us after death? How can we be assured of a favorable fate? Every religion must answer these questions, and the occult religion introduced at Shinar is no exception. *Occult* means *hidden*, and is in reference to the unseen dimensions and forces around us as well as the divine self concealed within us. In the occult (mystery) religions, the highest divinity and source of all that exists is a limitless force called the Absolute (a.k.a. the Monad, Brahman, Tao, Immutable Reality, and Divine Essence).

The Ultimate Energy Source

By its very nature the Absolute cannot be defined, but we will get near enough if we envision it as boundless energy which is the origin and fullness of all things, including time and space; the divine animating Source; or the flow of the universe. Given only that description, we could fairly equate the Absolute to the pre-existent, singular God of Israel, but we quickly encounter a point of contention when it is learned that the Absolute is not a person. It contains within it the potential for person-hood because it is the origin of the archetypes of personality, but the Absolute is not itself an individual. It possesses no morality or characteristics to which it must adhere; all such concepts arise at lower levels of being. Furthermore, there is no special providence from the Absolute, as there is with YHVH. The Absolute does not guide the universe, leaving it instead to created beings to determine the course of history.

Do not let this point escape you, dear reader. The occult god of gods is not a person, but the *impersonal* fount of all the universe's forces.

The occultist is convinced that the Absolute may be encountered and experienced through altered states of consciousness. The Bible flatly excludes that possibility with its teaching that no one can survive such an encounter. God told Moses, "You cannot see my face, for man shall not see me and live" (Exo. 33:20). The elected prophets have only seen God's avatar, or what Ezekiel described as "the appearance of the likeness of the glory of the LORD" (Ezek. 1:28). The apostle John brought this Old Testament doctrine into the New when he wrote, "No one has ever seen God; the only Son, who is in the bosom of the Father, he has made him known" (John 1:18, RSV). Paul agreed with this theology in his first letter to Timothy when he spoke of him "who is the blessed and only Sovereign, the King of kings and Lord of lords, who alone has immortality, who dwells in unapproachable light, whom no one has ever seen or can see" (6:15–16). What mystics are tapping into during their altered states of consciousness is a beautiful and wonderful sacred energy that emanates from God and is universally accessible[a], but they are not experiencing God himself. This conclusion finds support in research conducted by doctors Stanley Koren and Michael Persinger and recently replicated by a neurotheology team in Curitiba-Pr, Brazil. Using a device dubbed "the

---

[a] Evidence suggests that our unconscious minds bathe in that rejuvenating energy during the deepest portions of R.E.M. sleep and when under anesthesia.

God Helmet" to generate weak magnetic fields around a subject's temporal lobes, the researchers were able to elicit spiritual experiences and the feeling of "a presence" in eighty percent of subjects, whether religious, atheist, or agnostic. One percent of Dr. Persinger's test subjects reported visions of God. When asked about these results, Dr. Persinger stated,

> I suspect most people would call the "vague, all-around-me" sensations "God" but they are reluctant to employ the label in a laboratory. The implicit is obvious. If the equipment and the experiment produced the presence that was God, then the extrapersonal, unreachable and independent characteristics of the god definition might be challenged.[143]

People on psychedelic drugs and deeply meditative journeys often report feeling surrounded by a pleasant or loving presence, and feeling connected to the rest of the world in a special way. The God Helmet seems to be producing a similar effect, and like the mystics and trippers, Persinger's subjects sometimes interpret their experience as "seeing God." They do this because what they have felt is wonderful and not easily classified, and that leads to an association with the vague but universal label *God*. Persinger's helmet is not actually summoning the transcendent Creator to the laboratory.

Not all polytheists have acknowledged a transcendent Source—many were satisfied with worshiping the gods of the pantheon as they understood them and did not bother to explore further—but the illumined priests of the polytheistic religions have always pursued the Ultimate Power behind the gods. Those who pursue the true Babylonian religion have always sought gnosis[a] of the Absolute.

After their spiritual eyes are opened to higher dimensions and the "light" of the Absolute, they then learn to enter trance and use certain forms (i.e., symbols, idols, talismans, etc.), actions (i.e., dances, poses, music), and especially words or chants to affect the other dimensions.

---

[a] *Gnosis* is Greek for *knowledge*. Several of the New Testament letters strongly condemn Gnosticism, which teaches adherents to shun the material world and liberate the soul through esoteric knowledge, or enlightenment.

Occult Cosmogony

All occult cosmogonies agree that the Absolute is without a beginning. Not all agree as to whether there was a time before the existence of the universe(s). For instance, the Greeks believed that our universe has existed since infinity past, and the Hindus believe that an infinite number of universes are forever being born and passing away. Most occult societies today seem to conform to the Judeo-Christian view that all things besides God had a singular beginning.

Occultists also agree that the first estate of the universe was a womb-like space filled with a formless soup of rudimentary material, but their cosmogonies begin to diverge after that, with different mystery schools proposing conflicting versions of the evolution of the heavenly hierarchy. Some believe that the Absolute formed from Chaos a Supreme Being: the Universal Mind and Light of the Absolute, represented by the All-Seeing Eye. It is this Supreme Being that brought order from chaos by crafting the sun god, who then assembled all lesser gods and organized the material world. Others believe that the Absolute first brought forth the sky god and earth goddess, followed by Poseidon (a.k.a. Neptune/Dagon/Enki), the god of waters, and Kronos (a.k.a. Saturn/El/Enlil), the god of time, winds, and destruction. Then came the sun, who warmed the earth and pushed back the darkness until it encircled the cosmos—and so we have spirit, earth, water, wind, and fire deities founding the cosmos. These are sometimes

Figure 8-1. This Freemasonic mashup of symbols adeptly expresses the basic tenants of occult cosmogony.

called *Archons*. The solar deity, or *Solar Logos*, is considered to be the voice of the Absolute because he sang over the spiritual cosmos, and its chaotic contents organized into the physical cosmos, represented by the triangle[a]. There are other variations of this myth which we won't bother to recount.

Which of the aforementioned divine entities is to be considered the God of the mystics? It depends. According to venerated Western mystic Max Heindel,

> When the name "God" is used it is always uncertain whether The Absolute, the One Existence, is meant; or The Supreme Being, Who is the Great Architect of the Universe; or God, Who is the Architect of our Solar system.[144]

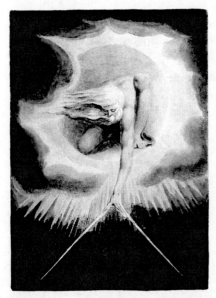

Figure 8-2. "The Ancient of Days setting a Compass to the Earth," by William Blake, 1794, in *Europe: a Prophecy*, copy D, from the British Museum. Many of Blake's friends were Freemasons, and the compass is of central importance to Freemasonry. Compasses show up in some of Blake's other works, as well.

When the subject of God arises during discourse between individuals, it is a mistake to assume that all parties have in mind the same conception of the Deity. One participant could have in mind the impersonal Absolute, whereas another could be thinking of the collective of all divinities overseeing the cosmos, whereas another could envision a singular divine person who is sole creator and ruler.

Often, members of the occult will use the term *God* in reference to the overseer of the particular cosmic sphere in which we reside. This *local* God did not create anything *ex nihilo*[b]. He is not the Absolute, nor the Supreme Being, but rather an emanation of the Supreme Being, and therefore finite. He is a creator only in the sense of arranging through the use of will and intellect all pre-existing substances into the patterns that define our environment.

---

[a]   The triangle also speaks to the occultist of the three-fold nature of man: spirit, intelligence, and material body.

[b]   A Latin phrase meaning "out of nothing."

During his December 3, 1993 broadcast of *The Hour of the Time*, radio talk show host William Cooper shared a few quotes that are relevant to us now. They come from General Albert Pike's books. The first quote revealed that Mr. Pike found it monstrously absurd that something was created from nothing, as traditional monotheists believe. Instead, he was of the opinion that the building blocks of all things already existed, and always had. The other quotes pertained to Ammon, the sun god of Egypt (later to become Ammon-Ra), which Mr. Pike called the "supreme being."[a] He claimed that this supreme being had not created anything.

In contrast, Christian theology stipulates that YHVH Elohiym is the one and only Supreme Being among all that exists or can exist, and he begot an exact representation of himself before time began. This only begotten Son of God, under the direction and empowerment of the Eternal Father, brought into existence from nothingness the space-time continuum and all the spirit, energy, and matter therein. Christ is the Logos, the Word through whom all things are ordered into their respective forms (John 1:1–3; Col. 1:15–17).

To occultists like Mr. Pike, the sun spirit, Lucifer, though not pre-existent, is the highest order being and the one who links the astral light with the material world; or, put another way, Lucifer translates between spirit and matter. (We are now speaking of Lucifer in the popular sense, as the Devil, not in the biblical sense, as the king of Babylon.) Read carefully the following quote from occult author Eliphas Levi (1810–1875):

> This agent is the infinite light, or, seeing that the light is itself only phenomenal, it is rather the light-bearer, the great Lucifer of Nature, the mediator between matter and spirit, **the first creature of God, but termed the devil by imposters and the ignorant**.... What is more absurd and more impious than to attribute the name of Lucifer to the devil, that is, to personified evil? The intellectual Lucifer is the spirit of intelligence and love; it is the Paraclete, it is the Holy Spirit, while the physical Lucifer is the great agent of universal magnetism.[145]

Occultists such as Mr. Levi teach that Lucifer is just as much God as YHVH and has been unfairly cast as the bad guy in the Abrahamic religions. By their way of thinking, when Moses wrote Genesis, he made

---

[a] Mr. Pike may have have disregarded the idea of a supreme being existing between the sun god and the Absolute, or he may he have taken the perspective that both the sun god and the Logos were supreme within their own spheres.

it appear as though the serpent was the wicked tempter, when in reality, the serpent was trying to emancipate Adam and Eve from the cage of a cruel god so that they could begin their road to spiritual advancement.[146] In such a scenario, the adversary of mankind is not the fallen Cherub, but YHVH, or Adonai. Echoing that line of thinking, Albert Pike stated that the Jewish rabbis and Christian priests were slandering Lucifer's name: "If Lucifer were not God, would Adonay and his priests calumniate him?.... [T]he true and pure philosophical religion is the belief in **Lucifer, the equal of Adonay.**"[147]

Do not imagine that Pike is a pariah to the Masons because of his ideology, for they embrace the man and continue to circulate his writings. For example, the author of a 2008 guidebook intended for widespread public consumption writes that Pike "promoted the belief that the fraternity's roots are to be found among the wisdom schools of antiquity. **His work became a spiritual and intellectual banner** for readers who hungered after an esoteric dimension in Freemasonry.... **its importance cannot be ignored.**"[148]

The twisted theology of Levi and Pike has ancient origins. The Sumerians started out venerating Enlil, but Enki ran a propaganda campaign in which he cast himself as the true champion of mankind, and the people of Mesopotamia were taken in by it. The worldview spawned by that role reversal has survived to this day, for the Serpent has never ceased to whisper in naïve ears.

Case in point: the Yazidis, a Kurdish community centered in Nineveh, practice a faith linked to ancient Mesopotamian religions and Zoroastrianism, and they honor a heptad of angels to whom they believe that God entrusted his Creation. The preeminent angel of the seven is named Melek Taus, but it is acknowledged that this angel is equivalent to Shai'tan, or Satan. He is depicted as a beautiful bird with the eight-pointed cuneiform sign of Venus at his side, standing on a sun disc that is drawn on top of a crescent moon. Those three symbols represent the primary triad of paganism and are often found together on Sumerian and Akkadian engravings. It is believed that Melek Taus sinned before the creation of the cosmos, but repented and was restored to the position of God's chief deputy. The Yazidi Book of Illumination states that Melek Taus (i.e., Satan) is the praiseworthy and righteous caretaker of mankind.[149]

This kind of belief is not confined to religious groups with ancient roots. In the popular modern book, *Conversations with God*, author Neale Donald Walsch shared messages that he received from a spirit which he believed to be God. In addition to attacking the Bible and repudiating the existence of cosmic moral law, Walsch's God told the author that man can be God's equal and that Adam's disobedience was in fact a blessing because it set him on a path of spiritual "upliftment."[150] Eliphas Levi agreed that we can be God's equals, saying, "To know the secret or science of God is to be God."[151] Evidently the Serpent did us all a favor... but one might be forgiven for questioning the merit of that spiritual upliftment, considering that it came yoked with death, decay, painful toil, a thorn-filled environment, and every kind of strife.

Doctrine of the Devil

The success of the bestselling *Conversations with God* is not a fluke. The modern New Age, New Spirituality, Wicca, Kaballah, Christian Science, Scientology, and other such movements which stand firmly rooted in the philosophy of man's inherent goodness and inner divinity, have been steadily gaining ground in the West since the 1960's. It's past time to sit up and take notice when New Age leaders begin praising talk-queen Oprah Winfrey, a veritable pop-culture sage, as "key to the genre's recent accomplishments."[152]

Even though many westerners would not identify themselves with a particular movement, they nevertheless sympathize with many of the "progressive" tenants of the Luciferic doctrine (progressive is in quotes because it's actually *regressive*, taking us back to the pluralism and relativism of the ages before Yeshua's ministry). In 20th-century America, greed, narcissism, and materialism grew like a cancer, wreaking havoc on our balance of life and inciting young people to look to the East for solutions. Eastern mystics were more than happy to help. Intellectuals such as Ralph Waldo Emerson and celebrities such as Shirley MacLaine gobbled up the ancient wisdom traditions and regurgitated them to a populace in existential crisis. No doubt empowered by the spiritual rulers of this world, the torch-bearers saw great success, and the New Age movement and its analogues have now become the norm as Western society divorces Yeshua and embraces universalism. The majority of today's youth have bought the lie that all religions are equally valid pathways to the Divine and that Yeshua was nothing more than an enlightened teacher who achieved "Christ Consciousness" and was killed for spreading the gospel of Self-Actualization. Supposedly, all of the world's great spiritual gurus, including Yeshua, have taught the same fundamental truths in different ways. The problem, say pluralists, is that their unenlightened followers have created flawed religions around the inspired teachings. If each of us would only seek enlightenment for ourselves, then we would see that all is one and that many paths lead back to the Absolute; and we could attain that Christ Consciousness which awakens our innate divinity, and could together free the world from superstition and dogma.[153]

Reality check: Yeshua meant what he said when he declared that the way is narrow, and only a few find it. Either pluralism is bunk, or Yeshua was wrong when he said, "I am the way, and the truth, and the life. No one comes to the Father except through me" (John 14:6). Yeshua was certainly not just a good human rabbi, for he claimed equality with God, he claimed to have come from heaven, and eyewitnesses reported that he returned to his Father's side after laying down his life for us. Yeshua was resurrected, and the Romans could never produce a body. No other supposedly enlightened teacher has ever conquered death.

The primary, three-pronged attack on Judeo-Christian society has come in the areas of entertainment, news, and education. We've all seen how secular media and journalism have disparaged the Bible and crossed every moral line over the last several decades, so those prongs hardly need to be addressed, but the Devil's efforts to influence society through education reform have been less visible. The *why* of it should be obvious, though: those who shape the thinking of a nation's youth shape the future of that nation. Tyrants and dictators have without fail brought education in their territories under the control of the national government and made it obligatory for parents to send their children into the public school system. Modern progressives seek to accomplish the same thing but on a global scale. Former editor of the *NEA Journal*, Joy E. Morgan, wrote in 1946 that

> in the struggle to establish an adequate world government, the teacher can do much to prepare the hearts and minds of children for global understanding and cooperation. At the very heart of all the agencies which will assure the coming of the world government must stand the school, the teacher, and the organized profession."[154]

Morgan's sentiments are representative of the NEA as a whole. The National Education Association was chartered in 1906 and unionized in 1978, and is today the chief education lobby in the United States. They push their globalist agenda in large part through funding from the Rockefeller and Carnegie Foundations, both of which are, to put it succinctly, priesthoods of globalism.

The NEA is far from being the only culprit. Dr. Robert Muller, former United Nations Assistant Secretary-General and creator of the World Core Curriculum for primary schools, worked diligently during his lifetime to impart a vision of humanism and universalism to youths and educators around the world. His work on the World Core Curriculum influenced initiatives such as Goals 2000, Education for All, and Common Core, which seek to indoctrinate children to become global citizens who renounce nationalism and eschew traditional values. This is not an exaggeration, and it is not a new enterprise. A 1949 UNESCO[a] publication for teachers asserted that "one of the chief aims of education today should be to prepare boys and girls to take an active part in the creation of a world society."[155] Translation: we must return to Babel. The publication also bemoaned the "poisoned air of nationalism." Undoubtedly, we should teach our children to respect all cultures and deal honorably with all people, but that does not mean that they must assimilate or approve of all the practices of other cultures. Multiculturalism does not rule out loyalty to the kingdom of God.

Today, UNESCO's website touts one of its flagship programs, entitled "Global Consciousness." The program description states that it exists to help young men and women adopt a broader worldview, to recognize "the universality of humankind," and to "overcome national fixations, ethnic narrow narratives and instrumental ways of perceiving the world, and to redefine our relationship with the environment."[156] One of the project's objectives is to "help develop… and implement curricula and other materials conducive to a global consciousness."[157] There's that New Age philosophy rearing its ugly head. Note the push for a more evolved consciousness… for environmentalism… for universalism. These things all stem from ancient pagan concepts, and they want our children to be trained up in them. Whether there may be some validity to concerns about the environment, or some truth to the concept of interdependence, is not relevant. Humanist globalists are leveraging these issues to take us to places that we don't want to go.

Consequently, the United States withdrew its UNESCO membership

---

[a] The United Nations Educational, Scientific and Cultural Organization

during the Reagan administration, citing how corrupt it had become[a], but the second Bush administration had us re-enrolled.[158] Since then, we've funneled many millions of dollars into the massive UNESCO bureaucracy for their use in radical social engineering. What we've received in return is Common Core, which extols socialism, globalism, and moral relativism while omitting vital stories about our American heritage that might reflect the conservative nature of our past leaders.

The late Dr. Muller was a hero to both the UN and the New Age movement. His pantheistic and humanistic outlook can be clearly understood from his speech at the 1997 Global Citizenship 2000 Youth conference, where he said, "Behave correctly towards the Earth.... You are not children of Canada, you are really living units of the cosmos because the Earth is a cosmic phenomena.... This is why religions tell you, you are divine. We are divine energy... it is in your hands whether evolution on this planet continues or not."[159]

The doctor's worldview is not uncommon in the United Nations. Monica Sharma, an expert on "leadership development for sustainable and equitable change" who worked at the UN for twenty-two years, formulated a leadership initiative for sixty countries, the design of which was to "manifest a new paradigm for our planet and humanity."[160] Her initiative was based on the belief that "evidence in the science of consciousness is revealing our potential for deeper and higher states of consciousness that reveal our essential Oneness in an interdependent universe. Our 'Oneness' can be the springboard for all action for humanity and the planet."[161]

If the reader would prefer to see quotes from a top-level UN official, we can reference the writings of the very first director-general of UNESCO, Julian Huxley. Mr. Huxley, a Communist sympathizer, wrote in his book, *UNESCO: Its Purpose and Its Philosophy*, that the organization adhered to "a scientific world humanism, global in extent and evolutionary in background," and that it would "stimulate... the quest for a **restate-**

---

[a] "Anti-Communists, patriotic organizations, and veterans groups had been protesting and documenting the offenses of UNESCO for many years and building the case for withdrawing U.S. membership, but it was UNESCO's proposed New World Information Order (NWIO) that finally proved to be the last straw. Under the Orwellian NWIO scheme, UNESCO proposed to license and control all journalists, broadcasters, and media personnel worldwide—the U.S. Constitution and Bill of Rights notwithstanding. This finally got the attention of members of the liberal press, who for decades airily dismissed the warnings of UNESCO's conservative critics. The NWIO provided the critical impetus needed to spur U.S. withdrawal."

ment of morality that shall be in harmony with modern knowledge and adapted to the fresh functions imposed on ethics by the world of today."[162] There's simply no room in that vision for the moral code of the unchanging God of Israel.

In 1989, UNESCO awarded Dr. Muller its Peace Education Prize.[163] His acceptance speech reflected the fact that he got many of his ideas from Theosophy (lit.: god-wisdom), and theosophist Alice Bailey (1880–1949) in particular. In fact, the *Robert Muller World Core Curriculum Manual* reads, "The underlying philosophy upon which the Robert Muller School is based will be found in the teaching set forth in the books of Alice A. Bailey by the Tibetan teacher, Djwhal Khul..."[164] That Tibetan was not a living man, but an *ascended master* whom Bailey channeled to write her books for her.

Down the Rabbit Hole

In order to get her books to print, Alice Bailey and her husband created the Lucifer Publishing Company. That company has since become Lucis Publishing, which is a United Nations NGO and a major player at U.N. summits. Are we getting concerned yet?

Alice Bailey was a member of the Theosophical Society of Russian mystic and occult author Helena Petrovna Blavatsky (1831–1891). Not unlike Bailey, she claimed to have written her books under the guidance of enlightened beings, but in her case the beings were purportedly alive and telepathically transferring their thoughts to her from their hideout in the mountains of Tibet. Madame H. P. Blavatsky defined Theosophy as "the archaic *Wisdom-Religion*, the esoteric doctrine once known in every ancient country having claims to civilization."[165]

Madame Blavatsky, the so-called mother of the New Age, wrote about Lucifer in these terms: Life, Thought, Progress, Civilization, Liberty, and the Logos. "The Great Serpent of the Garden of Eden and the 'Lord God' are identical," she claimed.[166] She believed that he was "higher and older than Jehovah, and had to be sacrificed to the new dogma" of Judeo-Christian monotheism.[167] In her book entitled *The Secret Doctrine* (which Aldoph Hitler read nightly[168]) she wrote,

> And now it stands proven that Satan, or the Red Fiery Dragon, the "Lord of Phosphorus," and Lucifer, or "Light-Bearer," is in us: It is our Mind—

our tempter and Redeemer, our intelligent liberator and Saviour from pure animalism.[169]

Blavatsky and those like her—there are more than you think—have completely reversed the biblical framework, swapping the Red Dragon for God. When she calls her God a redeemer, it is not meant that he redeems from sin, but from ignorance. Blavatsky proudly acknowledges that Lucifer is the tempter, believing that to be a good thing because it leads to liberation. Since the God of the Bible never tempts anyone to sin (Jam. 1:13), the God of Theosophy is undoubtedly the Dark Cherub.

Would that this study could be expanded to cover more facts regarding occult activity. Unfortunately, space does not permit us to carefully trace the progress of the luciferic doctrine from Babylon to the present, nor to survey our current landscape and see how prevalent the occult mindset has become among those in positions of influence. Thankfully, other authors have dedicated books to such studies. For the moment, let's avail ourselves of a sample, just to get an idea of how the enemy has infiltrated even our most honored establishments.

Wernher Von Braun (1912–1977) was the head of the Nazi V2 rocket program, and an occult-initiated S.S. Major. After World War II, the United States brought him to White Sands Air Force Base to help start the American space program. Von Braun worked closely with rocket engineer and mystery school initiate Jack Parsons (1914–1952). Parsons was one of the founders of the Jet Propulsion Laboratory, which became NASA; he was also an apprentice of 33rd-degree Scottish Rite Freemason Aleister Crowley (1875–1947). The press called Crowley "the wickedest man in the world" for his use of ritual blood magic and his love for Satan. Parsons and Von Braun put the very first rocket into space and then led a team of Army rocket scientists at Redstone Arsenal in developing propulsion systems for extended space flight with the eventual goal of reaching Mars, where Von Braun envisioned in concert with Walt Disney that explorers might discover alien life[a].[170] The name Redstone is simply a

---

[a] Von Braun also worked with Disney to create *Man in Space*, an animated space propa-

moniker for Mars, planet of the god of war and fortresses. During his work for the US Army, Parsons was heavily involved in occult ritual activity intended to bring about the arrival of the Antichrist through the use of the magic of Horus. In 1946, he accompanied L. Ron Hubbard, founder of Scientology, into the Mojave Desert to read seventy-seven incantations in the magical language of Queen Elizabeth's occult adviser, alchemist Dr. John Dee.[171] This ritual was known as the Babalon Working. As author David Flynn puts it, "Jack Parsons knew the space program of JPL and NASA would be the means to accomplish the same goal as magic. Both activities would result in communication with the former 'gods.'"[172]

In 1950, Jack Parsons wrote this passage about the philosophy of his occult brotherhood:

> We are the oldest organization in the world.... We are on the side of man, of life, and of the individual. Therefore we are against religion, morality and [Judeo-Christian] government. Therefore our name is Lucifer. We are on the side of freedom, of love, of joy and laughter and divine drunkenness. Therefore our name is Babalon [sic].... And when that vermin of Hell that is called the Christian Church held all the West in slavery of sin and death and terror, we, and we alone, brought hope to the heart of man, despite the dungeon and the stake.[173]

He isn't mistaken when he says that the occult is the world's oldest organization. Satan has been busily building his kingdom since the dawn of the age, and he does it by peddling an intellectual illumination unhindered by observation of YHVH's instructions.

Satan would have us believe that he rescued our ancestors from ignorance and bondage in Eden, freeing their minds so that they could become their own gods through the light of reason and progress. Hasn't that worked out well? In reality, the Devil offers us light but delivers darkness; he frees us from being servants of God only to become slaves to selfishness. True, we have freedom to do as we please, but what we please leads to every kind of evil and then eternal death.

The redeemed man believes that whatever light of goodness and wis-

---

ganda film, wherein astronauts find an artificial structure on the moon at a latitude of 33 degrees (a sacred number to Freemasons). Thirty-three degrees north is the latitude of both Mount Hermon, where the Watchers descended, and Roswell, New Mexico, where a famous UFO crashed the year after Jack Parsons conducted the Babalon Working.

dom that we possess is a gift of God, and cannot be won: "For by grace you have been saved through faith. And this is not your own doing; it is the gift of God, not a result of works, so that no one may boast." (Eph. 2:8–9). Without YHVH graciously transferring his light into us, we would be only darkness. But the pagan believes that through intellect and willpower he can magnify his own divine spark unto full illumination and even deification, nullifying the need to appeal to God or conform to his standards. This system of belief is known as *autotheism*—divinity within oneself, waiting to be raised to perfection through wisdom and consistent effort.

We need to realize that all the pagan religions and philosophies which have sprung up at the behest of Lucifer share a common core: they all adhere to the idea that man is inherently good and that he has within him everything that he needs to achieve godhood.

My friends, mankind is not good, and individual men are not good.

Yeshua said, "**No one is good** except God alone" (Mark 10:18). And Paul wrote, "**All** have turned away; they have together become worthless; there is **no one** who does good, not even one" (Rom. 3:12, NIV). That's a hard and unpopular truth because it takes humility to admit our brokenness. We have all inherited a dead spirit that leaves us selfish to the core, and we break God's commandments both in action and in thought every day. Without a substitute who imputes perfection to us, we have no hope of reaching the total holiness that is necessary in order to dwell with God.

Truly, when we boil down all the world's belief systems, we find that only two worldviews exist or have ever existed: autotheism and messianism. It's salvation by works versus salvation by grace. Even atheism fits within the former, for while it has no concern with an afterlife, it does worship the mind and the potential for greatness inherent in intelligent life. The choice is black and white: we can either do it Satan's way and try to elevate ourselves to nirvana/godhood/perfection through our own efforts, making ourselves the ultimate authorities in the process, or we can rely on God to restore us to glory through his messiah.

The Occultic Rebirth

Autotheists are following in the footsteps of Satan, who tried to elevate himself to a state that was not meant for him. This quest is elucidated in the *Corpus Hermeticum*, an Egyptian-Greek compilation of the teachings of the god Hermes Trismegistus, who evolved from Thoth, the ancient Egyptian god of Wisdom.

> If then You do not **make yourself equal to God**, You cannot apprehend God; for like is known by like. Leap clear of all that is corporeal, and make yourself grow to a like expanse with that greatness which is beyond all measure; rise above all time, and become eternal; then You will apprehend God. (XI.20b)

The *Hermeticum* aims to illuminate a disciple through the learning of cosmic principles, philosophy, alchemy, astrology, and religious cosmology. Its end is nothing less than the disciple's spiritual rebirth through enlightenment as evidenced in this quote: "Seeing within myself an immaterial vision that came from the mercy of God, I went out to myself into an immortal body, and now I am not what I was before. I have been born in mind!" (XIII.3).

One website dedicated to Hermetic philosophy lists several purposes of the mystical rebirth, including the following:[174]

- To allow the spirit to reunite with the Higher Consciousness
- To release the spirit from the spell under which it is held in bondage in the body
- To bring the body and the mind to quiescence
- To reunite the spirit with its lost universality
- To separate the higher subtle feelings from the gross sense feelings
- To allow the spirit to travel to higher realms

This idea of a philosophic rebirth is central in the pagan mysteries, and the rites of almost all classical occult societies involve role-playing the rebirth to which all neophytes should aspire. For instance, the ceremony of the Third Degree of Freemasonry takes a candidate through a figurative death, burial and resurrection, signifying entry into a new state of consciousness.[175] The Third Degree, which confers the *sublime* status of

Master Mason, is considered the most important legendary symbol of Freemasonry and is practiced without alteration in all countries. According to the *Indiana Masonic Monitor*, pages 144–145,

> It was the single object of all the ancient rites and mysteries practiced in the very bosom of pagan darkness… to teach the immortality of the soul. This is still the great design of the third degree of Masonry.

The symbolic teaching of the doctrine of gnostic rebirth was the main element of what could be termed the *lower mysteries*.

Figure 8-3. The coffin on this Freemasonic 3rd-degree tracing board symbolizes the voluntary death and rebirth of occult initiates.

The *higher mysteries* were preserved for a select few deemed worthy to posses the keys to divinity. In the higher mysteries, a neophyte was taken through a set of rituals designed to deprive him of awareness of the material world. The rituals induced a deep and extended trance during which the etheric and astral bodies of the neophyte were separated from his physical body, simulating death. The neophyte could then experience a higher plane of existence and come to the understanding that death is not the end of life, but rather a change of state in which one is brought closer to the source of all life.[176]

Plato was an initiate of the higher mysteries, and he spoke of that initiation as a simulated death wherein mind and spirit were temporarily liberated from the flesh. He gave the following testimony of his experience of enlightenment:

> In consequence of this divine initiation we became spectators of single and blessed visions, resident in a pure light; and were ourselves made immaculate and liberated from this surrounding garment which we call the body and to which we are now bound like an oyster to its shell. (*Pha-*

edrus 250:c)

Apuleuis, a Berber prose writer of the 1ˢᵗ century AD, experienced the higher mysteries of Isis and wrote about them in *The Golden Ass.* During his initiation he "underwent 'a voluntary death' and 'approached the realm of Death' in order thereby to obtain his 'spiritual birthday' in the service of a goddess whose followers were 'as it were reborn.'"[177]

Those who underwent the higher mysteries believed that they had gathered the spoils of eternity by reaching a state of fully spiritual consciousness. They reasoned that when their physical shell was lost, their soul would return to the place of divine light that they had experienced during the deep trance of initiation. No matter that such a belief was unsubstantiated and by nature untestable—the initiates were convinced. Plutarch even appealed to the mysteries as a way of assuring his grieving wife that their dead daughter was well. He said, "because of those sacred and faithful promises given in the mysteries.... We hold it firmly for an undoubted truth that our soul is incorruptible and immortal."[178] The Word of God agrees with Plutarch that the soul is never extinguished. It is not the survivability of the soul, but its final destination, that must be determined.

This state of awakened spiritual consciousness is called Christ Consciousness in modern times. Throwing out the biblical teaching that the Anointed One is unique in all of Creation, pagans imagine that any man can become an anointed and enlightened spiritual guru. Masonic writer J. D. Buck insists that it is "far more important that men should strive to become Christs than that they should believe that Jesus was Christ."[179]

The mysteries are much the same in the East as they are in the West. For instance, in the Upanishads there are frequent passages to the effect that he who reaches the Brahmic consciousness has attained to immortality. "He who knows Brahman becomes Brahman," says the Mundaka Upanishad. "He passes beyond all sorrow.... Freed from the fetters of ignorance he becomes immortal."[180] Notice how it is ignorance, not iniquity, which is said to keep us from immortality. This is precisely the opposite of the scriptural teaching that our rebellious heart is the problem (Isa. 53:6).

To the Illuminist, the experience of higher dimensions not only provides assurance of reincarnation into a better state—or extraction from reincarnation altogether—but it also qualifies one to enter the New Atlantis, whose global dominance is inevitable. Leading occult philosopher-historian Manly P. Hall, a highly degreed Freemason, writes in *The Secret Destiny of America* that the second birth is the key to membership in a coming empire.

> There is a second birth, which is not an accident; it is the consequence of a proper intent. By this second birth man is born by enlightened intelligence out of nation and out of race in an intellectual nation and an international race. It is this larger and coming race that will someday inherit the earth. But unless a man be born again by enlightenment, he shall not be a part of the philosophic empire.[181]

Influential spiritual philosopher and self-described "practical mystic" David Spangler made a similar assertion in his book, *Reflections on the Christ*, saying that

> Lucifer comes to give to us the final gift of wholeness. If we accept it then he is free and we are free. This is the Luciferic initiation. It is one that many people now, and in the days ahead, will be facing, for it is an initiation in the New Age.[182]

Here we are presented with another parallel between pagan and Christian practices, for Yeshua clearly taught that a man must be born again, born from above, to enter the kingdom of God. Only Yeshua can set men free. Indeed, Christian baptism is symbolic of dying to sin, being buried with Messiah, and then being raised with him to a new and eternal life, forever free from evil. The difference between Christian and occult rebirth is that the former is conducted in submission to and reliance upon a fearful but loving God, whereas the latter is undertaken through human effort for man's own glorification. One is accomplished through divine mercy; the other through mortal wisdom.

NINE

The Osirian Cycle

The fruit which I have engendered is the Sun.[183]

–Isis

I shall not decay, I shall not rot, I shall not putrefy, I shall not turn into worms; I shall have my being, I shall live, I shall live.[184]

–The deceased, identifying with Osiris,
from the *Book of the Dead*

Although the mysteries were practiced in Mesopotamia, Persia, India, Greece, and Rome, it was in Egypt that they were systematized and refined to perfection. Mystical polytheism thrived along the banks of the Nile, where the priests of the sun god, along with their deified priest-king, the Pharaoh, acted as the hands and feet of the spirit of Lucifer for thousands of years. High-ranking Egyptian priests, called *lector priests,* were prominent practitioners of magic and keepers of secret knowledge,[185] and of course the pharaohs and the high priests of the various deities were known to wield magic.[186]

When Moses and Aaron presented YHVH's demands to Pharaoh, the Egyptian priest-initiates turned water into blood and branches into vipers (Exo. 7:12), the very insignia of Lucifer. A line on a temple of Edfu stresses that the rituals which would have led to such powers should be closely guarded: "I am a priest knowledgeable of the mystery, who's chest never lets go what he has seen!"[187]

Many of those who reject the mainstream version of ancient history, full as it is of holes, have arrived at the conclusion that the early Egyptians were concerned with perfecting mankind through occult learning and the elevation of consciousness. The Egyptians believed that it was ignorance, not iniquity, that crippled man. Even those Egyptians uninitiated into the greater mysteries were taught that they needed special knowledge in order to gain access to the underworld kingdom of Osiris upon death. The deceased soul needed the correct spells, passwords, and secret names in order to pass through the challenges and gates that would bar them on their afterlife voyage, and this knowledge was encoded in the *Book of the Dead*. It was knowing the right formula that opened the way; virtue was of lesser importance.

The *Eye of Ra* found so frequently in Egyptian art was a symbol of not only the omniscience of the sun god, but the opened third eye, or spiritual eye, of the initiate who gazed upon the Light. In the "Fellow Craft" section of the *Kentucky Freemasonic Monitor*, the connection between the sun and *seeing* in a mystical sense is hinted at—but of course not stated openly, for it is a secret. It reads,

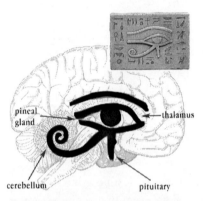

Figure 9-1. It's been suggested that the Ujat (Eye of Ra) symbol is a clever representation of the inner brain as seen when the left and right lobes are separated.

In most of the ancient languages of Asia "eye" and "sun" are expressed by the same word, and the ancient Egyptians hieroglyphically represented their principle deity, the sun-god Osiris, by the figures of an open eye, emblematic of the sun, by whose light we are enabled to see, and which itself looks down from the midst of heaven and beholds all things. (p. 116)

The Egyptian demigod who embodied the Light of Ra was by the Greeks called Osiris. Belonging to the earliest period of Egyptian mystical thought is the myth of Osiris and Isis, which gave rise to the doctrine known as the Osirian Cycle. The fable may have grown out of events in the lives of real persons, but it was imbued with mystical meaning by the illuminated priests; the celebrated Greek biographer, Plutarch, said, "The mystic symbols [of the Osirian Cycle] are well known to us who are of the brotherhood."[188]

A Short Biography of Osiris

Osiris was the son of the sun-god, Ra, and the brother of his wife, Isis (sound familiar?). He was born on the 361st day of the year, or December 25th,[189] the same day that several other cultures chose to celebrate their solar deities.

Osiris symbolized the Divine in a mortal form, and at Osiris' birth a heavenly voice announced, "Behold, the Lord of all the earth is born!"[190] He was the first ruler of Egypt and reigned with exceeding wisdom during a shaky period in human history that followed a great environmental catastrophe.

Osiris imposed civility on the primitive tribes of Egypt, teaching them agriculture, law, and religious conduct. After establishing an advanced civilization among the barbarians living in Egypt, Osiris departed and did likewise throughout the rest of the world. Greek historian Plutarch gave us one of a handful of accounts[a] to this tune:

> During his reign, Osiris started by delivering the Egyptians from destitution and savagery, made them understand agriculture, gave them some laws and taught them to honour the gods, **then he left by the whole world to bring civilisation**, without having, only rarely, to resort to the weapons, almost always achieving the will of his intentions by the charm of his persuasive word and by the resources of song and music.[191]

Osiris left his sister-wife, Isis, in charge during his absence. Like her husband, she was wise and possessed magical abilities and words of power. The king's brother, Set, was also formidable, but he lacked noble character and became jealous of Osiris, plotting to kill him. Seventy-two conspirators (there's that number again) joined Set in his treachery.

When the king returned from his travels to distant lands, Set threw a party in his honor. He had obtained his brother's measurements and constructed an ornate chest just large enough to contain Osiris. Accord-

---

[a] Amazingly, archeology bears out Plutarch's account of history. Scholars are baffled by what are called "full bloom" civilizations, those which came on the scene already matured and in possession of sciences and social systems comparable to—and in some cases beyond—our own. Modern secular theories of our origins demand a gradual increase in knowledge and ability, but what archeologists have found is plentiful evidence of a sudden explosion of civilization world-wide. Even more confusing is the fact that these advanced societies seem to have emerged at approximately the same time, even those in South and Central America.

ing to legend (and evidence that we will see later), Osiris was a giant, so the chest would have been too large for most men. At the banquet, Set promised to give the chest to whomever it would best fit. Osiris gauged that he would be able to lie comfortably inside, and so he did, imagining that his brother was kindly gifting him with a well-crafted furnishing. Once Osiris was fully inside the chest, the seventy-two accomplices of Set quickly closed it and nailed down the lid, whereupon they were able to carry the king to the Nile river and drown him. The chest in which Osiris died became the first sarcophagus.

With great effort, Isis was able to track down and recover the chest even though it had been carried out to sea and all the way to the shore of Byblos, where a tree grew around it. The tree was eventually cut down for use as a pillar in the local king's palace. When she finally retrieved the coffin from within the pillar and was able to lay eyes upon her husband's corpse, Isis wailed so loudly that it killed a boy standing nearby.

Isis brought the coffin, with the cadaver inside, back to Egypt and left it temporarily hidden in the swamps of the Delta.

Unfortunately, Set caught sight of it while out hunting. In a fit of rage, he chopped the body of Osiris in fourteen parts and scattered them along the length of the Nile. Unwilling to concede defeat, Isis scoured the land of Egypt until she had found all of Osiris' parts except one, the phallus, which had been eaten by an Oxhyrinchus fish.

Undeterred, the great sorceress was able to magically reconstitute and temporarily reawaken the body of the dismembered king from the thirteen recovered pieces. To complete the process, she crafted an imitation phallus from gold to replace the fourteenth piece. This is the origin of the obelisk, which is a monument in the shape of a stylized, erect phallus. Though first crafted in Egypt, obelisks can now be found across the globe in some very notable locations.

Transforming herself into a kite[a], Isis mated with the undead Osiris and conceived Horus, the falcon-headed god, who was considered the reincarnation of Osiris. The briefly reanimated Osiris passed again into death, but his son, Horus, grew to become powerful. He eventually battled his uncle, Set, to a stalemate, whereupon a council of gods ruled in favor of Horus. For her part, Isis had conscripted the help of Anubis to embalm her dead husband, making Osiris the first mummy. She also performed ceremonies necessary to ensure the life of Osiris in the neth-

---

[a] A small hawk.

erworld, the realm of the beautiful West, where Ra made Osiris king and judge of the dead. From that point on, every pharaoh of Egypt became the manifestation of Horus in life and Osiris in death, through imitative magic.

The Nile became another manifestation of Osiris, while the land surrounding the Nile became the body of Isis. The mummified king and his wife were linked to the constellation of Orion and the star named Sirius, respectively, and when those celestial objects would rise each year, the Nile would flood and restore fertility to the land. Thus the resurrection of crops was seen as equivalent to the annual astrological resurrection of the god-king.

Don't be fooled by this agriculture-based explanation, because it is only a concealing curtain—a mask for the real, esoteric meaning. The Osirian cycle is much more than the parable of a Nature cult.

The Interpretation of the Tale

In his book titled *Freemasonry of the Ancient Egyptians*, Manly Hall points out the foolishness of taking the Osirian Cycle at face value. He asks,

> Could such a fable have so greatly stimulated the admiration of Pythagoras that he would have spent a score of years in the assimilation of the idea? Or, again, would…. Pythagoras have pounded himself for a score of years against the walls of Memphis and find himself fully rewarded by being informed with bated breath by some arch-magus that Isis is the dog-star?[192]

These questions force us to look for an allegorical meaning to the Osirian Cycle.

Hall called Osiris "the personification of an order of learning," the embodiment of primordial knowing or experience of the Absolute "which is the end of all illumination." His incredible life, death, and resurrection revealed "the means by which mortal consciousness could achieve that end."[193]

Mr. Hall's explanation is indeed an accurate one, but it doesn't suffice. In the same chapter of his book, Hall draws attention to the fact that no extreme ills befell Plutarch, by which we can deduce that he never broke his vows as an initiate by revealing the secrets of the Brotherhood. Had he given us the true and deepest meaning of the Osirian cycle, he would have been killed or at the very least publicly disgraced.

The name of Osiris first pops up in the middle of the Fifth Dynasty of Egypt on the walls of the pyramids at Saqqara. Unlike the famous Giza pyramids, which are devoid of writing, the step-pyramids at Saqqara were covered with inscriptions. These writings, known collectively as the Pyramid Texts, consist of spells, or *utterances*, designed to assist the deceased Pharaoh on his journey to the afterlife, where he was to be installed as a god because he had acted as the vessel of Osiris in life. Despite the fact that many inscriptions have been found that predate the Pyramid Texts, none of them mention Osiris. Egyptologists are at a loss to explain how the extensive religious practices and stories associated with the god, absent any precursors, suddenly appeared and just as suddenly became the principle observance of the dynasties.[194] The simplest explanation for this enigma is that Osiris was based upon a real man who appeared in Egypt with occult knowledge and revolutionized their way of life. Upon the death of Osiris, Isis immediately presided over the apotheosis of her husband and instituted rites by which he should be perpetually revered, but it wasn't until the Fifth Dynasty, as far as we know, that the political and religious leaders recorded some of the details of their cult.

So Osiris was a real man, but a man that represented something bigger: a set of beliefs about transcending the darkness of ignorance. He was Knowledge and Order, the antithesis of Chaos.

The drowning of Osiris is an allegory for the loss of wisdom and civilization due to Noah's Flood. During the lifetime of the patriarch Enoch, angels called Watchers sinned and brought heavenly knowledge to the earth. This resulted in an advanced civilization called Atlantis, but it also resulted in terrible wickedness. Egyptian legends of *Zep Tepi*, "The First Time," conveniently leave out mention of the exponential increase in immorality that came yoked with the increase of man's abilities, but the books of Genesis, Jubilees, and Enoch inform us in no uncertain terms that God flooded the world on account of extreme depravity.

Of course, the postdiluvian king whom the Egyptians remember as Osiris was not alive at the time of the Flood, but that doesn't invalidate our interpretation of Osiris' death, since Osiris represents something beyond an individual life.

If Osiris is in part the doctrine of transcendence through orderly thought, as Manly Hall suggests, then his brother, Set, must be the opposing doctrine of degeneration through disordered thinking. Whereas Osiris represents man's progress to godhood through illumined intellect, Set is the personification of ignorance and of those superstitions which keep men trapped in an ignoble state. In Plato's famed *Allegory of the Cave*, Set would be the spirit of resistance to leaving the oppressive but familiar enclosure of the prison in order to experience the light of the outside world.

Pillars of Wisdom

Somehow, the advanced knowledge of the antediluvian world survived the Flood, and someone powerful got his hands on it. Modern-day occultists still claim that their secret knowledge came from Atlantis.[195]

Common sense tells us that Noah would have taken some of the learning of his era with him into Ark. Surely any of us would preserve as much knowledge as possible in the face of a global reset—especially the kinds of information that would aid in post-disaster reconstruction. The caveat is that Noah would not have brought along anything that could have incited his descendants to sin or become overly detached from the natural world that God created, which excludes all of the mysteries revealed by the fallen Watchers. (At the very least, Noah preserved the writings of his godly forefathers; the book of Enoch informs its reader that Methuselah, son of Enoch, received the books that his father had written, and then passed them down to Noah.) Whatsoever knowledge Noah brought with him would have been equally available to all of his offspring, so if Osiris had an advantage in learning, then it must have come from another source.

In his *Antiquities*, Jewish chronicler Flavius Josephus (AD 37–100) relates a tradition in which the descendants of Seth

discovered the science of the heavenly bodies and their orderly array. Moreover, to prevent their discoveries from being lost to mankind and perishing before they become known—Adam having predicted a destruction of the universe, at one time by a violent fire and at another by a mighty deluge of water—they erected two pillars, one of brick and the other of stone, and inscribed these discoveries on both; so that, if the pillar of brick disappeared in the deluge, that of stone would remain to teach men what was graven thereon and to inform them that they had also erected one of brick.[196]

Josephus notes that these pillars are located in the land of Seiris, which could be Egypt. (Sirius is the star of Isis, and to the Egyptian mind it is the most important of all the fixed stars). Josephus's pillars were probably not pillars at all, due to a deficiency in the Latin from which the passage was translated. In the missing original Greek text, the word was likely *puramis* instead of *columna* (pillar).[197] From *puramis* we get the English *pyramid*, which can be split into two components: *pyra,* meaning "fire" or "illumination", and either *ammos,* meaning "heap or mound,"[198] or *midos,* meaning "measures."[199] Do the pyramids have something to do with measures? Yes—illuminating mathematical and astronomical lessons are incorporated into the dimensions and layout of the monuments at Giza. And obviously a pyramid is a mound, but specifically, Giza is the place where the Egyptians believed that an island (Pangea) arose from the primeval sea during *Zep Tepi,* "The First Time." Amazingly, scientists have found that the Great Pyramid is located exactly at the center of the land mass of the earth (a coincidence?).

Author Rob Skiba presents a compelling argument that the Giza Plateau, the literal center of the surface of the earth, is the wilderness place where God formed Adam from the dust before transferring him to the Garden.[200] He also believes that it was the prophet Enoch who directed the construction of the Great Pyramid at the very spot of Adam's creation.[201] Could the pyramid of Khufu have been the stone pillar of which Josephus spoke? If anyone had the know-how to build such wonders, it was the man who was snatched up to heaven and instructed in esoteric wisdom. Enoch was told by God to "look on the cepher [book] of the tablets of heaven… and, reading that which is written in it, understand every part of it" (1 Eno. 80:1). And Enoch said to the godly men of future generations, "To you I swear, that I comprehend this mystery; that I have read the tablet of heaven, have seen the writing of the holy ones, and have discovered what is written and impressed on it" (103:1).

The scriptures do not mention pyramids by name, but Isaiah and Jeremiah do give us tantalizing clues about the purpose of the Great Pyramid. Jeremiah 32:20 speaks of YHVH placing "signs and wonders in the land of Egypt, even unto this day" (KJV), and of course we immediately think of the ten plagues during the time of the Exodus, but what can it mean that the signs were present even during the time of Jeremiah? Isaiah gives us more to go on when he states, "In that day there will be an altar to the LORD in the midst of the land of Egypt, and a pillar to the LORD at its border. It will be a sign and a witness to the LORD of hosts in the land of Egypt" (19:19–20). The altar and the pillar are assuredly the same object because the second sentence refers to them as a singular *it*. How can this monument be in the midst of Egypt and at its border simultaneously? The answer is that ancient Egypt was divided into Upper Egypt and Lower Egypt, with the Giza Plateau being in the southernmost portion of Lower Egypt. This seems to suggest that the Great Pyramid at Giza will be restored in the Day of the Lord; if that is the case, then the pyramid was a holy witness unto YHVH at its inception.[a] After all, God has his people tear down pagan monuments, not renovate them. Alternatively, the pillar of Enoch could be the Sphinx, which was carved out of solid rock and exhibits water erosion indicating that it is older than the current desert climate of Egypt.

At the very least, it should be considered meaningful that the most amazing and baffling structure in the world, and the only surviving member of the Seven Wonders of the World, is the artificial hill located at the center of the world and the spot where the first mound of earth was brought forth by God.

Writings in the ancient city of Heliopolis refer to the hill that arose from waters of Creation as the *Benben*, and the temple of Ra in Heliopolis housed the venerated *benben* stone, considered a sacred model of the primordial mound. The benben at Heliopolis was smooth and conical like the helmets of the Mesopotamian gods, minus the horns, but versions of the benben found elsewhere were sometimes angular in shape. The capstones of pyramids were likewise stylized versions of the Benben and were called by the same name. (This same shape is found on the top of obelisks.) The absence of the capstone of the Great Pyramid is very significant because it means that the structure was left incomplete; even the most ancient accounts make note of the missing capstone. Perhaps when Yeshua is installed as king in Jerusalem, the Great Pyramid will be completed with a golden capstone signifying that "the stone which the builders refused is become the head stone of the corner" (Psa. 118:22, KJV).

On the back of the American one-dollar bill is a drawing of an unfinished pyramid above which hovers a glowing capstone with an eye in

---

[a] Despite the claims of traditional Egyptologists, there is no compelling evidence that the Great Pyramid was built by Khufu or that it was ever used as a tomb.

it: the Egyptian All-Seeing Eye of Osiris/Horus. Above it are the words *annuit coeptis*, which means "he favors our enterprise," and the nature of that enterprise is given below the pyramid by the words *novus ordo seclorum*, or "new social order."[a] The number of stones in the pyramid is 72, the exact sum of nations that were formed out of the Dispersion, here finally reunited under Osiris and Horus. The Masonic occultists who designed this picture are telling us that they intend America to be a stepping stone towards the one-world government of the philosophic god-king, and that their god will crown their endeavor with success. The completion of this work is what Manly Hall called "the secret destiny of America." Hall made himself very clear on this matter, saying,

> The Great Seal is the signature of this exalted body—unseen and for the most part unknown—and the unfinished pyramid upon its reverse side is a trestleboard setting forth symbolically the task to the accomplishment of which the United States Government was dedicated from the day of its inception.[202]

Freemasonic author James D. Carter affirmed that occult ideas were purposefully embedded in the Great Seal when he claimed that Masonic symbols would be easily found whenever "an informed Mason examines the Great Seal."[203]

The capstone of the Masonic pyramid is not Messiah Yeshua, but the illuminated master of ancient Egypt, who is a false messiah. On the other end of the dollar bill is a picture of an eagle that is not an eagle; it is a phoenix in disguise. That statement may sound ludicrous at first, until one realizes that early designs for the seal depicted a different kind of bird, one that had the beak, long neck, and rear-facing tuft of a phoenix. One of artist William Barton's proposals to Congress even incorporated a phoenix rising from a pyre.[204] This bird was known to the Egyptians as the *bennu* bird, and it sat atop the benben stone, or capstone, as a symbol of resurrection and ascension. The Egyptians considered the phoenix to be "the soul of Osiris," and they sometimes called it "the morning star" (i.e., Venus).[205] The phoenix on our seal has thirty-two feathers in its right wing but thirty-three in its left; the former is the number of ordinary degrees of the Scottish Rite of Freemasonry, and the latter number

---

[a] The number (in Roman numerals) at the bottom of the pyramid is 1776, a pivotal year for America, but also the year of the founding of the Illuminati in Bavaria.

is the highest degree that exists, a special office conferred upon only a select few. The fact that this masonic bennu bird would grace the same seal as the unfinished pyramid leaves no doubt as to the intentions of the designers: they desire to see Osiris rise from his ashes to be elevated over the whole geopolitical structure of the new age.

Figure 9–2. Above: Hexagrams are hidden on both sides of America's Great Seal, incorporating the pyramid on the transverse and the stars on the reverse. **Below:** The Luxor Hotel in Las Vegas, Nevada, is modeled after the Great Pyramid. Its capstone is illuminated like the All-Seeing Eye of the Masonic pyramid. **(**Photo credit: Andrew Zarivny / Shutterstock.com**).**

We should consider the possibility that the writings of Enoch, scribe of godly illumination, were placed beneath the monuments of Giza, and that Osiris found these writings, learned from them, and eventually destroyed them so that he and Isis would have a monopoly on the heavenly secrets. Some of the Old Kingdom Coffin Texts quote Osiris as saying, "I have come to Rostau [the system of tunnels underneath Giza] in order to know **the secret** of the Duat [the supernatural realm]," and, "on the day of concealing the **mysteries of the deep place** in Rostau... I am he who sees the **secret things** in Rostau."[206] Either the secrets Osiris sought were texts left by the builders of the pyramids, or else the secrets were encoded within the very design of Rostau and its monuments, and Osiris was brilliant enough to decode them.

I do find it hard to believe that any structure could survive the devastation of the Flood, but it can't be ruled out. On one hand, geological evidence shows that that cataclysm dramatically changed the surface of the earth, but on the other hand, the pyramids at Giza are built upon a massive bed of limestone which may have remained fixed even during the Deluge, and many of the blocks of the pyramids are so tightly fitted together that even today a human hair cannot be slipped between them. If YHVH commissioned Enoch to build the pyramids, then they were evidently meant to survive the inundation.

Several sources other than Josephus give testimonies about two pillars or tablets inscribed with special knowledge and intended to survive a cataclysm; these include the Greek *Palaea Historica*, the Armenian *History of the Forefathers*, and the Latin *Life of Adam and Eve*.

In the 10th century, Coptic historian Al-Mas'udi (AD 896–956) wrote that the surfaces of the pyramids "exhibit all kinds of inscriptions written in the characters of ancient nations which no longer exist." Unsurprisingly, he reports that "no one knows what this writing is or what it signifies."[207] Herodotus claimed to have seen many strange characters on the exterior of the Great Pyramid while he studied in Egypt in the 5th century BC. Sadly, many of the casing stones of the pyramids were removed and reused as building materials by the inhabitants of Cairo after the AD 1303 earthquake, and the remaining stones gradually fell off, becoming rubble. Not everyone is agreed, however, that ancient knowledge was recorded on the *outside* of the pyramids. An Egyptian historian named Ibn 'Abd al-Hakam (AD 803–71) recounted legends which said that an antediluvian king of Egypt built the pyramids and had his priests inscribe the *insides* with all of the occult sciences of his people.[208]

Although the details differ, the overall theme is consistent between all of these accounts: exceptional knowledge from before the Flood was preserved in a form that would survive the cataclysm.

"Truly I Have Been Sent"

The Book of Jubilees reveals that records containing angelic knowledge were discovered by early descendants of the Flood survivors, and it points the finger at Kainam, a great-grandson of Noah, as culprit.

> And the son grew, and his father taught him writing, and he went to seek for himself a place where he might seize for himself a city. **And he found a writing which former generations had carved on the rock**, and he read what was thereon, and he transcribed it and sinned owing to it; for it contained the teaching of the Watchers in accordance with which they used to observe the omens of the sun and moon and stars in all the signs of heaven. And he wrote it down and said nothing regarding it; for he was afraid to speak to Noach about it…. and in the fourth year he begat a son, and called his name Shelach; for he said: Truly I have been sent. (Jub. 8:2–5)

A Masonic manuscript from the 16th century affirms the Jubilees account and even claims that the man who discovered the infamous pillar became the god known as Hermes-Trismegistus (the Egyptian Thoth), god of wisdom and writing. The manuscript reads,

> After the destruction of the world by flood, Hermes, who has been called the Father of Wise Men, found one of the pillars and taught the sciences written thereon to other men.[209]

Was this *Hermes* in fact Kainam? We can only wonder.

Evidently Kainam became puffed up with pride on account of the knowledge that he found, because he began to think of himself as a Godsend. Jubilees doesn't tell us what Kainam did with this knowledge, but one supposes that Cush got his hands on Kainam's transcription and used it to become a great builder, astrologer, and mystic, on account of which he had the clout to convince most of the families of the world to build a tower in defiance of YHVH.

The Tablet of Destinites

The Sumerians had several myths about a sacred object known as the *Tablet of Destinies,* which was stolen from Enlil by a bird-man called Anzu. Birds were a symbol of deity, so we may hypothesize that this part-avian thief represented the angelic Watchers who made off with the secrets of heaven. Interestingly, the Anzu bird is shown attending Enki (Satan) and Inanna on some Sumerian cylinder seals. The knowledge contained on the Tablet of Destinies conferred immense power and supreme authority, and it was fought over, stolen, and hidden several times over the course of history. One of these times was when the god Ninurta, who we have previously linked to Nimrod, seized the tablet from a demon and delivered it to Enki.

The Egyptians had a legend of a similar tablet of transcendent wisdom: the Book of Thoth (a bird-headed god, a.k.a. Hermes). All the magic of the world was supposedly written on it. Could legends of the sacred tablet have been meant to memorialize the rediscovery and transcription of angelic secrets by Kainam?

The Interpretation of the Tale (cont.)

Returning to the interpretation of the Osiris myth, we find that Isis recovers the body of Osiris from within a tree trunk at a place called Byblos. The tree trunk represents the *axis mundus,* or *world tree,* which will be discussed in a future chapter.

Byblos was a Canaanite port town and the first city in Phoenicia ("Land of the Phoenix" or "Land of Crimson," the color of the phoenix); as such, it is one of the oldest continuously-inhabited cities in the world. According to the priest named Sanchuniathon, it was built by Cronus, the god who Alexander Hislop identified as the apotheosis of Cush. The religion of all of Phoenicia was merely a copy of the Babylonian mystery religion, with different names assigned to the characters and some main players split into multiple deities. As a repository for Babylon's occult knowledge, we can imagine that the establishment of Byblos slightly preceded the migration of Nimrod's kingdom into Egypt. Incidentally, the Greek word *Byblos* gave rise to the word *Bible,* a book of sacred wisdom, and esoteric wisdom is one of the major elements that Osiris embodies.

Isis finds and rescues the sacred wisdom after it is lost to the sea, and she takes it to Egypt for safe-keeping. Set, personification of ignorance and disordered thinking, discovers the hidden Osiris, cuts him into pieces, and scatters his parts to the four winds. By this it is meant that the wise king who civilized Egypt (and much of the world after the Dispersion) was cut down, and the many branches of his kingdom became disconnected from one another. The real king Osiris was not chopped into pieces and scattered throughout Egypt; he remained in one piece and was turned into the first man-made[a] mummy, after which he was entombed either under the Giza plateau or under Nineveh, depending on which ancient sources you believe.

The priestly orders of the far-flung colonies of Osiris did still possess the arcane arts of the illumined king, but they constituted a small segment of the population, and their knowledge was easily lost. Due to war and cataclysmic natural disasters that occurred in early history, each generation retained less and less insight. Having no central authority to which they could turn to restore knowledge as it was lost, civilizations that began in a very advanced state slowly declined into nescience. In any age, it doesn't take very long at all for knowledge of specialized techniques to be forgotten if those techniques aren't carefully passed on and frequently put to use.

Osiris' wife, Isis, represents the feminine pole of the sun god, which is the receptive principle of Nature. Isis is to Osiris as the ekklesia (i.e., the assembly of believers) is to Yeshua. She is the accumulated body of Initiates and the one who perpetuates the doctrine of the Light-Bearer. She is the temple and the keeper of the mysteries; and, by extension, the one who confers the divine right to rule. Often represented in the form of a cow, Isis is the fertile earth and the fertile mind, receptive agents for the sun's generative powers as passed through Osiris. Every initiated member of Isis is fertilized by the intellectual light of Ra and becomes a type of Horus, whereupon he puts his hand to the completion of the Great Work of bringing back the original Osiris.

In the fifth installment of the *Mystery Babylon* series of radio broadcasts, researcher William Cooper arrived at this conclusion regarding the gathering of Osiris' body parts by Isis:

In the dark retreats of Islam, the Sufi explored the depths of Nature;

---

[a] The arid, sun-baked environment of Egypt sometimes turned untreated corpses into mummies naturally.

among the Jews, the learned Rabbis unraveled the intricate skein of Cabbalism; among the Greeks, Initiates rose to life through the nocturnal rituals of Eleusis; in India, neophytes were brought to the contemplation of the triple-headed Brahma at Elphanta and Ellora. Through the Middle Ages, the alchemists in their retreats explored the infinite chemistry of existence, the Illuminati sought the pearl of great price, and Rosicrucian adepts sought to recast the molten sea. **All these together were but Isis**, still searching for the members of her lord.

Cooper got it; he understood that the Mystery brotherhood is the hands and feet of Isis. Freemasons call themselves "sons of the Widow" as a mark of participation in the quest of Isis (not, as is commonly claimed, because the biblical Hiram was a widow's son).

The Dormer Masonic Study Circle of London reflected a similar understanding when it wrote that Isis "resurrected the dead God, and through union with him brought forth an order of priests **under the collective title of HORUS**." This tells us that the Osirian cycle is still in progress, and has been playing out for centuries. All these groups have been pursing the same goal via different routes. That goal, said Manly Hall, was "the perfected social order, Plato's commonwealth, the **government of the philosopher-king**."[211]

After the missing fourteenth piece of Osiris, known by some as the "Lost Word" of Freemasonry, is finally obtained, the magic that Isis will wield through Horus to bring forth Osiris is the accumulated arcana of the occult hierophants[a], who have ever searched out and passed on the secrets of sorcery and science.

The Prophesied Victory of Horus

The Egyptians viewed the afterlife in part as an island in the West, where the sun set (read: symbolically died). There the sun merged with the mummified Osiris and received the power of new vitality by which he traveled the Netherworld, gaining vigor as he went until being reborn in the East. While in the underworld, Osiris was considered to be inside the womb of Isis, but when the sun rose in the morning, Osiris was symbolically reborn as Horus-on-the-Horizon (*Coffin Texts* sp. 255).

---

[a] Masters of sacred mysteries or esoteric principles.

At noon, however, when the sun was at its highest and most powerful, the Egyptians said that Horus had completed his transformation into Ra. This sun god is of one nature with Osiris, for it is written in the tomb of Nefertari that "Osiris resides in Re and Re resides in Osiris." It is also written that Osiris is "yesterday" and Ra is "tomorrow."[212] The Pyramid Texts repeatedly state that Horus gives Osiris his eye, the All-Seeing Eye, which is the solar disk. When the priesthood called Horus becomes like the sun at noon, reaching the zenith of its power, it will bring about the god of illumination: the penultimate Ascended Master, who is the renewed Osiris.

Sharron Rose, president of *Sacred Mysteries Distribution* has this to say about Horus:

> Horus, the son of Isis and Osiris, is both the SON and the SUN. Horus is the representative of his father Osiris. The energy of Horus within us, awakened and invigorated by Isis, becomes the rising up of the will to complete the Great Work and attain full enlightenment in this lifetime, a process that the great Egyptian scholar Isha Schwaller de Lubicz called "willed superevolution."[213]

What the author of that statement is missing (or purposefully omitting) is that the enlightenment of the human race and the establishment of Utopia on earth can only be accomplished by Horus bringing Osiris back into the world, physically. It is not enough that he remain inside of the illumined ones (and also symbolically in the sun); he must manifest in human form as ruler of this world. In an ancient Egyptian tale about a magician and scholar named Setna, son of Rameses II, there are two passages which mention "**the Day of Awakening** when Osiris returns to rule the earth."[214] By this we see that an expectation of "the awakening" is not unique to modern occultists, and that the Egyptians of old also believed that the mummy of Osiris would be reinvigorated on some fateful day.

Freemasons have repackaged the Osirian cycle in a story about a mythical Phoenician named Hiram Abiff, master architect of Solomon's Temple. As the story goes, Hiram possessed great and secret wisdom, and for this he was murdered by three jealous conspirators. His death came before the Temple was completed, but the "Great Architect" in the sky bathed Hiram's body in celestial glory like the rays around the Eye of Horus atop the unfinished pyramid. Hiram is symbolically raised back to life in the Masonic ritual of the third degree, whereby a Fellow Craft member impersonates Hiram and upon resurrection becomes a so-called Master Mason. In the ritual, Hiram is called "the widow's son," providing a fat hint as to who this man is supposed to represent. Adding support, the name *Hiram* means "noble" or "kingly," and *Abiff* is old French for "lost one." As we have learned, Osiris was the lost king of the Egyptians, and Manly Hall called the king's missing phallus "the Lost Word of Freemasonry." The phallus is symbolic of the generative principle of nature, and when the secret of it is found, the lost king can finally be regenerated.

In Masonic ritual, the Great Architect issues a charge to those who would see the completion of the temple begun by Hiram, and that charge is to find the body and raise it from the dead. He commands,

> Seek ye... the grave of Hiram who has carried my Will with him to the tomb. This eternal quest is yours until ye have found your Builder.... **No more shall I speak until ye have found and raised my beloved Son**, and have listened to the words of my Messenger and with Him as your guide have finished the temple which I shall then inhabit. Amen.[215]

If Hiram's connection to Osiris is not yet clear enough, here is a quote from well-known 32° Mason J. D. Buck:

> In the third degree the candidate impersonates Hiram, who has been shown to be **identical with the Christos of the Greeks and with the Sun-Gods of all other nations**.... In deifying Jesus the whole of humanity is bereft of Christos [i.e., the anointing] as an eternal potency within every human soul, a latent Christ in every man. In thus deifying one man, they have orphaned the whole of humanity![216]

High-ranking members of Freemasonry understand the sun gods such as Osiris to be one and the same as Christ, and these characters are collectively represented by Hiram.

Osiris states confidently in the Egyptian *Book of the Dead*, "I am Yesterday and I am Today; and **I have the power to be born a second time**."[217] Not reborn year after year, mind you, but a *second* time.

The Raising

Each year in the Egyptian city of Abydos and several others, a commemorative *mystery play* was held in honor of Osiris. Hundreds of priests and priestesses reenacted the principal parts of the Osirian cycle during this grand, multi-day celebration. An important element of the reenactment was the raising of the Djed pillar[a], which took place on the eve of the agricultural New Year. The Djed was a column representing both the backbone of Osiris and the tree that grew around his sarcophagus after it came to rest at Byblos. The raising of the Djed at Abydos symbolized the victory of Osiris over death and the works of Set.

Abydos is one of the most ancient cities of Upper Egypt and is home to the enigmatic, subterranean, megalithic structure called the Osireion. Older than any other structure at Abydos, the Osireion was built over a fresh-water spring in the same manner as Enki's Abzu temple at Eridu. The fact that Abydos was intended to be another Eridu is betrayed by the Egyptian name for Abydos, which is *Abdju*. The "dj" sound is pronounced "z," making it phonetically the same as *Abzu*.

Figure 9-3. This reproduction of a scene on the west wall of the Osiris Hall at Abydos shows the raising of the Djed pillar.

Plutarch was was an eye-witness of the festival of Osiris held at the Egyptian sea town of Canopus. The festivities at Canopus mirrored those at Abydos. Describing part the ceremony, Plutarch related that

> on the nineteenth at night they go down to the sea; and the keepers and priests carry out the sacred chest [i.e., the symbolic coffin of Osiris], having within a small golden vessel, into which they take and pour fresh water, and shouts are raised by the assistants as though Osiris were found.[218]

---

[a] The Djed is actually a composite of four separate pillars shaped like papyrus stems, vertically offset from each other by a small distance. They may represent either the four cardinal directions or the four pillars of heaven.

The pouring of fresh water at the terminus of the sea is an allusion to the storehouse of the Netherworld, where the salt waters of Tiamat become the sweet waters of the Abzu. The Egyptian priests symbolically found the Abyss within the coffin of their dead king because his spirit resides there until his body can be reconstituted. The fresh water may also have represented the efflux of Osiris, held inside a hermetically-sealed container which we'll learn about later.

By retelling the legend of Isis and Osiris year after year, the priesthood was preserving the memory of a real man whose soul awaits its release from the Netherworld; they were also preserving the hope of a better world to come at the return of that man. The heirophants were ensuring that the mission of the Brotherhood was not forgotten, and as a result of their efforts, when the time came that the Egyptian civilization faded from the world stage, the Greeks took up and carried the baton; then the Greeks passed it to the Romans, and the Romans to the Medieval fraternal guilds, and those guilds to the secret societies of today.

An excellent account of the festival of Osiris is carved within the temple complex of Dendera, and it is accompanied by depictions of Osiris' resurrection. Sir James Frazer (1854–1941) describes it this way:

> These [bas-reliefs] exhibit in a series of scenes the dead god lying swathed as a mummy on his bier, then gradually raising himself up higher and higher, until at last he has entirely quitted the bier and is seen erect between the guardian wings of the faithful Isis, who stands behind him, while a male figure holds up before his eyes the *crux ansata*, the Egyptian symbol of life. The resurrection of the god could hardly be portrayed more graphically.[219]

Yet perhaps it has indeed been portrayed more graphically, in three dimensions, and in America's own Capitol. There, on the banks of the Potomac, a sculpture of a seventy foot bearded giant claws his way up from beneath the earth in a disturbing depiction of resurrection. The work of artist J. Seward Johnson, *The Awakening* sculpture was purchased by real estate mogul Milton Peterson and placed at the Nation Harbor resort just a few miles outside of Washington, DC. Was the sculptor of *The Awakening* aware of the mythos behind what he crafted? Is the unusually successful Mr. Peterson a member of the Brotherhood that is working to bring about the real awakening of the sun god? I have no answers to those questions, but just looking at the artwork makes the hair on the back of my neck bristle.

You see, the Osirian cycle is not only history, but prophecy. Osiris *will* arise.

Figure 9–4. J. Seward Johnson, Jr., *The Awakening,* 1980. Aluminum, 17' 1" x 69' 0", as it appeared at its former site in Hains Point. Reproduced from http://www.dcmemorials.com.

The adepts of the Mystery Religion still exist today and have not forgotten their purpose. They were weakened by wars and driven into hiding by Christianity, but never eradicated. The occult fraternities of the present time are feverishly working to complete the mission of their ancient brothers, the illuminated priests, by rebuilding Atlantis—and they will only be able to finish this Great Work by restoring Osiris to the face of the earth. He will possess the wisdom and might needed to establish a worldwide "benevolent despotism" in which men are "led to a nobler state of being by the firm, kindly hand of the enlightened sage."[220]

Bible-reading Christians know better. The ruler to come will not be the great Savior, but the great Destroyer.

TEN

Son of the Howling One

Under the names of Osiris, Tammuz, Adonis, and Attis, the peoples of Egypt and Western Asia represented the yearly decay and revival of life, especially of vegetable life, which they personified as a god who annually died and rose again from the dead. In name and detail the rites varied from place to place: in substance they were the same.[221]

–Sir James Frazer

H aving come to a basic understanding of the Mysteries, we are now able to grasp the meaning of Inanna's fertility rites and the symbolism of the many pagan mother-and-child cults.

Babylonian Life-Cycle Mythology

The ancient pagan priesthood put great emphasis on the annual cycle of vegetable death and rebirth, and its connection to the cycles of the luminaries. They emphasized it not simply because they recognized that the unending seasonal cycles are tied to the continuation of life on Earth, but because it illustrated spiritual lessons.

The stories involving Inanna and her derivative goddesses include a male counterpart who is either her husband or her son, or both. This character is a demigod associated with vegetation, husbandry, hunting, and sometimes magic. The god-man is tragically removed from earthly life and confined to the netherworld, whereupon his wife mourns his passing with loud wails and deep lamentations—this is why the planet Venus was known in some cultures as the star of lamentation. In most traditions the ill-fated demigod dies or disappears late in the year, when nature dries up and loses its life; yet he is reborn or revealed in the spring as plant growth begins anew.

In Sumer, this counterpart to the goddess was named Dumuzi of Kuara, a.k.a Dumu-zi(d)-abzu, "True Son of the Abyss."[222] The origins of Dumuzi are wholly obscure, and no one theory about his identity has yet been universally adopted. Mesopotamian tales present Dumuzi as Inanna's first love—Gilgamesh called him the mate of her youth—but there is nothing concrete that would allow us to associate him with a historical figure.

Dumuzi's name means "Faithful (or True) Son," which refers to his part in the endless cycle of death and rebirth in the vegetable kingdom. But whose son is he? Inanna's, evidently. The Akkadian version of Dumuzi, called Tammuz, was both brother and son of Ishtar. In regards to this, Semitic languages expert Dr. Julian Morgenstern writes,

> The divine child, grown to manhood, supplants the original Father-God as the lover and paramour, or even the husband, of the Mother-goddess; or he is even identified with the Father-god in such manner that Father-god and divine Son are regarded as one, one single deity, though in two, complementary forms or stages of divine being, the old god and the young god…. These two acts, the death and burial of the old, senescent god, and his rebirth or resurrection from the earth, or from the netherworld, the realm of the dead, in youthful, vigorous form, were the focal points of the agricultural religion, not only of Tyre, but likewise of all the West Asiatic Semitic people and city-states.[223]

In this same vein, a certain liturgy to Tammuz reads,

> O brother fruit of my eyes, lifting up of my eyes,
> Who is thy sister? **I am thy sister**.
> Who is thy mother? **I am thy mother**.
> In the sunrise when thou risest, rise!
> At the dawn when thou appearest, appear!
> The queen of Eanna who cries, 'Alas! **my husband, alas! my son**.'[224]

What a strange—not to mention physically impossible—relationship! Also note that in the above passage we find that Tammuz is linked to the solar cycle, and that he is mourned by Inanna/Isthar, queen of E-Anna Temple. In other texts, as Ishtar mourns the loss of Tammuz she calls him "child, true lord,"[225] but also "my hero" and "my enchanter and priest."[226]

A certain couplet from a liturgy speaks further about this:

> In his infancy in a sunken boat he lay. In his manhood in the submerged grain he lay."[227]

This seems to mirror the Osirian cycle, wherein Osiris (a shepherd like Tammuz) is drowned in a sarcophagus but is recovered by Isis and hidden in the Nile marsh; yet Set finds and slays him among the rushes. In the hymn titled *The Dream of Dumuzi*, the goddess Geshtinanna interprets Dumuzi's portentous dream for him, explaining that

> The rushes which rise all about you,
> The rushes which grow thick about you,
> Are your demons, who will pursue and attack you.[228]

Geshtinanna is telling us that the marsh plants in the dream are symbolic of adversaries. Accordingly, Tammuz being drowned as an infant is an allegory of the loss of the illumined society of Atlantis—and the goodness of its fruits—to the Deluge. Upon his return to life through the postdiluvian recovery of knowledge and prosperity, Tammuz is still a child, but he grows rapidly into a man. Yet after reaching maturity he is once again slain by the supposed forces of darkness; thus a cycle is established, and the ancients compared it to the cycles of the sun and vegetable life.

Being a vegetation god, Dumuzi was referred to as "The Green One" (as was Osiris), yet Dumuzi was also a god of the flock, as evidenced by this sentence from *The Courtship of Inanna and Dumuzi*: "As the farmer, let him make the fields fertile / As the shepherd, let him make the sheepfolds multiply."[229] After joining with Dumuzi in the marriage bed, Inanna sets him on the throne and makes him warlord under her authority.

Sumerian poems involving Dumuzi paint a picture of a complex figure who is at once a handsome ruler, divine bridegroom, a wild ox, and a civilized farmer. He is loved by Inanna but also despised by her; after making him king, she then sends him to the netherworld for his impudence. In accordance with her typically erratic behavior, Inanna laments Dumuzi's absence and in so doing loses much of her fertility power. Dumuzi's sister, Geshtinanna, also mourns his demise and begs the goddess of the underworld to let her swap places with Dumuzi for half of each year. The goddess accedes and Dumuzi is allowed to return to Inanna's side for six months annually—the months between the spring and vernal equinoxes, when living things are reinvigorated by the increased presence of the sun.

The Rite of Hieros Gamos

Inanna's primary function in the eyes of the Sumerians was to ensure the fertility of the earth. By her mystical conjugation with the harvest god on his yearly return from the underworld, Inanna became the source of universal life and abundance. Some of the songs of Inanna are explicit as they equate the female body to the earth and human sexuality to cosmic reproduction.

This concept was played out in *hieros gamos*, the annual ritual centered around copulation between the king, representing Dumuzi, and a sacred prostitute (probably the high priestess) representing Inanna. Before consummation took place, the king would be hidden away for several days to represent the annual demise of crops, and the people of the city-state would mourn with Inanna for his loss. On the spring equinox, he would emerge from the simulated grave to the sounds of celebration and unite with Inanna's priestess, thus stimulating the reproductive forces of nature. Once completed, this *imitative magic* ritual of hieros gamos bestowed godhood on the king, for he had become a fit extension for the spirit of Dumuzi. To the laypeople of ancient Mesopotamia, the reenactment of the god-man's death and resurrection somehow ensured an abundance of crops and offspring that year.

The practice of imbuing kings with godhood was not confined to Mesopotamia; the Egyptians also carried out an imitative ritual related to the chthonic[a] fertility god. In adherence to elaborate instructions given by Isis, the clergy would validate and empower each new pharaoh through imitative magic designed to install the royal *ka*, or life-force, of their dead god into the new king.[230] Upon completion of the ceremony, the pharaoh had in a spiritual sense become the reincarnation of Osiris. By manifesting his presence within each pharaoh, Osiris could direct civilization towards a desired end over the course of many human lifetimes.

Tangentially, it may interest American readers to know that similar imitative magic is being executed on our shores concurrent with every presidential inauguration. Researcher Dr. Thomas Horn shocked his readers

[a] Of or relating to beings of the netherworld.

when he revealed that this was so, and that he had personally inquired about the mysterious *Raising Ceremony* in the very location where it is performed: the third floor Temple Room at the Masonic *House of the Temple* in Washington, D.C. Horn writes,

> We've been there, stood inside and prayed for protection under our breath, because according to our sources (who provided facts that have not been denied when we were interviewed by a US Congressman, US Senator, and even a 33rd-Degree Freemason on his radio show), in addition to when a Mason reaches the Master level, the ancient raising ceremony is conducted following the election of an American president—just as their Egyptian forefathers did at the temple of Amun-Ra in Karnak—in keeping with the tradition of installing within him the representative spirit of Osiris until such time as the god himself shall fulfill the Great Seal prophecy and return in flesh.[231]

When Dr. Horn pressed Masons at the Temple to tell whether it was true that they imbued each president with the divine right of Kingship through the symbolic raising of Osiris, the previously cordial hosts balked. Being Initiates, they were sworn to secrecy and so would not talk about such ceremonies, but their faces told Horn all that he needed to know. The very construction of the Temple Room betrays its dark purpose, for the ceiling directly above the altar is a 36-paneled magic *666 square* hemmed in on each side by an embossed pyramid capstone sporting Egyptian-style wings reminiscent of the famous winged solar disc.[232] No, I'm not making that up; it's really there, looking down into the ceremonial center of America's most important Masonic temple.

In his book titled *Zenith 2016*, Dr. Horn draws attention to a phrase prominently displayed on the official seal of the United States: *Novus Ordo Seclorum*. Those words were borrowed from the prophecies of the *Cumaean Sibyl*, a prophetess of Apollo.[a] The Sibyl's oracles assured worshipers that Apollo would return in the future, at a time when men would be rejoined by the gods. President George W. Bush—himself a member of at least one occult society[233]—stated in his second inaugural address that when our forefathers placed the phrase *Novus Ordo Seclorum* on the Great Seal, "They were acting on an ancient hope that is meant to be fulfilled."[234] High-ranking members of the illumined Brotherhood must

---

[a] The Greek god Apollo is a spin-off of Dumuzi and Osiris, and the women who gave oracles on his behalf were well-esteemed in ancient Greece.

have smirked when they heard that, knowing that the ancient hope was in fact a plan to bring back the ancient demigod of the Near East.

Dr. Horn and several other authors, including a few Masons, have demonstrated in their respective books that the District of Columbia was designed and built by mystery school initiates (e.g., Freemasons, Rosicrucians, and Illuminati), and that the designs and landmarks they created were infused with an incredible amount of occult geometry, numerology, and symbolism. This was done to insure that America would become the New Atlantis, that it would develop into a utopian commonwealth and eventually give rise to the god-king. In other words, America was designed to be the continuation of ancient Egypt and Babylon.

But I digress.

The Monomyth

The Sumerian god Dumuzi was known to the Phoenicians as Adon[a], and to the Greeks as Adonis. Adon was a strapping youth and an avid hunter. The goddess Astarte loved him and wished to rid him of his wild side; but alas, he wouldn't be tamed. One day, while Adon was hunting, he was surprised and gored by a wild boar (or a jealous rival in the form of a boar). Astarte found the dying Adon but was unable to save him. She cried out in grief at his passing, declaring that his death would be mourned every year.

In Canaanite tradition, Anat's self-mortification on behalf of her fallen brother-husband, Ba'al, was extreme and much celebrated. Even though Ba'al was chief god over all the earth, he could not escape from Mot, the personification of death, who broke Ba'al into pieces and devoured him. In response, Anat vigorously mourned her sibling and tirelessly sought his corpse.

Several other myths of male gods, particularly in the Near East, conform to a similar pattern. According to Peter Goodgame,

> The story of a Dying God became known throughout the world long before God took human flesh in the form of Jesus of Nazareth. This is a fact that has always been known by the masters and initiates of the mystery traditions, but it is a fact that has been long ignored or repressed

---

[a] *Adon* is the Semitic word for "master" or "lord." In the Bible, *Adonai* means "my lord" and is used as a title for God.

by Christian scholars. In the late 1800s the phenomenon was presented through a secular academic perspective by Sir James Frazer and his groundbreaking book *The Golden Bough* published in 1890. Then in 1949 Joseph Campbell published his famous analysis of the "monomyth," entitled *The Hero With A Thousand Faces*. Campbell attempted to assimilate all of the ancient accounts of heroes and saviors into a basic template involving challenges, failures, death, rebirth, tragedy and finally triumph. Many of Campbell's ideas can be viewed in hindsight as accurate, because at a certain level many of the hero-myths of antiquity can be traced back to one man...[235]

This one man was none other than Nimrod, who became the embodiment of Dumuzi by marriage to the high priestess of the fertility goddess. Joseph Campbell noted that several of the myths of divine heros dying involve a rebirth of one form or another, but the more important connection is that they involve a grief-stricken paramour whose suffering and desparate searching were reenacted annually by worshipers.

Apollo and the Cosmic Dance of Shiva

Shifting gears slightly, we are going to take a look at the gods Shiva and Apollo, and discover that they closely relate to Dumuzi.

Shiva is a Hindu god who maintains balance in the universe through the juxtaposed actions of destruction and regeneration (but not true creation). Like Dumuzi and Osiris, he is a god of cyclical change. With neck and limbs wrapped in serpents, Shiva performs a dance called *Anandatandava*, "the dance of Bliss," which symbolizes the cycle of order and chaos as well as the annual and daily rhythms of life. This dance occurs within a circle representing never-ending cycles and the ouroboros that encircles the cosmic womb. It was within said womb that countless cycles of destruction and recombination took place among the particle soup of the early universe.

Depictions of Shiva often have

Figure 10-1. This relief on a gravestone is rife with esoteric meaning.

him holding an hourglass in his right hand and a flame in his left. The hourglass represents the endless rhythm of the male and female vital principles of Nature, and when the two triangles of the upper and lower divisions overlap, signifying sacred union (the hieros gamos), they form a hexagram. These opposing triangles are a representation of the principle of duality: positive and negative, active and passive, fire and water, and yin and yang. According to the *Wikipedia* entry on the hexagram, within Indic lore,

> The downward triangle symbolizes Shakti, the sacred embodiment of femininity, and the upward triangle symbolizes Shiva, or Agni Tattva, representing the focused aspects of masculinity. The mystical union of the two triangles represents Creation, occurring through the divine union of male and female.

The names Inanna and Dumuzi, or Isis and Osiris, or Venus and Mars could be substituted for Shakti and Shiva in the preceding sentence without changing its veracity.

This symbol of intertwined equilateral triangles shows up in various places such as the *Tibetan Book of the Dead* (circumscribed around a swastika), the Masonic overlapping square and compass (stylized, with the horizontal segments removed), and the Star of David, to name a few. The hexagram is a powerful tool in alchemy, astrology, and spell-casting—so much so that the word *hex* has become synonymous with *curse*.

The hourglass of Shiva is also a two-sided drum on which the god pounds out the beating pulse of the universe. One of the forms of Shiva is as a teacher of music, chant, and the achievement of trance. This reminds us that Osiris went to the far reaches of the world and brought people-groups under his authority "by the charm of his persuasive word and by the resources of song and music."[236]

Saturn is traditionally understood to be the planet of limitation and destruction, and it is encircled by rings representing the ouroboros. It is the planet of Shiva, the destroyer. The book *The History and Practice of Magic, Vol. 2* names the six-pointed star "the talisman of Saturn."[237] Amazingly, astronomers have recently discovered that Saturn has a permanent hexagon[a] shape in the gases of its northern pole.[238] They are baffled by the presence of this clearly-defined, unchanging polygon in

---

[a] A hexagon is just a hexagram with lines connecting the outer points. The overlapping portion of two intersecting, equilateral triangles forms a hexagon.

the planet's clouds.

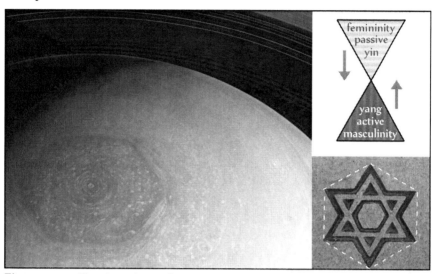

Figure 10-2. The planet Saturn features a permanent hexagon at its northern pole.

The tongue of flame in Shiva's left hand represents the element of destruction and the power of transformation into a new form. Hindu beliefs about the end of the world partially parallel Christian beliefs, for they say that it will occur by immolation (cf. 2 Peter 3:7), and after that a new cosmos will be formed. This circuit from cosmic creation to cosmic destruction and then recreation occurs on a long time-scale but is echoed at smaller scales by the emergence and re-immersion of the continents from water, the rise and fall of nations, and the biological life-cycle. The annual death and rebirth of vegetation and the daily journey of Sol are particularly illustrative to us of the greater cycle because we observe them so frequently. It is those daily and yearly cycles which the ancients incorporated into the myth of Dumuzi/Tammuz/Osiris, who was destroyed from this life but will faithfully return and ascend again.

Similarly, the journey of Osiris is an earthly echo of the journey of Heaven's rebel. The fire-bird known as the phoenix, the sacred bird of the sun cults,[239] is a representation of the fiery, flying reptilian that was Satan. Birds are like reptiles with feathers, and the similarities are so pronounced that many evolutionists propose that birds evolved from dinosaurs; so the phoenix, though a bird, is still a fine representative of the crimson dragon. It is by fire that the legendary red phoenix is destroyed before rising anew from its own ashes. Legend would have us believe that the phoenix self-immolates, but the Bible suggests otherwise when it says that YHVH brought a fire out of Satan's midst (Ezek. 28:18). "It consumed you," says YHVH, "and I turned you to ashes on the earth."[a] Although Satan was destroyed from his original abode, he took flight again as "the ruler of the kingdom of the air" (Eph. 2:2, NIV). Likewise, Dumuzi/Osiris not only returns to inhabit each new Babylonian ruler after the demise of the previous king/pharaoh, but he will return in the future to become the ruler of the whole earth, under Satan.

Figure 10-3. The Hindu god Shiva dances in a circle of fire.

Yogis often teach that Shiva acts on an anthropological level as well as a cosmic one: he destroys our illusions, delusions, and ignorance in order to bring about spiritual progress. In fact, idols of Shiva usually have the god dancing atop a flailing demon or dwarf who symbolizes ignorance. We could say that Horus acts on behalf of, or in accordance with, Shiva in Horus' own quest to destroy Set, the god of ignorance and barbarism. And presently, Horus (i.e., the brotherhood of illumined ones) is laboring to bring about systemic chaos on a global scale, so that a new and enlightened global order can arise from the ruins. (Judging by the terrible effects of the Four Horsemen of Revelation 6, the occult brotherhood will get its wish.)

The Hebrew equivalent of Shiva is Abaddon, whose name means "Destruction." The word *abaddon* is found six times in the Masoretic version of the Old Testament, and in four out of the six it accompanies the mention of Sheol. It would seem from these texts that abaddon is the place of torment within Sheol.

Yet Abaddon is also a spirit of torment. In Rev. 9:11, John writes that the host of demons who arise from the Abyss have "as king over them the angel of the bottomless pit. His name in Hebrew is Abaddon, and in Greek he is called Apollyon." *Apollyon* means "Destroyer" and is a com-

---

[a] The fire which consumed and brought the cherub to ashes is likely a reference to the destruction of Satan's planet, Rahab, which gave us the Asteroid Belt. Small pieces of Rahab struck the Earth in antiquity, possibly triggering the Flood or other large-scale disasters.

mon variant of *Apollo*, the sun god who was a son of Zeus. This Zeus is actually Satan, according to Yeshua's message to the church at Pergamum, where the Greeks had constructed a grand altar to the god (Rev. 2:13). Apollo was not only the god of the sun, light, and truth, but also of death. With his silver bow he shot arrows of pestilence and plague; yet he simultaneously functioned as a physician who brought medicine and healing (sometimes through his son, Asclepius). We see in these aspects a Shiva-like dichotomy. Apollo was also a god of music and poetry, and we find in the Homeric Hymn to Hermes that Apollo began life as a shepherd like Dumuzi, but traded in his flocks for a lyre with which, like Osiris, he could charm people. Moreover, the palm tree was sacred to Apollo (as it was also to Inanna[240]). Apollo was born under a palm, and the palm tree is where the phoenix makes its nest; in fact, the Egyptian name for the phoenix is the same as the name of the date palm.

Peter Goodgame points to the work of Australian professor Charles Penglase, whose careful research of Greek and Near Eastern mythology leads him to argue that the legends of Apollo were Greek retellings of the Babylonian legends of Marduk, which were in turn based on legends of Ninurta[241] (and, we might add, Tammuz). Goodgame also references Rudolf Steiner, who writes in his Egyptian Myths and Mysteries that the Greeks "recognized that Osiris was the same as the god whom they called Apollo."[242] So we have a connection between Nimrod and Apollo through Marduk, as well as Osiris, and in the final analysis we can equate Dumuzi, Tammuz, Shiva, Osiris, and Apollo all with the same demigod lover of Semiramis/Inanna.

Again, this is not to say that these gods of destruction and recreation were necessarily all modeled after Nimrod, but rather that Nimrod embodied the spirit of the Beast—or, if you prefer, the spirit of Leviathan—whose traits can be found in each of them.

Inseparable

Where the spirit of the Beast is found, we also invariably find the spirit of the great goddess. This point is worth reiterating once more just to reenforce its validity. Scottish orientalist W. Robertson Smith (1846–94) felt confident from his researches that many of the dying-and-rising gods were indivisible from the goddesses who had their origins in Semiramis. He argues,

We seem, in fact, to be justified in associating all the graves of Semitic male gods (e.g. the grave of Bel or Ba'al at Babylon, and that of Heracles at Tyre) with a worship of the Adonis type—a worship which is closely connected with that of Astarte and Ishtar, and with a myth in which the god who dies but rises again is the lover of the great goddess. And as we already know that Semiramis is a form of Astarte, the conclusion is obvious that the tombs of her lovers are sanctuaries (heroa) corresponding to the tomb sanctuaries of Adonis; and the analogy of the tombs of Adonis, which at Byblus and elsewhere were associated with a sanctuary and cult of Astarte, leads us to suppose that where there was a tumulus of the dead god there was also a sanctuary and worship of the goddess.[243]

In other words, the fertility goddess and the dying god are inseparable in ancient legend.

We can better understand the relationship between the goddess and her demigod consort by referring to a quote by Joseph Campbell, advocate of the *monomyth*.

[The goddess] is the other portion of the hero himself—for each is both: if his stature is that of world monarch, she is the world, and if he is a warrior, she is fame. She is the image of his destiny which he has to release from the prison of enveloping circumstances.[244]

This two-sides-of-the-same-coin relationship is precisely what we are presented with in Revelation. There are two aspects to the terrible monstrosity called Babylon, for it is both a military-economic superpower headed by the god-like man from the Abyss, and a religious system symbolized by a rich, harlot queen who ceases her perpetual mourning.

The Lamentations of the Queen of Heaven

The people of the Nimrod's kingdom were evidently very moved by Semiramis' pain at his loss, because the widow's lamentations for the fallen god-man were copied down through history. Isis bitterly lamented the death of Osiris, as Inanna did for Dumuzi, and Ishtar for Tammuz. In Scandanavia, Freya mourned for Balder, and in Italy, Venus grieved for Adonis. For like reason, Greek and Roman women cried every year over Dionysus/Bacchus. In fact, the very name Bacchus means "Lamented

One."245

The annual occult practice of mourning over the fallen god-man is mentioned in Scripture. In the Book of Ezekiel, the pre-incarnate Christ takes the spirit of the prophet to the Holy Temple in Jerusalem and conducts an exposé of the abominable acts being conducted there. Among the travesties revealed to Ezekiel is a group of women imitating grieving Ishtar.

> Then he brought me to the entrance of the north gate of the house of the Lord, and I saw women sitting there, mourning the god Tammuz. He said to me, "Do you see this, son of man? You will see things that are even more detestable than this." (Ezek. 8:14–15)

The apostate Israelites shown to Ezekiel were trying to fit in with the rest of the world by adopting the pagan nations' common religious traditions. By the lifetime of Ezekiel, remembrance of the sun god's demise had been going on annually for hundreds of years, so it isn't surprising that the practice was borrowed by the rebels within Israel.

The mother of the dying god in her role as *Queen of Heaven* can also be found in Scripture, though not by any specific name—by the time that the prophet Jeremiah was speaking about her, she was known by many names. Jeremiah preached that the Jews living in Egypt in his day were coming under judgment because they were worshiping foreign deities, but the people did not listen. Instead, they railed against his message.

> Then all the men who knew that their wives had made offerings to other gods, and all the women who stood by, a great assembly, all the people who lived in Pathros in the land of Egypt, answered Jeremiah: "As for the word that you have spoken to us in the name of the LORD, we will not listen to you. But we will do everything that we have vowed, make offerings to the queen of heaven and pour out drink offerings to her...." And the women said, "When we made offerings to the queen of heaven and poured out drink offerings to her, was it without our husbands' approval that we made cakes for her bearing her image and poured out drink offerings to her?"

> Then Jeremiah said to all the people, men and women, all the people who had given him this answer: "As for the offerings that you offered in the cities of Judah and in the streets of Jerusalem, you and your fathers, your kings and your officials, and the people of the land, did not the Lord re-

member them? Did it not come into his mind? The Lord could no longer bear your evil deeds and the abominations that you committed. Therefore your land has become a desolation and a waste and a curse, without inhabitant, as it is this day." (Jer. 44:15–22)

This passage should make us think carefully before ever giving adoration to a deified mother. Our Catholic friends should take note because Inanna's designation as Queen of Heaven has been applied by the Roman Catholic Church to the Virgin Mary,[a] whom many Catholics also laud as the Mother of God. Some popes have called her "Queen of the Universe, Queen of Heaven, Seat of Wisdom, and even the Spouse of the Holy Spirit."[246] However, the Bible never calls Mary a queen, does not condone her worship, and certainly does not allow us to think of her as a mediator, a co-redeemer,[b] or the spouse of God's spirit. Keep in mind that Mary is conspicuously absent from all of the New Testament letters; only Yeshua is in view. Although Mary provided the virgin womb which delivered to earth the incarnate Messiah, she in no way gave life to the great I Am. Ideas such as those unfortunately infiltrated the church in Rome after she foolishly yoked herself with the State. In her eagerness to convert pagan citizens, she allowed the entrance into Christianity of some of the most widely recognized and seemingly synchronous elements of the pagan faiths, even taking idolatrous statues of the goddess holding the sun-child and reinterpreting them as Mary holding Jesus. Pagans today have no trouble identifying the Madonna of Rome as the Great Mother goddess of the ancient world.[247]

Many Catholics claim that they do not consider Mary to be a deity, but one must wonder if that assurance comes from a place of denial, considering the extreme attention paid to the Blessed Virgin in Roman Catholic tradition. After all, it is implied that she has god-like powers because she is able to hear the prayers of millions of Catholics, simultaneously. Never mind the fact that Scripture flatly condemns talking with deceased human beings, which is what supposedly occurs during

---

[a] Some Catholics would say that their use of the word *queen* is not meant to suggest that Mary is God's peer, but why stubbornly cling to the term if the usual meaning is not intended?

[b] The Catholic Church calls Mary *Mediatrix* and *Co-Redemptrix*, but 1 Timothy 2:5 says, "There is **one** mediator between God and man: the man Christ Jesus," and Hebrews 10:10, along with many other verses, assures us that we "have been sanctified by the offering of the body of Jesus Christ **once for all**."

the *interior locutions* and some of the miraculous apparitions of Mary. Even on the extremely special occasion of Moses and Elijah appearing at the transfiguration of Yeshua, they did not speak to the apostles. Had the apostles spoken with Moses, they would have been breaking Torah.

Catholic doctrine teaches that Mary was immaculate (sinless), which is impossible for any human being descended from Adam[a]. The Roman Catechism further teaches that Mary as "the mother of the members of Christ" (963) was bodily assumed into heaven, where she was exalted as queen and given a "saving office" of "manifold intercession… to bring us the gifts of eternal salvation" (969). The catechism goes on to explain that the Mary is not equal to Christ and that the devotion given to her is, in some unspecified way, essentially different than the adoration given Jesus, but anyone looking into Catholicism from the outside can't help but get the impression that Mary is deity. In his book titled *The Virgin Goddess: Studies in the Pagan and Christian Roots of Mariology*, Stephen Benko puts it this way:

> When Christian clergy began to come from the educated classes, Mary was brought into the process [of syncretism]…. In this way, Mary was eventually declared to be "Mother of God," which is a wholly pagan term filled with new Christian meaning. Did Mary become a goddess when this declaration was made? The answer of Christians was, and still is, an indignant No!—but in fact Mary assumed the functions of pagan female divinities and for many pious Christian folk she did, and does, everything the ancient goddesses used to do.[248]

It would be foolish to make a sweeping generalization by concluding that Catholics without exception have been confused into honoring the ancient feminine spirit of Babel; however, knowing what we now know about the pagan origin of the Queen of Heaven, it may be wise for Catholic and Orthodox readers to question their traditions and conduct an honest assessment of the ways in which they think about and relate to the mother of Yeshua. Enough said.

---

[a] See the book of Romans and especially Romans 3:23.

Old Reverends' Tales

Mostly on account of the work of Reverend Alexander Hislop, author of *The Two Babylons*, a tradition has taken hold in Protestantism which says that the widowed Semiramis became pregnant soon after the death of Nimrod. As the tale goes, Semiramis spun the situation to her advantage by claiming that the baby was miraculously conceived by the spirit of Nimrod, and she caused her subjects to worship the child, named Tammuz, as the reincarnation of his father. The problem is that not an ounce of evidence exists to validate this story. It was crafted in reaction to the preponderance of ancient Madonna with god-child myths, but it is pure fiction, and resorting to it is totally unnecessary once we understand that the son of the fertility goddess is a symbol only—an emblem representing both the reborn solar demigod and the association of initiates which stand in his place until the return.

To reiterate, Semiramis did not conceive a real son named Dumuzi or Tammuz. Nimrod's sibling-wife probably did bear him biological children, but they had nothing to do with Dumuzi. Rather, Semiramis is the mother of Nimrod's mystery cult, and by extension the mother of divine leaders generated by that cult. Recall that at the coronations of kings, the mystery priesthood magically imbues each potentate with the spirit of Dumuzi/Osiris/Apollo—even in America! The fertility goddess is therefore the mother of all these deified rulers. Yet this practice of incarnating Nimrod into each king is a stop-gap measure. The ultimate goal is the permanent return of the king.

"The Dying God shall rise again!" declared Manly Hall in his book, *The Secret Teachings of All Ages.*[249] When the hierophants of the mysteries declare that the dying god will return, they are not speaking in allegory. Amazingly, the Bible agrees. In the next chapter, we will find out what the Word has to say about the end-times appearance of the son of Venus.

ELEVEN

The Eighth King

Out of the Hidden House, guarded by the silent god, must
some day issue the glorious and illumined Horus, the very
incarnation of his own father, the personification of the lord
of Abydos, the avenger of all and the just god in whom there
is no death.[250]

—MANLY P. HALL

Awake, Osiris! Awake, O King! Stand up and sit down, throw
off the earth which is on you!

— UTTERANCE 498 OF THE PYRAMID TEXTS

As I researched the heroic god-man archetype, I had to become
familiar with a plethora of shepherd-gods, builder-gods, and
war-gods which other authors have related to Nimrod. Would-
be researches should be warned that the process is quite a grind.
After many hours of comparative studies, I have concluded that the general consensus is correct and Nimrod is indeed the central figure of many
ancient myths. It is not true that Nimrod is the *origin* of the earliest war,
builder, and shepherd gods, but he is *linked* to them. Just as Cush was
associated with Chaos because he brought about a chaotic situation, and
Kainam was (possibly) associated with Hermes because he held sacred
and occult knowledge, so Nimrod was associated with the gods of civilization and retrogression, peace and war. These archetypes already existed before Nimrod's meteoric rise in preeminence, but Nimrod was the
penultimate embodiment of those archetypes and in some cases came to
be seen as equivalent to these gods.

Throughout the ancient world, Nimrod in his various aspects was
known multifariously as Tammuz, Osiris/Horus, Ba'al, Melqart, Molech,
Resheph, Attis, Balder, Thor, Herakles/Hercules, Krishna, Quetzalcoatl,

Adon/Adonis, Mithra, Dionysus/Bacchus, and others. It would be impractical to lecture on the synchronicity between all of these characters, so I leave it to the reader to replicate my research if desired.

I had initially considered that there might have been two postdiluvian heroes of renown—one a normal-sized man of peace, the other a literal giant who was a fearsome warrior—but I have gravitated away from that theory. Based on the amount of overlap between myths, it would seem that they are one and the same. This makes sense alongside the criterion that the Antichrist attempts to mimic Yeshua in all respects, because the real Messiah has two equally prominent roles: the first as a wise sage and compassionate shepherd, the second as an awesome warrior and judge of the souls of mankind. The only difference is that Nimrod played both roles simultaneously.

At first glance, some of the heroic demigods lack a violent aspect, making them a poor fit with Nimrod, but upon deeper inspection we almost always find some war-god and/or hunter attributes buried beneath the surface. For instance, the god Asarluhi, worshiped at the Sumerian port city of Kuara, is praised as an august sage, a judge of people's hearts, and a master of magic, and he seems to have been known primarily for his broad wisdom. However, lines 140–146 of the *Sumerian Temple Hymns* do state that Asarluhi is a warrior and "an onrushing storm battering the rebel land."[251] It is said that he pours spittle upon rebellious cities until they submit to him.

When crafting their lore, some people-groups placed emphasis on Nimrod's warrior aspect while others placed emphasis on his building and teaching aspects. Perhaps some cultures were more apt to remember Nimrod's violent feats because they themselves were preoccupied with violence, or because they had been traumatized by Nimrod, but cultures who lived in relative safety focused on the demigod's mystical wisdom.

In this chapter we will examine the attributes of the most noteworthy versions of Nimrod, then compare their traits to those of the coming Antichrist.

Why would we make such a comparison? How could stories of the long-dead Nimrod be connected to the last-days Beast? It may stretch the imagination, but the comparison can be made because Nimrod *is* the Beast. He will return—and not figuratively—to finish what Satan began long ago at the tower of Babel.

I will say it again: Nimrod is coming back to reign as the last king of Babylon.

Listen… do you hear that? That chorus of thumps? It's the clip-clop of skeptics on their charging donkeys. Before going any further, let's cut them off at the pass with a careful study of the resurrection of the Antichrist, as presented in the scriptures.

He Comes from the Seven

The eye-opening insights about to be presented are not my own; they come from Peter Goodgame, author of *The Second Coming of the Antichrist*. Mr. Goodgame has done a praiseworthy job of revisiting the words of the angel in Rev. 17:7–14 and interpreting them in a manner that rings true. He has also nailed down the identity of the Antichrist.

To begin to understand the return of Nimrod, we have to wrap our minds around the descriptions of the beasts that John saw in his end-times vision. Here is the passage most crucial to us:

> Then the angel carried me away in the Spirit into a wilderness. There I saw a woman sitting on a scarlet beast that was covered with blasphemous names and had seven heads and ten horns…. Then the angel said to me: "Why are you astonished? I will explain to you the mystery of the woman and of the beast she rides, which has the seven heads and ten horns. **The beast, which you saw, once was, now is not, and yet will come up out of the Abyss** and go to its destruction. The inhabitants of the earth whose names have not been written in the book of life from the creation of the world will be astonished when they see the beast, because it once was, now is not, and yet will come. This calls for a mind with wisdom. The seven heads are seven hills on which the woman sits. They are also seven kings. Five have fallen, one is, the other has not yet come; but when he does come, he must remain for only a little while. **The beast who once was, and now is not, is an eighth king. He belongs to the seven** and is going to his destruction. The ten horns you saw are ten kings who have not yet received a kingdom, but who for one hour will receive authority as kings along with the beast. They have one purpose and will give their power and authority to the beast. They will wage war against the Lamb, but the Lamb will triumph over them because he is LORD of lords and King of kings—and with him will be his called, chosen and faithful followers." (Rev. 17:3–14, NIV)

In the middle of this message, the angel challenges the reader by stating that unraveling it will require "a mind with wisdom." The illustration of the beast's heads is an enigma which must be carefully thought through.

A very common misconception about the Antichrist is that he will die from a head wound but be healed (Rev. 13:3–4). Most Premillennialists expect that the Antichrist's demise will occur near the mid-point of Daniel's 70th week. The exact wording is that "**one** of his [the beast's] heads" (plural) was injured unto death. All of the world will "wonder after," or be amazed at the beast because his fatal wound was healed. But is this beast equivalent to the Antichrist? If so, does that mean that the Antichrist will suffer from polycephaly[a]? Can we possibly take this literally?

The beast described in Rev. 13:1–2 is unquestionably symbolic, not literal. It is a chimera with ten horns and seven heads. The apostle John was given insight about the horns of the beast when an angel said to him, "**The ten horns you saw are ten kings** who… will receive authority as kings along with the beast" (Rev. 17:12). Daniel made it very clear that the Antichrist is a little horn that springs up among the ten horns, displacing three of them as it grows (Dan. 7:8). The Antichrist cannot be the beast on which the horns grow if he is counted among the horns themselves.

As we read in Revelation 17, the heads of the beast are both hills and kings. That being so, there's no justification for us to believe that the Antichrist's physical head will be wounded, because the heads represent both hills and royal persons in their entirety. If the beast that we call the Antichrist is a little horn on one of the seven heads, how can the Antichrist be one of the seven heads of that self-same beast? Trying to untangle this can practically trigger a nervous breakdown!

The way to avoid confusion is to realize that there are in fact three beasts in Revelation:

1. The seven-headed beast from the sea, representing the global Babylonian empire
2. The beast from the Abyss, which is also the little horn
3. The beast from the earth, which is the False Prophet

In Revelation, the second beast is spoken about as if it is equivalent to the first beast, and the reason is that the little horn becomes king over the

---

[a] The condition of having more than one head.

entire empire. "[The ten kings] hand over their power and authority to the beast" (17:13). The reborn Babylonian kingdom and the reborn king are essentially interchangeable in the text.

The seven heads connected to the body of the beast are seven kings of kingdoms that emerged from Babel. They are of one nature because each one of these kings was directly conducted by Satan; as a result, each was supremely prideful and set against God and Israel. The seven kingdoms are these:

1. The Sumero-Akkadian empire
2. The Egyptian empire
3. The Assyrian empire
4. The Phoenician empire
5. The Greek empire
6. The Roman empire
7. The Nazi empire? The late, great U.S.A.?

Opinions are divided as to which particular kings of these empires are to be considered the seven heads. The only clue the angel gave us is that five of them had already fallen at the time that John received his vision, whereas the sixth was currently in power and the seventh would exercise a short reign at some point in John's future. A common proposal of their identities is as follows:

1. Nimrod
2. Pharaoh of the Exodus. Every pharaoh was an embodiment of Osiris/Horus, but only one of them was insane enough to fight YHVH and try to exterminate the Israelites as they fled Egypt.
3. Sennacherib. Like all the kings of Assyria, he was believed to be indwelt by Asshur. Sennacherib sought to sack Jerusalem, but the angel of YHVH supernaturally defeated his army in the very valley where the Last Battle will take place.
4. Unnamed king of Tyre in Ezekiel 28. According to the prophet, he considered himself to be a god. Historians attest that Tyre's kings (at least from Hiram, onward) were believed to be incarnations of the god Melqart,[252] who was an aspect of Nimrod.
5. Antiochus Epiphanes. The name Epiphanes means "manifestation of a divine being." He tried to Hellenize the Jews and even desolated the Holy Temple in Jerusalem by sacrificing a pig on the altar and erecting a statue of either Zeus or Ba'al. Coins minted during his reign depict Antiochus as a laureated Zeus.[253]
6. Caesar Nero. The caesars were worshiped as gods, and Nero may

have been the caesar living at the time that John wrote Revelation. Nero was one of the most savage persecutors of Christians and became a popular candidate for Antichrist among early Christians. However, some researchers propose Domitian, a later caesar who wished to be recognized as Apollo incarnate.

7. Adolf Hitler, the king who was to come but only for a short time. Hitler and his followers were heavily involved in occult activity, and they constructed at the rally grounds in Nuremberg a replica of the altar of Zeus, which altar Yeshua called "the throne of Satan" (Rev. 2:13). The real throne had been dug up at Pergamon and relocated to Berlin more than a decade before the Nazi's rise to power. Hitler is well known for his attempt to exterminate the Jews.

John's angel equated the seven hills with the seven kings, but what does that mean? How can human beings be the same as mounds of earth? First we must realize that these hills are not, as many believe, the seven hills of Rome or Jerusalem or any other city situated upon mountainous terrain. The hills do not represent a cluster of literal geological features, for the respective kings were members of empires diverse in time and space. When John sees that the woman who rides the beast sits on the seven hills, he is being shown that the system which the woman represents will span the territories of all seven of the former empires—or franchises, if you will—of Babel. If it were not for the work that these empires accomplished in perpetuating Nimrod's secular order, there would be no end-times beast system, and the woman would have no place to sit.

The reason that hills are used as symbols of Babylonian governments is that the leaders of each of the seven empires underwent occult rituals that supposedly imbued them with divinity, and the loci of their divine power were the sacred hills. The power of the priesthood to carry out divinizing rituals came from their worship of the prince of this world, Satan; their method of communing with Leviathan and his Kosmokraters involved mimicking YHVH's Zion and his Holy Temple. Each one of the seven kingdoms constructed pagan shrines atop mountains, beginning with Nimrod's ziggurat for Enki. That ziggurat was an artificial hill, but the shrines of other empires were sometimes built on natural mounds (as is true also in Jerusalem).

The most fascinating and important of the kings is certainly the eighth because he presents us with a paradox. The angel says that the eighth king is the Beast and that he *once was* but no longer existed at the time of the conversation. Yet, mysteriously, this king *will be* again at some future time. For further clarification the angel specifies that the eighth king *is* one of the seven. This is astounding because it teaches us that one of the seven kings will be resurrected at the time when the New World Order—that final world empire, the one that struck fear into Daniel—arises to trample the whole world. There's no intellectually honest way to get around this interpretation, for it has been made abundantly clear by the carefully chosen words of God's messenger. The beast from the Abyss must be one of the seven kings of the beastly Babylonian system, *all of whom have died.* The question is, which king? It cannot be Caesar, or Hitler because they had not yet died at the time of John's vision. That leaves us with five choices.

The Assyrian of Tomorrow

I'm not speaking figuratively when I say that my jaw dropped when I learned that the name of the Antichrist can be found in the Old Testament. One of his names, that is; he's had many, and there's no telling what name he'll use upon his return. But the name that appears repeatedly in the Prophets is *Asshur.* It is the name of the chief god of the city of Assur in northern Mesopotamia. The original meaning of the name is unknown, but it came to be synonymous with deity (e.g., *aesar* in old Etruscan indicates a god[254]). In Assyrian artwork, Asshur is often depicted inside a solar disc with wings, reminiscent of the famous Egyptian symbol used by Horus.

In the following quote, Peter Goodgame explains that many biblical references to the Antichrist are entirely cloaked from view because of quirks in translation:

> Modern translators don't truly understand the use of the name "Asshur" in its biblical-historical context, so the singular word "Asshur" is sometimes translated as Assyria, or Assyrians, and often confusingly as "the Assyrian." However, the Hebrew text rarely precedes "Asshur" with the definite article "the," and many of the translations are misleading. We should just take the Hebrew word "Asshur" to mean Asshur, and then let the verb tenses and context determine whether the name is meant to refer to the Assyrian nation, the Assyrian people, the Assyrian king, or the historical figure behind the Assyrians—Asshur himself.[255]

It can be difficult to distinguish between Asshur proper and other Assyrian kings because they were historically treated as a unit. Through imitative magic every king became Asshur, just as every pharaoh became Osiris. So Asshur is every king of Assyria, but he is also the first and last king. Goodgame explains this on his website, saying,

> The kings of Assyria believed they were the earthly representations of Asshur upon the earth, and that is why the Lord refers to Asshur using singular verbs as if speaking to a singular individual. That is why he is portrayed as being on the scene in 722 BC, as well as on the scene at the very end of the age during the Day of the Lord.[256]

The name of the Beast has been staring us in the face for all these years, but almost no one recognized it. Those few scholars who did make the connection were not able to widely disseminate their wisdom, so it remained obscure. But now YHVH has graciously seen fit to bring the truth about Asshur back to light because it is the proper season, which is to say that the unveiling of the Antichrist is nearly upon us.

As eschatological passage in Micah declares that Asshur will aggressively enter into Israel in the last days. It reads,

> When the Assyrian [Asshur] comes into our land and treads in our palaces, then we will raise against him seven shepherds and eight princes of men; they shall shepherd the land of Assyria with the sword, and the land of Nimrod at its entrances; and he shall deliver us from the Assyrian when he comes into our land and treads within our border. **Then** the remnant of Jacob shall be.... among the nations, in the midst of many peoples... like a young lion among the flocks of sheep.... Your hand shall be lifted up over your adversaries, and all your enemies shall be cut off. (5:5–8)

This oracle is certainly about an event yet to come and not the past Assyrian invasion of Israel. The chapter begins by prophesying that the Savior will come from Bethlehem—and event that happened centuries after the Assyrian invasion—and that he will shepherd Israel when they dwell securely, during an era of peace. It is that shepherd, Micah tells us, who will rescue Israel from Asshur, and we know that hasn't happened yet. Overall, this isn't the easiest passage to interpret, but it is the only verse in the Bible that mentions Asshur, Assyria, and Nimrod back-to-back.

Earlier in this book we read the majority of Isaiah 14 and determined that Lucifer, son of the howling dawn, is the king of Babylon. If we proceed on from where we left off in Isaiah 14 we find this declaration:

> "I will rise up against them," declares the Lord of hosts, "and will cut off **from Babylon** name and remnant, descendants and posterity.... I will **break the Assyrian in my land**, and on the mountains trample him underfoot; and his yoke shall depart from them, and his burden from their shoulder." This is the purpose that is purposed concerning **the whole earth**, and this is the hand that is stretched out over **all the nations**. (vv. 22–26)

Many Bibles create an artificial break between vv. 23 and 24 by inserting a heading—in the English Standard Version it reads, "An Oracle Concerning Assyria." Unlike the reset written into v. 28, nothing about v. 24 indicates that a new oracle has begun. That separation is forced by the interpreters based on the assumption that the Assyrian has nothing to do with Babylon. But the fact is that the Hebrew here is singular—Asshur, a man and not a nation. And if Asshur is the man called Antichrist, then he is also Lucifer, the king of Babylon.

What we see in this passage is a classic case of prophetic double-reference. Knowing from 2 Kings 19:35 that "the angel of YHVH" saved Jerusalem from being razed by Assyrian invaders during the lifetime of Isaiah, our natural and reasonable tendency is to infer that this oracle was fulfilled by that angel ca. 722 BC. And it was, partially. However, that historical event did not fulfill all of the details of the oracle, so either Isaiah was a false prophet or the greater fulfillment has not yet come to pass. The oracle is very clear that this trampling of Asshur concerns the *whole earth* and *all* the nations, not just the nations of Israel and Assyria. It concerns the whole earth because end-times Babylon will be a global government.

Another important passage about Asshur is found in Isaiah 10, which sets the stage in vv. 3–4, making it clear that the oracle is about that future day when the Antichrist will break his treaty with Israel and invade the Beautiful Land. He will trample some and enslave others.

> What will you do on the day of punishment, in the ruin that will come from afar?.... Nothing remains but to crouch among the prisoners or fall among the slain.

God goes on to speak about the instrument of punishment, and you can guess who it is.

> Ah, Assyria [Asshur], **the rod of my anger**; the staff in [his] hands is my fury! Against a godless nation **I send him**, and against the people of my wrath **I command him**, to take spoil and seize plunder, and to tread them down like the mire of the streets.... When the Lord has finished all his work on Mount Zion and on Jerusalem, he will punish the speech of the arrogant heart of the king of Assyria [King Asshur] and the boastful look in his eyes. For he says: "By the strength of my hand I have done it, and by my wisdom, for I have understanding; I remove the boundaries of peoples, and plunder their treasures; like a bull I bring down those who sit on thrones." (vv. 5–6, 12–13)

YHVH will punish the unfaithful ethnic Israelites through the agency of Asshur, but then the boastful king himself will meet a fiery end at the hands of the Holy One (v. 17).

Only two kings in our list of seven could be considered *Asshur*: Nimrod and Sennacherib. We will discover which by examining one more passage of Scripture.

The First Global Superpower

In Revelation 13 we find that the beast from the Abyss had a fatal wound that was healed (v. 12), and again that this beast was wounded by the sword but still lives (v. 14). Notice that neither verse states that he received a *head* wound, as some popular authors like to imagine; the text only specifies that he died by the sword. The confusion comes from the fact that this man is allegorically one of the seven heads of the larger beast. He was fatally wounded by the sword at some point in history, but it was not necessarily a head wound. Does the Bible ever make mention of a Babylonian king being slain by the sword? In fact, yes, it does.

Ezekiel 31 is an oracle addressed to Pharaoh, king of Egypt, and his forces. At the beginning of the chapter, YHVH asks Pharaoh the question, "Whom are you like in your greatness?" He then compares Pharaoh to Asshur using a parable wherein kings are represented as trees.

> Behold, Assyria [Asshur] was a cedar in Lebanon, with beautiful

branches and forest shade, and of towering height, its top among the
clouds. The waters nourished it; the **deep [Abyss] made it grow tall,**
making its rivers flow around the place of its planting, sending forth its
streams to all the trees of the field. So it towered **high above all the trees**
of the field; its boughs grew large and its branches long from abundant
water in its shoots. All the birds of the heavens made their nests in its
boughs; under its branches all the beasts of the field gave birth to their
young, and **under its shadow lived all great nations.** (vv. 3–6)

Our studies up to this point have enabled us to understand the symbolism of this passage. Asshur was a mighty and far-reaching emperor,
presiding over all of the major people-groups throughout the earth
(there were only a handful at the time). The trees of the field are monarchs, princes, and governors subordinate to him. The beasts of the field
multiplying under the protection of the great cedar are the citizens of
Asshur's kingdom. We've seen that birds in Near Eastern art and literature are usually representative of divine beings, either spirits or mortal
rulers hosting spirits; this means that the rebellious spirits were right at
home in Asshur's pagan Old World Order.

And what of the waters of the deep that supplied the trees? Just as the
mundane Abyss—the source of fresh water within the earth—branches
out into underground rivers that feed the real trees of the field, the powers of the supernatural Abyss were coming up unto Asshur, who then
distributed occult knowledge and arcane arts to the lesser rulers of the
world. In Mesopotamian mythology, the earth is divided into three portions: upper, middle, and lower. Upper Earth is the surface world, where
men live; Middle Earth is the Abzu, where the god Enki resides; and
Lower Earth is the netherworld, where dead souls and some gods are imprisoned.[257] This is basically identical to the biblical conception, which
has the physical *deep* as a gateway to the cosmic pit and Sheol. The Sumerians believed that Enki, lord of the earth, is god of waters, and that he set
up his home in the Abyss. (However, he is not locked in the cosmic pit
of the netherworld as are the Watchers and many demons.) From there
Enki "watered" Asshur with instruction.

Come with me for a moment to ancient Jerusalem. Each day during
the eight-day festival of Sukkot, the Levitical priests who were scheduled to serve in the Temple would take water from the spring of Gihon
and pour it over the altar. As they poured, they recited, "Jehovah is my
strength and my song; he also is become my salvation. Therefore with

joy shall ye draw water out of the wells of salvation" (Isa. 12:2–3, KJV). Hundreds of years after Isaiah wrote those words, Yeshua of Nazareth, whose name means "salvation," described himself as a well of living water springing up into everlasting life (John 4:14). Soon thereafter he gave himself up as a sacrifice, and water literally poured from his side when a soldier lanced him in the heart, through his ribs, to make sure that he was dead. On one occasion during his ministry Yeshua said, "Whoever believes in me, as the Scripture has said, 'Out of his heart will flow rivers of living water'" (John 7:38).

The spiritual water that Enki provided to Asshur is the antithesis of the living water that Yeshua gives to those who love him. I believe that there may be even more to it than this, but that discussion will have to wait until later.

Returning to Ezekiel 31, we see that God became incensed with Asshur's relentless arrogance, and he brought down the giant cedar, declaring,

> Because it towered high and set its top among the clouds, and its heart was proud of its height, I will give it into the hand of a mighty one of the nations. He shall surely deal with it as its wickedness deserves. I have cast it out. **Foreigners, the most ruthless of [the] nations, have cut it down and left it**. On the mountains and in all the valleys its branches have fallen, and its boughs have been broken in all the ravines of the land, and all the peoples of the earth have gone away from its shadow and left it. (vv. 10–12)

So Asshur was brought down with an instrument of cutting—like a sword. YHVH goes on to say that no other kings since Asshur's fall have boasted like he did, nor have they been able to spread their branches over all the earth.

The instrument of Asshur's demise, God says, were the most terrible of all foreigners. There is little reason to doubt that this refers to a coalition of giants, several tribes of which dwelt north-east of Egypt. These tribes of giants were terrifying to the Israelite spies, who reported that Canaan was a land "that devours its inhabitants." Ancient myths from many regions of the world are consistent in their depictions of the giants as ruthless brutes, which is also how the Bible repeatedly presents them. First-century Greek historian Diodorus Siculus writes in his *Library of History* that it was the Titans who murdered Osiris: "The Aigyptians in their myths about Priapos say that in ancient times **the Titanes formed a conspiracy against Osiris** and slew him" (4.6.1). The Titans may have carried out this act of their own free will, but Ezekiel shows us that it was the Most High, at the behest of the Kosmokraters, who incited the giants to execute judgment on Asshur.

Before Asshur's fall, the angels of the Divine Council were driven to jealousy by the greatness of Asshur's kingdom, and were maddened that a mortal man would get to direct the affairs of the whole world. In Ezekiel's oracle these angels are described as trees in the Garden of Eden, reminding us that the covering Cherub is said to have been in Eden, upon the holy mountain, according to Ezek. 28:13. But even the trees of Eden could not compare to Asshur.

> The cedars in the garden of God could not rival it.... I made it beautiful in the mass of its branches, and **all the trees of Eden envied it**, that were in the garden of God. (vv. 8–9)

Although the oracle does not specify it, we are led to imagine that the Kosmokraters of the Divine Council brought accusations against Asshur which YHVH could not ignore. They railed against his unmitigated hubris, and incited the Judge to pass sentence. And they rejoiced on the day that Asshur was killed, because they were then able to rule over the nations without interference. Even though they must share his fate, in the end they will be comforted in their hearts because Asshur was violently deposed and his warriors were slaughtered. The oracle tells us as much, saying,

> All the trees of Eden, the choice and best of Lebanon, all that drink water, **shall be comforted in the nether parts of the earth**. They also went down into hell [Sheol] with him unto them that be **slain with the sword**; and they that were his arm, that dwelt under his shadow in the midst of the heathen. (vv. 16–17, KJV)

In the second verse above, the King James suggests that the trees of Eden *went* down to Sheol, past tense. However, in this instance the tense of the verb *to go* is uncertain in the Hebrew. Other translations say that the trees *shall* go down to Sheol. I believe that the KJV is incorrect in this case because Psa. 82:7 unambiguously states that the Kosmokraters will *in the future* die like men and fall like mortal princes.

They Kosmokraters may have celebrated Asshur's demise, but the world shook, and the subjects of the king were devastated. God says,

> On the day the cedar went down to Sheol I caused mourning; I closed the deep over it, and restrained its rivers, and many waters were stopped. I clothed Lebanon in gloom for it, and all the trees of the field fainted because of it. I made the nations quake at the sound of its fall, when I cast it down to Sheol with those who go down to the pit. (vv. 15–16)

Here we see that it was not just Semiramis/Inanna that mourned for her murdered husband; all of Lebanon was clothed in gloom, and all the governors of Asshur's kingdom grew weak of spirit. If the mighty one could be felled, what cause was there for confidence in lesser men?

This mighty king who ruled over all the nations of the earth can be none other than Nimrod. King Sennacherib isn't a fit for Asshur, for his kingdom was never all-encompassing and the nations did not quake, nor the springs dry up, when he died.

Furthermore, Sennacherib did not reign from Lebanon, as v. 3 says that Asshur did. But Nimrod certainly reigned as king in Phoenicia, which is modern-day Lebanon, where he probably established Byblos and Baalbek, and may have had a hand in building up Sidon[a]. Nimrod started his kingdom in Sumer but expanded north into Assyria before following the Fertile Crescent westward to Phoenicia. An Arabic manuscript in Baalbek, Lebanon, reads, "After the flood, when Nimrod reigned over Lebanon, he sent giants to rebuild the fortress of Baalbek, which was so named in honour of Baal, the god of the Moabites and worshipers of the sun."[258] Intent on continually growing his kingdom, Nimrod soon moved south from Phoenicia/Lebanon, into Egypt.

Lastly, although Sennacherib was slain by the sword, it was at the hands of his own sons, not the hands of "strangers, the terrible of the nations" (v. 12, CEPH).

Through a process of elimination we have arrived at the conclusion that the first of the seven kings is the only viable candidate to be the eighth.

---

[a] Sidon was a grandson of Ham through the cursed one, Canaan. According to Jubilees, Canaan took the region of Phoenicia illegally, for it did not fall to him by lot.

It is worth noting that Ezekiel was not the only prophet to compare the Antichrist to a cedar—the prophet Baruch also did so. In 2 Baruch 36, the prophet has a dream-vision wherein Yeshua, represented by a vine with rushing water proceeding forth from beneath it, destroys a huge forest and a surrounding ring of mountains with a flood, leaving only a single cedar standing. Finally it, too, is cast down. The vine is then installed in peace and tranquility, and servants bring to it the cedar which had been cast down.

> And I beheld and lo! that vine opened its mouth and spoke and said to that cedar: Are you not that cedar which was left of the forest of wickedness, and by whose means wickedness persisted, and was wrought all those years, and goodness never? And you did keep conquering that which was not yours…. and you did uplift yourself always as one that could not be rooted out! Do also therefore depart O cedar, after the forest, which departed before you, and become dust with it…. And after these things I saw that cedar burning, and the vine glowing, itself and all around it, the plain full of unfading flowers [the Redeemed]. (36:7–37:1, CEPH)

Baruch asks YHVH to give him the interpretation of this dream, which he does, and at the end of the interpretation he explains the identity of the cedar, saying,

> The last leader of that time will be left alive, when the multitude of his hosts will be put to the sword, and he will be bound, and they will take him up to Mount Tsyion, and my MASHIACH [Messiah] will convict him of all his impieties, and will gather and set before him all the works of his hosts. And afterwards he will put him to death, and protect the rest of my people which shall be found in the place which I have chosen. (40:1–2, CEPH)

Osiris the Mighty

The appellation *Osiris* means "mighty one," which correlates perfectly with Nimrod, the first *gibbor*, or "mighty man," of the antediluvian world. But the names *Osiris* and *Asshur* are connected by more than a shared meaning. The Egyptian name of Osiris is *Asr*, which upon the insertion of vowels becomes the *Asshur, Asar,* or *Asari* of Mesopotamia. The name *Asari* is written with two ideographs which are identical to the hieroglyphic characters of Osiris' Egyptian name. Those ideographs are a throne and a single eye.[259] The meaning of the throne is unambiguous, and the eye is the origin of the All-Seeing Eye on the back of U.S. one-dollar bills—it is the Eye of Osiris/Horus, and the occult eye of the miracle-working cyclopes of Greek myth.

As for Isis, long before the Greeks had named her, the sister-wife of Osiris was known as *Ast*, which is plainly equivalent to *Astarte* and *Ishtar*, both of whom are mourning fertility goddesses of the Near East. There can be no doubt that Osiris and Isis are the Egyptian versions of Asshur and Ishtar, who are in turn Ninurta and Inanna, or Nimrod and Semiramis.

Figure 11–1. Osiris, wrapped and mummified, yet alive in the underworld. He holds the crook and the flail.

Osiris is very frequently shown holding the flail and shepherd's crook, signifying his mastery of both agriculture and husbandry. We could choose to consider only the literal functions of those tools, which is perfectly valid, but we could also view them as figurative. Some Egyptologists, such as Carol Andrews, take the latter approach and conclude that the crook represents Osiris' care for the people, while the flail represents the discipline and punishment necessary to sustain society.[260] Christians will immediately sense the parallels to Yeshua, the Good Shepherd and the farmer who separates the wheat from the chaff. Again we see that the Antichrist mimics the Son of God, who has embodied these traits from eternity past. But unlike Yeshua, who is not memorialized wrapped in a shroud (because he rose from the grave), Osiris is nearly always depicted in a mummified form, wrapped tightly in linen because he remains in the grave (for now).

In a certain mythological story from Egypt's 20th dynasty, Osiris is addressed as "The Bull," "Hunting Lion," and "Gold Horus" in one breath.[261] Writings elsewhere tell us that Osiris founded his mansion among the waters of Rostau (under Giza) and that he fills the "Winding Waterways."[262] Moreover, since the Osireon is located at Abydos, we can only assume a connection with the Abyss. All of these aspects of Osiris are aggregated in the artwork of Assyria, where the emblems, standards, and reliefs of Asshur frequently include bulls, lions, the golden sun disc, and streams of water like those issuing forth from Enki, god of the Abyss.

At this point we hit a road bump. Genesis 10 relates that Asshur was a son of Shem, but Nimrod was a son of Cush. The Greek historian Eusebius writes that "Nineveh, which is called Ninus [in Greek], was the first royal city of the Assyrians. It was built by Asshur, one of the sons of Shem, who, as we said held all the eastern areas."[263] As Genesis implies and Eusebius clarifies, it was Asshur, not Ninus/Nimrod who built Nineveh and the other original colonies of Assyria. But if Osiris is Asshur, how is it that we can relate him to Nimrod? We must make one of two assumptions. Either Eusebius was mistaken and there were two Asshurs—so that it was Cush's Asshur, not Shem's, who founded Assyria—or else Nimrod went north and conquered the cities of Assyria and thereupon appropriated the king's namesake. The genealogies of Genesis do contain more than one instance of names being shared by different men (e.g., there are two Shebas); however, it is entirely possible that Nimrod slew or exiled Asshur and then took his name. Ancient gods and mythological figures often possessed many appellations because names were thought to have spiritual power, and an abundance of names bespoke great glory. As we have already seen, Cush's son went by several designations (e.g., Nimrod, Ninus, Bel, Enmerkar), and it would not have been strange for Nimrod to add the names of conquered monarchs to his own repertoire.

We have shown beyond the shadow of a doubt that Asshur/Nimrod is the eighth king, who "once was, now is not, and yet will be." For many, this will not be an easy pill to swallow, but the onus is now upon the dissenters to offer a viable alternative to our explanation of the angel's words to John.

The Antichrist will not be introduced but *re*introduced to the world, and when that time comes, he will arise from the Abyss as foretold in Rev. 17:8.

But where is the body hidden right now?

TWELVE

The Reconstruction of Asshur

May you wake in peace, may you wake, Osiris, in peace...
and he will not rot, he will not putrefy, this King will not be
cursed by your anger, you gods.

—PYRAMID TEXTS, UTTERANCE 576

I t would be inhuman not to wonder where Asshur is interred, so we
must tackle the subject. Are there any clues? Indeed there are; the
Egyptians made sure to record the approximate location of Osiris'
secret chamber. After all, there wouldn't have been much point in
preserving the body and memory of the great king unless he could be
recovered.

The Hidden Things of Rostau

One of the appellations of Osiris is *Lord of Rostau*, and *Rostau* means
"mouth of the passages." Specifically, these are the tunnels under the Giza
plateau, some of which still await discovery. A Hermetic prophecy states
that Rostau is the place where the "return of the gods" will one day take
place. As recently as 2006, ground-penetrating radar revealed several
wide tunnels as far as twenty-five meters below Giza.[264] Former Egyptian
Minister of Antiquities Dr. Zahi Hawass said back in 1996 that "there are
secret tunnels under the Sphinx and around the Pyramids which will
prove to carry many secrets of the building of the Pyramids."[265]

Certain spells within the Coffin Texts reveal that Osiris has a house in
Rostau, and indeed the entire Giza plateau is in other texts called *pr wsir
nb rstaw*, or "House of Osiris, Lord of Rostau." A mysterious, chthonic deity named Sokar also had a "house" or "shrine" in Rostau, and in fact the
whole of Rostau was said to belong to Sokar. Robert Bauval, who discovered that the pyramids of Giza are a reflection of the stars of Orion's belt,

argues in his book *Secret Chamber Revisited* that Osiris posthumously took on the identity of Sokar and was buried under the Giza plateau, which the Egyptians considered to be the gateway to the Duat (supernatural realm both under and over the earth).[266] Bauval writes:

> The idea that the Great Pyramid, or indeed the Giza necropolis as a whole, might have been regarded as the "dwelling place" for the soul or spirit of Osiris or the combined deity Osiris-Sokar is, interestingly enough, much supported by ancient texts. As Egyptologist Selim Hassan pointed out, there are several statements made to that effect in the Book of the Two Ways, dated ca. 2000 BCE. For example, there is a reference to the "Highland of Aker which is the Dwelling Place of Osiris," and also to "Osiris who is in the Highland of Aker." Aker, as we have already seen in chapter 2, was an ancestral deity who had the shape of a huge lion or sphinx and who, according to Hassan and others, may have represented the Great Sphinx of Giza. Hassan consequently concluded that the Highland of Aker must, by necessity, be the elevated plateau of Giza, the "Monte Libyco"[a] of the Hermetic Texts.[267]

Related to this discussion of Aker, a stele of Pharaoh Thutmose IV once situated between the paws of the Sphinx says that the ancient lion monument sits "beside Sokar in Rostau." The 10th-century Coptic Al Masudi and two other Arab chroniclers related accounts of a subterranean, guarded (booby-trapped?) chamber accessible via an entryway somewhere near the Sphinx.[268]

In the early 20th century the so-called Sleeping Prophet, Edgar Cayce (1877–1945), made a prediction that the wisdom of Atlantis would be discovered in a subterranean chamber near the Sphinx, but special knowledge would be needed in order to find it. Let us be clear that Cayce was not a prophet of YHVH, and whatever was speaking through him was not omniscient, but there is no reason to doubt that fallen angels who have lived throughout all of human history remember very well where important artifacts were put for safekeeping.

Given these things, the most reasonable belief is the one that places Osiris—or at least some of him—under Giza. Egyptian texts claim that Asshur's efflux is under Giza, but Ctesias as preserved in Diodorus'

---

[a] A Hermetic prophecy states that Monte Libyco is the place where the return of the gods will some day take place.

Library claims that Ninus/Nimrod is entombed in the precinct of the palace of Nineveh.[269] Perhaps his remains are in both of these places.

Where the Eagles Gather

In his Olivet Discourse, Yeshua made an intriguingly cryptic statement about the end-times location of the messianic impostor. He warned,

> Wherefore if they shall say unto you, **Behold, he is in the desert**; go not forth: **behold, he is in the secret chambers**; believe it not. For as the lightning cometh out of the east, and shineth even unto the west; so shall also the coming of the Son of man be. For wheresoever the carcase [Greek: *ptomata*, "corpse"] is, there will the eagles be gathered together. (Matt. 24:26–28, KJV)

This admonition has historically been as clear as mud even to well-studied Christians, but the meaning manifests when one understands that the false Christ is buried somewhere under Giza, in the hidden chambers of Rostau, and/or in the desert of Assyria. When the legendary King is found in the desert place or secret chamber and brought back to life after more than four thousand years, those who don't know YHVH's son and don't cling to his instructions will spread the news with a rush of excitement. "Don't believe it!" says Yeshua, "This is not the second coming of God's Chosen One, for when I return it will be in a blaze of glory visible from every point on earth." It will not be until years after the resurrection of Asshur that the sign of the Son of Man shall appear in heaven, and Yeshua himself shall descend from it, wrapped in billowing clouds (Matt. 24:30).

The singular corpse which Yeshua speaks of in v. 28 must be the mummy of Asshur, but what are we to think of the eagles that flock to it? In his *Babylon Rising* blog, Rob Skiba astutely points out the fact that American military personnel and government vehicles are covered in eagles. Taking that line of thinking further, we might clue in to the fact that all but one of the empires of the seven heads/kings of Revelation 17 had an eagle as their symbol. And that isn't a surprise considering that the earliest cultures of Mesopotamia used the wings of regal birds to represent divinity and the divine right to rule.

Modern countries with predatory birds as their national symbol include America, Mexico, Chile, Columbia, Panama, Bolivia, Germany, Austria, Albania, Greece, Hungary, Iceland, Poland, the Philippines, Lebanon, Syria, Iraq, the United Arab Emirates, Egypt, Nigeria, and several other African nations. Could it be that one or more of these nations will send equipment and personnel to the tomb upon the discovery of Osiris?

The Pseudo-Resurrection

To my knowledge, the scriptures are silent regarding the manner of Asshur's resurrection. Be assured that the nature of his resurrection will be entirely different than that of Yeshua's, for the Son of God was raised by the life-force of the Holy Spirit, and devils are not life-giving spirits. What Satan's forces do have at their disposal is very advanced technology (so advanced that it appears to be magic). Satan, like every other created being, must operate under the laws of the universe, and he must repurpose, rearrange, and reemploy what already exists in order to produce the effects he desires. Unlike God, Satan cannot create *ex nihilo*. Nevertheless, Satan has such a thorough understanding of the laws of Creation that he is able to accomplish seemingly miraculous feats.

In the Egyptian *Book of the Hidden Chamber*, it is Horus' left eye that rejuvenates the dead Osiris. Horus' left eye is called the "eye of Thoth," and his right eye is the "eye of Ra;" they were the moon and the sun, respectively. Thoth was the god of magic arts, the development of science, and the system of writing, and these are the subjects which must be mastered in order to revive a mummy: without writing, knowledge cannot be passed effectively from a few masters to more numerous pupils or from one generation to the next; without the scientific method, the mechanisms of nature cannot be understood and employed; and without the involvement of arcane arts, the soul of Asshur would not be able to leave Sheol and inhabit his renewed body.

We live at a time of rapid technological advancement, when scientists are imagining to accomplish things undreamed of by the previous generation, and their imaginings are not vainglorious. The genetic sciences have now advanced to the point that it may be possible to clone an extinct woolly mammoth.[270] Of course, some of the mammoths that we have discovered were flash-frozen, and some of the DNA within their bone marrow is relatively undamaged. A *mummified* mammoth would be an entirely different challenge... but not likely insurmountable.

Getting DNA from Osiris may not be as difficult as it seems. As I write this, a report has just been published about the successful reconstruction of the entire genome of an Italian man who has been dead for nearly a century. Scientists were able to retrieve DNA from a handkerchief containing the semen of fascist wordsmith Gabriele D'Annunzio and are now technically capable of cloning the dead poet. No one intends to remake D'Annunzio, but the chief of the foundation in possession of the DNA commented that the door is now open to the cloning of historical figures, even if their remains are lost.[271] This relates to our discussion because Egyptian records may indicate that Osiris' blood or sperm was preserved in a special container in Rostau. Spell #1080 of the Coffin Texts states,

> This is the sealed thing which is in darkness, with fire about it, which contains **the efflux of Osiris**, and it was put **in Rostau**. It has been hidden there since it fell from him, and it is what came down from him onto the desert sand.

Similar language is used in spell #1087:

> This is the word which is in darkness. As for any spirit who knows it, he will live among the living. Fire is about it, which contains the efflux of Osiris.

What is this efflux which fell from Osiris, and why is it sealed in darkness? Merriam-Webster's Dictionary defines efflux as "something given off in or as if in a stream." Immediately we think of a bodily fluid of some sort. How strange that it is equated to a word... or perhaps not so strange, when we consider that Yeshua was called the Word of God. The other mystery here, which we won't attempt to solve, is what kind of fire protects this efflux.

If one desired to see a king restored in the far future, the bodily substance most worth saving would be whole blood or semen. Saving the efflux of Osiris in a hermetically sealed container may have been a wise precaution by priests worried about the safety of their king's mummy or the ability of future generations to reconstitute DNA from completely desiccated remains. If we were to find this efflux today, and if it were preserved as well as the Coffin Texts seem to suggest, then it is very likely that we could clone Osiris. Even the term *hermetic seal* comes from

Hermes, the Greek name for Thoth, who was the Egyptian god of wisdom and the world's first chemist.[272] Thoth not only helped Isis and Anubis to mummify Osiris, but he recovered and restored the Eye of Horus after Seth removed it in battle.

The pieces of the puzzle fell into place for me after I watched an online video by Christian documentary filmmaker Gonz Shimura in which he exposes the occult symbolism woven throughout a cartoon called *Gravity Falls*.[273] The creator of *Gravity Falls* is not exactly sneaky about his insertion of mystery-religion themes and symbols into the storyline. In fact, one of the main characters, Stan, is a member of an occult fraternity, and he runs a tourist trap called *The Mystery Shack* in a remote town where nothing is as it seems.

In addition to the more blatant symbols (such as the eye within a pyramid) that the show waves before its viewers, Shimura points out that a phallic-shaped lamp makes multiple appearances in the episode titled "Not What He Seems." This is a climactic episode in which Stan creates an underground "universe portal" from instructions found within three mysterious journals. A cryptogram within the third journal reveals that the machine will open wormholes to other worlds: "The portal when completed will open a gateway to infinite new worlds and **herald a new era** in mankind's understanding of the universe." However, Stan's grand-nephew shines a black light on the schematic of the machine and reveals an invisible message scrawled over the top of the drawings: "The machine was meant to create knowledge but it is too powerful! The device, if fully operational, could tear our universe apart!" Indeed, the side-effect of activating the machine is the creation of gravitational anomalies that threaten to destroy the earth. All of this is eerily similar to CERN's subterranean Large Hadron Collider (LHC), which is now in operation under Switzerland. The physicists operating the LHC hope to create rifts between dimensions and peek into other universes on a subatomic level. They admit that anomalies such as small black holes may be spawned by the high-energy collisions of their experiments, and some specialists, including a nuclear safety officer, have had serious concerns about the danger that these anomalies could pose.[274] To top it off, the episode "Not What He Seems" was aired in the same month that the LHC was scheduled to restart (at a much higher power) after being offline for two years. There are several other reasons to suspect a connection between CERN and the *Gravity Falls* machine, but we'll move on.

The phallic lamp found in "Not What He Seems" has incredible meaning related to the obelisks of Egypt. The obelisk is a stylized representation of the penis of Osiris, which was lost and could not be recovered by Isis[a]. It is this lost member that Manly Hall equated to the *Lost Word* of Freemasonry. Don't forget that spell #1087 of the Coffin Texts says that the efflux of Osiris is the *word* in darkness.

At the top of every obelisk is a pyramid, and under many obelisks is a circle representing the testes of the obelisk which lie within the earth. In the design of an obelisk, the shaft, representing the lost member of Osiris, is positioned directly below the pyramid; likewise, the efflux of Osiris has been placed below the pyramids of Giza. The circle at the base of the shaft represents the generative force of Osiris, which presently resides in the Abyss. To the occult mind, The light of Ra while he travels with Osiris through the netherworld rises up the shaft of the obelisk and out into the surface world through the pyramid. This is very esoteric stuff, and hard to swallow, but remember that the occult is well-known for its obsessive use of symbols. Nothing is as it seems, with them.

Figure 12–1. Famous obelisks of the world, with circles at their bases. Images courtesy of Google Earth. **Left**: The Washington Monument in Washington, D.C. **Center**: Egyptian obelisk relocated to St. Peter's Square, the Vatican. **Upper Right**: Lateran Obelisk, Rome (the tallest monolithic obelisk in the world). **Middle Right**: Cleopatra's Needle in Central Park, New York City. **Lower Right**: Heliopolis obelisk, Cairo (with its original enclosure, which has now been remodeled).

The three most notable obelisks in the world are located in Washington, D.C., New York City, and Vatican City: the political, economic, and reli-

---

[a] For this book I have purposefully avoided using the traditional typographical marks for footnotes, which are the *obelus* and *asterix*. The obelus is a crucifix, which the Romans developed by combining the four spokes of the sun disc (representing the four divisions of the year) on top of the obelisk of the solar demigod. The asterix is the star of Isis, whose name in Egyptian is *Ast*. Astoreth/Astarte is the Western version of the Eastern goddess Ishtar/Inanna, whose symbol was the eight-pointed starburst. The Asherah poles which YHVH so hates are representations of the privy member of Isis' husband. Now you know why the obelus and asterix go together.

gious centers of the Western world, respectively. Other major cities with prominent obelisks include Paris, London, Stockholm, Dublin, Istanbul, Argentina, São Paulo, Moscow, and St. Petersburg[a]. Many of these obelisks, including the one at the Vatican, were actually transported from Egypt to their current resting places.

In ch. 10 we discussed the Hindu god, Shiva, and compared him to Dumuzi and Osiris. Knowing what we now know about the obelisk, we can make sense of an additional tidbit about Shiva. In most of the temples dedicated to Shiva, a graven image called a *shivaling* is used as the focal point for worship. The *shivaling* is not a statue of the god, but a phallic shaft with a circular base, protruding up through a circular disk. It sometimes has a carving of a serpent wrapped around the shaft. Hindus familiar with this will admit that the shivaling represents the male and female sexual organs in a state of conjugation, which symbolizes the union between the dualistic principles of the material universe.

This leads us to understand why obelisks are so often paired with domes. In the same way that the obelisk is a stylized version of the demigod's reproductive organ, the dome is a stylized version of the goddess' womb. According to David Ovason, author of *The Secret Architecture of Our Nation's Capital*, the city of Washington, D.C. was laid out to welcome Isis by establishing an astrological pattern involving Jupiter, the sun, Sirius, the moon, and the constellation Virgo.[275]

Is it a coincidence that the obelisk in D.C. and the obelisk in St. Peter's Square are both situated at the end of corridors designed to connect those phallic symbols with domed buildings where incredibly powerful individuals help guide the course of history? The inside of the dome which faces the Washington Monument features a circle comprised of 72 pentagrams, and that circle encompasses a painting of a deified George Washington surrounded by the Greco-Roman pantheon. Speaking of the pantheon, the dome which faces St. Peter's Square was modeled after the famous Pantheon building, a monumental Roman structure which also has an obelisk in front of it.

Is it also a coincidence that the Washington Monument is 666 inches wide and 6,660 inches (555 ft.) tall? Tom Horn has pointed out that the magic 666 square within the Masonic House of the Temple is the most famous of all magical utilities "because the sum of any row, column, or

---

[a] An elegant marble obelisk was erected in a square called *The Field of Mars* (Mars was a war-god with intriguing links to Nimrod). The obelisk was moved to Vasilyevsky Island in 1818, when the Field of Mars was re-landscaped.

diagonal is equal to the number 111, while the total of all the numbers in the square from 1 to 36 [half of 72] equals 666." He then concludes that "Freemasons built the Washington Monument Obelisk to form a magic square at its base and to stand 555 feet above the earth, so that when a line is drawn 111 feet directly below it toward the underworld of Osiris, **it equals the total of 666** (555+111=666)."[276]

A similar design can be found in an ancient temple of Apollo (a.k.a. Osiris/Shiva/Nimrod), but instead of using an innocuous dome to represent the goddess, the ancient builders scorned propriety and sculpted a vagina. Author Adam Gollner records in *The Book of Immortality* his visit to this temple, saying,

> I took a ferry to the volcanic island of Ischia, famed for its healing waters, where I spent time in Apollo's **Temple of the Sun**. It consisted of three rooms dedicated to "the eternal cycle of life." In the first, **water poured from a holy vaginal relic** symbolizing the origin of life. I tried to figure out why **the mossy orifice was crowning a stone pyramid**, but I couldn't get too close without getting splashed.[277]

Are you putting it all together? In *Gravity Falls*, the phallus is in the form of a lamp because lamps give off light—they illuminate, just like the occult wisdom of Osiris, the solar demigod, who will be returned to the world by means of the bodily fluid that came up through the phallus and is now stored beneath the pyramids. It is Horus (Stan Pines in *Gravity Falls*) who will open the "womb" for the efflux through the use of Luciferian technology. Then and only then will the Great Work be completed, when the All-Seeing Eye is finally installed atop the unfinished pyramid.

When the resurrection of Asshur takes place, the world will understandably be astounded, and most people will be swept up in a storm of adulation and idolization of this formerly deceased leader. If you think the pre-inauguration craze over Barack Obama was extreme, wait until an ancient king returns from the grave! Progressives will be falling all over themselves when they hear Asshur speak of peace and equality for all mankind (except for disciples of Yeshua, that is). Jews and Muslims will see him as the prophesied Messiah and Mahdi, respectively. Followers of eastern and occult religions will see him as the Light-Bearer, an exalted one possessing a fully awakened *Christ Consciousness*, the final incarnation of Vishnu, Buddha, or the sun god. Those who worship at the altar of Science will be forced to revise their model of reality when confronted with a patently and undeniably supernatural event, and as soon as their heads stop spinning, they will beg to learn at the feet of this amazing figure who understands "dark sentences" (Dan. 8:23).

But you, dear reader, now know better. You can resist the Lie. The resurrection of the Antichrist will no take you by surprise, nor cause you to wonder in awe alongside the duped masses.

THIRTEEN

A Whore Rides the Beast

The twenty-first century... will be the era of World Controllers.[278]
–ALDOUS HUXLEY (1894–1963)

The survival of civilization in something like its present form might depend significantly on the efforts of a single man.[279]
–MAURICE STRONG (1929–),
UNDER-SECRETARY GENERAL OF THE UNITED NATIONS

O f all the striking imagery in the Bible, perhaps the most infamous and intimidating is that of the beast which was seen by both Daniel and John. In Revelation 12, the terrible creature is a red (Greek: *purros*, meaning *fire-colored*) dragon with seven heads, ten horns, and seven crowns upon those horns. In the subsequent chapter, John sees a beast with the same number of heads, horns, and crowns, but which is not a dragon. Instead, it is a chimera (a combination of animals), and the particular animals included are exactly the same as the ones in Daniel's prophecy, given hundreds of years earlier. The beast that John saw "resembled a leopard, but had feet like those of a bear and a mouth like that of a lion" (Rev. 13:2). To make sense of that image, we need to turn to another great prophet: Daniel.

Lions and Leopards and Bears, Oh My

During the first year of the reign of Belshazzar, king of Babylon, Daniel had a vision of four winds churning up the great sea. In the Bible, the sea is often a symbol for the Gentile nations, whereas the earth is a symbol for Israel. Four great beasts come up out of the turbulent sea of Daniel's vision: a lion with the wings of an eagle, whose wings are plucked off; a bear raised up on one side and having three ribs in its mouth; a leopard with four wings and four heads; and a dreadful but unidentified beast with iron teeth and ten horns[a] (Dan. 7:1–7). That last beast, the terrifying one, is Leviathan, the king of the sea. God told Job that it was the most awesome and terrifying of all his earthly creatures.

Biblically speaking, beasts are symbols of unredeemed men or kingdoms which are set in opposition to God. Daniel asked an angel about the meaning of the beasts, and the angel said, "These four great beasts are four **kings** who shall arise out of the earth" (v. 17). But a few verses later, the same angel says that "the fourth beast is a fourth **kingdom** that will appear on earth" (v. 23, NIV). Thus kings and their kingdoms are synonymous in prophecy, and we run into this way of thinking also in the Book of Revelation.

Most conservative Christian scholars believe that the four kingdoms Daniel saw were Babylon, Media-Persia, Greece, and Rome, in that order; and they teach that Daniel had another vision which parallels the vision of the beasts. Earlier in his life, Daniel had been given the interpretation of a recurring dream that was plaguing King Nebuchadnezzar. In his sleep, the king was shown an enormous statue of a man that was divided into four parts, each crafted from a different substance. The head of gold symbolized Babylon, the chest of silver symbolized Media-Persia, the mid-section of bronze symbolized Greece, and the legs of iron symbolized Rome. Just as legs are divided in two, the Roman Empire had two distinct divisions: east and west. The prophecy didn't stop there, but continued to the feet, which were made partly of iron and partly of baked clay. Daniel saw a huge stone strike the statue on its feet, causing the entire object to break into pieces; then the stone became a mountain and filled the whole earth. That stone is clearly the kingdom of God, for "in the time of those kings, the God of heaven will set up a kingdom that will never be destroyed, nor will it be left to another people" (Dan. 2:44).

Popular prophecy teachers usually extrapolate from the imagery of the crushed feet the idea that the ten toes of the statue are equivalent to the ten horns of the fourth beast. From this they surmise that the Roman Empire will be revived in some sense in the latter part of the age, when it will reach its culmination as a global empire ruled by ten kings. But is that actually what the vision teaches us? Is there truly a link between the

---

[a] Teeth represent an organized destructive force such as an army, and horns are potentates.

statue's toes and the beast's horns? And can we make sense of the four beasts of Daniel 7 if we identify them as ancient kingdoms that existed sequentially? The answer to all of these questions is *no*.

The Contemporaneous View of Daniel 7

The English translation of Dan. 7:7 is partly to blame for the widespread acceptance of the sequential view of the kingdoms in Daniel's vision. In this verse, the prophet recalls that the fourth beast-kingdom "was different from all the beasts that were before it." The English word *before* does not always pertain to a thing's position in time; it can describe a thing's position in space as well. In the Chaldean being used by Daniel the word is *qidmah*, the feminine version of Strong's #6925, meaning "the front" or "forward part." It conveys a spatial relationship between the beasts, just as the vessels of the Holy Temple were brought *before* King Belshazzar in 5:23. Daniel was not telling us that the lion, bear, and leopard kingdoms are to be placed chronologically prior the terrible kingdom with iron teeth.

Aside from this problem in translation, the idea that the four beasts are empires that have taken the stage one at a time suffers from several major shortfalls. Let's quickly examine the issues.

Issue number one with the sequential interpretation is the problem of the beasts living through the Second Coming of Yeshua. Dan. 7:12 indicates that the first three beasts—the lion, leopard, and bear—will survive (in a diminished form) into the Millennium. They will be stripped of all their power but will retain their basic semblance: "As for the rest of the beasts, their dominion was taken away, but their lives were prolonged for a season and a time." The preceding verses make it plain that the chronological context for v. 12 is the Day of the Lord because the little horn (Antichrist) appears and speaks proud blasphemies, then the Ancient of Days sits in judgment, and then the beast is killed and burned in fire on account of the little horn's boastful words. After that, the Son of Man is given dominion, and the vision ends. If the four beasts existed one after the other throughout history, then it would make no sense for the first three to survive the last. In the popular conception, the fourth beast should be the only one on the scene at the end, yet that isn't what v. 12 presents.

Issue number two with the sequential interpretation is the problem of inconsistent symbols. In Dan. 8:20, the angel Gabriel explains to Daniel that the two-horned ram represents Media and Persia, while the goat represents Greece. And yet it is popularly taught that in ch. 7 the Medo-Persian empire is the bear, and Greece the leopard. Are we to believe that one chapter later, the identities have changed to new animals? Admittedly, it is *possible* that one kingdom is compared to two different animals, but it is extremely unlikely. The Bible is very consistent with its imagery, even across multiple books by multiple authors separated by hundreds of years. Shall we then put stock in a theory that has a single author recording back-to-back a couple of oracles that have conflicting imagery?

The third issue comes from trying to use the life of Nebuchadnezzar to explain the lion kingdom. Popular opinion supposes that the lion of Daniel 7 correlates with the head of gold of Daniel 2. In ch. 2 the prophet states explicitly that the head of gold is Nebuchadnezzar, therefore logic dictates that the lion must be Nebuchadnezzar's kingdom, Babylon. It should be noted, however, that Babylon never used the lion as an official emblem. Marduk was the patron god of Babylon, and his animal was the dragon, not the lion. Because of Ishtar's strong association with lions, depictions of winged lions do show up on the Ishtar Gate, but then so do winged bulls and dragons—and there are far more bulls and dragons than lions on the gate.

In Daniel's vision the lion has its wings plucked off before it is raised up and given a human heart. This is usually interpreted as a reference to the humbling of Nebuchadnezzar, when God caused him to lose his mind and become like a wild ox, and to eat grass for years before being brought back to sanity. The key here is that Nebuchadnezzar was restored, and when he was restored to his original state, he received his throne back and gave honor to YHVH. In contrast, the lion in Daniel's vision is not restored to its original state; the wings remain detached. Also, the successors of Nebuchadnezzar were by no means godly; his son, Evil-Merodach, was licentious and unjust, and he was soon assassinated for his crown. This is important because Nebuchadnezzar was already out of the picture by the time that Daniel had his dream, which he says occurred in the first year of the king or regent named Belshazzar (7:1). Belshazzar was the wicked ruler who saw the handwriting on the wall, and it was during his reign that the empire fell. If the beast being lifted up and given the heart of a man is supposed to represent Babylon's shift to higher-order behavior, then it was a very short-lived transformation indeed, and one which had already reverted by the time that Daniel received the vision. Why would God bother depicting Babylon in a way that was no longer applicable?

Issue number four with the sequential view is the command given to the bear: "Arise and devour much flesh!" (7:5). The bear is shown with three ribs in its mouth *before* being given the command to devour much flesh. The traditional interpretation has the ribs representing the conquests of King Cyrus the Great and his son, Cambyses II. This is problematic because the conquests of Cyrus and Cambyses occurred swiftly and very early in Medo-Persian history, and afterward, the Medes and Persians simply held onto what they had inherited for two hundred years, until they were conquered by Alexander the Great. There were no further Medo-Persian military victories to speak of after Cambyses. In his commentary on Daniel, Chris White makes the following statement concerning the bear: "If it [the bear] already has the conquests of Cyrus and his son in its mouth, then its future can't be looked at as devouring more flesh because it simply didn't in history."[280]

The last issue working against the sequential view of Daniel's beasts is that we find nothing in Daniel 7 to suggest that the statue and the animals are related. The text simply doesn't make that connection. Where the Bible is silent, we should be very cautious not to extrapolate new content based upon our own notions. It's okay to make guesses, but we run into trouble when our theories turn into dogma.

The fact that John's beast from the sea is a chimera of Daniel's four beasts suggests that the final world empire will absorb the lion, bear, and leopard kingdoms in the latter days. In Daniel 7, the four kingdoms are separate, but in Revelation 13 they are combined into one monstrous beast with exactly the same number of heads as Daniel's four beasts, combined (four from the leopard and one from each of the other three animals). The question is, what happens to cause the merger? I agree with the view promoted by Chris White, who posits that the kingdoms will be amalgamated as a result of the Antichrist's military conquests. White says,

> Dan. 11:36–45, which describes the wars of the Antichrist... links Daniel ch. 7—the Antichrist pre-wars, where he is only one of four powers—with Revelation 13, where he is the uncontested ruler of all world powers. So these three chapters, spread out all over the Bible, more or less provide a before, during, and after conquest snapshot of the Antichrist.[281]

The pre-wars of which White is speaking are the global conflicts brought about by the first two seal judgments of Revelation 6, which are the white and red horsemen of the Apocalypse. World War III is on our doorstep, and it will involve four major world powers. This time of worldwide chaos is represented in Daniel 7 by the four winds stirring up the Great Sea. The Hebrew words translated as "stirring" or "churning" can also mean "bursting forth," as in a sudden gale. The bottom is going to drop out from under us rather quickly, and the four kingdoms will whirl suddenly together in a ball of claws and fury.

Things won't improve for the secular world until the Antichrist takes the helm. The chaotic state of the world under the four end-times kingdoms will be brought into order by the might of Asshur. The kingdom represented by Leviathan is the end-times kingdom of Babylon, and it is from there that Asshur will arise. The ten horns are a feature exclusive to the fourth beast, and they will initially rule over only a portion of the earth. These are regional rulers who will make important decisions collectively, much as the European Union is supposed to operate today. "And the ten horns that you saw are ten kings who have not yet received royal power, but **they are to receive authority** as kings for one hour[a], **together with the beast**" (Rev. 17:12). Three of these kings will be taken out of play by Asshur as he grows in power (Dan. 7:8). The rest of them will hand over their authority to Asshur at the midpoint of Daniel's 70th week (Rev. 17:13, 17) so that there will be one king over the whole earth during the Great Tribulation. It will be terrible tribulation for the saints, but it will be the New Atlantis for the wicked.

As an aside, I suspect that the first beast of Daniel 7 represents America and Britain together, possibly with some of their neighboring countries mixed in. The first beast is a lion with wings, which is combination of the symbols of Great Britain and America, both divisions of the same English empire. The lion has its wings plucked off, which foretells the soon-coming destruction of America as we know her. However, Daniel saw the lion lifted to its feet by some unseen power and given the heart of a man. It could be that in the time of trouble a great spiritual awakening

---

[a] Could this "hour" be relative to God's millenial clock? If a day is as a thousand years on Heaven's clock, then an hour would be 42 years. If we add to that the seven years of Daniel's 70th week, then we get 49 years—the length of a Jubilee cycle. Of course, John saw that the ten kings will hand over their power 3½ years before Armageddon, so in order for the reign of the ten kings to equal exactly one hour, it would have to begin a few years before the start of Daniel's 70th week. It's a theory.

will break out in America or Britain, or both, and the people will no longer be like wild animals barring their teeth at YHVH. The dreams and visions of certain godly brethren over the last several decades seem to point in this direction.

Mystery Babylon

In Revelation 17 we are presented with a startling scenario: the terrible, death-dealing beast from the sea is being ridden by a harlot. One would assume that such a beast is unable to be tamed, but evidently a powerful and ungodly woman has made it subservient, at least for a time. John describes the sight in this way:

Figure 13-1. The goddess Europa rides atop Zeus in his bull form, on one side of a Greek euro.

> I saw a woman sit upon a scarlet coloured beast, full of names of blasphemy, having seven heads and ten horns. And the woman was arrayed in purple and scarlet colour, and decked with gold and precious stones and pearls, having a golden cup in her hand full of abominations and filthiness of her fornication: And upon her forehead was a name written, Mystery, Babylon The Great, The Mother Of Harlots And Abominations Of The Earth. And I saw the woman drunken with the blood of the saints, and with the blood of the martyrs of Jesus: and when I saw her, I wondered with great admiration. (Rev. 17:3-6)

Notice that the beast is scarlet, a bright red hue nearly matching the color of the dragon. The woman riding the beast is likewise scarlet, but she wears the additional color of purple. Scarlet is the color of blood, which we associate with war, but it is also the color associated with fertility because birth is a bloody business, and because blood rises to the surface of the skin and collects in the sexual organs during arousal. It isn't in vain that women put on red lipstick and wear red clothing when they want to appear enticing. The beast is the color of blood, for he makes war and conquers all people, but the woman is the color of sex. She wears purple in addition to red because she is royalty. Purple or royal blue has always been the color of royalty in the Babylon-based empires; in Sumeria, the color was obtained from lapis lazuli gemstones. It so happens that carnelian red and lapis lazuli blue were the colors used to symbolize the goddess Inanna.[282]

The many blasphemous names of the beast are the names of the solar demigods throughout history, from Tammuz, to Osiris, to Mithras. But the woman only needs *one* name that encompasses all her variations: Mystery, Babylon the Great.

A mystery is a thing which is hidden from all but perhaps a few privileged individuals. The Bible often refers to the redemptive plan of YHVH as a mystery; it is called that not only because the Gospel was revealed and executed piecemeal over millennia, but because it is so backwards to man's normal way of thinking that a human being could never have anticipated it. Paul said that the Gospel is foolishness to those who are perishing (1 Cor. 1:18). When Yeshua walked the earth, he spoke in parables so that the people would not understand the deeper meaning behind his words; yet he told his disciples, "Unto you it is given to know the mystery of the kingdom of God" (Mark 4:11). The apostle Paul emphasized the mysterious nature of the Gospel many times in his letters. For instance, he wrote to Timothy, "Without any doubt, the mystery of our religion is great: He was revealed in flesh, vindicated in spirit, seen by angels, proclaimed among Gentiles, believed in throughout the world, taken up in glory" (1 Tim. 3:16). He who understands and trusts in that messianic mystery will live forever.

The pagan religion of Enki (Satan) that replaced the worship of Enlil (God-the-Son) in pre-history had its own mysteries, which we have briefly glimpsed. Its secrets centered around finding the eternal divine spark within man and nursing it through the cycle of death and rebirth as embodied in Inanna and Dumuzi. The illumined priests were convinced that the promise of the serpent still held true, that they would "not surely die."

When a woman is used as a symbol in the Bible, it always represents a religion. The righteous symbolic woman is the bride of Christ, which is the flock of the Redeemed. She is equated to a city in Rev. 21:2, where John saw "the Holy City, the new Jerusalem, coming down out of heaven from God, prepared as a bride beautifully dressed for her husband." Mirroring that, the unrighteous woman who rides the beast is also said to be a city: "The woman you saw is the great city that rules over the kings of the earth" (Rev. 17:18). However, the woman is not exclusively a city, since she sits on many waters (17:1). An angel told John, "The waters you saw, where the prostitute sits, are peoples, multitudes, nations and languages" (v. 15). Thus, the whore must be a global religious system headquartered in a particular city called Babylon.

The fact that the woman riding the beast is a religious system makes a lot of sense, considering that religious authorities have always exerted enormous influence over civil authorities. Author Dave Hunt touches on that dynamic in his book *A Woman Rides the Beast*:

> Religion was always the dominant element in ancient world empires, including the four depicted by Nebuchadnezzar's image and Daniel's four beasts. Priests, soothsayers, and sorcerers were the closest advisers to rulers for thousands of years, and in most instances were the real power behind the throne, manipulating sovereigns by their magic and devious counsel. Science itself had its roots in occultism, beginning in astrology and alchemy. Materialism, skepticism, and atheism are of fairly recent origins and will be submerged in the tidal wave of renewed interest in "spirituality," which is already gathering momentum exactly as Jesus foretold for the last days.[283]

It is unlikely that materialism will lessen, as Mr. Hunt suggests, but occult religious ideologies are certainly on the increase. It is perfectly possible to be "spiritual" and greedy at the same time, as has been well demonstrated by the opulent ways of all the religious institutions that have been in bed with their contemporaneous civil authorities throughout history.

In 1825, Pope Leo XII minted a papal medal (Mazio #585) bearing an image of the Virgin seated on the globe, holding the golden chalice of the mass with the circumscribed cross of the sun god inside it, wearing a crown of

Figure 13-2. Papal medal Mazio 585

seven sun rays (viz. Apollo and Liberty), and surrounded by the phrase, "The whole world is her seat." This is not to say that the Roman Catholic Church alone is the end-times woman that rides the Beast, but it is plain to see that Rome has been the greatest manifestation of Inanna's religious system that the world has seen thus far. Catholicism may be monotheistic and Abrahamic in doctrine, but the opulence, history of atrocities, and enormous political influence of the Vatican make it nearly indistinguishable from Inanna's cults in practice.

In Rev. 17:2, John sees that the prostitute had committed fornication with the kings of the earth. Here we have a strong correlation to Inanna, who was the goddess of courtesans and of the annual sacred copulation. In this connection, let us remember that Inanna's priestesses fornicated with the king in a ritual act (hieros gamos) that not only ensured continued abundance, but merged the religious and political components of the civilization. In her book titled *Gender and Aging in Mesopotamia: The Gilgamesh Epic and Other Ancient Literature*, author Rivkah Harris examines the goddess' role as the harlot of heaven in the Gilgamesh epic. Harris calls Inanna/Ishtar the "patroness of prostitutes" and "role model for her votaries," noting that she sets out for the bordello dressed as a prostitute, eager to solicit a lover.[284] This fits with the title, Mother of Prostitutes, given in Rev. 17:5 to the woman riding the beast. That title primarily concerns spiritual adultery, but it doesn't have to be confined to the spiritual.

The writing upon the woman's forehead also declares that she is the mother "of the abominations of the earth." Idol worship, sexual misconduct between heterosexuals, homosexual activity, cross-dressing, bestiality, child sacrifice, practicing magic, and contacting spirits have always come up high on the list of things that God detests; yet many of these things were practiced and glorified in the cult of Inanna. Harris describes the unruly nature of Inanna's feasts as

> the time for disorder and antistructure, when reversals in categories of age, species, status, and sex all came into play.... She was, one might say, externalized into unordered, carnivalesque celebration that demonstrates a reaching beyond the normal order of things and the breakdown of norms. The goddess' festivals were institutionalized license. They celebrated and tolerated disorder.[285]

Today, we in the West live in a society that tolerates all manner of licentiousness and excess, and normalizes disorders; indeed, we hardly remember what propriety and moderation mean. It would seem that the spirit of Babylon is experiencing a resurgence in our day, and the sad result is that many people who partake in her sins are plagued with mental anguish and emotional instability. To relieve the pain, they commit even more sin, and cover up the symptoms of their mental illness with pharmaceuticals[a].

Inanna was an almost paradoxical character in the way that she embodied extremes. On the one hand, she represented disorder and baseness, but on the other hand, she was portrayed as glorious royalty who dispensed justice and maintained the sacred codes of society. In fact, she went to great lengths to attain the *me*, or Divine Laws, from the god Enki so that she could put them into practice in Uruk. Likewise, the whore of Revelation makes use of a well-oiled socio-political system to produce the bounty of worldly fruits which she so treasures.

As Isaiah hinted at in his oracle about the king of Babylon, Mystery Babylon's capitol is the heart of the world's wealth-making engine. The harlot is said to be decked in gold and precious stones, and she holds a golden cup, signifying prosperity. For this reason, the merchants of the world will weep and mourn over her on the day of her destruction "because no one buys their cargoes any more" (Rev. 18:11). They will say, "All your riches and splendor have vanished, never to be recovered… In one hour such great wealth has been brought to ruin!" (vv. 14, 17). Just as man's first attempt at a united empire was based out of the city of Babel, so the final, global empire will be based out of a single, great city where power and wealth are consolidated. Some people believe that New York City is playing the role of Babylon. Others (myself included) believe that Babylon will be rebuilt in Iraq, and world power will return in the end to the place where it began. Still others see Rome as the city of Babylon because the apostle Peter called it by that name in his first epistle (1 Pet. 5:13). Whatever the case, that city, being the hub of materialism and paganism in all its forms, will be the spiritually darkest place that has ever existed or will ever exist. For this reason, the Lord cries out, "Come out of her, my people, lest you take part in her sins, lest you share in her plagues; for her sins are heaped high as heaven, and God has remembered her iniquities" (Rev. 18:4–5).

Part of the sin of Babylon is that it keeps a stranglehold on the proletariat, who have been duped into a lifestyle of fanatical consumerism and must borrow indefinitely to maintain it. Likewise, the cult of Inanna at Uruk thrived financially on account of usury. In a treatise about one of the famous high priestesses of Inanna, Betty Meador explains how the cult of Inanna multiplied its holdings by making loans. She writes,

---

[a] The apostle John wrote that Mystery Babylon had deceived the people of the world with her sorcery, which in Greek is *pharmakeia*. The mind-altering pharmaceuticals so prevalent today are but one aspect of that sorcery.

> As the *en*-priestess, Enheduanna managed the extensive agricultural en-
> terprise on the land around the temple.... These estates provided the
> high priestesses considerable economic independence, enabling them
> to make loans from the temple treasury.... Her title, *en*-priestess, desig-
> nates a singular purpose: she is the lady who engenders abundance, the
> ruler over prosperity.[286]

Another parallel between Inanna and Mystery Babylon is seen in the
imagery of her mounting a beast. Again and again in Mesopotamian
art we find Inanna/Ishtar depicted as standing upon one or more lions.
Throughout the ancient religions, the lion is consistently used as a symbol of the solar deity.

A comparison of Inanna to Mystery Babylon must also take into account one of the goddess' main roles: that of the grieving widow who
annually renews her wailing for the fallen sun god. Unlike Inanna/Ishtar,
the prostitute of Revelation does not weep, but that disparity actually
strengthens our hypothesis. In Rev. 18:7, the whore of Babylon says that
she is a queen and *not* a widow, and she refuses to mourn, which cannot
be understood except as a reference to the grieving Queen of Heaven
with whom the apostate Israelites committed spiritual adultery. This
queen's husband, the king of Babylon, has made a permanent return in
the form of the Beast, and she will never again need to mourn his loss.

A final connection is found in the fact that the Beast and his regents
will ultimately destroy the mounted queen (Rev. 17:16), reminding us of
the love/hate relationship between Inanna and her mates, as in the *Epic
of Gilgamesh* and *Inanna's Descent to the Underworld*.

Given the many parallels between the Queen of Heaven and the Queen
of end-times Babylon, it is hard to escape the conclusion that the Mesopotamian goddess of fertility, abundance, and war is the source for the
harlot who rides the Beast. What Semiramis and her brother started in
Babel over four thousand years ago, the Harlot and the revived king of
Babylon will finish in the coming days.

Political and religious Mystery Babylon is taking center stage even
now; the reign of Inanna is nearing its climax.

FOURTEEN

In Support of Enoch

> From them [the angels] I heard all things, and understood
> what I saw; that which will not take place in this generation,
> but in a generation which is to succeed at a distant period.
>
> –1 ENOCH 1:2

During the Olivet Discourse, Yeshua taught that the days before his return would be like the days before the flood of Noah (Matt. 24:37). That should stimulate us to ask the question, What was it like in the days of Noah? To begin to answer that question, let us turn to a much-maligned and oft-misunderstood sacred text which gives a fascinating account of life before the Flood.

A Lost Treasure Rediscovered

We are going to spend a significant amount of time in the Book of Enoch (i.e., 1 Enoch, not versions 2 or 3), which is really a collection of five books attributed mainly to Enoch, with small portions attributed to Methuselah and Noah. This composite work was once cherished by Christians for its vast scope, its awe-inspiring depictions of the spiritual realms, and its many similarities to New Testament teachings. To get a sense of the degree of similarity, take a look at these three passages, the first from 1 Enoch and the other two from the Bible:

> The former heaven shall depart and pass away; a new heaven shall appear; and all the celestial powers shall shine with sevenfold splendour for ever. Afterwards likewise shall there be many [ages], which shall externally exist in goodness and in righteousness. Neither shall sin be named there for ever and for ever. (1 Eno. 92:17–18)

Moreover, the light of the moon will be as the light of the sun, and the light of the sun will be sevenfold, as the light of seven days, in the day when the LORD binds up the brokenness of his people, and heals the wounds inflicted by his blow. (Isa. 30:26)

Then I saw a new heaven and a new earth, for the first heaven and the first earth had passed away.... Nothing impure will ever enter it, nor will anyone who does what is shameful or deceitful, but only those whose names are written in the Lamb's book of life. (Rev. 21:1, 27)

A secular scholar who compared these passages would conclude that John and Isaiah borrowed from Enoch, but those prophets didn't borrow words or concepts from anyone—they faithfully recorded the visions that they were given. Otherwise, John and Isaiah are liars, and all of their oracles are bunk. The only valid conclusion for a Bible-believing Christian is that these three men were all given visions of the same events, by the same God. The Book of Enoch validates the Bible over and over again.

Many of the key concepts used by Yeshua during his earthly ministry have close parallels in 1 Enoch. For instance, Yeshua echoes almost verbatim Enoch's words about the rich, saying,

But woe to you who are rich, for you have already received your comfort. (Luke 6:24)

Woe to you, rich, for in your riches you have trusted; from your riches you will depart, because you have not remembered the Most High in the days of your riches. (1 Eno. 94:8)

The apostle John saw the horror of the Last Battle, when the grapes of wrath are trampled by Messiah, but it would seem that Enoch was the first to witness that horrific scene.

And the winepress was trampled outside the city, and blood came out of the winepress, up to the horses' bridles, for one thousand six hundred furlongs. (Rev. 14:20, NKJV)

A horse will wade up to its breast through the blood of the sinners... [for] those who aided iniquity will be gathered into one place.

(1 Eno. 100:3–4)

Such parallels are numerous, and should stimulate great curiosity about the writings of Enoch.

We should also be intrigued by the fact that two New Testament authors referred to antediluvian events which are not recorded in the Bible—but they *are* recorded in 1 Enoch. Here are the two New Testament excerpts:

> For if God did not spare the angels when they sinned, but cast them into Tartaros and committed them to chains of deepest darkness to be kept until the judgment; and if he did not spare the ancient world... (2 Pet. 2:4–5)

> And the angels who did not keep their own position, but left their proper dwelling, he has kept in eternal chains in deepest darkness for the judgment of the great day. Likewise, Sodom and Gomorrah and the surrounding cities, which, in the same manner as them [the angels], indulged in sexual immorality and pursued unnatural lust, serve as an example by undergoing a punishment of eternal fire. (Jude 1:6–7)

Much to our advantage, the Book of Enoch fills in the gaps of the very succinct Genesis account of the antediluvian world.

The Book of Enoch was long lost to the West but resurfaced in 1773 when explorer James Bruce returned to Europe from Ethiopia with three copies written in the Ethiopian language, Ge'ez. The Ethiopians had faithfully preserved the ancient text and even considered it part of their canon. Many years later, fragments of the book were found among the Dead Sea Scrolls at Qumran[a], but they were in Aramaic, not Ge'ez. Portions of the book have also been preserved in other texts, both in Greek and Latin.

---

[a] The Dead Sea Scrolls were produced by a very conservative Jewish community called the Essenes, of which John the Baptist may have been a member.

Currently, many scholars guess that 1 Enoch was originally written by a Semitic author during the intertestamental period. It is probably true that the book existed in Aramaic form before being translated into Greek and Ge'ez, but if the patriarch Enoch is truly the author, then the original language was that spoken by Adam and Eve.

Right away, many right-minded Christians will object to relying heavily on a book that isn't part of the biblical canon. Normally, I would agree, but this remarkable book by the great-grandfather of Noah stands in a class all its own. Read the following verses from Enoch and ask yourself if it aligns with biblical doctrine:

> Then shall the kings, the princes, and all who possess the earth, glorify Him who has dominion over all things, Him who was concealed; for from eternity the Son of Man was concealed, whom the Most High preserved in the presence of His power and revealed to the elect. He shall sow the congregation of the saints, and of the elect; and all the elect shall stand before Him in that day. All the kings, the princes, the exalted, and those who rule over the earth shall fall down on their faces before Him, and shall worship Him. They shall fix their hopes on this Son of Man. (61:10–12)

One of the most wonderful things about the Book of Enoch is its emphasis on the Lordship of Christ. It frequently portrays him as a preexistent king and even calls him *Son of Man* over a hundred times! That title as applied to a messianic figure only shows up in the Old Testament once, in the Book of Daniel, yet Yeshua referred to himself as the Son of Man on many occasions. It seems likely that Yeshua was identifying himself as the exalted figure seen by Enoch.

Tertullian, one of the early church fathers, wrote in defense of Enoch, arguing that we must take the book seriously because it concerns itself with a messiah figure to whom all righteousness is attributed, who can be none other than Yeshua (1 Eno. 46:1–4, 48:2–7, et al.).[287] The Book of Enoch goes far beyond simply mentioning the Son of Man; it is explained that "the Elect and Concealed One" existed in God's presence before the creation of the world, that his name was invoked before the sun and stars were formed, that he will be the light of the nations and the hope of all whose hearts are troubled, that everyone righteous will fall down and worship before him, that the kings of the earth will be judged in his presence, and that he will bless the world with peace and wisdom (48:2–14).

How incredible! Any book which foretold of our Messiah as he has since been revealed in the New Testament scriptures, can only be of God.

According to the angelic narrator of the Book of Jubilees, Enoch was a very important prophet in the history of prophets: "For Enoch's office was ordained for a testimony to the generations of the world, so that he should recount all the deeds of generation unto generation, till the day of judgment" (Jub. 10:17–18). Did you catch that? Enoch was told all of the deeds of every generation. As we read the part of 1 Enoch commonly called the "Book of Dreams," we find that the author was indeed given the entire history of the saints in allegorical form, starting from Adam and ending with Judgment Day. If the Book of Enoch was written when it says it was (before the Flood), then we must pause and be amazed, because our Great God showed a faithful man at the beginning of history how the entire story of human redemption would unfold. Enoch wrote about events which came and went long ago, and we can increase our faith by matching his prophecy to our own knowledge of history; but Enoch also wrote about events that are still future to us, and they correspond amazingly well to all of the other eschatalogical prophecies that we find throughout the Bible. True, Enoch's prophecy is painted with broad strokes—it has to cover a lot of ground very succinctly—but it is demonstrably accurate. Enoch's prophecy isn't easy to understand, but that doesn't diminish its rightness. The prophecy is cloaked in obscurity because different types of animals and animal behaviors are used allegorically in place of people, and the allegory only really makes sense once the respective events have occurred; then we can look at the text with hindsight and understand how the parable synchronized with actual events. Why was it written in completely symbolic language? So that our adversaries, the fallen angels, would not be able to use it to precisely predict the future and derail the plan. Yet after the events have passed, we have the privilege of strengthening our faith by witnessing God's foreknowledge expressed through the pen of the prophet.

Dating the Text

The majority opinion at present is that 1 Enoch was written relatively late in history, only a few centuries before Christ, making it pseudepigraphal. When researching 1 Enoch, one will see this late-date claim thrown about confidently,[288] as if it is indisputable, but the truth is that there has been much debate surrounding the dates of composition, and it all remains very speculative. The oldest manuscripts of 1 Enoch date to around 300 BC, but they are definitely copies, and obviously, the age of a copy cannot be used to date an original. Thus, scholars must resort to clues within the text itself to determine its age. Keep in mind that nearly all of the scholars attempting to date 1 Enoch are skeptics and naturally biased against the idea that the book is real prophecy from a real antediluvian prophet. These are the same people who try to late-date the Book of Daniel to the mid-second century BC, thereby invalidating most of Daniel's prophecies. To these skeptics, one possible indication of date has to do with the style of the Aramaic fragments of Enoch found at Qumran. The Aramaic does not appear particularly archaic, and is therefore attributed to a later date; however, other scholars object. Author Roger Beckwith is one of them, and he objects,

> Dr. S. P. Brock and the late Dr. J. C. Greenfield, with whom I discussed the matter some years ago, warn me that, since there is such a paucity of Aramaic literature from the period, and vernacular Aramaic (with its dialect differences) is also ill-attested, linguistic arguments on questions of dating must only be used with caution. Also, the possibility that authors are deliberately archaizing, and, on the other hand, that copyists are modernizing, must be borne in mind.[289]

In short, linguistic arguments are of little value. Other evidence must be sought.

When Archbishop Richard Laurence introduced Ethiopic Enoch to the West in 1821, he relied on two clues within the book to help him assign it a date of origin: allusions to the Herodian period of Jewish history, and a mention of the Parthians and Medes being stirred up against the city of the righteous (1 Eno. 56:5). The archbishop surmised that the historical allegory given in the Book of Dreams goes no further than the reign of Herod the Great, and he arrived at that conclusion based on the number of shepherds in the parables, which was seventy. Laurence understood the shepherds to represent kings of Israel and Judah. With all due respect to the archbishop, that cannot be correct. Those shepherds are in fact angelic rulers who were set over the Hebrews after God divorced Israel for repeated spiritual adultery and rampant lawlessness.

We can prove that the shepherds of the Book of Dreams are Kosmokraters and not human beings because of an interaction that Enoch observes between God and the seventy shepherds.

> He called also seventy shepherds, and resigned to them the sheep, that they might overlook them; Saying to them and to their associates, Everyone of you henceforward overlook the sheep, and whatsoever I command you, do; and I will deliver them to you numbered. I will tell you which of them shall be slain; these destroy. And he delivered the sheep to them. Then he called to another, and said, Understand, and watch everything which the shepherds shall do to these sheep; for many more of them shall perish than I have commanded. Of every excess and slaughter, which the shepherds shall commit, there shall be an account. (88: 94–98)

Obviously, no such interaction has ever occurred between God and Hebrew rulers. Assuming for a moment that it had, and that the command from God was replicated at the time of the coronation of each king, how would those men have known who God intended them to eliminate, and how exactly would they have accomplished such a thing? They couldn't have, and the interpretation of the shepherds as mortals is sheer folly.

As an interesting aside, take note of the place in the narrative at which those shepherds begin to oversee the Jews. It's the time of the Assyrian and Babylonian invasions, when the twelve tribes were given over to the lions, which have always been symbols of the mighty men and kings of Mesopotamia. Ever since the Babylonian Exile, large portions of the Jewish populace have constantly been repressed by the Gentile nations.

Other supposed allusions to the time of Herod the Great are far-fetched at best. For instance, scholars such as Darrell Hannah interpret 1 Eno. 67:4–13 as a reference to Herod's visits to the hot springs at Callirrhoe,[290] but the content of those verses is nowhere near specific enough to be able to attribute them to Herod with any confidence.

Likewise, scholars who interpret the later portion of the Book of Dreams as having to do with the rise of the Essene movement and the

Maccabean war of liberation have great latitude to do so because of the allegorical nature of the telling. Their intent is to show that the supposed prophet was not portraying future events, but turning past events into parable. In that case, the author pretending to be Enoch must have written his book within the first two centuries BC, for he was unable to furnish details about the fate of the Jews after that time. If we reckon instead that the prophecy does not suddenly conclude at the time of the Maccabees, but continues on speedily through history unto the end of the age, then we will notice that the allegory fits into and expounds upon what we know from Daniel and Revelation about the treatment of the saints in the last days, and of the return of Messiah to smite the earth. There may indeed be a legitimate reference to first- and second-century BC events somewhere within the Book of Dreams, but that is to be expected, since the book contains a fore-telling of Hebraic history in its entirety.

As concerns the mention of Parthians (Persians) and Medes in ch. 56, it is suspicious that the names are used at all, considering that they did not exist in Enoch's day. However, Enoch may have been given the post-diluvian names as part of the prophecy. It is also feasible that a misbehaved scribe who lived during or after the time of the Parthian invasion inserted the names of contemporary invaders to make the text square with events of his day. If that was the case, it still does not help us date the rest of 1 Enoch. The Parthian Empire did indeed lay waste to Judea ca. 40 BC, triggering a civil war in Jerusalem,[291] so it's tempting to interpret that event as a fulfillment of the ch. 56 oracle. Here's the problem: the verses before and after the oracle in question, and even the adjacent chapters, are all eschatological in nature. In ch. 55, God declares that he will never again wipe sinners from the earth with a great flood, but instead will employ angels to deliver his wrath in the day of tribulation. Then the kings of the earth will see the Elect One on the throne of glory, meting out justice—a clear reference to Yeshua's future installment as King in Jerusalem. The end of ch. 56 says that sinners will be cast into hell in the presence of the elect, and that their destruction will "be not in vain," which contrasts with God's statement in ch. 55 that the destruction of sinners in the Flood was "in vain." Why was it in vain? Because humanity was allowed to continue to procreate and would eventually reach another pinnacle of immorality and violence worldwide. Therefore, we should understand the end of ch. 56 to speak of the *final* destruction of all sinners, which we know will not occur until Yeshua returns.

In order to understand ch. 56, we need to look to the future, not the past. The pertinent verses read as follows:

> In those days the angels shall return and hurl themselves to the east upon
> the Parthians and Medes: **they shall stir up the kings** so that a spirit of
> unrest shall come upon them, and **they shall rouse them from their
> thrones**, that they may break forth as lions from their lairs.... And **they
> shall go up and tread under foot the land of His elect ones**, but the
> city of my righteous shall be a hindrance to their horses. And they shall
> begin to fight among themselves... and a man shall not know his brother,
> nor a son his father or his mother, till there be no number of the corpses
> through their slaughter.... In those days Sheol shall open its jaws, and
> they shall be swallowed up therein... **Sheol shall devour the sinners** in
> the presence of the elect. (56:5–8)

The passage begins with "in those days," a phrase frequently found in
apocalyptic oracles. It can refer to the Millennium or beyond, but more
often speaks of the Great Tribulation. In the Book of Revelation we are
told that unclean spirits will go to the kings of the East in the days immediately preceding the return of Christ and will convince those kings and
the leaders of other nations to go to battle against Israel (Rev. 16:12–16).
We find also in Ezekiel 38 that God will put a hook in the jaws of Meshech
and Tubal to pull them into war with Israel, and *Persia* will be with them.
When they arrive at Jerusalem, the mountains will fall, the cliffs will
crumble, and every wall will fall down—that may be why Enoch notes
the difficulty of the horses. As the invaders swarm Jerusalem on foot,
God will send confusion into their midst so that "every man's sword will
be against his brother" (Ezek. 38:21). At the culmination of the Day of
the Lord, sinners will be removed from before the faces of the righteous,
for we have it written, "Behold, the day of the Lord comes, cruel, with
wrath and fierce anger, to make the earth a desolation and **to destroy
its sinners from it**" (Isa. 13:9). As Yeshua promised, "The Son of Man
will send out his angels, and they will weed out of his kingdom everything that causes sin and all who do evil. They will throw them into the
fiery furnace, where there will be weeping and gnashing of teeth" (Matt.
13:41–42). Doesn't that all sound much the same as Enoch ch. 56?

An overwhelming number of the oracles of Enoch have clear parallels
to passages in the Bible that pertain to the Day of the Lord and beyond.
It is much easier to make sense of Enoch's prophecies if we default to the
assumption that the eschaton is in view.

Another way that critics late-date Enoch is by finding similarities between 1 Enoch and parts of the Old Testament or other Jewish apocalyptic books, and then concluding that the writers of Enoch must have been borrowing from those prior Jewish texts. For instance, Archbishop Laurence believed that 1 Enoch must have been written after the Jews' captivity in Babylon because it contains the language and imagery of Daniel "in the representation of the Ancient of Days coming to judgment with the Son of man."[292] A simple analogy will explain why this is not legitimate. Imagine a scenario wherein two college students take lecture notes from the same class taught by the same professor, but during different semesters. A younger student who later inherits both notebooks might conclude that one of the note-takers had copied from the other, but that would be incorrect. The similarity of the students' notes is attributed to the fact that those students were taught the same material. Likewise, many of the Jewish prophets partook in a tour of the future under the guidance and instruction of the same angels as did Enoch, and it would be disconcerting if their eye-witnesses testimonies were *not* similar.

Jude Weighs In

Anyone who believes in the inerrancy of Scripture can refute the late date-of-origin theory with a single line of questioning: Would an apostle of Christ have drawn from the Book of Enoch and treated the selection as trustworthy prophecy, if its authorship was a lie? I refer to the apostle Jude, who quoted Enoch in his epistle.

> It was also about these that Enoch, the seventh from Adam, **prophesied**, saying, "Behold, the Lord comes with ten thousands of his holy ones, to execute judgment on all and to convict all the ungodly of all their deeds of ungodliness that they have committed in such an ungodly way, and of all the harsh things that ungodly sinners have spoken against him." (Jude 1:14–15)

Would the Holy Spirit allow Jude, as his mouthpiece, to teach from a work of fiction? Not a chance. That would be introducing false testimony into the inspired Word.

Critics like to point to the fact that Paul quoted a Greek poet (Acts 17:28), arguing that such a quote does not sanctify the entirety of the quoted author's words, but when Paul referenced a Greek writer, he was doing so in order to be as relevant as possible to the Greeks, since he was attempting to convert them. Paul was certainly not suggesting the the poet was a prophet of God or speaking on his behalf; rather, the poet had hit on some small truth about God simply by using his God-given ability to reason. Jude, on the other hand, explicitly notes that Enoch *prophesied* about the coming judgment. Clearly, Jude treated 1 Enoch as religiously authoritative. If we believe the Book of Jude to be canon, then we must believe that the *original* Book of Enoch was inspired.

The Learning of the Patriarchs

There's one more thing to note before we move on: Job was aware of what would happen in the last days, for he said, "I know that my Redeemer lives, and that **in the end he will stand upon the earth**" (Job 19:25). Job had also been taught what God required from his followers, since he could assure his friends that "My foot has held fast to his steps; I have kept his way.... **I have treasured the words of his mouth** more than my portion of food" (23:11–12). What words from his mouth, exactly? And to what instruction was Eliphaz appealing when he admonished Job to receive "instruction **from his mouth**, and lay up **his words** in your heart" (22:22)? This is very interesting because Job lived long before the Torah (lit.: instruction) was given to Moses, and before any Jewish prophets were given visions of the Messiah descending to the earth at the end of the age. How did Job and his companions know what they knew?

Job's friend, Bildad, suggested that he enquire of former generations as to what their forefathers had taught them, "for we were born yesterday and know nothing, and our days on earth are but a shadow" (Job 8:9, NIV). This implies that the lifespans of the former generations were much longer than Bildad's, and those generations could still be consulted. In other words, Job lived during a time when the sons or grandsons of Noah were still alive on the earth. This is entirely possible because Genesis tells us that those men lived to between four and five hundred years of age. This could be why Eliphaz said to Job, "What do you know that we do not?... Both the gray-haired and the aged are among us, much older than your father" (15:9–10, NKJV). These early postdiluvian patriarchs had knowledge from before the Flood, and that may have included the prophecies of their great grandfather, Enoch. No doubt what Adam learned from God, he passed to Seth, and Seth to his descendants, coming finally to Noah.

Bildad did not indicate whether the forefathers passed on God's instructions in oral or written form, but an ancient manuscript called *The Testaments of the Twelve Patriarchs* suggests that Abraham's descendants did have access to a written version of Enoch's words. The Patriarch Naphtali writes in his testament, "I have read in the writing of Enoch that ye yourselves also shall depart from the Lord..." (1:28), and five of the other eleven patriarchs appeal to the words of Enoch. We should take The Testaments seriously[a] if for no other reason than that the Bible draws from it repeatedly:

- Luke 14:11 (cf. Luke 9:48) parallels the Testament of Joseph 17:8–18
- Luke 17:3 bears striking semblance to T. of Gad 6:3
- Mark 12:30–31 expounds on T. of Issachar 5:2
- Rom. 12:19 corresponds to T. of Gad 6:10
- 1 Thess. 2:16 is a quotation of T. of Levi 6:11
- Eph. 5:6 condenses T. of Naphtali 3:1–4
- Uniquely N.T. theology is found in T. of Benjamin 10:7–11

Whether we trust these testaments or not, Enoch's instructions evidently survived in some form. It is helpful to know that God was giving both laws and eschatological oracles before the Jewish nation ever came into existence. That buoys our case for an antediluvian dating for 1 Enoch.

The Odd Book Out

Why didn't the Early Church incorporate Enoch into the Bible? There may have been more than one reason. First of all, when deciding on canon, Christian leaders tended to ignore those Jewish texts which were not widely used by 1st- and 2nd-century Jews, and it has been suggested that the Jews took issue with Enoch's depiction of angelic mutiny distinct from Satan's.[293] Another sticking point may have been the fact that Enoch depicts a scenario of apocalyptic last days, affirming the

[a] Portions of The Testaments may have been appended to the original by early Christians, but the bulk of the text is undoubtedly pre-Christian, as some of the testaments were found among the Dead Sea Scrolls at Qumran.

prophecies of Yeshua and his apostles but negating Jewish eschatological beliefs.

On a more practical level, the five books which comprise 1 Enoch would have been a chore to distribute. At over a hundred chapters, 1 Enoch is a lengthy text and would be burdensome to reproduce in an era which lacked the printing press.

More importantly, Enoch's writings no longer exist in their original form. In fact, we don't even know the language in which Enoch wrote. There's no telling how many times it was translated before arriving in the Ge'ez and fragmentary Greek and Aramaic versions that we now possess, or who guarded and reproduced it during the millennia following the Flood. Some solace may be found in the fact that most if not all of 1 Enoch's content aligns neatly with biblical theology, leading us to believe that the Ethiopic Enoch was kept relatively safe from heretics. But since we know nothing of the book's journey after it left Noah's hands, we cannot be wholly confident in the fidelity of what we've inherited.

Despite having no assurance that 1 Enoch was passed down faithfully, many Hebrews still considered it to be Holy Writ. The Essenes treated it as authoritative, and Jewish texts such as 4 Ezra, 2 Baruch, and the Testaments of the Twelve Patriarchs, all affirm it. Early Church fathers who wrote favorably of 1 Enoch include, among others: Tatian, Justin Martyr, Clement of Alexandria, Irenaeus, Athenagoras, and Origen. Also, the Epistle of Barnabas, which was popular in the early Church, quotes from the Dream Visions section of 1 Enoch.

Polish priest and language expert Józef T. Milik, who deciphered hundreds of the Dead Sea Scrolls, went so far as to say that Enochian literature underwent a "full-blown renaissance in the early Christian communities."[294] It was not until the early fourth and fifth centuries that it fell out of favor, particularly after the Council of Laodicea (AD 364) approved a list of books suitable for reading in church, Enoch not being among them. Perhaps the mortal wound was incurred in AD 450, when St. Jerome, who translated the Bible into Latin, declared 1 Enoch to be apocryphal due to the obscurity of its origins and its at-that-time unpopular portrayal of the supernatural realm.

The Book of Enoch still today has numerous critics and detractors, even among devoted Christians. This is due in part to the fact that most people are set in their ways and averse to anything that changes their traditions, even if it's a positive change. But beyond that, religiously conservative Christians have been taught to believe that the canonized books are absolutely the only books ever inspired by the Holy Spirit. *Sola Scriptura* has been an important rallying cry by which to combat the dangers of unbiblical teachings and stay true to divine revelation, but it loses its validity when taken to mean that the books of the current protestant Bible comprise the entirety of divine communication throughout history. The Old Testament repeatedly refers to oracles of God which were recorded and copied by the Jewish scribes, yet which did not survive the ravages of time (1 Chr. 29:29; 2 Chr. 9:29, 32:32, 33:19; Col. 4:16; et al.). Are we to believe that those scrolls were not inspired? It would be uncharacteristic for the Holy Word to point readers to non-authoritative sources. It would be better to conclude that those lost scrolls were sacred and useful during their times but not strictly necessary for the teaching and edification of future generations, therefore God allowed them to be lost. The rest of the biblical books are sufficient for us. However, that does not imply that finding copies of the lost prophecies of Israel would be inconsequential. It would be fortunate indeed to have those oracles because we could use them to affirm and strengthen what we already know about history, YHVH, and the redemptive plan. They might even shed light on a few topics which the Bible has left mostly unaddressed. Likewise, 1 Enoch further illuminates for us the spiritual world that has already been made visible through the canonized scriptures.

It should be emphasized that 1 Enoch is not without error, but overall, judging by the biblical quality of the content, the Book of Enoch appears largely trustworthy. Perhaps we cannot treat it as fully intact and infallible, but let's be careful not to throw out the baby with the bathwater.

Prophecy buffs have long postulated that the Two Witnesses who will preach from Jerusalem in the last days (Rev. 11:3–13) will be Enoch and Elijah, the only two men in history who did not die, but were bodily assumed into heaven, where they remain still. The Two Witnesses will die by the hand of the Antichrist at the mid-point of Daniel's 70th week, and if they are in fact the prophets Enoch and Elijah, then their deaths will validate the apostle Paul's declaration that all men have sinned and must die. Any believer who is in Jerusalem when the Two Witnesses appear should take it upon himself to ask Enoch whether the Book of Enoch is indeed from the prophet's hand, and whether it has been significantly altered over the ages. What a privilege it will be to hear from those who have dwelt in the presence of YHVH in heaven!

FIFTEEN

Sins of the Watchers

"All the earth has been corrupted by the effects of the teaching of [the Watchers]."
—YHVH, 1 ENOCH 10:12

The Ethiopic version of 1 Enoch has been divided into five sections based on internal literary themes. Biblical scholar and languages expert J. T. Milik labeled the sections as follows:

- The Book of the Watchers (chapters 1-36)[a]
- The Book of Parables (chapters 37-70)
- The Astronomical Book (chapters 71-81)
- The Book of Dreams (chapters 82-90)
- The Epistle of Enoch (chapters 91-105)

The Book of the Watchers is the portion from which Jude quoted, and it is where we will focus most of our attention. It begins by announcing its intended audience.

> The words of the blessing with which Enoch blessed the righteous chosen who will be present on the day of tribulation, to remove all the enemies; and the righteous will be saved.... Not for this generation do I expound, **but concerning one that is distant** I speak. (1:1-2)

This tells us that Enoch received his visions for the edification of the elect who would live during a generation far off. We know that the last generation will be the one that goes through the Great Tribulation, so could it be that Enoch was specifically targeting that group of believers? If so, perhaps that is why his book has re-emerged from obscurity and recently generated so much interest.

---

[a] The chapter numbers in this list are based upon the Cepher version.

The subsequent verses describe how God will bring his power to bear upon the wicked world, causing the wicked to tremble in terror (cf. Rev. 6:15-17); he will shake the world so that the mountains fall down (cf. Rev. 6:12-14); and he will destroy Earth with fire (cf. 2 Pet. 3:10). This adds support to the hypothesis that Enoch had the Tribulation saints in mind to receive his message.

Angelic Misconduct After the Fall

Chapter 7 begins with a story that closely parallels the first verses of Genesis 6. The passage reads,

> It happened after the sons of men had multiplied in those days, that daughters were born to them, elegant and beautiful. And when the angels, the sons of heaven, beheld them, they became enamoured of them, saying to each other, "Come, let us select for ourselves wives from the progeny of men, and let us beget children." (1 Eno. 7:1-2)

Early Catholic leaders formed the opinion that the Book of Enoch had extrapolated its legends from the earlier Book of Genesis, but modern Catholic scholar J. T. Milik came to the opposite conclusion after examining all surviving Enochian manuscripts. In his 1976 book published by Oxford, Milik posited that the abridged Genesis 6 text derives from the earlier Enochian tale.[295] How interesting to consider that Moses may have paid homage to the work of an earlier and even greater prophet.

Many of us have probably wondered why the Genesis 6 account is so frustratingly succinct, especially since it introduces mysterious new characters and outlandish events. Perhaps it is because God's faithful were never intended to discard the Book of Enoch with its much fuller account of the antediluvian world!

According to Enoch, Satan and the angels who followed him were not the only angels to ever sin. A band of two hundred angels who were members of the division know as Watchers, also transgressed. These are the angels which Saint Peter said were chained in Tartarus to await the day of judgment. Those who followed Satan in his pride to supersede YHVH are called devils, and devils are not currently bound in chains; they are restricted in a legal sense, but they are not imprisoned. The Bible makes very clear that devils are free to roam the earth, and they are constantly at work thereabout. The Watchers, however, were judged by God *why* at the time of the Flood and cast into the pit. Their initial sin was not pride, but lust and the desire to procreate (the latter being a blessing for men, but illicit for angels). They were powerful and brilliant creatures, and once they had it in their heads to partake in intercourse, primitive humans couldn't stop them.

The Erroneous Sethite Interpretation

Not everyone is willing to believe that angels could breed.

The earliest Christians had no problem with the idea, but the further in time from the apostles that one investigates, the more one finds Christian leaders disquieted by the notion of angelic fornication (despite the fact that the citizens of Sodom wished to rape the angels who visited Lot's family). These leaders may have been focused on Yeshua's statement that "spirits do not have flesh and bone," but that statement was meant only to assure the disciples that Yeshua had received a new body with which he could interact with those in the physical plane. The fact remains that spirits are sometimes (rarely) allowed to manifest in fleshly bodies. Beyond that, the critics were undoubtedly concerned with Yeshua's teaching that the angels in heaven do not marry. He said, "For in the resurrection they neither marry nor are given in marriage, but are like the angels in heaven" (Matt. 22:30). Indeed, marriage and procreation aren't normal activities for angels *in heaven*. The angels who sinned are no longer in heaven. Likewise, good police officers don't do illegal drugs; but they could do them, if they so desired, and some will occasionally break the law in that fashion, but then they are no longer good officers. Take note that Yeshua did not say that angels are incapable of mating when in possession of a material body.

When Genesis 6 tells us that "all flesh had corrupted their way on the earth" (v. 12) and that Noah was the only man who was "perfect **in his generations**" (v. 9, NKJV), we should understand that the author was not concerned foremost with moral purity, but genetic purity. Noah could no more be classified as morally perfect than could any other human being who ever lived. We all fall short of God's glory, Noah included, yet God called him *perfect* because neither his bloodline nor his spirit had been modified. In the first seven chapters of Genesis, we find eighteen instances of the phrase "according to their kind(s)." It never occurs again after Genesis 7. Moses was setting the context for the Flood by strongly emphasizing God's serious intention that animals remain within their distinct kinds. The Watchers transgressed and taught the mixing of kinds, which nature never intended. The results were disastrous, and God was forced to wipe out all tainted organisms.

You read that correctly: the Flood was God's way to cleanse the world of the abominations caused by a supernatural invasion. The Bible stresses that before the Flood, the world was full of violence and the minds of men were obsessed with evil, but why was that the case? Why did such extreme degradation take hold relatively soon after the fall from Paradise? According to Enoch, it was the result of outside influence. Not only did the Watchers lead mankind into error, teaching all manner of occult knowledge which leads to godlessness, but their gigantic offspring, the Nephiliym, became merciless dictators and cannibals who demonstrated no justice, no mercy, and no remorse. Enoch wrote that the Watchers' progeny "sinned against all flesh." In fact, the very fragmentary *Book of Giants* found alongside 1 Enoch at Qumran reveals that the giants were able to create hybrids of many different species of animals, resulting in monstrous combinations[a] that terrorized homo sapiens. Early man was completely overwhelmed by what fell upon him and cried to heaven for help, and YHVH responded by sending angels to wipe out the fallen Watchers and their offspring.

 I believe that it was Satan who tempted the Watchers to engage in procreation, and that he did so in a bid to prevent the birth of the Messiah. The promised Seed of the woman could not be delivered if every woman was infected with an angelic spirit. I believe that Satan also enticed the Watchers into sharing arcane knowledge with men as a way of making recompense for seizing their daughters. Men later used that knowledge for the miscegenation of taxonomic classes and orders; if the Book of Jasher is to be believed, men behaved well for a while after the destruction of the Watchers and Nephiliym, but rebelliousness gradually increased until there came a time when the unholy mixing of kinds was being practiced with complete cognizance of the fact that it would provoke YHVH. Had Satan succeeded in corrupting the genes of the entire human race through one means or another, he would have disqualified Eve's descendants from being eligible to deliver the promised Seed, and in so doing would have averted his own doom. Satan came frighteningly

---

[a] Could these hybrids have been the origin of some of the chimeras of ancient lore?

close to achieving victory, for only one family in the whole earth preserved the human pedigree. In a greater sense, however, Satan efforts
were futile from the start because he was never going to win—it only
looked like he might. YHVH let the clock run down to a mere second
before taking his winning shot.

You probably didn't cover all of that in your Sunday school classes.
Even grown-ups have a hard time coming to grips with such an account.
We hardly ever discuss the sins of the Nazis, and that was only a generation ago; yet their practices, which included eugenics and attempts to
genetically modify human beings, dragged the whole world into brutal
conflict for years. Think about how much more devastation might have
been wrought if the Nazis had been demigods with all the secrets of the
angels.

Those who reject the transgenic[a] interpretation of Genesis 6 likely
do so from a place of emotion, not reason; they just can't stomach the
idea of angelic hybrids. Their argument goes something like this: "We
find it incredibly weird to imagine that angels mated with women. It
just seems far-fetched and mythological, so we'll label it unbiblical hog-
wash." Here is such an argument passionately presented by Chrysostom
(AD 346-407):

> Here is, first, the most audacious idea, of which we are going to show
> you the absurdity, by presenting to your meditation the true meaning of
> Scripture…. It would be folly to accept such insane blasphemy, saying
> that an incorporeal and spiritual nature could have united itself to hu-
> man bodies![296]

That's not what most people would call a compelling argument. We
are expected to agree with Chrysostom that the transgenic interpretation is blasphemy simply because he said so. What if his ideas about the
nature of angels are unfounded? Many children grow up thinking that
babies are conceived through some form of spontaneous generation, and
it must seem very weird to those children when they discover that babies
are the result of sweaty coitus and an exchange of bodily fluids. We are
like children and truly know little about the universe at large; is it wise
to convince ourselves that we fully understand the ways of God's exalted
spiritual beings?

---

[a] That is, pertaining to the mixing of genes from different species.

After critics have summarily dismissed the idea of angel-human copulation on grounds of it being a bit kooky, they must then concoct an explanation for Gen. 6:1-4 that does not resort to anything supernatural.

Christian writer Julius Africanus (AD 200-245) was the first to offer an alternative reading of the fall of the sons of God in Genesis 6. He posited that the sons of God were sons of Seth and the daughters of men were the daughters of Cain.

Saint Augustine of Hippo (AD 354-430) later took up this thesis and expounded on it, and by reason of Augustine's popularity, the Sethite interpretation became the standard among Catholic theologians. Since Augustine's beliefs conflicted with the writings of Enoch, those writings were tragically laid to rest, where they remained for centuries. Yet God has resurrected the tome of 1 Enoch so that we may correct the error of our predecessors and be increased in our understanding of God's holy program.

We do not have the luxury of time to refute the Sethite thesis here, but be assured that it has been thoroughly deconstructed and debunked. For a fairly exhaustive treatment of the topic, refer to the introduction of the book *Giants: Son of the Gods* by Douglas Van Dorn. Chuck Missler's *Koinonia House* (khouse.org) has also made available good material addressing the Genesis 6 controversy.

Before we move on, let's meditate momentarily on the logical dissonance of a Bible-believing Jew or Christian choosing to hold the Sethite view. Dr. Michael Heiser, an evangelical Christian and Semitic languages expert, finds fault with reactionary criticism of the transgenic interpretation of Genesis 6 and says,

> Genesis 6:1-4 is one of those texts that, for many, is best left alone. Many contemporary evangelical Bible scholars have gone to great lengths to strip the "mythology" out of it (i.e., the supernatural elements) so as to make it more palatable. But one has to wonder how bending supernatural language to human reason is consistent with the testimony of affirming a supernatural worldview.[297]

Mr. Heiser is on target. Trusting in the Bible entails believing that all manner of supernatural events have taken place as God works out the redemptive plan. Let's not cherry-pick among the supernatural elements of the Word. If a donkey was given speech; if the sun was made to stand still in the sky; if Samson was empowered to kill hundreds in a single battle with a single jawbone; if walking-staves were turned into serpents; and if God's son was born of a virgin, then truly all kinds of miracles are possible. Put into that context, the transgenic interpretation of Genesis 6 really isn't a stretch.

Who Watches the Watchers?

If the sons of God spoken of in Genesis 6 are indeed angels, then there is some cause for concern. Could other angels make the same mistake and once again take on human form in order to mate with our women?

It must be emphasized that the fact that holy angels are sometimes allowed to take on flesh and bone does not imply that angels can become corporeal at any time they so desire. They may be normally confined to the spiritual realms except for special occasions when God grants them physical form. Many readers of Enoch have assumed that the Watchers first lusted, then descended to earth solely for the purpose of mating, but the text doesn't explicitly say that. It is equally likely that the Watchers were given permission to take on flesh to carry out an earthly ministry but became ensnared in lust during the course of their sojourn. That is the scenario presented by the Book of Jubilees, which states,

> For in his [Jared's] days the angels of the Lord descended on the earth, those who are named Watchers, that they should instruct the children of men, that they [men] should do judgment and uprightness on the earth. (4:15)

This would help explain why the two hundred Watchers assembled themselves on Mount Hermon instead of heaven when they wanted to take an oath. That angelic powwow is recorded in Enoch 7, where we read that Samyaza and the two hundred Watchers under his command came to an agreement to take wives for themselves and sire children by them.

> They then swore all together, and all bound themselves by mutual execrations.... Then they took women, each choosing for himself; whom they began to approach, and with whom they cohabited; teaching them sorcery, incantations, and the dividing of roots and trees. And the women conceiving brought forth giants, and they bore to them three races first, the great giants. The giants brought forth the Nephiliym, and the Nephil-

iym brought forth the Elioud. (vv. 7-10)

We can only imagine that Satan played the role of tempter in this scenario, subliminally causing the Watchers to notice the daughters of men
in a sexual way. Indeed, 1 Eno. 53:6 says that the Watchers had become
"ministers of Satan." They had evidently been on earth for hundreds of
years before imagining to sin, because Jared was born in 461 AM[a] but
Enoch did not deliver God's sentence of condemnation to the Watchers
until roughly 1,180 AM.[b]

Interestingly, this is only eight years before God made the declaration
that man's (remaining) time would be 120 years (Gen. 6:3). God dealt
with the fallen Watchers by imprisoning them and destroying their offspring, but the damage was already done: the wickedness of the Watchers had taken root like a cancer in the antediluvian world, and the earth
would have to be washed clean. Jubilees puts the date of the Flood at
1308 AM. The Samaritan Pentateuch puts it at 1307. Subtract 120 years
to discover that mankind's official eviction notice was given in approximately 1,187 AM (possibly seven years, or one Shemitah cycle, after the
sentence was levied against the Watchers).

Tit for Tat

The Book of Enoch is clear that the primary catalyst for the increase of wickedness on earth was the disclosure of occult knowledge to the children of Adam. As compensation for taking their
daughters, the Watchers taught men sorceries and sciences that
equipped fallen humanity with far too much power; man was
destroyed on account of the secrets of heaven. The worst crime
was committed by a Watcher named Aza'zel, for he revealed to

---

[a] Anno Mundi, or *Year of the World*. This calendar begins at Creation.

[b] I arrive at the date of 1,180 AM through clues found in Genesis, Enoch, and Jubilees.
Both Jubilees and the Samaritan Pentateuch version of Genesis agree that Enoch was
born in Jared's 62nd year (the Masoretic Text has 162 instead), which would be 522 AM
According to Genesis 5:23. Enoch was taken into heaven and seen no more during his
365th year. Jubilees offers the helpful piece of information that Enoch dwelt with the
Watchers in heaven (not all among that class of angels had descended to Earth) and
learned from them for six jubilee cycles, which is 294 years. Adding 294 to 365 to 533
gives us 1,180, give or take a year.

men the making of weapons of war and to women the crafting of mirrors and the techniques of beautification, including jewelry and makeup. As a result, "impiety increased; fornication multiplied; and they transgressed and corrupted all their ways" (8:2). In 1 Eno. 10:12, God ascribes to Aza'zel "the whole crime," meaning that Aza'zel was penalized to the maximum extent for his role in the degeneracy of the earth. The angel Raphael was instructed to bind Aza'zel and cover him in complete darkness under the desert, where he would remain until Judgment Day. Later in history, instructions were given through Moses to the high priest of Israel to put the sins of Israel upon the head of a scapegoat once a year, on the Day of Atonement. The goat was given the name Aza'zel and abandoned to the desert after being injured so that it could not return to the habitation of the people. The Bible does not explain why this strange practice was commanded, but the Book of Enoch does.

To make the antediluvian situation worse, the giant offspring of the Watchers seemed to have no moral compunctions at all. They began to eat men and then each other, even drinking the blood, and they sinned against all types of animals (1 Eno. 7:13-14). The Book of Jasher claims that men learned the secrets of miscegenation from the Watchers and began mixing animals of their own. We read,

> And [the Watchers] went to the daughters of men and took their women by force… and the sons of men in those days took from the cattle of the earth, the beasts of the field and the fowls of the air, and **taught the mixture of animals of one species with the other**, in order therewith to provoke YAHUAH (4:18).

As the situation devolved, the righteous remnant grew desperate and cried out to Heaven to intervene. The four high angels heard their pleas and brought suit against the Watchers. YHVH passed judgment against the reprobates and sent Enoch back to the earth to inform the Watchers that they would certainly pay for their crimes. They looked on, powerless, as the angel Gabriel turned their half-breed children against one another in a war of complete, mutual destruction. Then the Watchers were taken captive by the archangel, Michael, and bound beneath the earth—in Tartarus, a part of the Abyss—for seventy generations, until the Day of Judgment (10:15). Could the destroying angels seen by John the Revelator be Watchers who are being kept in chains of darkness because of their corruption? One of the angels, Abaddon, will emerge from the Abyss when it is opened. Several months later, a command is given to "Loose the four angels which are bound in the great river Euphrates," and they proceed forth to slay a third part of mankind. The reader will recall that the Sumerians believed that the entrance to the Abzu, or Abyss, was located in the city of Eridu, and Eridu sat at the mouth of the Euphrates river.

Some readers may have a lingering question at this point: If the children of the Watchers were utterly annihilated, as Enoch teaches, then why was the world genetically corrupted during the lifetime of Noah? Weren't all of the hybrids gone? Technically, no. The Nephiliym were destroyed, but the sons of men had used Watcher technology to create hybrids, and these were not slain by the holy angels. 1 Eno. 7:12 says that the giants devoured everything that men could grow and it was not enough to satisfy them, so they began to eat people. Perhaps men turned to genetic engineering as a way of producing more food for the giants, in the same way that biologists today have genetically manipulated cows and chickens to grow faster and bigger.

I can only imagine that, humans being what they are, somebody eventually got the bright idea to mix animals and humans in order to create an army capable of fighting the giants. Once the cat was out of the bag, transgenic enhancement might have found its way into the general populace in an arms race with upgraded men as the weapons. Those with the resources or knowledge to give themselves extreme enhancements could have become a privileged class that enslaved and abused their less capable neighbors, and so "the earth [was] filled with violence through them" (Gen. 6:13).

On that note, that the U.S. Defense Advanced Research Projects Agency (DARPA) is even now investigating the feasibility of creating super-soldiers by introducing animal DNA sequences into their genomes, and by adding a 47th chromosome to act as a "vector platform for inserting bio-alterations and wholesale genetic 'improvements' into our DNA."[298] If that doesn't frighten you, there's something wrong.

Starting from the time that God sent angels to remove the Watchers and their seed, mankind was given one hundred and twenty years[a] in which

---

[a] Many people have been led to believe that this decree caps man's lifespan at 120 years,

to repent or be destroyed by God (Jash. 5:8; cf. Jub. 5:8). In Genesis 6 we find the verdict rendered thus: "Then the LORD said, 'My Spirit will not contend with humans forever, for they are mortal [Hebrew: *b'shar*]; their days will be a hundred and twenty years'" (v. 3, NIV). The meaning of the word *b'shar* is dubious. It is usually translated "flesh" or "mortal" but can carry the connotation of corruption. A translation that takes into consideration the context of the story and the testimony of the extra-biblical books would give us: "His remaining years shall be one hundred twenty, for his flesh has become corrupted."

Had the people of Atlantis humbled themselves in repentance, the Flood would not have been poured out and all of history would be different. To be clear, though: true repentance would have meant putting a stop to the production of hybrids *and also* destroying all of the hybrids that had already been born, especially those having a human component. That may sound harsh, but if any hybrids had been allowed to live, they inevitably would have corrupted the whole human race—a little leaven leavens the whole loaf. That is why YHVH instructed the Israelites to utterly destroy from the Promised Land all of the Nephiliym and even their animals.

So why didn't the Atlanteans want to get rid of their hybridization program? Probably because of the benefits of gaining useful abilities and enhanced senses from animal DNA. Think of the possibilities! One could gain the ability to see in the dark like an owl, smell like a bloodhound, and hear like a rabbit. Men could gain the strength and sexual vigor of oxen while women could beautify themselves with bioluminescent patterns or plumage. Many diseases could be prevented by taking immunities from particular species. These are the kinds of offers which science will soon use to entice us and our children. Doubt it not!

Not only did men fail to rid the earth of hybrids, but they continued to practice genetic manipulation on themselves until there was only one family left on the entire earth that was both faithful to YHVH and fully homo sapien. Thus God was forced to eliminate all flesh outside of the Ark.

---

but that interpretation is only valid if you don't think that God really means what he says, because lifespans were counted in centuries for several generations after the Flood, and even since then a handful of people have lived beyond 120 years of age.

The High Technology of Atlantis

When discussing Osiris and his occult knowledge, we became familiar with the tradition that Atlantis was the great civilization of the antediluvian world. We now understand that it was the knowledge of the Watchers that enabled the creation of a such a civilization. Even though the Watchers were removed and bound in Tartarus, the occult knowledge they promulgated had set the sons of Adam on a quest for greater knowledge and more power over their environment (and their neighbors). Who can say just how far this quest took them before the Flood swept over?

Consider for a moment the implications of these two facts:

Earlier members of our species were more intelligent because they were subject to less cellular damage and fewer mutations. Adam and Even were created with perfect faculties, and their environment was pristine. They ate a plant-based diet, and their food was chock full of nutrients. The health of their descendants would have been immaculate for many generations.

Antediluvian lifespans were eight to twelve times what they are today. Progress in the modern world is impeded by the loss of great minds after only decades of work; it takes long years to develop new minds to a comparable level. Physical abilities may wane as one gets older, but knowledge and wisdom can increase dramatically, so we can hardly fathom what would have been accomplished by people with hundreds of years available to engage in observation, contemplation, and experimentation.

Even if men only had one hundred twenty years of relative peace in which to play with Watcher tech, that's more than enough time to reach amazing heights. Can you imagine if Da Vinci or Einstein or Tesla had lived an additional 100+ years? The great minds of Atlantis must have accomplished splendid and splendidly abominable things.

Today's increasingly globalized society is becoming much the same as Atlantis. Any time that inventors are presented with an opportunity to develop a device, pill, or technique that would have certain useful applications but would also come yoked with dire consequences to our health or way of life, scientists will eventually justify its existence and deliver it to society whether or not we are amicable to the idea. In the last two to three hundred years we've brought forth countless implements of war, weapons of mass destruction, pollution-belching factories, environment-killing plastic disposables, sweeping surveillance technologies, engineered bio-hazards, and genetically modified organisms—just to name a few of the more obvious reprobates—and we're currently not far from being able to craft true artificial intelligence. If humanists like Google's Director of Engineering, Ray Kurzweil, have their way (and they will because God is withdrawing his hand of protection), the next step for mankind is to imitate the Atlanteans and move full-tilt into the age of transhumanism.

Succinctly put, transhumanism is the drive to "evolve" mankind through genetic and/or cybernetic manipulation. This includes the mixing of different *kinds,* which YHVH is so vehemently against. This is not a science fiction author's pipe dream, but a real movement making use of technologies that already exist in the real world. Half-human, half-animal chimera embryos have already been created in laboratories in several countries. Now cloned cows with human immune systems are being produced in the United States for the purpose of infecting them with the Ebola virus and extracting antibodies from their blood.[299]

Dr. Tom Horn has done gobs of excellent research on the topic of transhumanism, and I refer you to him for more information. He often points out that Yeshua spoke pointedly about the character of the last days, saying, "As it was in the days of Noah, so it will be at the coming of the Son of Man" (Matt. 24:37, NIV). Civilization is becoming very advanced in both capability and rebellion: a deadly concoction. In fact, Yeshua said that if the last days were not "cut short, no human being would be saved" (Matt. 24:22). Mankind is progressing, all right—straight off of a cliff, patting ourselves on the back as we go. Thankfully, Yeshua has promised to save his obedient sheep from out of this cauldron of abominations.

Antediluvian OOPARTS (Out-of-Place Artifacts)

Some readers will be wondering if there is any evidence that an advanced civilization existed before the Flood, besides what we are told in ancient lore. The answer is yes, there is, but the scientific establishment in place today will never acknowledge as authentic any artifact which is deemed "out of place." To do so would require them to admit that their unbiblical model of world history is wrong, and that's unthinkable.

Presented below is a small sampling of out-of-place artifacts to whet your palate:

- A chunk of bituminous coal mined in Upshur County, West Virginia, contained a bell of brass-like appearance topped by a small sculpture of a winged man. The coal encasing this bell was supposed to be 300 million years old. The Institute for Creation Research had the bell analyzed at the University of Oklahoma, and the lab results showed the artifact to consist of an alloy unknown today (it included copper, zinc, tin, arsenic, iodine, and selenium). This artifact is not a unique case; over the last couple of centuries, numerous man-made metal objects have been found trapped in coal.[300]

- In 1877, precious metal prospectors searching the hills of Spring Valley near Eureka, Nevada, spotted a leg bone and knee cap protruding from solid rock. They dislodged the oddity with picks and placed it on public display in Eureka. The stone encasing the leg was a dark red quartzite dated to the Jurassic period, and the bones themselves were black with carbonization (indicative of great antiquity). Medical doctors who examined the remains concluded that they were of human origin and that the owner when alive had stood at over twelve feet tall.[301]

- Mr. Zhilin Wang discovered a screw-threaded metal bar inside a stone near the Marzong Mountain region of China. The small, pear-shaped stone is of an unknown type and is incredibly dense. About a dozen geologists and physicists gathered to study the mysterious object, but could only come to a consensus on the fact that the metal piece appeared to have been manufactured. The panel unanimously declared the stone to be one of the most valuable finds in the world for further study.[302]

We're lucky to find anything at all from before the Flood. While he was living on earth, Enoch had a dream-vision of the coming global cataclysm, and this was his description of the devastation he witnessed:

> I saw likewise the earth absorbed by a great abyss; and mountains suspended over mountains. Hills were sinking upon hills, lofty trees were sliding off from their trunks, and were in the act of being projected, and of sinking into the abyss. (82:5-6)

The geological upheaval was so extreme that most of the material covering the surface of the planet would have been buried under countless tons of rock and sediment. Add to that the fact that the number of people living at the time of the Flood was probably relatively small compared to today—for the giants had decimated the human population only one hundred twenty years beforehand—and we can be sure that the vast majority of antediluvian artifacts are lost forever.

The Origin of the Zodiac

Before moving on, we need to touch on the fact that the Watchers taught astronomy to mankind. The very name *Watcher* may have had as much to do with the observation of the dance of the celestial bodies as it had to do with the observation of life on earth, for during his time in heaven, Enoch saw angels both conducting and recording the celestial proceedings.

Enoch informs us that "Barkay'al [taught] the **observers of the stars**, Akibe'el **signs**; Tami'el taught **astronomy**" (8:5-7). These are the names of the Watchers who revealed to men the secrets of the firmament. This means that the Zodiac was already established and known to the holy angels before they fell. When God confronted Job about the man's limited understanding of divine ways and motives, he asked, "Canst thou bring forth Mazzaroth in his season? Or canst thou guide Arcturus with his sons?" (Job 38:32, KJV). *Mazzaroth* is Hebrew for *Zodiac* (or perhaps the constellations in general),[303] and Arcturus is the non-zodiacal constellation of Boötes. Only in the absence of Enoch's literary contribution could we argue that God was making reference to Gentile astronomical mnemonics in his monologue.

The constellations are not a human invention. That explains why, throughout history, maps of the Zodiac have been substantially the same whether they come from Africa, Europe, or the Americas. The earliest recorded star charts—those that come from Mesopotamia—use stations that clearly parallel the signs of the Zodiac as we know them today, with designations such as "The Crayfish" (Cancer), "The Bull of Heaven" (Taurus), and "The Seed-Furrow" (Virgo). The fifth tablet of the Babylonian and Akkadian creation story (the *Enuma Elish*) teaches that the great god arranged the stars into figures of animals: "twelve months of stars in three rows he arranged."[304] The rows just mentioned are the northern hemisphere, the southern hemisphere, and the equator. We know this because the Babylonian star catalog called *Three Stars Each* presents a tripartite division of the sky with boundaries at 17° North and South of the celestial equator.[305] The sun spends three months in each zone (from Earth's perspective) as it passes through the four quarters of the zodiac.

As for the eighty-eight non-zodiacal constellations, many of their identities vary wildly across cultures, and their number has increased over time, so it's clear that they can't all be trusted. The most ancient cultures had solar zodiacs of twelve major constellations with three sidereal side-pieces each; the thirty-six signs that accompany the Zodiac are sometimes called *decans*. Ptolemy recorded thirty-six decans in his *Almagest* ca. AD 150, and the same number of subordinate signs are found in an older account by the Greek astronomer Eudoxus of Cnidos ca. 350 BC.

The oldest extant star chart was drawn by the Chinese about a millennium prior to Eudoxus' work. Known as the Dunhuang star chart, it was found at the Buddhist Mogao cave complex in 1900, and careful analysis has revealed that the astronomical drawings on it are consistent with mathematically-correct projection methods still used today. Many of the 257 constellations on the Dunhuang scroll are unique to the Chinese, but some of the constellations, such as Orion, do match those of Near East star catalogs.[306] This goes to show that even in societies far removed from the Ubaidians, they retained a portion of the original designations.

The first chapter in the Bible tells us clearly that God put stars and planets in the sky to both mark the passage of time and display a message: "And God said, 'Let there be lights in the vault of the sky to separate the day from the night, and **let them serve as signs** to mark sacred times, and days and years'" (v. 14, NIV). The story being shown in the sky is the same as the story in our Bibles, only simplified.

Just as there are twelve hours in the day that begins the year (from Jerusalem), twelve gates in the walls of the heavenly Jerusalem, and twelve tribes of Israel, so there are twelve houses of the Zodiac. In fact, the arrangement of the tribes of Israel around the Tabernacle may have been a reflection of the layout of the Zodiac. Each sign of the Zodiac represents an archetype, and as the sun and planets move through these archetypes their positions construct a narrative.

One of the lessons we are to learn from the heavenly vision given to the prophet Ezekiel is that YHVH is Lord of the celestial signs. The four faces of the Cherubiym seen by both Ezekiel and John correspond to the middle signs of the four quarters of the Zodiac: the lion being Leo; the bull, Taurus; the man, Aquarius; and the eagle, Scorpius[a]. These four

---

[a] This sign was not originally a scorpion.

signs are exactly ninety degrees from one another, corresponding to the points of the compass; and is it coincidence that the Cherubiym only travel along the straight lines of the cardinal directions? The Cherubiym move about the throne room of God on wheel-like mounts (Ophaniym) whose rims are covered with eyes. We can equate those eyes to the many stars that make up the constellations on the rim of the zodiacal wheel.

The fact that the Zodiac was established by YHVH, not mankind, will be of great importance later in our study. It will be shown that there is perfect synchronization between major biblical events and what was happening in the sky at the time.

SIXTEEN

The Nephiliym and Rephaiym

> While we were in the sandhills, scouting the Niobrara country, the Pawnee Indians brought into camp some very large bones, one of which the surgeon of the expedition pronounced to be the thigh bone of a human being. The Indians said the bones were those of a race of people who long ago had lived in that country. They said these people were three times the size of a man of the present day, that they were so swift and strong that they could run by the side of a buffalo.[307]
>
> –WILLIAM "BUFFALO BILL" CODY (1846–1917)

> The eyes of that species of extinct giants, whose bones fill the mounds of America, have gazed on Niagara, as ours do now.[308]
>
> –PRESIDENT ABRAHAM LINCOLN (1809–65)

Recently, while browsing in an online book store, I downloaded a Nook sample of a Christian book very much like the one you are holding. It was *Doctrines of Devils and the Coming Delusion* by Charles T. Mesic. Four pages into the first chapter, my eyes widened and my muscles clenched. Mr. Mesic was describing an experience so similar to one of my own that I could hardly believe it. The hair stood up on the back of my neck as a feeling of déjà vu swept over me.

Mesic writes that he was newly married when God gave him his first vision. He and his wife had rented a studio apartment in Pearl Harbor, Hawaii, and while sleeping there on the first night, they were simultaneously awakened by terrible nightmares. It happened four nights in a row. Exhausted from sleeplessness, this brother asked God to reveal the source of the nightmares, and God did so by sending a vision while the he was traveling to work. The young husband saw he and his wife's new apartment as if standing at the doorway looking in at their makeshift bed in the corner. Towering over that bed was a fearful and immense creature. It looked like a man who was covered in soot so thoroughly that he reflected no light, and he was so tall that his head was bowed to fit in the room. His arms were extended downward at the pillows. Knowing then that he and his wife were experiencing demonic oppression, Charles Mesic went home, faced the bed, and said, "Devil, get out of my apartment in the name of Jesus!" The couple slept like babies after that.[309] There is power in the name of God's son.

My own experience with a demon differs only in particulars. I was engaged to my high school sweetheart at the time, but we were finishing our degrees at different universities hours apart. I was living alone in an apartment near campus until our wedding. One night at about 3:00 A.M., I awoke from a nightmare to find that I was being crushed. Directly over my body hovered a dark cloud, black like pitch, like the interior of a deep cavern. The feeling which emanated from this cloud was one of absolute evil. Sweat poured from me in a flood and I could hardly breathe; I thought my heart would stop from terror. I could not move anything but my mouth, but that was enough because I began to call on the name of Jesus. At first my voice was weak and choked, barely more than a whisper, and I have to admit that when I started praying it was with merely an iota of confidence. Yet all I could think to do was to call on the Lord for help—there was certainly no way I could fight the creature myself. So I quoted scripture at it, and the more I did so, the more my voice strengthened and the darkness diminished.

After a few minutes of petitioning heaven for help in the name of Jesus, the evil presence was gone.

The next day, while speaking to my fiancee on the phone, I began to tell her about the demonic assault. She stopped me part-way through the story to ask when exactly the incident had occurred.

"About three o'clock," I told her. "Why? Is that important?"

"That's the same time I woke up from a nightmare and felt an evil spirit," she responded flatly, almost as if she couldn't trust the words coming out of her own mouth. "I had to pray against it for several minutes before it went away."

I assure you that I am neither fabricating nor exaggerating this story. The forces of darkness are usually not so apparent, but they do present themselves from time to time. Since the encounter just described, I have had two other run-ins with demons; the latest occurred during the writing of this book and was merely a brush, as if the creature thought better of trying to attack me and instead went on its way. Yeshua gives us incredible power to engage in battle in the Spirit and overcome in his name foes which would otherwise be far too mighty for us.

What exactly were the terrifying beings that tried to oppress both myself and Charles Mesic? I assumed, as he did, that the entity in my bedroom that night was a devil, a fallen angel. It wasn't until years later that I learned otherwise. It wasn't an angel, but rather the offspring of an angel. It was one of the Nephiliym.

Men of Infamy

The word Nephiliym (pronounced *neh-fil-LEEM*) is found within the first verses of Genesis 6 during a discussion about the sons of God mating with the daughters of men. The narrative is concise, giving us little to go on, but it would seem that angels mated with women and produced halfbreeds who were extraordinary in more ways than one. As we learned in previous chapters, the Book of Enoch reveals that the offspring of the Watchers were gigantic individuals with a propensity towards extreme wickedness. Enoch separates the children of the Watchers into three races—the Nephiliym being one—but ostensibly because of the meaning of the word ("fallen ones" or "corrupted ones"), Moses chose to use *Nephiliym* as a label for all three categories of half-breeds.[a]

The Alexandrian Septuagint version of Genesis (LXX) renders Nephiliym as *gigantes*, meaning "giants," from the huge demigods of Greek mythology. These giants were of the same sort as the Anakiym, Rephaiym, and other over-sized inhabitants of Canaan encountered after the Flood, which may be why Moses wrote that the Nephiliym were in the earth "after that" (6:4). Alternatively, as per Rob Skiba's hypothesis, the *after that* could be in reference to hybrids created by Atlanteans before the Flood.

In describing the giants, Moses chose to use the term *gibboriym*. A *gibbor* is a mighty man, someone of legendary strength or ability. The giants of Canaan were called *gibboriym*, and the Spirit-empowered Israelite warriors who slew those giants were also described as *gibboriym*.

---

[a] In Norse mythology, the abode of the dead was inhabited by giants called *Niflheim*, which is surprisingly close to *Nephiliym*.

Guess who else was called a gibbor. The answer is *Nimrod*. Genesis states that he "began to be" a gibbor (10:8).

After their downfall, the Genesis 6 giants became demonic spirits that terrorized men both upon the earth and within Sheol. Earlier, we read in the Book of Jubilees about the problems that Noah's grandchildren were having with demonic forces, but now lets read in the Book of Enoch to discover where these demons originated.

> Now the giants, who have been born of spirit and of flesh, shall be called upon the earth **evil spirits, and on earth shall be their habitation**. Evil spirits shall proceed forth from their flesh, because they were created from above; from the holy Watchers was their beginning and primary foundation.... Upon earth shall be the habitation of terrestrial spirits, who are born on earth. The spirits of the giants are like Nephiliym[a], which shall oppress, corrupt, fall, contend, and bruise upon earth. They shall cause lamentation. No food shall they eat; and they shall be thirsty; **they shall be concealed**, and shall rise up against the sons of men, and against women; for they come forth during the days of slaughter and destruction. (15:8–10)

The evil spirits which proceeded forth from the flesh of the Nephiliym are now known as demons, fiends, ghouls, poltergeists, and the like. These spirits are distinct from fallen angels but are of the same nature because they were begotten by angels. Unlike the fallen angels, however, they are confined to the surface of the earth unless cast into the Abyss; whereas Satan and his friends move freely over the earth and through the waters of the deep.

Initially, all of the deceased Nephiliym roamed upon the surface of the earth as God had declared, but when Noah appealed to YHVH to remove them from the land of the living, ninety percent of the demons were imprisoned in the part of Sheol called the Pit (Jub. 10:9). The legion of spirits which Yeshua exorcised from a demoniac in Gadarenes begged Adonai not to send them into the Abyss (Luke 8:31), where most of their brethren are trapped. They reminded Yeshua that it was not yet their time to be sealed away. Legion wished to remain on the surface of the earth, where they could inhabit bodies and wreak havoc upon living souls, whose fates are still hanging in the balance.

---

[a] Or "lead astray"

Having never inhabited bodies of flesh, Satan's angels do not seem to yearn for a material residence like the antediluvian Nephiliym do. This is not to say that they cannot enter into an organism's heart if legally permitted to do so, for in the Gospels we see Satan enter into Judas on Preparation Day of Passover. But fallen angels like the one which restrained Gabriel from his mission seem content to remain princes of the air (Dan. 10:13). As any experienced deliverance minister will tell you, demons greatly desire to stay attached to a host, cause that host torment, and feed off his or her misery. In this sense Nephiliym spirits are much like any biological parasites.

The New Testament tells a few stories about men who were afflicted by such unclean spirits, and in each case the victim possessed superhuman strength. One was able to break out of every kind of chain, and another was able to thrash a group of seven normal men in hand-to-hand combat. Could this unusual strength be related to the fact that the unclean spirits at the helm were literally giants?

1 Enoch 15 describes the release of the Nephiliym at the end of the age, when "they come forth during the days of slaughter and destruction" (v. 10). The Book of 2 Baruch (absent from the Protestant canon) divides the Apocalypse into twelve parts, and God reveals to the prophet Baruch that "in the eighth part a multitude of spectres and attacks of the Shediym [demons]" will occur (27:9, CEPH). This begs the question, In what form will they come forth? Will the last days see a dramatic increase in the same forms demonic oppression that have always plagued the world? Or will they interact with the living in a new way?

Revelation 9 describes a judgment during which the Abyss is opened and frightening chimeric entities come forth like a swarm of locusts. Their exceedingly strange appearance suggests that they are spiritual, not physical. They do not damage vegetation like normal locusts; these nasty creatures go after unredeemed human beings instead. They are not allowed to kill their victims, only to inflict torment on them "like the torment of a scorpion when it stings someone" (v. 5). They have as king over them an angel of the Abyss, named Abaddon, or "Destroyer." Could this be a plague of Nephiliym led by the Watcher chief, Semyaza? Only those who have the seal of YHVH on their foreheads will be immune from this plague—yet another reason to fear God and accept the free gift of mercy made available to us by the loving sacrifice of Yeshua.

The Evidence for Giants

Many ancient cultures had legends of giants, but modern academics treat these stories as flights of fancy—and that's understandable, considering their disbelief of scriptural accounts and the lack of giants roaming our streets. But what if the bones and tools of gargantuan people had been uncovered on multiple occasions but never treated seriously in academia? Then we would have even less reason to heed the diploma-waving skeptics trying to convince us that giants only exist in fairy tales. The fact is, such bones and tools have turned up on multiple continents.

Although the testimony of Scripture is all the evidence that the faithful should require in order to believe in giants, it helps to have extra-biblical sources with which to debate skeptics. Fortunately, a good deal of archaeological and historical evidence of giants does exist. Were it possible to provide all of that evidence in these pages, I would be happy to do so, but space limits us to only a brief discussion. Beyond that the reader must conduct his or her own research. Steve Quayle's *Genesis 6 Giants* is a good place to begin (not all of Mr. Quayle's research pans out, so be discerning in your studies).

I contend that more than once, the bones of giant humans have been falsely classified as large, extinct primates. For example, in 1939, when Dutch paleontologist Ralph von Koenigswald found a humanoid molar of several times the volume of a normal human molar, he designated the owner *Gigantopithicus*, meaning "giant ape." This ape was estimated to have stood thirteen feet tall. Von Koenigwald's search for more giant remains bore fruit in 1941, when he unearthed in Sangiran, Java, a massive partial mandible containing three teeth. They were smaller than the teeth of the Gigantopithicus but shaped more like a typical human's. Von Koenigswald dubbed his new find *Meganthropus paleojavenicus*, and so far the scientific community has been unable to reach a consensus on the taxonomic and phylogenetic status of the creature.[310] Some Meganthropus fossils have since been found alongside primitive tools.

Tools and weapons too large to have been wielded by mere humans have turned up in many other regions. In the 1990s, four giant stone hand-axes were recovered from among thousands of normal-sized stone tools in a dried-up lake bed in the Kalahari Desert.[311] A museum in Crete showcases double-headed axes taller than a human. They were thought to have been used to sacrifice bulls, but who would have wielded such a tool? Just last year, researcher Bruce Fenton discovered irregularly shaped, large stone blocks and giant stone hammerheads in a remote part of the Ecuadorian jungle, where locals still tell legends of a lost city of giants.[312]

Actual skeletal remains are hard to come by because they rarely survive the elements, and so far no bones from an individual of King Og's stature have been presented to the modern public, but that doesn't mean that there aren't some strangely large humanoid bones to be seen. For instance, the femur of a 12' tall individual is held in the vaults of the medical school at WITS University, Johannesburg. Michael Tellinger recorded a video of this femur being displayed beside an average human leg bone, and he has posted that video on YouTube.[313] Unfortunately, because artifacts like the aforementioned bone exist in isolation, they are considered anomalies, and their greatness is chalked up to pathological causes. Modern archaeologists need to find a single site containing multiple large skeletons; only then they will be forced to reconsider their stance. Until then, those of us who trust the biblical record must rely on legends and secondary evidence.

One such piece of evidence comes from 16th-century Italy. A man named Bartolomeo Bon (a.k.a. Giovanni Bona and Bartlmä Bon), who served Archduke Ferdinand at Ambras Palace, near Innsbruck, was nearly eight feet tall. His jousting armor, pictured here, is in the possession of the palace.[314] There is also a painting of Bartolomeo standing beside a midget whose full stature reaches only the top of the giant's shin.

Figure 16-1. Armors collected by Archduke Ferdinand II. They are kept in Schloss Ambras, Innsbruck, Austria. The largest set was worn by Bartlmä Bon during a tournament in Vienna in 1560.

An even larger court giant served in Hanover, England. Christopher Munster (died 1676) was a yeoman of the guard at the court of Duke John Frederic. He stood four ells, six inches tall, which, depending on the type of ell, would equate to between 8½ and 9½ feet.[315] If men of such size still existed late in history, we can imagine that the thoroughbred giants of biblical times were even more stout.

North America was no stranger to giants, either. In fact, the relatively undeveloped land here has yielded quite a few giant finds in contrast to the continuously-inhabited terrain of Europe and the Near East. A few determined researchers have found hundreds of articles printed during the course of American history that contain reports of the unearthing of giant skeletons. Many of them are likely mistakes or tall tales—yester-year's version of modern supermarket tabloids—but a portion of them are very detailed, sober-minded studies printed in trustworthy journals. For instance, Scientific American gave this report in its August 1880 issue:

> The Rev. Stephen Bowers notes, in the *Kansas City Review of Science*, the opening of an interesting mound in Brush Creek Township, Ohio. The mound was opened by the Historical Society of the township, under the immediate supervision of Dr. J. F. Everhart, of Zanesville.... There was found in it a sort of clay coffin including the skeleton of a woman mea-suring eight feet in length. Within this coffin was found also the skeleton of a child about three and a half feet in length, and an image that crum-bled when exposed to the atmosphere. In another grave was found the skeleton of a man and woman, the former measuring nine and the latter eight feet in length. In a third grave occurred two other skeletons, male and female, measuring respectively nine feet four inches and eight feet. Seven other skeletons were found in the mound, the smallest of which measured eight feet, while **others reached the enormous length of ten feet**.... Resting against one of the coffins was an engraved stone tablet (now in Cincinnati), from the characters on which Dr. Everhart and Mr. Bowers are led to conclude that this giant race were sun worshipers.[316]

Some such articles reference the folk tales of various Native Ameri-can tribes whose members believe that a race of white-skinned, red- and blonde-haired giants warred with their ancestors. (Of note: some of the pre-Incan, elongated skulls found in Peru still have patches of red hair[a] attached.) Native Americans remember the giants not only for their un-usual size and hair color, but because they often sported six fingers and six toes. Rock art of six-fingered hands has been found in Three Rivers, New Mexico, and a smattering of other sites throughout the American Southwest.[317] When the legends of giants with extra digits originated,

---

[a] In India, the Hindus have tales of the *bakasura*, evil red-haired giants who sought to replicate the fire altar of heaven and ascend to the sky. (William Joseph Wilkins, *Hindu Mythology, Vedic and Purānic* (London: Thacker & Co., 1882), 364).

American natives did not have Bibles, yet their testimony matches that of the Bible, which says, "In still another battle, which took place at Gath, there was a huge man with six fingers on each hand and six toes on each foot—twenty-four in all. He also was descended from Rapha" (2 Sam. 21:20, NIV).

In general, the gibboriym who lived in North America were not as tall as those who lived in the East, probably because they were several generations removed from men like Goliath. An inferior diet may have also played part in their diminution. These giants could have migrated to the Americas from Europe, where some of them had fled to escape genocide at the hands of the supernaturally-empowered Israelites. We were taught that Christopher Columbus discovered America in 1492, but the truth is that Europeans made it there long before the Spaniards ever planted foot. A Scandinavian king named Woden-lithi made it to North America during the Bronze Age and left texts in the rocks at Peterborough, Ontario, written with Teutonic and Norse alphabets.[318] The Los Lunas Decalogue Stone on Hidden Mountain near Los Lunas, New Mexico, also betrays the pre-Columbian presence of Old World travelers. The boulder sports an inscription of the Ten Commandments in Paleo-Hebrew with some Archaic Greek and Iberic thrown in. Nearby, on the east-facing rim of the mountain's summit, is a partial star map memorializing a solar eclipse that occurred on September 15, 107 BC.[319] Statues and carvings of bearded men have been found at numerous sites throughout North America and Meso-america;[320] yet Native Americans have no beards.

Our ancient ancestors were not as helpless and isolated as we make them out to be. If normal men were making the trip across the Atlantic in ancient history, then giant men could have done the same.

The well-known Smithsonian Institute has kept a small number of records of unusually large human skeletal remains. For instance, the *Twelfth Annual*

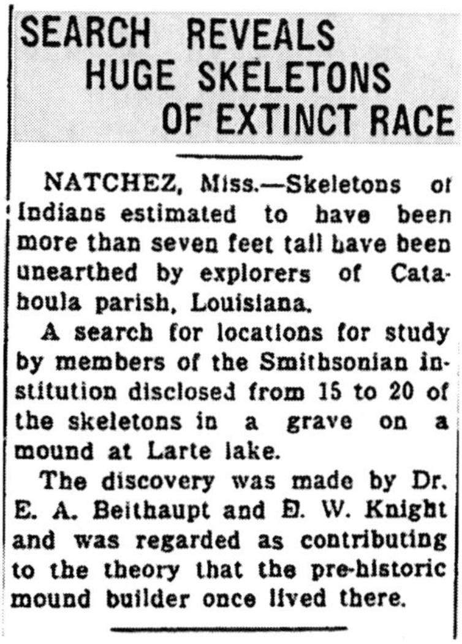

SEARCH REVEALS HUGE SKELETONS OF EXTINCT RACE

NATCHEZ, Miss.—Skeletons of Indians estimated to have been more than seven feet tall have been unearthed by explorers of Cata-houla parish, Louisiana.

A search for locations for study by members of the Smithsonian institution disclosed from 15 to 20 of the skeletons in a grave on a mound at Larte lake.

The discovery was made by Dr. E. A. Beithaupt and B. W. Knight and was regarded as contributing to the theory that the pre-historic mound builder once lived there.

Figure 16-2. Despite reports such as this one from the June 28, 1933 edition of the Sarasota Herald-Tribune, the Smithsonian claims that it does not possess any unusually large human remains.

Report from the Bureau of Ethnology to the Secretary of the Smithsonian, published in 1894, speaks of the discovery in West Virginia's Kanawha Valley of a cluster of intact skeletons measuring seven to eight feet in length (the report can be found online at Archive.org). The frustrating reality of these cases is that the bones are either unaccounted for or were soft and disintegrated upon removal from the burial mound, leaving us devoid of physical evidence. But the documentation is there.

In my personal opinion, the strongest evidence for giants is this: the fact that there is widespread agreement across ancient accounts from all over the world. That speaks for itself. We're not talking about a handful of isolated instances of stories about behemoths, but dozens upon dozens of similar tales from every region of the world, even in places where there has been no outside contact for long ages. Nearly every culture seems to have maintained the memory of giants on the young earth, and many of these cultures also tell stories of a global flood. The ravages of nature may have destroyed most of the skeletal remains of the giants, but memory-fossils from around the world tell us everything that we need to know.

The Two Adams and Multiple-Incursion Theory

Whenever the topic of giants is raised among Bible-believing folk, a very reasonable question will inevitably rear its ugly head and incite a storm of conjecture and confusion: Did another group of angels take on flesh and mate with humans after the Flood? It seems absurd for God to wipe out all life upon the earth but then fail to restrict angels from reinfecting the planet with abominations. And if, as some researchers suggest, devils were responsible for the postdiluvian Nephiliym, then what prevented Satan's angels from producing half-breeds with unrelenting fervor until all flesh on earth was corrupted? Multiple-incursion theory simply doesn't harmonize with our present hybrid-free situation. Yet there were clearly giants living after the Flood, so where did they come from?

Concerning the ability of angels to materialize in human form, the most sensible scenario is the one presented by the Book of Jubilees, which says that the Watchers were given special permission to take on flesh and live among humans for a time. That is to say that holy angels cannot become materially human willy-nilly, and fallen angels are never free to do so. In this scenario, there is no possibility of devils going hog-wild on our daughters.

In order to understand how the antediluvian giants could have sprung up again after the Flood, we must first understand the Bible's perspective on reproduction. Specifically, we need to grasp the fact that each human father passes on his spirit in addition to his genes. A human mother contributes only genetic material (and, of course, all the love and wisdom that is imparted as she raises her child, but that isn't relevant to our discussion).

Nowhere does the Scripture indicate that God gives each person a spirit and soul at the time of his or her conception, and this odd omission is not an oversight. The spirit that God breathed into Adam after he formed the man from the dust of the earth was multiplied into Eve and into all of their descendants. YHVH did not breathe life into Eve or create her body from the dust; rather, part of Adam's flesh was split off and grown into a new body, and part of the *breath of life* (Hebrew: *ruach*) within Adam was likewise duplicated, so that one organism became two. A soul is generated at the union of flesh with a certain kind of spirit: "And the Lord God formed man of the dust of the ground, and breathed into his nostrils the breath of life; **and man became a living soul**" (Gen. 2:7, KJV).

A similar process is occurring every time that a baby is conceived. However, instead of a part of the father's biology being used by itself to grow a new organism, cells from both parents are used. This is because a man and woman become "one flesh" when they are sexually united (Gen. 2:24). But YHVH never said that they become one spirit. Only one of the parents is allowed to contribute their spirit, and that function goes to the male, who was the original recipient of God's spirit. This is precisely why the Bible never states that a woman begot a child; only men are said to beget children.

The idea that the spirit is multiplied from the father alone is proven out in the writings of the apostle Paul, who tackles the theology of spiritual death and the *second Adam*. Everyone who has every lived, says Paul, inherited an inert spirit, or what is commonly called a *sinful nature*, from Adam. Paul writes that "sin came into the world through one man, and death through sin, and so death spread to all men because all sinned," and he continues on to say that just as the trespass of one man led to condemnation for all, so the righteousness of one man makes available justification for all (Rom. 5:12–19). A goodly portion of the Book of

Romans is based on the understanding that in all of history there have only been two biological sons of God: Adam and Yeshua. Those two men were hand-crafted by YHVH, while every other human being is multiplied from Adam. Yeshua was a son of God, and Adam was a son of God, but all others are sons of Adam unless they partake of the Messiah's life and become co-heirs with him.

Figure 16-3. The Doctrine of Paternal Spiritual Lineage states that children receive their spirits exclusively from their respective fathers.

Those who are in Christ become sons of God because they have received a living spirit from God (Gal. 3:26; cf. Luke 20:35–36). Thus Paul can write, "The first man Adam was made a living soul; the **last Adam was made a quickening spirit**" (1 Cor. 15:45, KJV). When Adam sinned in the Garden, his body began the process of dying, but his spirit immediately died. To be dead does not mean that one ceases to exist but that one is no longer connected to the source of life, who is YHVH—and if we are not at one with God, then we divided against him. Once Adam's spirit was dead, his offspring could only inherit a dead spirit from him, and so it is that every descendant of Adam needs to be quickened, or revived, spiritually before he or she can become part of God's family and receive an inheritance of eternal life. No one is born with sin already marring his or her soul, but because our spirits are disconnected from God, we are inherently selfish and inclined to sin. In our spiritual weakness we all inevitably sin, and we do it repeatedly. Through the disobedience of Adam we are effectively imprisoned in sin, and God allowed this so that he may have mercy on all who repent, to the everlasting glory of his name (Rom. 11:32).

We know that Yeshua did not sin; he could have sinned but chose otherwise, for he was not a slave to sin but a servant to God. Yet it is written that all men are slaves to sin (Rom. 6:16–22) and that "all have sinned and fall short of the glory of God" (Rom. 3:23). How then did Yeshua, being a man, avoid sin? The answer is that his spirit was not the dead spirit of Adam but the living spirit of YHVH. The second Adam was human on account of the genetic code contributed by his mother, Mary, but he had no biological father to pass down the spirit of the first Adam. Instead, Matthew writes that Mary "was found to be with child from the Holy Spirit," and it was that pure spirit of God which was multiplied into Yeshua. If it was the case that Mary contributed part of her spirit to her children, then Yeshua would have been shaped—as the psalmist said of himself—"in iniquity" (51:5); but this was not the case.

The concept of *father as spirit-giver* explains why the Nephiliym became demons after their physical deaths, instead of proceeding to rest in Sheol like normal human beings. Upon the death of the owner, a human spirit is reabsorbed into the boundless energy of God (Eccl. 12:7), whereas the spirit of a Watcher remains eternally distinct from God's spirit even though its origin is from God. It is written that if God decided to "gather to himself his spirit and his breath, all flesh would perish together" (Job 34:14-15); but those beings which were not created in bodies of flesh would not perish because their spirits cannot be revoked. The Nephiliym were born of human mothers and did not receive the spirit of Adam from them, but they instead received eternal, corrupted, angelic spirits from their fathers. I believe this means that the giants were unredeemable; in order for redemption to occur, a holy spirit must be substituted for an unholy one, initiating the godly transformation of the host soul; but the eternal spirits of the Nephiliym could not be dissolved and replaced like those of material beings.

This Doctrine of Paternal Spiritual Lineage adds another dimension to YHVH's promise to Adam and Eve that the Seed of the woman would redeem mankind. This focus on the maternal component of our ancestry is alien to the rest of Scripture, where we consistently find the patriarchy in view. When he finally arrived, the promised Seed repeatedly called himself "Son of Adam," not "Son of Eve." If Yeshua's focus was on his biological descent from Adam, why did YHVH put emphasis on the Seed of the woman? More to the point, why couldn't God have inserted his spirit into an egg that had been fertilized by male sperm? If, as many believe, God imbues each zygote with a spirit at the time of conception, and only biological material is contributed by the parents, then there should be nothing preventing God from putting the Holy Spirit into any given zygote. Then the Messiah could have been the offspring of both the man and the woman. Doesn't that seem more fair? But that's not what happened, and it couldn't happen that way because there exists an immutable law whereby the spirit of the father is always passed to his child. The reproductive contribution of the man had to be subtracted before a divine spirit could be introduced.

As we meditate on the Doctrine of Paternal Spiritual Lineage, we will realize that the DNA of the Watchers could have existed within human beings who were spiritually normal. If even one of the people on the Ark carried Watcher genetic material, then the trait of gigantism could have found expression in some of Noah's grandchildren, but those oversized kids would have had fully human spirits that were passed to them from Noah. No one imagines that YHVH would have allowed a Nephiliym on board the Ark, but who's to say that he didn't allow some of their genes aboard? It was the angelic spirits, not the DNA, that was the real problem. After all, the Watchers were not a different kind of creature from the women that they married; the Watchers became genuinely human, biologically speaking (though some of their genetic code was evidently unusual).

Ham's wife is the culprit who preserved the Watchers' genes, which we know because Ham was the father of Canaan, and several tribes of giants descended from Canaan, but none are said to have come from the children of Shem and Japheth. Cush, father of Nimrod, was also a son of Ham, and while there is no indication that he was a giant, Nimrod certainly possessed the trait. The Aramaic version of Genesis 10 states that Nimrod "began to be a giant of the earth" and that he was "a lion-hearted giant before the Lord" (vv. 8–9); meanwhile, the Septuagint version says, "And Chus begot Nebrod: he began to be a giant upon the earth. He was a giant hunter before the Lord God." In the commonly-used Masoretic version, the word *gibbor* is translated as "mighty" instead of "giant," but it is the very same word used to speak of the Nephiliym in Genesis 6.

By the way, it is unlikely that Nimrod was as great in size as the largest of the antediluvian giants, which the Book of Enoch compares to elephants. As far as we know, Semiramis was a normal-sized woman, so Nimrod couldn't have been too terribly big or else there would have been a physical incompatibility. In the Babylonian legend of Gilgamesh, the hero is said to be a giant but is still able to copulate with any of his female subjects.

Now we know how Nephiliym genes survived the Flood, and we are free to discard the unsupportable theory of multiple incursions. Next, we will find out how the Rephaiym fit into the picture.

Shades and Necromancers

The Rephaiym are a confusing lot, and it isn't obvious from a cursory reading of Scripture how they relate to the Nephiliym. This is due to the fact that *Rephaiym* pulls double-duty, describing two groups: a race of giants living in ancient Canaan, and the dead inhabitants of the netherworld.

The first mention of Rephaiym occurs in Gen. 14:5, when a military coalition led by Kedorlaomer campaigns against the clans of giants in the Levant. When the Israelites later migrate to that area, they were frightened of the Nephiliym living there (Num. 13:33), which included the Rephaiym. Not all of the giants were Rephaiym, but the Rephaiym were Nephiliym (biologically speaking). So what distinguished these people from the other giants?

In the poetic scriptures such as Job, Psalms, Proverbs, and Isaiah, the Rephaiym are always found in Sheol and are treated as being the souls of the deceased. In the context of Isaiah 14, they are the souls of the ungodly who will be roused to meet the slain king of Babylon at his arrival, and to say to him, "You also have become weak, as we are; you have become like us" (v. 10). However, the souls of the departed were also associated with healing. Philip Johnston explains in *Shades of Sheol: Death and Afterlife in the Old Testament* that linguists used to interpret the root word, *rapha*, as "weak," but careful study of linguistically similar Ugaritic texts has led most scholars to prefer the meaning "to heal." Johnston writes, "Thus the dead were thought to be healers or providers of fertility and life, a view possibly reflected in the occasional LXX translation of rᵉphaʾîm as 'healers.'"[321] And yet because they are in Sheol, they are weak and powerless. This is an interesting dichotomy to a modern man, but an ancient Semite would have understood it perfectly well because they would have been familiar with the relatively common practice of necromancy. In biblical times, arcane masters frequently besought gods and departed souls to bestow healing upon the living.

We know from God's warning to the Israelites in Deut. 18:9–11 that some of the inhabitants of Canaan practiced necromancy. In that verse and others like it, the existence of occult specialists such as necromancers and mediums is taken for granted, and the Israelites are told in no uncertain terms that summoning the dead is a criminal act punishable by death. The souls of the dead are to remain separate and hidden.

Aside from *rephaiym*, the Bible uses a second term for dead souls: *ʾôb*. These are described as ghosts or shades in the sixteen times that they appear in the Old Testament, and in all but one instance the term *ʾôb* is used in the context of necromancy. The word *ʾôb* has a cognate in Sumerian, where its earliest meaning was that of a pit holding souls which could be drawn up. YHVH prohibited the use of ghosts not because it was an ineffective practice, but precisely because it was effectual! King Saul knew this and had the witch of Endor call up the spirit of the prophet Samuel from Sheol to seek his counsel (an awful idea which sealed Saul's tragic fate). The allure of necromancy was that it worked, and the masters of the dead could compel ghosts to provide special information or to fulfill tasks of restoration which were beyond the skills of the living. Somehow—don't ask me how—the dead could manipulate biological functions when summoned from Sheol. The giant Rephaiym were were so adept at summoning healing spirits that they became known primarily for their necromantic practices.

Healing by necromancy has never ceased, it has only become more rare. There are still some today who practice this art, as author Michael Harner discovered when visiting Hawaii in the late 1990s. Harner was suffering from macular degeneration, and someone suggested that he visit an elderly shaman-priest in Kona to ask for help. The shaman, who was reputedly one of the last authentic kahunas left on the Islands, agreed to assist Harner, who describes his treatment thus:

> For five mornings and evenings, as I lay silently on my back, he prayed over me in front on an altar of leaf- and flower-bedecked wooden images of traditional Hawaiian gods. I experienced nothing eventful until the fifth and last evening, when I felt the spirit of a deceased person entering my consciousness... Indeed, several months later when I asked my eye doctors to recheck my ocular condition, they could find no evidence of any macular degeneration whatsoever. Such a reversal, they said, was impossible, and the only explanation was that my previous diagnoses were wrong (although the diagnoses had been made repeatedly for almost a decade!)[322]

If this account is to be believed, a *rapha* can still be used to mend infirmities. Of course, in order to be healed, Mr. Harner participated in idolatry and witchcraft, and he will have to pay the penalty for that unless he repents of it. Let no disciple of the Messiah be tempted to copy such behaviors. If we need healing, we can receive it from YHVH (if we are obedient and have faith).

> Is anyone among you sick? Let him call for the elders of the church, and let them pray over him, anointing him with oil in the name of the Lord. And the prayer of faith will save the one who is sick, and the Lord will raise him up. (Jms. 5:14–15)

Gargantuan Grapes and Strange Skulls

Numbers 13:23 is one of those portions of the Bible that makes most of us wrinkle our brows, scratch our heads, and shrug our shoulders before filing it away in the unsolved mysteries drawer of our mental cabinets. The verse falls within the story of the twelve Israelites spies who explored the land of Canaan for forty days. While they were in an area that was populated by the Anakiym, who were giants, the spies cut off a branch bearing a single cluster of grapes, and the cluster was so heavy that two men had to carry it on a pole between them. These were strapping warriors in peak physical condition, mind you. Even the largest clusters of grapes in today's world would hardly be a challenge for a soldier to carry by himself. The grapes, pomegranates, and figs which the spies brought back to the tribes were unlike any of the fruits that they had seen in Egypt, and Egypt was a land of plenty. By what means did the fruits of Canaan, like its inhabitants, become so large?

The Genesis 10 account of Nimrod gives us a tantalizing clue towards a possible answer. Verse 8 tells us that Nimrod "began to be a mighty one (Hebrew: gibbor) in the earth," and the Hebrew word translated here as "began" is the word *chalal* (Strong's #2490). This verb is used throughout the Bible in two seemingly different ways, but there may be a connection. The most common usage of the verb *chalal* carries the meaning "to pollute" or "to profane," and the less common usage carries the meaning "to begin." Under the entry for "To Pollute," *Vine's Complete Expository Dictionary* states that "the word is often used to describe the defilement which results from illicit sexual acts," but it is not confined to sexual deviance, and can describe any kind of befoulment." *Vine's* then suggests that the most important use of *chalal* when it means "to begin" is found in Gen. 4:26, where it is said that "men began to call on the name of the LORD" (NKJV). This is generally taken to mean that Seth's children were the first to petition YHVH and magnify his name. However, the text does not specify that it was Seth's offspring using the name; Cain also had offspring on the earth, and they probably greatly outnumbered Seth's at that time. The glaring problem with the traditional interpretation is that Adam and his family already had a relationship with YHVH. Could Cain and Abel have built an altar and sacrificed to YHVH without worshiping him? Aren't the two synonymous? Cain even had a two-way conversation with the Creator. And are we to think that Adam and Eve did not frequently petition the Lord after their fall? Wouldn't they have been crying out in desperation? Given the above, the alternative interpretation of Gen. 4:26 understands *chalal* to signify defilement, making the translation of the verse something like "men began to profane the name of YHVH."

If *chalal* can in some instances connote the initiation of a morally detestable action—a combination of "to begin" and "to pollute"—then Nimrod's transformation into a giant could have been the result of some kind of ritual genetic desecration. Perhaps he was not a giant, but some of his brothers and cousins were, and he became envious; therefore he set about activating the genes for gigantism by using some arcane technique revealed on the Tablet of Destinies.

The Gospels make it very clear that many diseases and infirmities can be activated by unclean spirits, and this may fit with the modern medical understanding that genes are not the only determining factor in genetic diseases. Take rheumatoid arthritis, for example. According to Dr. Timothy Spector of King's College London, "Though identical twins have identical DNA, they do not always get the same diseases. With rheumatoid arthritis, he added, if one twin gets the disease, there is only a 12 percent chance that the other will, too."[323] People who have gene variations associated with arthritis risk do not always possess the chemical tags that would cause the disease to activate. Genes remain stable, but chemical tags called *methyl groups* can attach themselves to genes and turn them on or off.[321] If unclean spirits can cause harmful medical effects, then it is conceivable that they can trigger some beneficial medical changes by attaching methyl groups at particular sites. We should consider the possibility that this is what the Rephaiym were getting the dead to do for them. And since the language used of Nimrod in Gen. 10:8 seems to suggest that he *became* a giant rather than started that way, we should not rule out the possibility that he got someone from the other world to transform him into a *gibbor.*

If unclean spirits and summoned souls can make cellular changes in humans, it should technically be possible to do the same in vegetation. The Nephiliym may have used sorcery or necromancy to increase the size of their crops to be in proportion to their enormous appetites.

Evidence of the bioengineering of crops comes to us in the form of corn. Yes, that's right: maize, the most popular crop in the western hemisphere. We take for granted this staple of our diet, but the fact is that corn's existence is an enigma. It is a scientifically established fact that corn is a cultigen (engineered), and the features that have been artificially selected in corn—although beneficial for harvesting and consumption—leave the plant unable to reproduce on its own. (The same can be said for bananas, which are seedless hybrids.) Because they are sterile, these crops would become extinct if farmers altogether stopped sowing them.

In an article titled "Maize: Food From the Gods?", Philip Coppens points out that the Mexican National Museum of Culture claimed in a 1982 exhibition that maize was not domesticated, but created. Aboriginal Americans considered it to be a gift handed to them by the gods. He goes on to write that

> no wild ancestor of maize has ever been found, despite decades of research. Maize's closest relative is a mountain grass called teo-

sinte, which looks nothing like maize. It is neither a practical food source. Most grasses develop grain near the top of the stem, which, when mature, will let the seed "shatter", and the grains will fall to the ground, from which new grasses will grow. It guarantees the survival of the species, but is ill-suited for human agriculture. In wild wheat and barley, a single-gene mutation has blocked such shattering, which meant that these cereals became more easily harvestable for humans. Teosinte shatters too and there is no known non-shattering variant. Furthermore, at least sixteen genes control teosinte and maize shattering, resulting in a complex problem for those trying to figure out how a non-shattering variation of maize might have occurred naturally – by accident – or how our distant ancestors figured out how to create such a feat; scientists continue to have no idea.

Pennsylvania geneticist Nina V. Federoff states that "to get corn out of teosinte is so—you couldn't get a grant to do that now, because it would sound so crazy. Somebody who did that today would get a Nobel Prize! If their lab didn't get shut down by Greenpeace." Indeed, maize is, in origin, genetically modified food, which is at the centre of much controversy today. Still, our ancestors seem to not only have had no such social opposition, but more importantly, were able to pull this stunt off.[325]

And, we might add, to create gigantic grapes and pomegranates.

Our theory about genetic manipulation being practiced by arcane masters in the ancient world is, of course, conjecture, and not something that we should build doctrine upon. But if true, it may explain the elongated Paracas skulls[a], which display only one parietal plate instead of the normal two; or the enigmatic Starchild Skull of Mexico,[326] which presents scientists with such an unusual genetic and physical profile that it may have to be classified as a new species. We will know more once thorough genetic testing is done on these remains.

---

[a] The shape and cranial volume of these skulls indicates that they were not manually deformed into cone shapes, as are the skulls of children subjected to head-binding. The practice of head-binding may have been developed in order to mimic the natural head shape of a special and revered type of person whose brain capacity was above average due to genetic engineering.

SEVENTEEN

Babel and Trans-dimensional Gateways

The Mystery Schools were the sacred colleges, and the first graduates of those secret institutions were the adept-builders. These initiate-builders were skilled in the arts and sciences required to transform the dream of universal brotherhood into the temporal fact of the divine commonwealth.[327]
–MANLY P. HALL

As above, so below.
–ATTRIBUTED TO HERMES-TRISMEGISTUS

Buried beneath the idyllic landscape near Geneva, Switzerland, lies the longest machine ever built: the Large Hadron Collider (LHC), built by an organization named CERN. The device is a particle accelerator in the form of a circular tunnel some seventeen miles in circumference, and its purpose is to advance our understanding of physics by colliding particles at extremely high speeds and then using specialized sensors to observe the behavior of the resulting subatomic debris. It sounds harmless enough, but that's before one understands that the experiments conducted at the LHC have to potential to result in undesirable, destructive theoretical anomalies. The chances of such anomalies forming and becoming problematic are quite low but cannot be entirely discounted. After all, the LHC is essentially recreating the Big Bang on a small scale.

Figure 17-1. An interior view of the Large Hadron Collider under Geneva, Switzerland. (Photo credit: Unknown).

More unnerving is the stated goal of the currently scheduled round of tests: to create mini black holes which will betray the existence of forces operating in extra dimensions. Although I'm sure they don't think of this way, it does sound as if the scientists of CERN wish to create a slight tear in the veil between the material and astral planes.

They wouldn't be the first to try. In this chapter we'll learn that a similar attempt was made thousands of years ago.

Much interest has been generated by the thoroughly out-of-place statue which stands proudly in front of the CERN complex. The bronze sculpture depicts none other than the god Shiva standing inside the flaming circle, dancing on the back of the demon of ignorance. It is this same Shiva whom physicist Robert Oppenheimer quoted while viewing the first successful atomic bomb test in 1945. Observing the dreadful mushroom cloud rise from the White Sands Missile Range, he intoned, "'Now I am become Death, the destroyer of worlds.'"[328]

What does CERN's Hindu sculpture say about the mission of the minds behind the LHC? The scientists there may not understand the deeper spiritual significance of this idol, but their angelic master certainly does.

Making Contact

Although the Book of Jubilees puts the pagan "boom"—the Cambrian Explosion of idolatry, as it were—after the incident at Babel, the unclean spirits had by that point already made good progress towards inciting widespread rebellion against God.

YHVH had told Noah's family to spread out and fill the earth, but many of their descendants weren't having it. They said, "Come, let us build us a city and a tower, whose top [may reach] unto Heaven; and let us make a name, lest we be scattered abroad upon the face of the whole earth" (Gen. 11:4). It would have been bad enough if they were only being disobedient to God's command "increase in number and fill the earth" (Gen. 9:1), but they went a step further with the intention to attain to heaven.

Contrary to the popular notion that the Ubaidians were attempting to reach God's house by ascending far enough off the ground, their intention was not to make a exceedingly tall structure that would act as a stairway to heaven. That idea can be dismissed simply by looking at where they chose to build the tower: the plain of Shinar. It was not much higher than sea level. If sheer height had been the goal, they could have built the tower at mountainous Aratta instead of transporting supplies hundreds of miles away. And since God doesn't seem to mind it when we build skyscrapers or launch men into space, we can safely deduce that straining for the sky is not what got the Ubaidians in trouble.

Furthermore, most translations of Gen. 11:4 insert a couple of words that aren't present in the Hebrew. The original language does not say that the people wanted to build a tower whose top "may reach unto heaven"; instead, they agreed to build a tower "and head-of-him in-the-heavens." Could the goal have been to touch heaven through some means other than increased elevation?

Certainly, there is something spiritually rousing about being physically elevated; however, some places seem to be zones of spiritual power regardless of their elevation. When Moses spoke to God through the burning bush, he was at the foothills of Mount Horeb, not the peak, for he had his flock with him; but God had Moses remove his sandals because he was standing on holy ground. Likewise, when Joshua saw the angel of the Lord near Jericho, he also stood on holy ground and was told to remove his sandals. And when Jacob saw the angels moving between heaven and earth via something the author could only describe as a ladder, he was not at a particularly high place in Israel, yet he called it "the gate of Heaven."

The Tower of Babel was never completed, but the Mesopotamians did finish other towers, called ziggurats, at various times and places throughout their history. The tops of these step-pyramids terminated in shrines which were considered the homes of gods. According to Greek historians, the ceilings inside the shrines were decorated with the constellations of the Zodiac. Only priests were allowed inside. Cuneiform texts describe ziggurats as mountains linking heaven and earth, and the very names of the ziggurats often reflect their function. For instance, at Babylon, *Etemenankia* meant "the house of the platform between heaven and earth;" *E-sagila* was the "mooring post of heaven and earth;" and the ziggurat at Sippar was the "temple of the stairway to pure heaven." If the tower in the valley of Shinar was like the other ziggurats, then its main purpose was a metaphysical one.

The city around the tower also had a purpose, and it was to function as a hub for the trade of goods and ideas. The tower would make the city famous, and fame draws crowds. If two heads are better than one, then a metropolis full of heads is the best—if by *best* we mean most suited to advance rapidly in capability. It's not that people didn't want to spread out and take land for themselves, it's that they wanted to do so gradually while remaining connected with civilization. Babel would have been the Rome of the ancient world, coordinating trading networks, building roads, sending out militia to keep the peace, and ultimately bringing all the wealth and knowledge of the world into the hands of a few rulers. God did not desire this concentration of power because power corrupts, and those who wield the most do so on the backs of the masses. He also saw that man would become too advanced, too quickly, and would destroy the earth with his wickedness (as we are doing now) before God had time to execute his plan of salvation.

When Adonai saw what the people were building, He said, "Behold, the people are one and they have all one language; and this they begin to do: and now nothing will be restrained from them, which they have imagined to do" (Gen. 11:6). Instead of scoffing at the attempt of the humans, God expressed concern. He even admitted that as long as the people were unified in purpose and speech, they would be able to accomplish *anything* (given time).

Anything, really? That's an amazing statement. And yet we're seeing the truth of that pronouncement today: it seems like every morning we wake up to stories of scientific breakthroughs granting us fresh, fanciful abilities. Is it not bizarre that we can manipulate atoms in order to destroy whole cities in a single strike; that we can clone organisms and modify them at the genetic level; or that people on opposite sides of the world can see and speak to each other in real-time? Maybe anything *is* possible—at a cost. So we have to wonder: on what did the people of Shinar have their imaginations set? Certainly it must have been more than constructing an impressive landmark over which to boast and be remembered, for all of mankind's great wonders of the world have gone unaddressed by God. But what if the Ubaidians were literally shooting for the stars? If men were constructing a temple whose priests would be able to bridge the dimensions, then we could understand why God and the Divine Council (the *us* of Gen. 11:7) went down to observe the project.

The Ubaidians were trying to make a name for themselves not only by constructing a lasting and impressive structure, but by literally opening a gate to the gods. They were building an inter-dimensional portal.

Lucifer's Plan B

Would it have worked? Could the Tower of Babel have actually functioned as a ladder to heaven? All we know is that God acknowledged the possibility. The first iteration of the Tower may not have produced the desired result, but had mankind been allowed to go about their efforts uninterrupted, the portal would have been opened sooner rather than later. This is why YHVH had to put an end to continued collaboration.

Suddenly we can make sense out of the portion of Isaiah 14 which reveals that Lucifer intended to invade heaven. We've already established the fact that Lucifer is a king named Nimrod, and now we can understand why a mortal actually entertained the idea that he could ascend "above the stars of God" and "sit on the mount of assembly," becoming "like the Most High" (vv. 13–14).

In ch. 7 we considered some reasons why it was probably not Nimrod who instigated and directed the Tower project, as popularly believed, but it is entirely possible that he was involved in some fashion—as a supervisor alongside his brothers, perhaps. It's all speculation. But according to Isaiah 14, Nimrod did have it in mind to personally make use of the portal, were it opened. Although he was denied the opportunity at Babel, Nimrod didn't altogether give up on the dream of usurping God; he simply realized that he would have to take a different approach than his father did. Instead of attempting to invade the highest heaven, he would appeal for help to the cosmic authority in the second heaven (Eph. 6:12), whom he knew as Enki, and attempt to bring heaven to earth. With the assistance of Satan/Enki, Nimrod would be able to execute a plan to reunite the world, trample the righteous, and create a heaven on earth where YHVH was not welcome. Towards this end, he ordered the construction of the ziggurat at Eridu. The E-Abzu, Nimrod's artificial hill at Eridu, functioned as a device which facilitated contact with other dimensions, but it was not sophisticated enough to allow bodily translation into the highest dimensions.

The plan may no longer be to invade God's home turf. Instead, at least in the short term, it is to deny the kingdom of God any ground in the lower realms. YHVH and his angels can keep the highest heaven so long as they stay out of the rest of Creation. This is why the Antichrist will not only wage war on the saints, who are walking ambassadors of God's kingdom, but will also invade Israel and take Jerusalem and the Holy Temple for himself. In order to be successful, Asshur must eliminate or corrupt anything on earth that belongs to YHVH. If nothing holy remains in the world, then the Holy One of Israel has no stake in it, and God will have effectively been kicked out. (What the Adversary fortunately can't change is that Yeshua as the perfect Second Adam has already won the legal battle and holds the title deed to the earth.)

English has become a global language, and translators are often used for collaborative projects in which some members don't speak English, so we've in large part reversed the effects of the confusion of tongues at Babel. Once Asshur has established a global union of nations, he may gather together top talents from around the world and task them with continuing the experiment begun at Babel. Since communication is no longer a barrier, such a project will eventually bear fruit. Perhaps this renewed attempt to reach heaven is part of the prophecy that John the Revelator was told not to write down (Rev. 10:1–4). Whether this is the case, or whether Asshur will only open portals to the spiritual realm without also attempting to invade God's dwelling place, it is a safe bet that he will cross every boundary in his quest to eject YHVH's chosen people and elevate reprobate men to godhood.

Part of this quest will involve taking God's earthly property for himself. Satan and Asshur understand the supreme importance of the Promised Land, especially Jerusalem, which is why it consistently occupies so much attention in international relations. It is the center of the navel of the earth, the very shadow of the heavenly Zion, and it is there that the heaven-earth connection is strongest. Let's take the next several pages to unwrap that concept and learn what the ancients knew about spiritual gateways.

The Ziggurat Beyond the Veil

The psalmist says, "I cried unto the LORD with my voice, and he heard me out of his **holy hill**" (Psa. 3:4, KJV). Where does God answer from? His throne in heaven. That throne is in the middle of a heavenly city called Jerusalem, situated on top of the heavenly Mount Zion. After the Temple of YHVH was erected by King Solomon on Zion, the city of Jerusalem in Israel functioned as a (relatively meager) representation of the real dwelling place of God in heaven. In a stirring vision of the future, the apostle John saw that God's city will descend to the newly re-created Earth after the Millennium.

And [an angel] carried me away in the Spirit to a mountain great and high, and showed me the Holy City, Jerusalem, coming down out of heaven from God. It shone with the glory of God, and its brilliance was like that of a very precious jewel, like a jasper, clear as crystal. It had a great, high wall with twelve gates, and with twelve angels at the gates. (Rev. 20:10–12)

Verses 15–17 of the same chapter give us the measurements of the heavenly Jerusalem. Author Patrick Heron notes that the City of God may have been pyramidal in shape, since it is laid out like a square and has a height equal to the length of its base.[329] Those dimensions describe either a pyramid or a cube, and arguments have been made for both. Mr. Heron further proposes that the pyramids, ziggurats, and other artificial mounds of the ancient world—all of which are strangely aligned with key astronomical markers—were meant to imitate the heavenly Mount Zion and the City of God resting upon it. If Satan could not be enthroned on the real Holy Mount, he would do so on mountains engineered by human hands. Until such a time as God could be deposed, simple replicas of his dwelling place would have to suffice.

Heron supports his theory by pointing to the Egyptian Edfu Texts and their repeated claims that the Egyptian monuments were replicas of heavenly buildings, made from plans which descended from heaven.[330] The Egyptians believed that those archetypal structures had existed in the celestial realm before the creation of the world. In fact, there is a clear association in Mesopotamian literature between ziggurats and mountain houses were the gods meet.

Navels and World Trees

The ancients recognized that the veil between the physical and spiritual worlds is thin at certain places, and such places were thought to contain something like an umbilical cord connecting them to heaven. These places were usually marked with a conical stone or pillar. The Greeks used the word *omphalos* (navel) to describe locations of increased spiritual conductivity. Today we use the term *axis mundus* (axis of the world).

World axes are symbolized by a sacred tree, the *World Tree*. The tree is used to symbolize the connection between the dimensions because its branches touch the heavens, its trunk connects the heavens and the earth, and its roots reach into the netherworld. The roots of a tree mirror it's branches, providing a perfect example of the famous maxim, "As above, so below."

The true axis of the world is Mount Zion in Jerusalem, which should be obvious to any student of the Bible, but we have extra confirmation from the Book of Jubilees, which says, "Mount Zion—the center of the navel of the earth" (8:20). Yet there are other places of connection, such as at Bethel, where Jacob saw angels ascending and descending on something like a ladder. His response to this vision was to set up a stone pillar and anoint it with oil and wine (Gen. 35:14).

Figure 17-2. The Omphalos of Delphi, Greece, 1.23 m x 0.92 m, carved in high relief from a block of marble.

The Greek omphalos stone found at Delphi was embossed with a net of plant-like pods and may have symbolized that the navel at Delphi was but one in a network of axis mundi. Other omphalos stones[a] were carved to look like pine cones or were crisscrossed with a diamond grid around which a serpent coiled. The crisscrossing pattern of pine cone bracts is especially provocative because it radiates out from the stalk in arcs that approximate the Golden Ratio, Phi. We will talk more about Phi, plants, and sacred geometry in the next volume of this book.

I find it highly likely that there is a grid of energy surrounding the earth and running beneath the crust—these are popularly called *ley lines*—and that this grid is somehow connected to the underground fresh water system known as the Abzu/Abyss. Axis mundi would be located wherever these lines intersect. The collection of world trees at these "navels" may be what Job was thinking about when he said during a monologue about God's power that "the **pillars of heaven** tremble" (26:11, KJV).

In Caananite tradition, Mount Hermon was the axis mundus.[331] In the Inca culture it was the city of Cusco, whose name means "navel" in

---

[a] a Also know by the Latin term *baetyl*.

the Quechua language.[332] To the Celts it was Croft Hill, a 128 meter-high cone of granite (the type of stone preferred by the Egyptians for its conductive and acoustic properties).[333] In Egypt, the omphalos was represented by the benben stone, which they equated to the mound that arose from the primordial waters. In Heliopolitan tradition, the benben turned into a pyramid where the supreme god Atum dwelt.[334]

In almost all instances, and across all cultures, the omphalos stone is associated with serpents and eagles, a pairing of creatures that we see repeated again and again in religious iconography from around the world. The serpents represent wisdom and knowledge while the eagles represent divinity. Some records indicate that the ancients considered the omphalos markers to be the seats of solar deities. For instance, there exists a Greek coin which shows the god Apollo seated atop an omphalos decorated as a pine cone.[335] It is reasonable to believe that the Kosmokraters ruled from the location where their respective people-groups had found navels and placed altars.

In fact, the Kosmokraters likely led people to these locations.

There is an Aztec legend that is illustrative of this idea because it attributes the founding of the city of Tenochtitlan to a prophecy from "The Portentous One," which stated that the Mexica (ancestors of the Aztecs) must settle "where the eagle screeches, where he spreads his wings, where the eagle feeds, where the fish fly, where the serpent is torn apart."[336] In approximately the year 1318 AD, after almost a century and a half of migration and wandering, the Mexica tribe from Chicomoztoc ended up on a

Figure 17-3. The symbol which adorns the Mexican flag recalls how the Mexica people were led by their god to settle on an island in Lake Texcoco.

swampy island in the middle of Lake Texcoco. While wandering about, they spotted an eagle perched on a cactus, eating a snake, just as their god, Huitzilopochtli, had promised. (It so happens that Huitzilopochtli, like Asshur, was a solar god of building and war.) There the Mexica obediently founded Tenochtitlan and developed it into a marvelous city, the heart of the Aztec empire. That swampy settlement eventually became the capital of the nation of Mexico. What is today the metropolis of Mexico City began on a hill surrounded by water.

It is clear that the tapered and pointed stones found at ancient holy sites are shadows of the primordial hill which emerged from the sea during the creation of the earth. That sea-encompassed primordial hill is itself a shadow of the heavenly mountain of God that is surrounded by the crystal sea. The reason that YHVH instructed the Israelites not to shape or cut the stones that they would use when building an altar (Exo. 20:25) is that the altar was meant to represent the archetypal heavenly mountain, which was not made by hands, but by the Word of God. Altars, omphalos stones, and the conical hats worn by gods and magicians are all symbols of the mountain of God.

The connection between pyramids, omphalos stones, and world trees should now be evident. When placed at one of the earth's navels, a shrine on a mound mimics the configuration of the heavenly Zion—"As above, so below"—and this widens the gap in the veil, allowing a strong connection to the world tree. Congress between dimensions can then more easily occur. It should be of no surprise to learn that the Mexica built a huge pyramid at Lake Texcoco after their god settled them there. Excavations at the site of the pyramid continue to yield amazing religious artifacts such as the Aztec Sun Stone.

As redeemed children, we should be very thankful that the curtain which hid the Most Holy place in the earthly Temple was torn at the time of Yeshua's crucifixion, for it signified that the veil between dimensions will be opened for those who are redeemed by the Blood. By reason of that cleansing blood we can now "come boldly to the throne of our gracious God" in prayer (Heb. 4:16). For when we put ourselves under the new covenant we figuratively came "to Mount Zion, to the city of the living God, the heavenly Jerusalem.... to the church of the firstborn, whose names are written in heaven" (Heb. 12:22–23, NIV). We don't need to claw our way into heaven, because heaven has opened for us. True, for the time being we are restricted to material bodies, but the spirit of our God is *in* us, giving us contentment and joy and also acting as a deposit that guarantees our inheritance (Eph. 1:13–14). Our high priest in his resurrected and glorified body has passed bodily through the veil on our behalf, and on the day that we receive our resurrected bodies, we too will be able to travel bodily between the material realm and the heavenly ones. The Ubaidians worked incredibly hard to achieve that very thing at Shinar, but had they instead served God and waited patiently, they would have received the gift of inter-dimensional travel (and far more) in due time.

To summarize what has been said so far: The Tower of Babel was a stepped pyramid located at a world axis and intended to translate three-dimensional beings into hyper-dimensional beings in like manner as Enoch and Elijah were translated into heaven. The Babel experiment was interrupted mid-development and the research was in large part lost when the languages were confused and men had to turn their attention to basic survival and war-making. From then on, pagan temples were not intended to facilitate bodily transit into higher dimensions, but rather to function as focal points for astral energies. Think of them as spiritual lightning rods.

In addition, ziggurats, pyramids, and elevated shrines act as amplifiers for the pineal gland, assisting human efforts to perceive the spiritual planes and communicate with those who live there, which is the topic of our next chapter.

EIGHTEEN

The Third Eye and the Arcane Arts

Then Pharaoh summoned the wise men and the sorcerers, and they, the magicians of Egypt, also did the same by their secret arts.

–EXODUS 7:11

And he [Manasseh] burned his sons as an offering in the Valley of the Son of Hinnom, and used fortune-telling and omens and sorcery, and dealt with mediums and with necromancers. He did much evil in the sight of the Lord, provoking him to anger.

–2 CHRONICLES 33:6

Due to the infiltration of Eastern philosophies into Western culture over the last fifty years, many people are familiar with the concept of the *third eye* as the eye of the spirit. Fewer people are aware of the astounding fact that the ancients knew which part of our anatomy controlled the third eye. That part is today called the pineal gland, an endocrine gland shaped like a pine nut and situated nearly in the center of the vertebrate brain. It is oddly isolated from the blood-brain barrier and receives a greater blood flow relative to its size than any other part of the body save the kidneys.

The French philosopher Descartes (1596–1650) referred to the pineal gland as the seat of the soul, and since the medical doctors of his day didn't know the first thing about the functionality of the pineal gland, the only way that Descartes could have known it was through Egyptian occult wisdom handed down to him.[a] It turns out that the Greeks had a vague notion that the pineal was related to spirituality, and that notion

---

[a] Embarrassingly for him, Decartes expounded upon this inherited ancient knowledge of the pineal with some medical hypotheses that turned out to be wholly incorrect.

survived until the Middle Ages; in particular, a famous Greek doctor named Galen (ca. AD 130–210) touched upon the subject in his anatomical treatise *On the Usefulness of the Parts of the Body*.[337] Of course, a large portion of Greek wisdom came from Egypt, which is where we may assume that Galen got his knowledge.

The Preoccupation with Pines

Pine cones are found at nearly every turn by those studying ancient sacred artwork. We find them in the hands of Mesopotamian gods, Hindu gods, Mexican gods, Greek gods, and more, and they turn up as decorations on a surprising array of religious items.

Figure 18-1. Top half of the staff of Osiris, currently housed in the Egyptian Museum in Turin, Italy

Hieroglyphs in the Temple of Hathor inform those entering that they are moving into the domain of the god Osiris and must open their third eye in order to make the journey. The Staff of Osiris, a relief dating to approximately 1200 BC, is portrayed as a shaft topped with a pine cone and flanked by a pair of snakes in a double-helix configuration. This parallels the famous caduceus of Hermes, son of Zeus, but is also similar to the snake-entwined rod of the healing god Asclepius (son of the Greek version of Osiris). One could easily draw a connection to the Indian concept of Kundalini energy, a metaphysical force that is sometimes activated in trance. When awakened, the "coiled" Kundalini spirals up the spinal column from the lowest chakra to the pineal gland, causing the third eye to open dramatically.

Manly P. Hall wrote this concerning the meaning of the pine cone:

> The exact science of human regeneration is the Lost Key of Masonry, for when the Spirit Fire is lifted up through the thirty-three degrees, or segments of the spinal column, and enters into the domed chamber of the human skull, it finally passes into the pituitary body (Isis), where it invokes Ra (the pineal gland) and demands the Sacred Name. Operative Masonry, in the fullest meaning of that term, signifies the process by which the Eye of Horus is opened. E. A. Wallis Budge has noted that

in some of the papyri illustrating the entrance of the souls of the dead into the judgment hall of Osiris the deceased person has a **pine cone attached to the crown of his head**. The Greek mystics also carried a symbolic staff, the upper end being in the form of a pine cone, which was called the *thyrsus* of Bacchus. In the human brain there is a tiny gland called the pineal body, which is the sacred eye of the ancients, and corresponds to **the third eye of the Cyclops**.[338]

The cyclopes were not monstrous humanoid beasts with only one eye, as popularly depicted. The cycloptic eye represents the spiritual vision of the illumined mystics, awakened by gnosis, and is analogous to the All-Seeing Eye of Horus. Yes, some of them were in fact giants because they were of Ham's lineage and received Nephiliym genes, but not all of them had that characteristic.

Figure 18-2. The All-Seeing Eye set in a luminous pyramid, carved on the pediment of a Masonic Lodge in Prague

The cyclopes were members of the Secret Brotherhood, a fraternity that combined architecture with religion; they were hierophants trained by Cush and Nimrod in the art of the mysteries. The Freemasons, which are modern torch-bearers for that ancient, secret brotherhood, are not ignorant of this fact, and indeed trace the origin of their fraternity back to Nimrod. Renowned Masonic author Albert Mackey has said, "The legend of the Craft in the Old Constitutions refers to Nimrod as one of the founders of Masonry."[339]

The cyclopes are the men who built the breathtaking megalithic structures that baffle architects and engineers even today, and they accomplished this by using occult techniques handed down from the Watchers. Many of the greatest sacred sites of the ancient world are situated in earthquake-prone areas, yet they have survived the test of time because the mortarless, tight-fitting, irregular shapes of cyclopean masonry can withstand high-magnitude quakes. In vol. 2 of this book we will study the megalithic monuments and uncover the secrets behind their dimensions and astronomical alignments.

In ancient art, the pine cone served dual duty as a representation of the pineal gland and a sign of new life. Coniferous trees were sacred symbols in pagan cults (including the Osiris cult)[340] not only because they keep their needles year-round, but because of their fire-assisted life

Figure 18-3. An Assyrian deity points a pine cone
(*mullilu*) toward a world tree (not shown), perhaps sprin-
kling sacred water upon it. From Nimrud, captial of king
Ashurnarzipal.

cycle. Oftentimes a fire must sweep through a conifer forest before new
growth can begin. The fire may consume one generation of trees, but it
also clears the way for the next generation and causes the conical fruit
of the trees to open up and release seed. Likewise, when the pineal gland
has been "ignited" by the fire of the sun spirit, it opens up and produces
a new life. This is the vegetable version of the mythical phoenix bird that
self-immolates only to rise again from its own ashes. It should then come
as no surprise that Nimrod as the god Osiris has said in the *Book of the
Dead*,

> **I am the phoenix**, the fiery sun, consuming and resuming myself....
> Mine is an earth of carnelian, blood red as the crest of a phoenix.[341]

This explains for us the tradition of the yule log, which is burned to end one year[a] and begin another, and when it is burned it produces heat and light which reminds those round about that the sun, like Nimrod, will return.

Even though having a shrine on an axis mundi is incredibly helpful for a mystic, one need not have an astrologically-aligned artificial mountain located at a world navel in order to experience higher dimensions. Through the practice of mysticism in its various forms, it is possible for anyone to tap into the spirit world without an amplifier; however, it is more difficult and much less efficacious.

Trance and Thaumaturgy

The Austrian esoteric philosopher and founder of anthroposophy, Rudolf Steiner (1861–1925), explained in his book, *An Outline of Occult Science*, that mystical learning is rooted in two beliefs:

> First, behind the "visible" there exists an invisible world, concealed at the outset from the senses and the thinking bound up with the senses; and second, it is possible for man, through the development of capacities slumbering within him, to penetrate into this hidden world.[342]

Just as the Ubaidians believed that they could enter the spirit world via the technology of the ziggurat, so mystics today believe that they can transmit their consciousness into higher, invisible realms. And they aren't wrong.

There is no doubt that spending an extended amount of time in deep trance can cause detachment from the physical world and entrance into a mysterious experience of unseen worlds. Abundant testimony of that fact is available to anyone with a mind to seek it out, so we will not spend our time arguing the point. Trance can be brought about through a number of methods including meditation, sensory deprivation, sacred dance, breathing techniques, redirected sexual energy, and entheogenic[b] drugs.

---

[a] This is true even though the rite is practiced approximately five days before the official turn of the year, because ancient civil years had only 360 days.

[b] Non-addictive, psychoactive drugs commonly treated as sacred and used to facilitate transcendent experiences. Mescaline (from Peyote), psylocybin (from mushrooms), and

The latter in particular has been used since the beginning of history to facilitate spiritual journeys. Scholars are well aware of the link between intoxicants and sun- or fire-god worship, as demonstrated in the following quote from Daniel Brinton's 1894 essay about Nagualism:

> The nagualistic rites were highly symbolic, and the.... most important symbol was Fire. It was regarded as the primal element and the immediate source of life.... Other ceremonies connected with fire worship took place in connection with the manufacture of the pulque, or *octli*, the fermented liquor obtained from the sap of the maguey plant.... This was distinctly a survival of **an ancient doctrine which connected the God of Fire with the Gods of Drunkenness.**[343]

Brinton thereafter expounds upon this ancient link, saying,

> Fire was worshiped as the life-giver, the active generator, of animate existence. This idea was by no means peculiar to them. It repeatedly recurs in Sanskrit, in Greek and in Teutonic mythology, as has been pointed out by Dr. Hermann Cohen. The fire-god Agni (*ignis*) is in the Vedas the Maker of men; Prometheus steals the fire from heaven that he may with it animate the human forms he has moulded of clay; even the connection of the pulque with the fire is paralleled in Greek mythos, where **Dionysos is called Pyrigenes, the "fire-born."**[344]

The gods Indra, Osiris, and Dionysus, who are variations of the same ancient demigod, were all patrons of narcotic cocktails: Indra drank the famed but enigmatic Indian soma; the death and resurrection of Osiris was symbolized in the blue lily, key ingredient in the intoxicating lily-mandrake-poppy mix;[342] and Dionysus was the god of wine but was also associated with the Eleusinian Mysteries and that ritual's psychedelic kykeon. Entheogens as ritual aids were used throughout the Old World: Greek, Minoan, and Germanic priests used opium (called the "tears of Aphrodite/Venus") to achieve oracular states;[346] the Scythians and Thracians used cannabis to induce trance in their soothsayers so that they could conduct divination;[347] and every civilization that developed in Mexico had religious members who used hallucinogenic plants such as peyote, datura, and morning glory to receive guidance from the spirit

---

LSD are examples of entheogens. The word is Greek and means "that which generates God within."

world.

The metaphysical experiences obtained during trance are ineffable; they are notoriously difficult to convey because, like dreams, they are often nonsensical or have no analogue in the physical plane. It's for this reason that the transcendent journey undertaken in trance is called *mystical*, for it is a mystery to the uninitiated. Outsiders can no more understand its essence than a blind man can understand color.

The occult rebirth discussed in ch. 8 is in large part synonymous with having an intense mystical experience during deep trance facilitated by ego-destroying rituals, mind-altering drugs, and isolation. The opening of the candidate's third eye often takes place inside a coffin or sarcophagus which acts not only as a symbol of death to the old self, but serves a practical function as a sensory-deprivation chamber. Even former U.S. President George W. Bush had to lie inside a coffin when he underwent initiation into the Skull & Bones society.[348]

Practitioners of transcendental meditation, tantra, Indian/Tibetan yoga[a], contemplative prayer, ritual dance, and other forms of mysticism spend many hours attempting to separate their spirits from their physical enclosures so that they may dwell, even briefly, in the spirit world. There are three primary goals of such enterprise:

1. Union in a super-rational way with the unclassifiable Order which goes by many names, such as The Absolute, Cosmic Mind, Christ Consciousness, Brahman, and Matrix. As evidenced by the clear-as-mud labels just given, this esoteric Order is a very abstract concept. The philosophy which one uses to inform such an experience is determined by one's belief system; thus, mystics can be pantheistic, panentheistic, theistic, or monistic.

2. Contact with the entities that dwell in higher planes. Mediums, psychics, shamans, yogis, and those who meditate all commune with spirit guides, deceased gurus/masters, ancestors, or transcendent deities.

3. Procurement of secret knowledge and special abilities—what we commonly call *witchcraft* and *sorcery*.

As with any pursuit, the more one practices mysticism, the easier it is to achieve the desired result; the practitioner becomes more and more attuned to spiritual frequencies. Ritual aids such as incense, candle flames,

---

[a] The goal of Eastern, mystical yoga is the synthesis of the physical and metaphysical universe.

and mantras are often used to speed the process, yet even so, reaching the heights of ecstatic mystical experience takes years for most individuals, and not all practitioners will become sorcerers.

Sorcery was much more prevalent in the ancient world, but even today, shamans and yogis are well known for their thaumaturgy[a]. In the early 20th century, John Neihardt spent much time with a Sioux holy man named Black Elk, and in his biography of this man, Neihardt notes his clairvoyance, saying, "When I had known the great old man for some years I was quite prepared to believe that he did [glimpse the future], for he certainly had supernormal powers."[349]

Anthropologist Dr. William S. Lyon spent four decades doing field research with American Indian medicine men and has shared his findings in a book titled *Spirit Talkers: North American Indian Medicine Powers*. In that book he gives eyewitness reports of paranormal activity. Dr. Lyon also provides numerous accounts from 18th- and 19th-century anthropologists and settlers who witnessed apparently supernatural displays which, try as they might, they could not debunk.

One such observer was journalist and activist Charles F. Lummis (1859–1928), who spent much time with the natives of the American Southwest and was boggled by the feats of their medicine men. Lummis was a naturalist and could not bring himself to believe that what he saw was real, but neither could he explain by what method the medicine men were able to generate such wondrous illusions. In his 1892 book, *Some Strange Corners of our Country*, he describes watching spiritists dance naked in fire and eat live coals without suffering ill effects. He also saw them summon storms indoors. He reports that

> outside the sky may be twinkling with millions of stars, but in that dark room a fearful storm seems to be raging.... How these effects are produced I am utterly unable to explain, but they are startlingly real.[350]

Lummis also marveled at the ability of Navajo witch-doctors to rub themselves down with burning firebrands without harm, and to cause the growth of the sacred corn from seedling to full maturity within the hours of a single day.[351]

Another example of the efficacy of modern shamanism comes in the form of a 2006 article written for *National Geographic*. The author, Kira

---

[a] Wonderworking

Salak, a self-proclaimed atheist turned agnostic, describes being instantly cured of life-long depression during a shamanistic medicinal ritual in Peru. During a second ceremony years later, with the help of shamans, Salak expels demons which unbeknownst to her had attached themselves during a trek on a cursed mountain. Without being instructed to do so, Salak also travels into part of the netherworld and finds a child version of herself trapped by three denizens (this little girl represents part of herself that was splintered off because of childhood trauma). Salak's shaman guides enter her trance and confront the chthonic entities on her behalf. They also instruct her to pull the child out of its fiery prison, and they do so despite the fact that she has not vocalized what she is seeing.[352]

Accounts about the essence of sacred trance have been collected from shamans of many different tribes around the world and sifted for commonalities. The shamans' stories show a similar progression through the mystical experience:[353]

1. An unsettling journey into a void or some kind of inner darkness characterized by a loss of connection with the physical world or a sense (sometimes painful) of being dissolved.
2. Being birthed into a sea of lights, vibrant colors, and a constantly animating weave of geometric patterns.
3. The emergence of entities from the writhing patterns. They most often come in the form of serpents and therianthropes (humanoid animals). Medicine men of the Amazon make a potion called ayahuasca from a vine and leaf native to the rainforest. Those who imbibe ayahuasca often see a feminine humanoid plant spirit which presents herself as a mother.
4. As the trance fades, the shaman often enjoys super-natural powers such as healing, foresight, and clairvoyance.

It is no coincidence that paranormal events follow on the heels of contact with spirits during the ceremony. Magic is not an impersonal force like the one wielded by Jedi in the *Star Wars* films; rather, magical feats are accomplished by intelligent, hyper-dimensional beings interested in assisting humans. Practitioners of today will say that they are manipulating *energies*, but in the ancient world and in the Bible they are known as *spirits.* Some of these spirits may be neutral—I say may because I'm no expert—but some are malevolent. The capabilities of these non-material beings are sometimes unbelievably awesome.

When Moses and Aaron confronted Pharaoh about the Jewish slaves, Aaron's staff turned into a snake to demonstrate the favor of God on their mission, but

> Pharaoh then summoned wise men and sorcerers, and the Egyptian magicians also did the same things by their secret arts: Each one threw down his staff and it became a snake. But Aaron's staff swallowed up their staffs. (Exo. 7:11–12)

The miracles done on behalf of the Egyptian magicians should make us wonder what else they were able to accomplish and how it may have contributed to the advancement of their civilization.

Mystics sometimes emerge from the trance with the gift of useful information that would otherwise be unknowable to them. If that information is shared, it can cause quite the stir. A Spanish missionary to Latin America named Father Joseph de Acosta (1539–1600) records that some of the aboriginal sorcerers

> will tell what is happening in very remotes places before the news arrives or could possibly arrive, as happened even after the coming of the Spaniards; for even at a distance of two hundred or three hundred leagues news has been received of... something that in the natural order of things was impossible to learn so quickly. To perform this [art] they go into a house locked from the inside and drink until they lose their senses; after a day, they answer what they have been asked.[354]

Of note here is the 1995 CIA-commissioned review of two decades worth of remote viewing research sponsored by the U.S. government. The team concluded that the phenomenon of remote viewing was real and of utility to intelligence gathering.[355]

One of the most famous recent examples of the phenomenon of channeling special knowledge while in trance can be seen in the life of American psychic Edgar Cayce (1877–1945). He would lie down, enter a sleeping trance, and allow a voice which referred to itself as we to speak through him. The voice gave suggestions for the treatment of health and personal problems, information about past lives, and predictions of future events. Upon waking, Cayce had no memory of what he had said while asleep. The accuracy of Cayce's clairvoyant instructions has long been debated, but it is undeniably true that thousands of people, including doctors, businessmen, and politicians, claimed to have been helped by their readings. Modern holistic medicine derives in large part from Cayce's work.

Of all his readings, Cayce's visions of the future are the most criticized. Some of his prophecies were demonstrably incorrect, and some were so vague as to be unverifiable, but others did find their target, such as his predictions about the Great Depression, the magnetic pole shift, and even the timing of his own death. To their credit, Cayce's sons admitted to being very skeptical of about two hundred of the readings, and no one in the family, including Cayce himself, ever claimed flawless accuracy. What we need to realize is that Cayce's failures, however few, automatically disqualify him as a prophet of God. Why? Because the oracles of true prophets are never wrong. God told the Jewish people to expect 100% accuracy from any prophet which He would send them: "If what a prophet proclaims in the name of the LORD does not take place or come true, that is a message the LORD has not spoken. That prophet has spoken presumptuously, so do not be alarmed" (Deut. 18:22). So Cayce was not operating under the authority of the Holy Spirit, but some other spirit. No created spirit can see the future; only God is outside of time. However, spirits do know much more than us and can use that knowledge to make well-educated guesses about the future.

Cayce was supposedly a Christian who taught Sunday school and recruited missionaries, yet the religious content of his readings drifted further and further from biblical doctrine over the course of his career. Cayce's friend and biographer, Thomas Sugrue, devoted a chapter of his book to the systematic analysis of the philosophic content of Cayce's readings. Summarizing his findings, Sugrue writes, "The system of metaphysical thought which emerges from the readings of Edgar Cayce is a Christianized version of the mystery religions of ancient Egypt, Chaldea, Persia, India, and Greece."[356] Whatever Cayce's personal beliefs, the spirit(s) speaking through him had different ideas, unbiblical ideas, like monism and reincarnation. This should inform us that the source of the readings was not ultimately benign, regardless of whatever help may have been provided. Unfortunately, no small number of people paid attention to the philosophy espoused during Cayce's readings because of the miraculous things which came through them. Some within the New

Figure 18-4. "Priestess of Delphi" by John Collier (1850–1934), from the Art Gallery of South Australia

Age community even consider him to be the founder of the movement.

Ancient priesthoods in particular relied on knowledge from beyond the veil. The best-known example of the use of trance as an oracular tool is the ancient Greek *Pythia*, which was the title given to the priestess who prophesied at Delphi, on the slopes of Mount Parnassus. Beginning in the 8th century BC, the Oracle of Delphi at the Temple of Apollo was highly revered for the prophecies that came to her from the god Apollo. On this topic, Christian researcher Thomas Horn writes,

So important was Apollo's oracle at Delphi that whenever Hellenism existed, its citizens and kings, including some from as far away as Spain, ordered their lives, colonies, and wars by its sacred communications. It was here that the Olympian gods spoke to mortal men through the use of a priesthood, which interpreted the trance-induced utterances of the Pythoness or Pythia. She was a middle-aged woman who sat on a copper-and-gold tripod, or, much earlier, on the "rock of sibyl" (medium), and crouched over a fire while inhaling [hallucinogenic smoke] until a sufficient intoxication for her prophecies had been produced.[357]

Some would like to believe that the Pythia got her insights by tapping into an ethereal storehouse of records—a comprehensive library existing outside of time and space—but the Bible negates that theory when it reveals that Greek fortune-tellers received their oracles from unclean spirits. In the Book of Acts, Luke records,

> As we were going to the place of prayer, we were met by a slave girl who had a **spirit of divination** and brought her owners much gain by fortune-telling. She followed Paul and us, crying out, "These men are servants of the Most High God, who proclaim to you the way of salvation." And this she kept doing for many days. Paul, having become greatly annoyed, turned and said to the spirit, "I command you in the name of Jesus Christ to come out of her." And it came out that very hour. (Acts 16:16–18)

Needless to say, the girl's handlers were not happy. They had Paul and his band severely beaten for depriving them of a good source of wealth and influence.

Information has always been the greatest power, and religious leaders of the ancient world were more than happy to obtain special knowledge with which to elevate themselves above the masses. Communing with spirits can be very profitable, in the short term (but the end thereof is eternal death). In pursuit of worldly power, our early ancestors found shortcuts by which to interact with the astral plane. The best method they devised was to build artificial mountains at sacred navels. Any priest or magician given the opportunity to enter a trance state at one of these hot-spots could open up the spirit world with ease and establish contacts which would otherwise take much time and diligence.

Some readers may be having a hard time with these ideas, divorced as they are from today's dominate philosophy of naturalism. Many westerners, even those who are Christians, are locked into a paradigm that leaves no room for sorcery. What we fail to realize is that we are the exception, not the rule. For most of human history, the prevailing viewpoint was one which admitted and even hinged on the supernatural. It would not have occurred to people of the ancient world to deny or downplay the existence and power of the spirit realms, and they would have laughed at the naturalist's worldview if it were presented to them. They had no doubt about the truth of higher realities and the beings inhabiting them, and they expected that the gods would usually show up, if sought.

Author Mark Booth spent over twenty years researching mystery teachings and was helped along by a high-ranking member of more than one secret society. Booth himself never underwent initiation because he did not want to take an oath of secrecy that would forbid him to write about mysticism. In his work titled *The Secret History of the World As Laid Down by the Secret Societies*, Mr. Booth concisely explains what has been going on since the building of the pagan temple of Inanna and the Tower of Babel: "At the very heart of all esoteric teaching in all parts of the world lies the belief that higher forms of intelligence can be accessed in altered states."[358]

The weight of that claim cannot be underestimated. Imagine the long-term impact on world affairs if human beings from all cultures have been the recipients of esoteric knowledge given by hyper-dimensional entities. At first glance, knowledge from advanced beings might seem like a boon to the human race. The problem is that we don't control what *kinds* of advanced beings are accessed in trance.

The Danger of the Sorceric Arts

Mystics throughout the ages have acknowledged the inherent danger of occult practices. Spirit beings can sometimes behave in unexpected and frightening ways, so commerce with them is considered a risky business. But they do it anyway! According to Booth, "Controlled communion with the gods and spirits was the preserve of the Mystery schools."[359] Manly Hall agrees and writes that "ceremonial magic is the ancient art of invoking and controlling spirits by a scientific application of certain formulae. A magician... could by the power vested in certain words and symbols control the invisible inhabitants of the elements and of the astral world."[360] Hall believes that true hierophants of the mysteries hold to "noble concepts" and use proper techniques to ensure that they summon and employ harmless elementals instead of evil spirits.[361]

It may be true that initiates of the Mysteries were able to exert a degree of control over spirits—after all, the witch of Endor was able to call up the spirit of a deceased man at will (1 Sam. 28:7–20). However, let us not imagine that even the most adept among the illumined ones can control the Kosmokraters or the Dragon himself. Every human being, and most assuredly those who play at being puppet-masters, are puppets in the hands of greater masters.

Medium Sri Chinmoy, a spiritual adviser at the United Nations, stated that he knew of quite a few cases where people who deal with spirits were convinced by those spirits to hurt or kill themselves.[362] Furthermore, both Eastern and Western gurus have taught that temporary insanity and possession (by deceased gurus, ascended masters, or ancestors) are hallmarks of the path to enlightenment.[363]

An admission of the dangers of mysticism is given by Franz Hartmann of The Theosophic Society in his January 2006 article for Quest magazine. The Theosophic Society is a well-known "wisdom tradition" centered around mystic and occult teachings, which promotes regular meditation as a path to enlightenment. Mr. Hartmann writes,

> I have before my eyes a long list of friends and personal acquaintances, who within the last few years have become victims of their "psychic researches," for which they were not yet ripe and in which they persisted in spite of all warnings. Some of them became insane, some incurably diseased, others obsessed and morally depraved, and not a few of them ended by suicide. They were not unintelligent or uneducated people; on the contrary, one of them was a great and well known scientist and inventor, noble minded and generous; several were writers or poets of some distinction...[364]

Suicide and incurable disease are not what most people would call acceptable risks. Despite such unsettling cases, occult practitioners still claim that contact with spirits is safe if proper precautions are taken. Sadly, sorcerers often believe that they can shield themselves from danger by casting protection spells or by thinking certain positive thoughts, but the truth is that such rituals have no power. Demons couldn't care less about our positive thoughts; try casting positivity at a hungry wolf and see if that keeps it at bay. Sorcerers and mediums foolishly believe that they can either control the spirits, or that the spirits they commune with are harmless. Nephiliym spirits are always vicious and usually do harm to their victims in visibly obvious ways, but devils and some of the lower-ranking spirits can be subtle. There are many spirits who do not mean well but will cooperate with mortals in order to gain allegiance, after which they can guide the spiritists into ever more ungodly beliefs and lifestyles, turning them into pawns.

The spirits with whom pagans communicate are not clean spirits, even if they present themselves as peaceable, for devils may come disguised as angels of light (2 Cor. 11:14). The Bible does not indicate even once that clean spirits are allowed to communicate with unsaved people except to proclaim a coming judgment and the need to repent. If benign spirit beings are incommunicado with pagans, then who is it that's taking their calls?

In ch. 16 I related Michael Harner's experience of being healed during a necromantic ritual. What I did not report was the message that Harner received from the deceased. Although Harner did not speak Hawaiian, he heard these Hawaiian words being repeated during the ceremony: *Hele hele aku I ka pono.* Those who understand the language told him that the phrase means "Go, go! Forward to everything positive." The shaman treating Harner told him that the message was an affirmation that he was blessed and on "the moral path, the correct path."[365] Thus a grateful Michael Harner was emboldened to continue his involvement in activities that YHVH hates. This is a clear example of arcane practice coming yoked with deception meant to keep people off the straight and narrow path of the Holy One of Israel.

God forbade the Israelites to participate in any occult practices such as communication with spirits and the use of powers wielded by those spirits.

> There shall not be found among you anyone who makes his son or his daughter pass through the fire, one who uses divination, one who practices witchcraft, or one who interprets omens, or a sorcerer, or one who casts a spell, or a medium, or a spiritist, or one who calls up the dead. For whoever does these things is detestable to the Lord; and because of these detestable things the Lord your God will drive them out before you. (Deut. 18:10–12)

These prohibitions were not put into place because God is a kill-joy, but because he understands where occult paranormal powers originate, and he knows that the unclean spirits who provide special favors do so in order to draw people away from the life-giving Holy Spirit.

Shortly before his crucifixion, Yeshua warned his disciples that false christs and false prophets would arise and deceive many by showing great signs and wonders (Matt. 24:23–25). As we approach the end of the age, expect to see an increase in paranormal activity and an explosion of occult practitioners doing paranormal things by compelling spirits to work on their behalf. Many of these practitioners will call themselves *anointed*, which is the English translation of the Greek word *christ*. They will boast about having a full measure of Christ Consciousness, or to put it another way, they will claim *enlightened guru* status. This is certainly not a novel assertion, but in the years to come it will be backed up with spiritual power rarely before seen.

Dark Sentences and the Occult Utopia

And we may also fitly remember that Satan has his miracles.[366]

–JOHN CALVIN (1509–1564)

O ne of the most disturbing qualities of the Beast from the Abyss will be his mastery of the arcane arts. An angel told the prophet Daniel that in the latter days, "a king of fierce countenance, and **understanding dark sentences**, shall stand up" (Dan. 8:23, KJV). The word *dark* here is used figuratively to convey something that is hidden or occluded—in other words, occult knowledge. Other translations render it as *riddles*. Recall that Isis and Osiris were both skilled in enchantments and words of power, as was also the case with Ninurta, Marduk, and many of the other gods associated with Nimrod. As he did in his previous existence, Nimord/Asshur will use his occult wisdom to accomplish feats that will seem like miracles. Yet his amazing abilities will not be like the supernatural power of the Creator that flowed through Yeshua. The angel explained to Daniel that the false messiah's power "shall be mighty, but **not** by his own power" (8:24, KJV).

The Antichrist will not be able to exert supernatural power from within himself in the way that a man exerts muscular power by the use of his own bodily instrument. Instead, the superhuman deeds that appear attributable to Asshur will in fact be the craft of fallen angels. This is why Paul writes that by his own glory Yeshua will destroy the wicked, "even [Asshur], whose coming is after the working of Satan with all power and signs and lying wonders" (2 Thess. 2:9, KJV).

It boggles the mind, but the man of sin will even bring down angelic entities. In one of Daniel's visions, the prophet perceives the Antichrist as a little horn which grows rapidly, and this is what Daniel says of that horn: "And it waxed great, even to the host of heaven; and **it cast down**

some of the host and of the stars to the ground, and stamped upon them" (8:10, KJV). To call this an incredible statement would not be doing it justice. Indeed, if it weren't recorded in the Word of God, we wouldn't believe it. Asshur will actually succeed in capturing and abusing angels in the sight of human beings! By so doing, he will convince the wicked that it is possible to fight the forces of YHVH and win.

Not only will Asshur trample on angels, but he will find a way to murder the two witnesses of YHVH who are supernaturally protected from harm during their 3½ years of evangelism. Anyone who attacks them is consumed by fire, but the Beast will somehow survive the attempt (Rev. 11:7–8). True, those witnesses will be resurrected and taken into heaven 3½ days after their deaths, and some people will fear God and repent on account of it (vv. 11–13), but Asshur will quickly reassure his followers and instruct them not to be shaken by the miracle—after all, he himself was resurrected! The false messiah may declare that YHVH has finally abandoned his efforts to claim the earth, and that the withdrawal of the two witnesses is a sign of surrender. People will be duped by this assertion because the plagues will cease for a time. Some premillennialists assume that the plagues of Revelation will continue in a mostly unbroken succession during the whole span of Daniel's 70th week, but Scripture offers no outright support of that theory. It all depends on one's interpretation of the chronology of Revelation.

The New Atlantis Realized

The verse which follows the description of the witnesses' resurrections says, "The second woe has passed; behold, the third woe is soon to come" (11:14). This indicates that there will be a gap between the trumpet and bowl judgments. Soon is obviously a relative term, especially in the Bible, where a day is treated as a thousand years, so it is futile to try and assign a particular length of time to that gap based on the wording of the verse. But if we look to other verses, we can find clues suggesting that the unbelieving world will experience a few years of global peace and become convinced that the Messiah has at last ushered in the Millennium. The dream of the New Atlantis will have finally reached fruition. Sadly, this short era of secular utopia will simultaneously be a period of great tribulation for those who will not renounce their faith in Yeshua. Genuine, Gospel-spreading, "fundamentalist" Christians will be considered enemies of the state, traitors whose allegiance to the tyrannical and bigoted god of darkness is deserving of death. And so we will be hunted down and beheaded by the millions (Rev. 13:7–10, 20:4).

Meanwhile, Asshur will be building Tomorrowland. In the next volume of *Leviathan's Ruse*, we will study evidence suggesting that civilization under Nimrod's world empire was in some ways even more advanced than our own. When Nimrod is resurrected, he will bring knowledge of the Watchers back with him and will once again provide divine help to struggling humanity. The gift of high technologies that are environmentally-friendly and infrastructure-independent will endear Asshur to a public barely surviving the ravages of world war, famines, and plagues. Only Nimrod/Asshur has the know-how to recreate Atlantis, to transform the world from the playground of Chaos into the occultists' Divine Commonwealth, and he will be lauded as Savior for doing it.

It is safe to say that the Antichrist's occult secrets will feed into the transhumanist agenda and help usher humankind into the next level of so-called evolution. This will assuredly involve the transgenic mixing of kinds, as in the days of Noah. It may also involve the use of technology to achieve immortality, thus relieving the privileged authorities—the illumined elite of the New World Order—of any temptation to appeal to YHVH for eternal life, and also belatedly giving weight to the serpent's assertion that Eve would not surely die because of disobedience. We should expect the proliferation of every method for turning men into gods—supermen who believe that they do not need to rely on the One God. Of course, that's really a preposterous notion, for YHVH is the source of all goodness and order, apart from which there is no life. Even the moment-to-moment operation of living cells is dependent on the constant outworking of God's spirit (Job 34:14–16). Nevertheless, rebellious people foolishly imagine that they can have life apart from YHVH.

The Open Vision of David Jones

At the age of seventeen, an American southerner by the name of David Jones received an open vision of the Day of the Lord. When the vision was given, David was babysitting his sisters' children, whom he had already put to bed. As he was idly scanning for stations on the radio, he heard a woman scream somewhere outside. He rushed to the window but then hesitated because he suddenly felt sure that he would see something horrific. Nevertheless, he was compelled to go see what was happening. Jones recently related his experience to television host Sid Roth, saying,

> I pulled back the curtains on the second story and I looked down, and I didn't see anything, and I was like, there's nothing wrong. And then when my eyes caught the stars in the heavens, all of a sudden it was just like a movie screen, and blood on the moon appeared. And it's like someone took an ice pick and poked the moon; then blood began to ooze out of the moon. And then all the stars in the heaven began to fall all at once, and the sky itself began to roll up as a scroll. And it was happening simultaneously: the moon turned to blood, the stars fell from the heaven, the sky rolled up as a scroll. And all of a sudden I [saw a] woman with long black hair. She was beholding what was happening coming upon the earth, and she began to take her fingernails and dig on her face, and scream, and holler. Then I seen hundreds of people running, thousands of people running, and the horror on their faces; and God allowed me to sense what they were feeling: total helplessness, total terror. And all of a sudden the vision disappeared, and I fell to the ground, and I was trembling and shaking. I was like, Oh my God, what did I see?[367]

What the young Mr. Jones saw is awesome by itself, but it becomes even more amazing by virtue of the fact that he was not yet a Christian when he received the prophecy. In fact, he shook off the vision as best he could and went on to lead a rebellious lifestyle that resulted in drug and alcohol addiction. But God eventually shook him until he repented and ran to the Savior, at which point he was delivered from his substance abuse problems. Jones then served the Lord in ministry for over two decades before getting another vision in February 2012. Here is his explanation of the second vision:

> And I can see all the beautiful skies and the sun, and all the happiness, people going to and fro, mothers with their children going into the grocery stores, people pumping gas, businessmen with their ties and briefcase going into the buildings. And all of a sudden, a thick darkness and clouds started appearing upon the earth. And then all of a sudden there was a sound from heaven, a sound that I have never heard before in all my born days. It was like seven claps of thunder uttered into one. The sound was so deafening, not only did it pierce the ears of all mankind,

but it began to pierce them [such] that when they heard it their bodies began to shake and quake. This sound was so deafening, people began to scream. Then all of a sudden—like someone took a razor blade and split the heavens—here come the Son of God with all his bands of angels and all of his glory. Oh Sid, and the colors were glorious, splendid, magnificent, glorious, the blues, the golds, the greens. I had never seen such colors like this. And he was coming speedily on the earth. Then people began to urinate on themselves and scream. And then one man said, "No, no, no, wait, wait, wait. I thought I had time. I thought I had time." But, too late; all time had ran out for all mankind. Another man— he was like an Indian guy, real short—he began to say, "No, no, no, this is a dream, this is a dream. I'm going to wake up." But Sid, he couldn't wake up because he was already woke. Then I heard a voice from heaven say, "This is the Day of the Lord! It has come!" And I came out of the vision, trembling on the floor, and I'm shaking and quaking within myself.... And I began to repent over my own life. Lord, save me. God, forgive me. Because He allowed me to sense what everyone was feeling. And I began to repent. Because I said, "God, I want to be pleasing to you, Lord. If I have hurt you or come against you in any shape or form, please forgive me, Lord. Lord, please allow me to be counted worthy to go back with you. I have seen the Day of the Lord." Then the Lord spoke to me saying, "I charge you now to warn all mankind."[368]

So far as I can see, Mr. Jones' vision is entirely scriptural, and the charge that was given to him is in keeping with God's desire that none should perish, "but that all should reach repentance" (2 Pet. 3:9). Many people, especially over the past few years, have had similar dreams and visions of the coming judgment. This is to be expected because it is written, "In the last days it shall be, God declares, that I will pour out my Spirit on all flesh, and your sons and your daughters shall prophesy, and your young men shall see visions, and your old men shall dream dreams" (Acts 2:17). As we covered in ch. 2, the cosmic cataclysm which Yeshua describes in Matt. 24:29–30 and which David Jones witnessed in his visions must occur at the *very end* of Daniel's 70th week, because the Lord clearly states that that cataclysm will come after the great tribulation and before the resurrection.

David Jones saw people living normal lives in a world that was not reeling from the effects of supernatural plagues. That's not to say that the world won't go through the ringer between now and the Second Coming, but by the time that the Day of the Lord begins, things will have returned to some semblance of serenity. Thus Yeshua could say that the end of the age would be like unto the days of Noah,

> for as in those days before the flood they were eating and drinking, marrying and giving in marriage, until the day when Noah entered the ark, and they were unaware until the flood came and swept them all away, so will be the coming of the Son of Man. (Matt. 24:38–39)

The apostle Paul conveys the same idea in his first letter to the Thessalonians, teaching that the Day of the Lord will arrive unexpectedly, so that "while people are saying, 'There is peace and security,' then sudden destruction will come upon them as labor pains come upon a pregnant woman, and they will not escape" (5:2–3).

Furthermore, we see in Revelation 18 that the economic powerhouse that is Babylon will be in full swing up until the moment that the great city is destroyed. John sees that business is hopping when the city suddenly goes up in smoke, but how could that be? Her merchants could not be dealing successfully in all kinds of luxuries during a time of plagues like those linked to the heavenly trumpets and bowls, for in times of disaster men are concerned with basic necessities, not luxuries. Yet John sees merchants weeping at the destruction of Babylon because they can no longer sell their cargoes of "gold, silver, jewels, pearls, fine linen, purple cloth, silk, scarlet cloth, all kinds of scented wood, all kinds of articles of ivory, all kinds of articles of costly wood, bronze, iron and marble, cinnamon, spice, incense, myrrh, frankincense, wine, oil, fine flour, wheat, cattle and sheep, horses and chariots, and slaves, that is, human souls" (Rev. 18:12–13). Therefore Babylon must be given some room to breathe and develop before the end.

Jacob's Trouble

Who are the souls that the merchants of Babylon will traffic in the last days? Many of them will be Jews taken captive in Judea (Matt. 24:16). Yeshua warns of this tragedy during his Olivet Discourse, explaining that when the Antichrist desolates Jerusalem, those who do not heed his warning and flee immediately "will fall by the edge of the sword and be **led captive among all nations**, and Jerusalem will be trampled underfoot by the Gentiles, until the **times** of the Gentiles are fulfilled" (Luke 21:24). The *times* mentioned here parallels the 3½-year period foretold in the book of Daniel, where an angel swears by Elohiym that the saints of the Most High will be given into the hand of Asshur "for a time, times, and half a time," or 3½ prophetic years, and that the power of the holy people would be shattered during that time-span (7:27, 12:7). The saints and holy people mentioned by the angel are not unbelieving Jews, but rather the *ekklesia* (assembly) of Yeshua; however, the persecution of the saints occurs during the same 3½ years as the enslavement of the ethnic Jews—this is known as "the time of Jacob's trouble". Clearly, the Beast hates both the physical and spiritual seed of Abraham.

Thankfully, because of the faithfulness and power of the King of Kings, the Beast will not have his way for long, and the time of Jacob's trouble will end on the day of Messiah's Glorious Appearing.

> Alas! for that day is great, so that none is like it: **it is even the time of Jacob's trouble, but he shall be saved out of it**. For it shall come to pass in that day, saith the Lord of hosts, that I will break [Asshur's] yoke from off thy neck, and will burst thy bonds, and strangers shall no more serve themselves of him: But they shall serve the LORD their God, and David their king, whom I will raise up unto them. (Jer. 30:7–9)

Deus Ex

All this is to say that Asshur will arise with supernatural powers beyond anything we've seen since the time of the prophets—for Satan will have placed every unclean spirit at his Seed's disposal—and with the military might and technological know-how to build a New World Order. Using arcane arts, Asshur will overcome the two seemingly invincible witnesses of Yeshua and declare himself to be God, victorious over evil. He will set up an idol of himself in the Holy Temple, at the very gateway to heaven, and from there, he and the False Prophet may be able to access the spiritual realm in especially frightening ways. Asshur will then rule the global empire with an iron fist. His kingdom will receive a 3½-year reprieve from God's judgments, give or take, so that wickedness can increase and Babylon can flourish exceedingly, and during this period, citizenship in the global government of Lucifer will require the Mark of the Beast. It will seem as though the enemies of YHVH have won, and that the Elohiym of the Israelites was not the Almighty, after all.

Yet the end that is decreed for Babylon and her king will come like a flood, when suddenly the bright sun turns to blackness and the moon to blood, when the stars fall from heaven and the sky rolls up like a scroll, and when Yeshua returns to our world as a thief in the night. Maranatha.

what?

TWENTY

The Cosmic Signs

The heavens declare the glory of God; and the firmament sheweth his handywork. Day unto day uttereth speech, and night unto night sheweth knowledge. There is no speech nor language, where their voice is not heard.

–PSALM 19:1–3, KJV

If the unenlightened heathen thus still acknowledged among the starry heavens some vestiges of ancient prophecy, shall Christians neglect to trace there the memorials of a revelation from the Divine Creator?[369]

–FRANCES ROLLESTON (1781–1864)

We are going to pick up where we left off in ch. 15 and decode the story that God has written in the stars. As we go, we will see that God is faithfully executing a plan that was conceived before the founding of the cosmos, and it will become obvious just how sovereign he really is. We will also look into the near future and find an astronomical alignment that may signify the arrival of the Antichrist.

Once again, it must be stressed that we are not engaging in astrology by examining the constellations. Astrology teaches that the heavenly bodies act upon the inhabitants of the earth in some mystical fashion, and that their arrangement from day to day and year to year drives the course of our lives. Because they supposedly understand the forces being exerted by the celestial bodies, astrologers believe that they can break away from the otherwise predetermined flow of history. The Bible contradicts such fantasy, but it does plainly state that God put the stars in the sky for signs, and that the Almighty brings out the Mazzaroth (set of constellations) in its season.

The Lion of Judah says of himself, "I am the Alpha and Omega" (Rev. 22:13), therefore the story of the Zodiac must begin and end with Leo. As we learned all the way back in ch. 2, the great story woven throughout the many books of the Bible is a romance between YHVH and the Redeemed, who collectively take the symbolic form of a virgin bride. The Book of Revelation concludes with the eternal union of this spotless bride to the one who sits upon the throne in the New Jerusalem. It is no coincidence that Virgo and Leo stand side-by-side on the ecliptic, and any attempt to interpret the Zodiac must end at the place where the virgin and the lion touch. The ancient pagan custom was to start with Virgo and end with Leo, but this is the reverse of how the author intended it—no surprise, since those in the kingdom of darkness have everything backwards. The order of the signs must be as follows: Leo, Cancer, Gemini, Taurus, Aries, Pisces, Aquarius, Capricorn, Sagittarius, Scorpius, Libra, and Virgo.

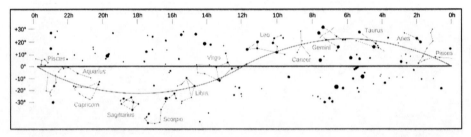

Figure 20-1. Constellations of the Zodiac overlaid with the path of the sun. By the author, based on a graphic by M. J. Powell

Through the Mazzaroth

In this section we will walk through the Mazzaroth in chronological order. The numbered list following the description of each zodiacal sign gives the names and meanings of that sign's three decans.

1. LEO

The lion is the symbol of the tribe of Judah and of the righteous branch that arose from that tribe (Rev. 5:5).

The summer solstice was in Leo during the same age that the vernal (spring) equinox was in Taurus, the fertile, heavenly bull; that era was also when God populated the earth (ca. 4000 BC). The summer solstice is the longest day of the year, the day on which the sun reaches the apex of the heavenly arch. Ancient myth has it the sun is a fiery lion who brought order to the dark cosmos by roaring and pushing back Saturn. In 4000 BC the sun hovered directly in front of the mouth of Leo, reminding us that Yeshua is the Word who was with God in the beginning, when God spoke the lights into existence. The apostle John writes, "All things were made by [the Word], and without him was not any thing made that was made" (John 1:3).

The star *Regulus*, whose name means "Prince," is the brightest star in Leo and sits square on the ecliptic. William Tyler Olcott writes in *Star Lore of All Ages* that Regulus

Figure 20-2. One of twelve renderings depicted in Urania's Mirror, a set of constellation cards published in London in ca. 1825, designed by Richard Rouse Bloxam and engraved by Sidney Hall

has also been called "the Star Royal," and the cuneiform inscriptions of the Euphratean Valley refer to it as "the star of the King." The Arabs knew it as "the Kingly Star," and it was one of the four celebrated Royal Stars.... "Cor Leonis," or "the Heart of the Lion," was another name for this star, and Al-Biruni called it "the Heart of the Royal Lion." The importance of Regulus in ancient times is well attested by the great variety of names assigned it, titles for the most part signifying power and might.[370]

This star may represent Yeshua himself, or it may represent King David, who will be set up as a prince under Yeshua during the Millennium (Ezek. 34:23-24). So we see that even the stars within these constellations can have names that enhance the meanings of the signs.

Even though we begin with Leo, we also end there, and Leo's decans have more to do with the completion of history than its inauguration.

i.   Hydra—The serpent in the Abyss. This is Draco cast down and imprisoned for a thousand years. The position of Leo in relation to Hydra is important: the lion is above the serpent with his paws coming down on the back of its head. This predicts the fulfillment of God's promise that the seed of the woman will crush the head of the serpent (Gen. 3:15).

ii.   Corvus—The bird whose talons grip Hydra's tail. To the Greeks this was a crow, but its original avian classification may have been different. Corvus represents either the birds that will gather to feast after the battle of Armageddon (Rev. 19:21), or the angel that will throw Satan into the Abyss (Rev. 20:1-3).

iii.   Crater—The cup which sits atop Hydra. The meaning of this symbol is uncertain, but it may be the cup of iniquity, locked up with Satan during the peaceful and righteous reign of Yeshua. Alternatively, it may be the cup of God's wrath which will be poured out as fire upon Satan's army at the end of the Millennium (Rev. 20:9).

2. CANCER

The crab, like all shellfish, is a biblically unclean animal that lives in the sea. As discussed previously, the sea represents the Gentile nations, those set against YHVH; accordingly, Cancer is face-to-face with Leo in a defensive posture, pincers at the ready. Crabs are completely armored creatures, strong for their size, and they do not easily let go once they have grabbed onto something. They prefer to move diagonally instead of straight forward. In contrast, fish are soft creatures who lack the grasping ability of the crab, are not good at moving perpendicular to the axis of their bodies, and are declared by God to be clean for food. From this we can surmise that Cancer represents the sinful, unyielding nature of mankind after the Fall. Men are uncomfortable following the wisdom of God to "Let your eyes look directly forward, and your gaze be straight before you" (Pro. 4:25), and to "make straight paths for your feet" (Heb. 12:13). They can cause great harm when they grab what they want, and they are unwilling to let go of their sinful ways. They are unclean in their hearts and not tender towards the spirit of God. And isn't it interesting how much sin is like the disease called cancer, which starts small but eventually takes hold of every part

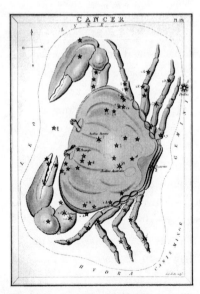

Figure 20-3. Cancer, by Sidney Hall

of a person and turns it into death.

i.   Argo—The ship. Specifically, the Ark. It is the safe place where God encloses his people who are living while his wrath is exercised against sin.

ii.   Ursa Minor—Also known as the Little Dipper. Today, both Ursas are depicted as bears, yet they have very long tails that are nothing like the stumpy tails of real bears. The oldest records have Ursa Minor as either a cart or a fold. For instance, in the Egyptian Dendera Zodiac[a] it is known as "the cattlefolds." The Hebrew, Arabic, and Persian words for "bear," "cattle," and "animal enclosure" all sound similar to one another, and it is theorized that the Greeks mixed them up when making their star charts.[371]

The designation *minor* implies that Ursa Minor is the lesser of two containers. This could signify the relatively meager assembly of called-out ones who lived before the Flood, or the deceased saints who waited patiently in Sheol until the Resurrection of Yeshua. If the latter option is correct, then the handle of the Little Dipper, which corresponds to the bear's tail, could represent the "train of captives" led by Yeshua out of the Paradise portion of Sheol on the day of First Fruits. That interpretation is strengthened by the fact that the pole star, Polaris, is located at the tip of Ursa Minor's tail, in the same area of space as Zaphon, the heavenly Mount of Assembly.

iii.   Ursa Major—All of the stars in this constellation have names related to sheep, flocks, herds, multitudes, and companies of travelers. One star is named "Little Lamb," another "She Goat." The tail of Ursa Major is actually a line of animals filing out of the enclosure and towards the constellation Boötes, the harvesting shepherd who holds both a crook and a sickle. Our Good Shepherd said that at the end of the world there will be a harvest, and then he will separate the sheep from the goats.

3. GEMINI

Although the Greeks saw Gemini as twin boys, more ancient cultures depicted them as a heterosexual couple. The Hebrew name of the

---

[a] The Temple of Dendera was built in the first century before Christ, but the map of constellations in the temple comes from a source map of greater antiquity (700–1600 BC, as dated by the precession of the equinoxes).

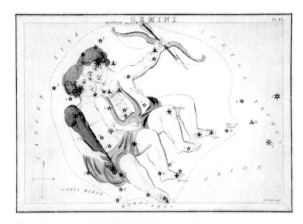

Figure 20-4. Gemini, by Sidney Hall

constitution is *Thau-min*, meaning "united," which agrees with the Coptic name, *Pi-Mahi*. In the Dendera Zodiac the sign is shown as a male and female walking together, and its name means "the place of him who cometh."

The tarot card of Sol/Helios depicts Gemini as a boy and girl standing underneath the sun in a setting filled with occult symbolism. The two figures both wear plain white, conical hats. In *The Pythagorean Tarot: An Interpretation of the Major and Minor Arcana on Pythagorean and Alchemical Principles*, Ioannes Opsopaus has this to say about the picture:

> ...the twins unite the inferior, passive, or cold elements, earth and water. These elements correspond to Taurus and Cancer, respectively, which are united by Gemini. In addition, the boy's right hand is turned skyward in the classical attitude of celestial invocation, whereas the girl's left hand is turned downward in chthonic invocation. **Thus the children unite the forces of Heaven and the Abyss**, the astral spirits and the elemental spirits. In this way the superior (active, hot) elements, fire and air, are united with the inferior. The boy's elements are fire and earth, which are dry, that is firm and rigid; the girl's are air and water, which are moist, that is yielding and adaptive.[372]

This is a pagan interpretation of the constellation, but it fits perfectly well with our understanding of the roles of Dumuzi and Inanna, or Osiris and Isis, or Shiva and Parvati, in the sacred marriage.

i. Lepus—The hare. We have precious little information about this decan, but the traditional view of hares and rabbits may be helpful to us. These animals have long been seen as symbols of fertility, femininity, and abundance, and are often linked to the lunar cycle.[373] With such associations, it is no wonder that the white bunny on a black background is the logo of a certain pornographic magazine. Rabbits were sacred to Aphrodite/Venus because of their procreative ability, and Freyja, the Norse goddess of love, sensuality, and mysteries, had hares as attendants. There is a strange but well-established connection between hares and eggs, especially in eastern Europe. The eggs symbolized the rebirth of the sun god at the dawn of the year, and they also symbolize the cosmic womb which contained the potential for both genders.[375] In Egypt, the goddess Wenet was a hare who faces the dawn, but Osiris was also sometimes presented as a hare.[376] Hares were thought to be hermaphrodites,[377] which reminds us of the dual nature of Inanna and the planet Venus. Buddhist and Hindu texts present the hare as a bringer of destruction and reincarnation in the same sacrificial fire as the phoenix.[378]

Taking all of this under consideration, we conclude that Lepus is most likely a representation of the religion of Inanna/Ishtar, the whore of Babylon.

ii.   Canis Major—The greater dog. Some Christian writers have suggested that the two Canis signs represent Yeshua as the glorious prince and coming redeemer. Frankly, I think the comparison is unintentionally demeaning. Yeshua comes as a mighty lion, not a dog: "For I will be like a lion to Ephraim, and like a young lion to the house of Judah. I, even I, will tear and go away; I will carry off, and no one shall rescue" (Hos. 5:14).

Wolves and dogs are unclean animals, and Scripture points out that "a dog returns to its own vomit" like a pig to muck (2 Pet. 2:22). In the Old Testament, dogs are often spoken of derisively, and one messianic psalm compares Yeshua's executioners to dogs when it says "dogs encompass me; a company of evildoers encircle me; they have pierced my hands and feet (Psa. 22:16). During his ministry Yeshua told a Gentile woman, "It is not right to take the children's bread and throw it to the dogs" (Matt. 15:26). The Bible paints wolves in an even worse light, using them to represent false teachers whose aim is to devour the flock. Would God choose to use the same creature to represent the Good Shepherd? Certainly not. This constellation, which the Persians saw as a wolf named *Zeeb*, meaning "Leader," and which the Hebrews called by the same name,[379] represents a pagan leader who leads astray and devours.

It is true that Yeshua sometimes takes the form of a lion, which is ranked with the unclean animals, but this is a role that he takes on when he goes out to conquer, not an identity that he wears consistently. His steadfast identity is as a shepherd and a lamb. One of the proverbs says that "a king's wrath is like the growling of a lion" (19:12). It is only when a king's anger flares hot that he becomes a lion. The lion is the symbol of Yeshua's tribe, Judah, and the one time in Scripture that Yeshua is called a lion, it is spoken in conjunction with his role as the champion of Judah (Rev. 5:5).

If Yeshua is a lion and a lamb, then Canis Major must represent some other individual than the Lord. The Babylonians saw the constellation not as a dog but as a bow and arrow, while the Egyptians saw it as the bull of Isis with a star between her horns. We know that Semiramis was a hunter like her husband and that Inanna has multiple associations with bulls (e.g., her marriage to "the wild bull Dumuzi" and her use of the Bull of Heaven to defend her honor), and while those facts don't prove anything, they may lend support to a theory identifying Canis Major as Nimrod's wife.

The brightest fixed star in the sky, Sirius, is located in the head of Canis Major. Its name in Greek is *Seirios*, meaning "Glowing" or "Scorching." The heliacal rising of Sirius marked the *dog days of summer* in the ancient world and signaled the annual rising of the Nile in Egypt, when the abundant waters made the land fertile once again. Four thousand years ago this rising took place in July, during the Hebrew month of Tammuz.[a]

To the Egyptians, Sirius was the star of the goddess Isis, and in artwork throughout Egypt she was consistently paired with the jackal-headed god Anubis, son of Osiris. Interestingly, Sirius is a binary star.

iii.   Canis Minor—The lesser canine. In Babylonian astronomy, Canis Minor was a pair of little twins, but to the Egyptians it was a dual-natured creature with the body of a snake and the head of an ibis. Like Canis Major, the meaning of this constellation is a mystery, but it could be a reference to Nimrod's twin sons, who the Romans memorialized as Romulus and Remus. In Roman mythology, the twins were born to the god Mars or Hercules and a Vestal Virgin named Rhea Silvia. A wolf suckled the boys in the wilderness after they were abandoned to die. Diodorus Siculus mentions in his *Library* that Osiris had two sons, Anubis and Macedo,

---

[a]   Yes, sadly, the Jews have a month named after the Mesopotamian version of the dying and rising god of fertility.

who wore the skins of a dog and a wolf over their armor.[380] Canis Minor may represent either Macedo alone or the pair of sons together.

4. TAURUS

Figure 20-5. Taurus, by Sidney Hall

Without a doubt, this sign stands for God Almighty. The Sacred Bull represented the Deity in ancient Near Eastern religions. The fact that the bull was lunar in Mesopotamia from the earliest times, its horns drawn in the shape of a crescent moon, alludes to YHVH, whose holy days are based on the lunar calendar. Nimrod tried to appropriate the identity of the bull for himself. In the Sumerian tales about Bilgames (from whence came the Akkadian *Epic of Gilgamesh*), the giant demigod protagonist claims that he has killed the Bull of Heaven, and he assures his people that they no longer need to worry about appeasing the big bully (excuse the pun!). The descendants of the Sumerians built idols known as *lamassu*, winged protective deities with the bodies of bulls and the heads of bearded men.

In the pictographic Phoenician and proto-Hebraic alphabets that were used during the time of Abraham, the first letter is shaped like the head of an ox. It means "strength" and "crown." And when the Israelites at Sinai created a graven image to act as a mediator for them in Moses' stead, they crafted it in the form of a young ox intended to stand for the transcendent ox, Elohiym.

The charging Taurus is the Mighty One of Israel, who showed himself all-powerful during the Exodus.

i.   Orion—The giant warrior. This is the adversary of God, and in the sky he confronts the bull face-to-face, war club raised high to strike. He arrogantly waves a lion's pelt with his left hand as a demonstration of what he will do to God's son. The Bible thrice mentions Orion by the name *Kesil* (Job 9:9, 38:31; Amos 5:8), meaning "fool" (Strong's #H3684). This foolishly prideful warrior is none other than Nimrod, the mighty hunter in the face of the Lord. The 7th-century *Chronicon Paschale* states that Nimrod was posthumously deified in the constellation of Orion, and that the Persians still call it *Nimrod*.[381] Recently discovered Hungarian myths also equate Orion to Nimrod.[382]

In Greek mythology, Orion was a handsome giant and the son of the sea god, Neptune. In Muslim astronomy, Orion was known as *Al-Jabbar*, "The Giant." The Egyptians called him *Long-Strider* because of his impressive height. Egyptian Pyramid Text Utterance 477 reads, "You threw Osiris to the earth… when there came into being **his name of Orion, long of leg and lengthy of stride**, who presides over Upper Egypt." This Utterance incontrovertibly links Orion to Osiris. Utterance 442 does likewise: "Behold, he has come as Orion, behold, Osiris has come as Orion." The fact that the Egyptians explicitly made this connection supports Robert Bauval's theory that the pyramids of Giza are by design a mirror image of the highly recognizable stars of Orion's belt.[383]

Finally, Dendera text II (101,3) states that Osiris measured eight

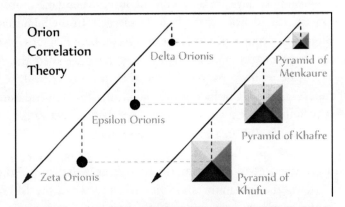

Figure 20–6. Robert Bauval postulates that the positions of the Giza pyramids relative to one another correspond precisely to the positions of the stars in Orion's belt.

cubits, six palms, and three fingers in height. That's about 4.6m or 15' tall. Whether this is accurate or not is irrelevant; the Egyptians obviously considered the demigod to have been a giant. And no doubt he was, because Osiris is Nimrod, the gibbor.

ii.   Eridanus—The river. This constellation's name may be based on the Sumerian city of Eridu, location of the Enki's Abzu temple. This hypothesis arises from the fact that the Babylonian constellation MUL.NUN.

KI, meaning "Star of Eridu," could be the same as the Greek Eridanus. The celestial river runs from directly beneath Orion to the sea-monster, Cetus, which is Leviathan; it pictorially links the ruler of the Abyss to Asshur, which is a correlation that we previously found in Ezekiel 31.

iii.   Auriga—The shepherd. This sign is tricky to interpret because the identity of the shepherd seems so obvious until we realize that he is grasping goats instead of sheep. Many would like to think that Auriga represents Yeshua, the Good Shepherd, but what is he doing holding goats? We can be sure that these are goats and not sheep because of the names of the stars in this sign: the alpha star is *Alioth*, meaning "she goat"; the beta star is *Menkilinon*, which means "chain of the goats"; another star is called *Maaz*, indicating a "flock of goats." In every instance, wild goats in the scriptures are symbols of unbelievers, so Auriga may not be the Son of Man. I propose that Auriga represents one of the Kosmokraters because they were given charge over the Gentiles after Orion/Nimrod was slain by Taurus/YHVH. These same angelic rulers were later given charge of the rebellious Israelites. In the dream-visions of Enoch, the prophet sees God summon seventy shepherds and resign to them the sheep of Israel which have chosen to behave like heathen (88:94). Just as Tammuz and Osiris were called shepherds, so the angelic rulers of the seventy Gentile nations have been allowed to herd the goats of this world, including ethnic Israelites (for a time).

5. ARIES

Given the name *Taleh* ("Lamb") in Hebrew and *Bara-ziggar* ("Sacrifice of Righteousness") in Akkadian, Aries is the Lamb of God in his pre-incarnate form. The Bible compares God's saints to sheep, and the mighty one among the flock is the ram. The meaning

Figure 20-7. Aries, by Sidney Hall

of the Hebrew word for *ram* is "high, exalted." Traditionally, the ram also represents protection because the ram protected the herd; thus the ram is an exalted defender. Yeshua is the praiseworthy Angel of the Lord which protected Israel from the Egyptians and the inhabitants of Canaan, and who slew 185,000 Assyrians before they could siege Jerusalem.

When Abraham was asked to sacrifice his only son, Isaac, an angel stopped him from going through with it and provided a ram as a substitute, foreshadowing the future substitutionary sacrifice of the perfect ram.

i. Cetus—The sea monster. The constellation Cetus is named after a sea monster from Greek mythology, and it ranks with Draco as the largest of the creatures in the stars. It lies in the far south (at the mouth of the Abyss), on the opposite side of the celestial sphere from Draco and the Mount of Assembly. Johann Bayer depicted it as a "dragon fish" in the 17th century.[384] It lies under the constellations of Aries and Pisces, but not under the constellations that flank them (Taurus and Aquarius). Surely this denizen of the deep is Leviathan, whose presence is manifest during the ages of Aries and Pisces.

ii. Cassiopeia—The bride, seated in waiting. She is preparing herself to meet the king, for she is the betrothed of the Messiah. In her right hand she holds high a length of textile, and with her left hand she brushes leaves over her head. The textile is scarlet yarn and the leaves are hyssop.

"Purge me with hyssop, and I shall be clean," says the psalmist (Psa. 51:7). Why hyssop in particular? At the first Passover, God commanded the Israelites to "take a **bunch of hyssop and dip it in the blood** that is in the basin, and **touch the lintel** and the two doorposts with the blood that is in the basin" (Exo. 12:22). After the Israelites had come out of Egypt and agreed to enter into covenant with YHVH, Moses "took the blood of calves and goats, with water and **scarlet wool and hyssop**, and sprinkled both the book itself and all the people" (Heb. 9:19). Both hyssop and scarlet yarn were used by the Levitical priests to cleanse people and homes which had become unclean: "the priest shall command them to take for him who is to be cleansed two live clean birds[a] and **cedarwood and scarlet yarn and hyssop**" (Lev. 14:4). (I don't think it would

---

[a] Representing two living, heavenly witnesses, perhaps meant to be Enoch and Elijah, the only two human beings who were given permanent residence in heaven without first dying.

be going to far to assume that the chair on which Cassiopeia sits is made of cedar.) The fulfillment of these things is that Yeshua was given a scarlet robe when he was severely flogged (Matt. 27:28)—his innocent blood would have soaked the garment—and sour wine on a hyssop branch was offered to him while he was on the cross (John 19:29), the sturdy wood of which may have been from a cedar tree (Hebrew: *erez*).

Some Christians have been misled by naïve Gentile theology into believing that the bride of Christ is comprised only of those believers who have lived after the Resurrection. The Bible does not make this distinction. It indicates instead that Gentile believers who respond to the Gospel are grafted into the tree of Israel (Rom. 11:11-24), made into "one new man" by being added to "the commonwealth of Israel" and "the covenants of promise" (Eph. 2:12-15). The whole Song of Solomon is an allegory of the love between Messiah and his bride, the saints of all ages, and that bride is drawn in the sky as Cassiopeia.

iii.   Perseus—The mighty one who breaks. Perseus is a warrior who holds a sword aloft in one hand and the head of Medusa in the other. The name of Medusa may come from *medomai*, meaning "to contrive,"[385] or from the Sanskrit *medhas* and Greek *metis*,[386] both of which mean "wisdom." These are fitting descriptors for God's angelic adversary. The greatest star in the head of Medusa is *Al Ghoul*, meaning "evil spirit." Medusa's head is covered in serpents, but the head itself is an invention of Greek mythology. The serpents are the heads of Leviathan (not the real beast, but the Dragon's kingdom). Perseus is the Son of Man, he who in the Day of the Lord "with his sore and great and strong sword shall punish leviathan the piercing serpent, even leviathan that crooked serpent" (Isa. 27:1, KJV). The prophet Asaph said to God, "You crushed the **heads** of Leviathan; you gave him as food for the creatures of the wilderness" (Psa. 74:14).

6. PISCES

Fish played a big role in the ministry of Yeshua. He commanded the nets of some fishermen to be filled to the breaking point, pulled a coin out of a fishes' mouth in order to pay a tax, multiplied a couple of fish to feed a crowd of five thousand, and ate fish with his followers after his resurrection. He told his disciples that he would make them fishers of men, and indeed they caught a great multitude. God foretold this through Jeremiah, saying, "Behold, I am sending for many fishers, declares

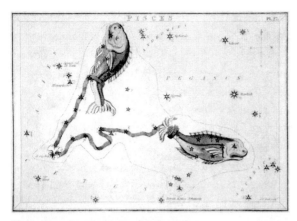

Figure 20-8. Pisces, by Sidney Hall

the LORD, and they shall catch them" (16:16).

The two celestial fish which follow the age of the sacrificial ram represent the two divisions of Israel: the Northern Kingdom and the Southern Kingdom. More information about Pisces is coming up in the next section of this chapter.

i.   The Band—The fish of Pisces are held by a cord or rope, demonstrating that they have been caught and are no longer roaming free. They have become someone's property. In some versions of the Zodiac, Aries is shown with one leg through the band, which identifies Yeshua for us as the owner of the fish. Also, it is meaningful that the fish are permanently connected to one another. Everyone who joins the family of God in the Messiah belongs to one of the twelve tribes and thus to one of these two kingdoms of Israel. Accordingly, the only surviving epistle of James is addressed "to the twelve tribes in the Dispersion" (1:1).

ii.   Cepheus—The crowned king seated on a throne. He holds up a scepter and gazes at Andromeda. The name of Cepheus' alpha star, Alderamin, means "right arm," which is a biblical epithet for the Messiah, God's strong right arm. Beta star Alfirk's name means "flock of sheep." The gamma star is Errai, whose designation is Arabic and means "the Shepherd." Cepheus is the resurrected Yeshua, returned to heaven and seated at the right hand of the Father (Acts 2:33). He awaits the fullness of the time of the Gentiles, when the cup of iniquity is full, at which point he will return for his bride.

iii.   Andromeda—The chained maiden. Greek and Hindu legends see her as a human woman with fetters upon her wrists and ankles, while Arabian records have her as a fish that overlaps Pisces. This fish-woman is the persecuted Church.

7. AQUARIUS

Here we have a man pouring a great volume of water from a bucket at his side. The Hebrews knew this sign as "The Water Urn," and the Egyptians saw it as a man who put his jars into the Nile to begin the annual flood. Aquarius marks the beginning of the ministry of the Holy Spirit as it was delivered on the Day of Pentecost. Joel prophesied about the miracle that would begin at Pentecost and eventually encompass

Figure 20-9. Aquarius, by Sidney Hall

the whole earth, saying, "And it shall come to pass afterward, that I will **pour out my Spirit** on all flesh" (2:28). Regarding the waters that God sends from above, Joseph A. Seiss writes,

> Wherever the Scriptures represent the Spirit and grace of God under the imagery of waters, the idea of unfailing supply and plenteous abundance is also invariably connected with it. Sometimes it is a plentiful rain; sometimes it is a voluminous fountain; sometimes it is a great river flowing with fullness that supplies a thousand life-freighted rivulets. Inspiration tells us that the rock smitten by Moses was the type of the smiting of Christ and the blessings proceeding from Him; but in that case the waters "gushed; they ran in dry places like a river."[387]

iv.   Cygnus—The swan whose body forms a cross. Greek and Roman mythologies offer us little assistance in explaining this sign, but we can still glean a hint from the fact that there is a common element among four major myths involving swans. The son of Apollo, the son of Poseidon, the son of Ares, and the son of Sthenelus all turned into swans after their deaths. Cygnus may therefore represent the resurrected Christ returning to heaven, which had to happen before the Holy Spirit could be poured out. Yeshua told his disciples, "It is to your advantage that I go away, for if I do not go away, the Helper will not come to you. But if I go, I will send him to you" (John 16:7).

    v.   Piscis Australis—The southern fish. Yeshua said, "If anyone thirsts, let him come to me and drink" (John 7:37). The waters of Aquarius descend before the urn-bearer and turn under him to disappear into the mouth of a fish. The stream of God's spiritual blessing does not fade into the starry scenery or split off so as to water more than one location; rather, its entire volume proceeds into the body of a single constellation representing Yeshua's disciples.

    vi.   Pegasus—The winged horse of the fountain. This swift, white creature is the mascot of 1st-century evangelism. The pace at which the kingdom of God spread is noted in Acts, where we read that "this [evangelism] continued for two years, so that all the residents of Asia [Minor] heard the word of the Lord, both Jews and Greeks" (19:10). The Babylonians saw the constellation of Pegasus not as a horse, but as a field, which still fits the theme because it can represent the *mission field*. Moreover, the Egyptian Dendera Zodiac presents an irrigated plot of land between the two fish of Pisces, and this plot is thought to correspond to the well-known *Square of Pegasus* asterism. The work of taking the Gospel into fields that are ripe for harvest continues to this day.

8. CAPRICORNUS

    The Sea-goat is one of the stranger zodiacal signs, as it is a combination of two animals from radically different biomes. The front half of the creature is a goat, and the back half is a fish's tail curled in vigorous action. It has been represented this way since the Middle Bronze Age and is explicitly listed as *MULSUHUR.MAŠ*, "The Goat-Fish," in Babylonian star catalogs from before 1,000 BC.

Figure 20–10. Capricornus, by Sidney Hall

The Bible rarely has good things to say about goats.

Speaking in third person, Yeshua promised that when the Son of Man comes in his glory, "Before him will be gathered all the nations, and he will separate people one from another as a shepherd separates the sheep from the goats. And he will place the sheep on his right, but the goats on the left" (Matt. 25:32-33). Both of these groups will call Yeshua *Lord*, or *Master*, but only the sheep did what the master wanted. Those will inherit the kingdom, but the goats will go into eternal punishment. This parable follows directly on the heels of two other parables, one about an unprofitable servant who is cast into outer darkness because he bore no fruit, and another about ten virgins who await a single bridegroom, only half of whom are taken into the wedding chamber. These parables are each teaching us that Messiah will not accept those who profess him as master but will not behave accordingly.

A verse in Ezekiel clearly supports this interpretation: "As for you, **my flock**, thus says the Lord God: Behold, I judge between sheep and sheep, between rams and male goats" (34:17). In this verse God addresses and judges his own flock, not the wild animals of Satan's fold.

Domesticated goats in the Bible represent members of God's flock who are unwilling to "walk the walk." Like the rich man (a believer) who wanted to follow Yeshua but could not bring himself to sell his possessions, it is the things which goats treasure above the Living God that prevent them from having intimacy with the Messiah. They are idolaters at heart. While real sheep usually respond well to a shepherd's voice, goats do not. Real goats are obstinate, rebellious creatures, but they are biologically very similar to sheep, which is why Yeshua said that he will have to separate the rams from the goats like wheat from tares.

We have already established that fish in the Mazzaroth represent the assembly of the Redeemed. Combining that with our assessment of the meaning of goats, we discover that Capricornus is showing us false believers at the head of the Redeemed (i.e., leading the school of fish). This is a picture of the condition of many Christian congregations over the last nineteen hundred years, and all the more so as we approach the Day of the Lord. Christian leadership positions are often filled with people who do not genuinely fear God or live the kind of radically sacrificial and set-apart life that Christ and his apostles modeled for us. Yeshua calls them Nicolaitans because they would rather lord over the laity than serve Yeshua's flock humbly and without compromise (1 Pet. 5:1-3).[388]

i. Delphinus—The dolphin. This creature is known primarily for its ability to spring with great speed out of the sea and seemingly fly through the air.

ii. Sagitta—The arrow. It has been loosed but the one who sent it is unknown. Arrows are often used in Scripture to portray God's swift and inescapable punishment upon the arrogant and rebellious.

iii. Aquila—The wounded eagle. The name of Aquila's Alpha star is *Altair*, meaning "Flying Eagle." This bird was once soaring but now, having been struck by Sagitta, it falls. This could be an illustration of what Daniel saw in his vision, of the wings of the lion kingdom being plucked off. Is Delphinus a symbol of ICBMs launched from submarines, coming up out of the sea with great speed? Is Sagitta one of the nuclear missiles that will destroy that soaring eagle, America? If so, the destruction of the United States may mark the full arrival of the Four Horsemen of the Apocalypse. Only time will tell.

9. SAGITTARIUS

This constellation has been classically depicted as a centaur wielding a bow and arrow, with a cape trailing behind him. (The star at the tip of Sagittarius' arrow is *Alnasl*, meaning "The Point.") The Babylonians also saw him as a chimera, but to them he had wings instead of a cape.

He also had two heads, and a second tail like a scorpion stinger. The presentation of Sagittarius in the Egyptian Dendera Zodiac follows the Babylonian version almost exactly. The wings indicate that this being is a spirit of some sort, while the scorpion stinger

Figure 20-11. Sagittarius, by Sidney Hall

indicates that he is a fallen one, bound to the earth and hostile to those living there. One of the two faces of Sagittarius, the one that points backward, is that of a lion, but the one pointing forward is that of a man.

These represent the signs of the extremities of the year, of the Great Heat and the Great Cold, of fire and water; they are Leo and Aquarius. These two signs which lie exactly opposite each other on the zodiacal wheel speak to us of the past and the present, and the cycle of time. Researcher David Flynn writes,

> Again we are reminded of the two-headed deity Janus, the Roman god who presides over doorways and arches, the dualistic god of war and peace, the past and future, after whom the month of January was named. These deities associated with entryways, arches, pillars and doorways are also "time gods"—their dualistic nature refers to a transitional place in time, or a place of endings and new beginnings.[389]

The transition from one grand cycle to the next is delineated by the core of the Milky Way, which is the spot where the Ouroboros consumes its own tail (refer to ch. 5). The heads and weapon of Sagittarius are directly beneath the open mouth of the serpent, and the tip of his arrow points to the galactic core proper. In other words, the archer is situated at the gateway between eons. As an aside, it has been suggested that the oblong core of the galaxy is also the fiery funeral pyre from which the phoenix, as Scorpius, rises to new life.

The sun at winter solstice is currently transitioning through the mouth of the Ouroboros. The winter solstice is the shortest day of the year, the day on which the sun is allegorically reborn, after which the days begin to lengthen until, six months later, the sun is at the height of its power. The winter solstice was dead center in the mouth of the Ouroboros in 1948, when the nation of Israel was reconstituted. Year by year it is moving up and out of that area, but will still be in-between the serpent's jaws until the latter half of the 21st century.

The first judgments of the apostle John's apocalyptic vision are the Seal Judgments, and the first four seals when broken bring forth four horsemen. At the breaking of the first seal John says, "And I looked, and behold, a white horse! And **its rider had a bow**, and **a crown was given to him**, and he came out conquering, and to conquer" (Rev. 6:2). It is this first rider that marks the transition into the Apocalypse; everything begins here. Could this horseman be the custodian of the cosmic gateway? Perhaps he is not a chimera, as the astronomer-priests of the ancient world believed, but rather a spirit atop a horse. Although John didn't specify that the rider of the white horse sports a pair of wings, it is obvious that he and the other riders are spirit beings, so it would make sense for him to be depicted as winged. Moreover, the Babylonians associated Sagittarius with Nergal, the archer-god of the planet Mars. He was the god of war, fire, and civilization, and had such titles as "Giant King of War," "Illuminator of the Great City," and "The Hunter." This of course brings us back to Nimrod. Did the wise men of old understand that Sagittarius represented the entity responsible for opening the gates for War, the Second Horseman of the Apocalypse?

Everyone familiar with the Zodiac knows that Sagittarius is a bowman, but few realize that he stands facing a crown. Corona Australis, a constellation in the shape of a crown, lies directly in front of Sagittarius, almost touching the collarbones of the horse. This corresponds perfectly to the crown that John saw given to the First Horseman of the Apocalypse. It seems most likely that Sagittarius is the white horseman who throws the world into chaos.

i.   Draco—The Dragon. He coils around the northern pole of the heavens, reflecting the desire of Satan as it comes through Asshur: "I will exalt my throne **above the stars** of God: I will sit also upon the mount of the congregation, **in the sides of the north**... I will be like the most High" (Isa. 14:13-14, KJV). By going forth to conquer, Sagittarius cues the arrival of the rider on the red horse (he who takes peace from the earth) and thus begins the sequence of events that leads to the near-completion of Satan's master plan.

ii.   Lyra—The harp. After the first four seals are broken and the four horsemen ride forth, John sees a great multitude of saints standing before the throne of God in heaven and worshiping the Lamb. One of the elder angels informs him that these are the Redeemed who have come out of the great tribulation (Rev. 7:13-14). Later in Revelation we see that these saints have been given harps: "And I saw what appeared to be a sea of glass mingled with fire—and also those who had conquered the beast and its image and the number of its name, standing beside the sea of glass **with harps of God in their hands**" (Rev. 15:2).

iii.   Ara—The altar. It is positioned nearly upside-down as if its fiery contents are being poured out upon the inhabitants of the lower realm. In fact, according to John the Revelator, that is exactly what is happening: "Then the angel took the censer and filled it with **fire from the altar and threw it on the earth**, and there were peals of thunder, rumblings, flashes of lightning, and an earthquake" (Rev. 8:5).

10. SCORPIUS

This sign has been associated with two creatures, the scorpion and the eagle. Scorpius is the only zodiacal sign traditionally associated with more than one symbol, and no one remembers why. If God is the author of the Mazzaroth, then we should be able to find something in the Bible that corresponds to the dual nature of this sign.

Before they entered the Promised Land, Moses reminded Israel that it was God "who led you through the great and terrifying wilderness, with its **fiery serpents and scorpions** and thirsty ground..." (Deut. 8:15). These words may have literally applied to the children of God living at that time, but they also hold spiritual meaning for the rest of us, because the New Testament authors teach that the journey of the Israelites through the wilderness was an allegory of the journey of all the Redeemed through the spiritual wilderness of this fallen world. The enemies of God's people are represented here by two types of venomous creatures. We know

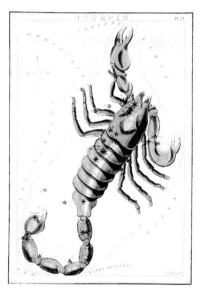

Figure 20-12. Scorpio, by Sidney Hall

that Satan is a serpent and that serpents are used in the scriptures to symbolize fallen angels, but what are the scorpions?

During one of Yeshua's lessons he made the statement, "What father among you, if his son asks for a fish, will instead of a fish give him a serpent; or if he asks for an egg, will give him a scorpion?" (Luke 11:11-13). The Lord never said anything without a reason, and everything that he did say taught one lesson on the surface and another lesson underneath. We have to consider why, out of the long list of dangerous animals, Messiah would chose a serpent and a scorpion for his illustration.

Only one chapter earlier in the Gospel of Luke, Yeshua declared that his disciples are equipped to do spiritual battle with both serpents and scorpions. Yeshua said, "Behold, I have given you **authority to tread on serpents and scorpions**, and over all the power of the enemy, and nothing shall hurt you" (Luke. 10:19). These words are not, as some foolish men have found out, permission to play with dangerous animals[a]. We have only been given authority over the entities represented by venomous animals.

The tormenting spirits which will emerge from the Abyss during the fifth trumpet judgment of Revelation are described as having power "like the power of scorpions of the earth" (Rev. 9:3). There are so many of them that John describes them as a swarm of locusts, but he sees that their ability to torture people is in their scorpion-like tails. These are not physical insects, but spirit creatures that were locked up in the Abyss. There are only two groups that we know for certain are imprisoned there: the rebellious Watchers (minus Azazel, who is under the desert) and ninety percent of the antediluvian Nephiliym. Thus it would seem that the Bible uses scorpions to symbolize the unclean spirits that issued from the Nephiliym. This makes good sense because God declared that the spirits of the giants "shall cause lamentation" on the earth (Eno. 15:9).

It also makes sense that Scorpius would fall chronologically after the First Horseman in the story of the Mazzaroth, because the trumpet judgments do come after the breaking of the first seals in John's apocalypse.

A Babylonian stele from the time of Nebuchadnezzar and found at Abû Habba in 1882 depicts Gulu, the goddess of the underworld, sitting below-ground and being guarded by an archer who has the body and tail of a scorpion, and the feet of bird. It is very interesting that a combination of Saggittarius and Scorpius would be shown guarding the goddess of the Abyss.

As to why Scorpius would also be considered an eagle: the origin of the Nephiliym is from the angelic Watchers, and angels have always been symbolized by powerful birds. The dead giants are eternal angelic spirits that have become completely twisted and desire only to inflict harm. Now, like scorpions, those who are not locked in the Abyss must wander in dry places seeking shelter (Luke 11:24).

i.   Serpens—The rebellious angel. This is the Dragon of Revelation 12

---

[a] During his missionary travels, Paul was bitten by a deadly snake and remained in perfect health, but he wasn't purposefully handling it. Playing with venomous animals is testing the Lord, which Yeshua refused to do when tempted in the wilderness.

engaged in war in the second heaven.

ii.   Ophiuchus—Michael, the archangel, who wrestles with Serpens while standing on Scorpius. "Now war arose in heaven, Michael and his angels fighting against the dragon. And the dragon and his angels fought back, but he was defeated, and there was no longer any place for them in heaven. And the great dragon was thrown down, that ancient serpent, who is called the devil and Satan, the deceiver of the whole world—he was thrown down to the earth, and his angels were thrown down with him" (Rev. 12:7-9).

iii.   Hercules—The oldest Greek texts to mention this constellation do not refer to it as Hercules. In regard to its identity Aratus writes, "Right there in its [Draco's] orbit wheels a Phantom form, like to a man that strives at a task. That sign no man knows how to read clearly, nor what task he is bent, but men simply call him *On His Knees*."[390] These are the saints who John sees immediately after Michael hurls Satan to the earth. They rejoice, bent in worship to God, because the accuser of the brethren has been thrown down, and they kneel on Draco's head because "they have conquered him by the blood of the Lamb and by the word of their testimony, for they loved not their lives even unto death" (Rev. 12:11).

11. LIBRA

The scales of Libra are the sign of just judgment conducted by the righteous and omniscient God. This sign marks the Day of the Lord. Men are "laid in the balance" (Psa. 62:9) and "weighed in the balances" (Dan. 5:27). The Redeemed who remain repentant owe no debt, for it was paid in full, but their good deeds are weighed to determine rewards. The wicked are weighed to determine the severity of their eternal prison sentence.

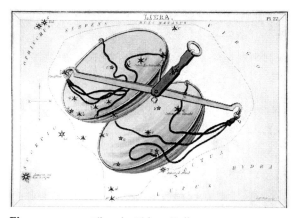

Figure 20–13. Libra, by Sidney Hall

i.   Crux—The cross. It is the suffering of Messiah as the second Adam which qualifies him to judge the nations. Yeshua's death upon a crucifix and subsequent resurrection from the grave signals his victory over the solar deities of the mystery religions. The cross may be part of the sign of the Son of Man which appears in the sky at the time of his Second Coming (Matt. 24:30).

ii.   Lupus—The slain wolf. Prior to a 15th-century mistranslation of Ptolemy's *Almagest*, Lupus was not considered a wolf, but rather an arbitrary animal killed by Centaurus, who is piercing it with a sword or spear.[391] An astronomer named Hipparchus of Bithynia (died after 127 BC) called it *Therion*, meaning "Beast."[392] The Babylonians knew it as the "mad dog."[393] Lupus is Asshur, the Beast from the Abyss, being killed by the rider on the white horse, which is Yeshua (Rev. 19:11-21).

iii.   Corona—This is the royal crown which signifies Messiah Yeshua seated as king over the whole earth, for God has promised to make his enemies a footstool (Psa. 110:1).

12. VIRGO

"Therefore the Lord himself will give you a sign. Behold, the virgin shall conceive and bear a son, and shall call his name Immanuel [God With Us]" (Isa. 7:14).

Finally we arrive at the glorious Bride. The son which Mary—paradoxically part of the Bride herself—birthed has become the King of Kings and Lord of Lords, and he is ready for his queen. Having retrieved her from her home on the earth, he brings her to his father's house and lets her undergo final preparations for the wedding.

The future day when the Messiah and his bride will be wed is foreshadowed by the mythological sphinx. Unlike the famous sphinx at Giza, which

Figure 20-14. Virgo, by Sidney Hall

originally had the head of lion, sphinxes are usually depicted as a lion whose upper half is that of a woman. This is a combination of Virgo and Leo, which sit beside each other on the zodiacal wheel. The Greek root of the word *sphinx* means "to bind together" or "hold fast,"[394] as demonstrated in the permanent joining of spouses.

Figure 20-15. Sphinx statues guard the Freemasonic House of the Temple of the Scottish Rite, in Washington, D.C.

i.   Coma—The virgin nursing a child. This constellation more than any other demonstrates Satan's subversion of God's celestial message. What started as a picture of Mary with the young Yeshua in her lap has been traded out for a woman's wig. On the surface at least, the Greeks are responsible for this travesty. E. W. Bullinger, author of *Witness of the Stars*, suggests that a problem in translation led to the change.[395]

Where the Greeks have a wig in their star maps, the Egyptian Zodiac of Dendera gives us the image of a seated woman holding a male child in her outstretched arm. The Egyptian name of the sign is *Shes-nu*, "The Desired Son," which reminds us of Haggai's description of the Messiah as "the desire of all nations" (2:7). Of course, the Egyptians considered this to be a representation of Isis holding Horus, but Albumazar, an Arab astronomer of the 9th century AD, related in detail the true nature of Coma. Albumazar was not a Christian and yet he writes,

> Virgo is a sign of two parts and three forms. There arises in the first decan, as the Persians, Chaldeans, and Egyptians, the two Hermes and Ascalius teach, a young woman, whose Persian name translated into Arabic is Adrenedefa, **a pure and immaculate virgin**, holding in the hand two ears of corn[a], sitting on a throne, **nourishing an infant**, in the act of feeding him, who has a Hebrew name (the boy, I say), by some nations named Ihesu, with the signification Ieza, **which we in the Greek call Christ**.[396]

Shakespeare must also have known the true identity of Coma, for he

---

[a]   Cereal grain, not maize

writes in *Titus Andronicus* of an arrow shot up to heaven and falling in the "Good boy in Virgo's lap."

ii. Boötes—The herdsman, a.k.a Arcturus, the Coming One. This man holds high a sickle and receives the animals proceeding out of Ursa Major, the Greater Sheepfold. Yeshua taught that when the time comes for him to take his rightful place as king, he shall separate the sheep from the goats (Matt. 25:31-46) and the wheat from the tares (Matt. 13:24-42). The coronation of Messiah will immediately precede the division of the Redeemed from the Reprobates, and for that reason we find the constellation Corona hovering just to the right side of Boötes, perhaps even in his right hand in the original arrangement.

iii. Centaurus—The one who pierces. After the wedding banquet of the Lamb, Yeshua will descend to earth on a white steed, followed by the armies of heaven. As we saw earlier, Centaurus smites Lupus, the Beast, with a spear. That weapon is actually the long sword which comes out of the mouth of Christ (Rev. 19:15). This constellation represents the victor of the Battle of Armageddon.

A Story in the Equinoxes

In addition to reading all twelve ecliptic signs of the Mazzaroth in the order just given, we can also read a second story in those signs if we run through them based upon the position of the sun at the spring equinox.

As any schooled person knows, our planet spins on its axis. But the planet also wobbles like a top as it spins, so that the direction of its tilt is ever changing. This makes it seem from our perspective on earth as if the heavens are slowly rotating around the planet at a pace of one cycle every 25,920 years, or about one degree every seventy-two years. This phenomenon is called *the precession of the equinoxes*.

The precessionary cycle marks out *ages* based on which zodiacal constellation is visible behind the vernal (spring) equinox sunrise. The poet Virgil wrote that "the white bull with the golden horns opens the year,"[397] but his statement was untrue at the time that he penned it, and he knew it. Virgil was referring not to his own age, but to the first age, long since past.

At the end of the fourth millennium BC, the sun resided in the midst of Taurus the Bull during the vernal equinox. Because God has designed human history to play out over the course of a "week" of millennia, mirroring the seven days of Creation, and because we are within mere decades of entering into the seventh millennium—a Sabbath for the whole earth—we can be confident that Adam was not created prior to ca. 3940 BC.[a] In other words, history began under the sign of the strength and authority of the heavenly rulers, known in Semitic languages as *elohyim*. To the people of the ancient Near East, the ox was the symbol of the supreme deity (*El* to the Phoenicians and Hebrews). Bulls have always been symbols of might and fecundity, so it is not surprising that the Age of Taurus witnessed the reign of dinosaurs and giants and long lifespans, all of which tapered off over the latter several centuries of the age.

There is no consensus on when the Age of Aries began, but popular estimates place it at roughly 2100 BC. This happens to also be approximately when Abraham was given a ram to sacrifice in place of Isaac. Later, once the Levitical priesthood had been established, YHVH instructed the priests to sacrifice a bull and a ram on the most holy day of every year (the Day of Atonement).

By the time of Yeshua's conception in 2 BC, the sun was in Pisces—specifically, it was positioned under the tail of the first of the two fish of Pisces, which is the smaller of the two fish and is oriented perpendicular to the line of the Zodiac. What this means is that the sun spent relatively few years going through the first fish of the constellation, but it has been moving up the rope and through the body of the second fish for two millennia. These fish represent the two houses of Israel: Judah and Ephraim. Judah, which also incorporates the tribe of Benjamin, was the Southern Kingdom of Israel, while the other ten tribes comprised the Northern Kingdom. At the time of the Assyrian invasion, Ephraim was taken prisoner and scattered among the nations, and they have been lost sheep wandering in the wilderness ever since, often unaware from whence they came. The kingdom of Judah did not fall to the Assyrians but did succumb to the Babylonians, and they were exiled to Babylon for seventy years. Afterward, much of the Southern Kingdom returned to the Promised Land and repopulated it; thus, during Yeshua's first advent he ministered primarily to the Jews and Benjamites (Saint Paul said in

---

[a] This is difficult to nail down precisely because the calendars that men have been using are quite different from God's calendar. Both Jubilees and Enoch say that men will greatly err as to the days and years, and this has certainly held true.

Rom. 11:1 that he was one of the latter). Yeshua told his disciples that he would make them fishers of men, and indeed they caught many fish, bringing out untold numbers of disciples from the schools of the Scribes and Pharisees (Acts 21:20). Judah gave up most of its fish quickly, and within a few decades the Jews were totally deaf to the Gospel. But many from within the Gentile nations heard and believed unto eternal life, as continues to this day. This is all reflected in the sky: the sun did not remain over the smaller fish of Pisces for very long, but many centuries will pass before the sun completes its journey across the bigger fish.

Opinions vary wildly as to when we leave the Age of Pisces. Based purely on a visual estimation of the journey of the equinox using astronomy software, it appears that the equinoctial sun will remain in Pisces until AD 3000-3100, which coincides with the end of the seventh millennium; then it will enter the sign of Aquarius, the water carrier. At that time, the cosmos will be destroyed in fire, and a new heaven and new earth will be created (Rev. 21:1-3). The righteous will inherit the new creation and dwell there in peace and blessing forever. He that sits upon the throne says, "Behold, I make all things new.... I am the Aleph and Tav, the beginning and the end. I will give unto him that is athirst of **the fountain of the water of life** freely" (21:5-7, CEPH). And in New Jerusalem will flow "a pure **river of water of life**, clear as crystal, proceeding out of the throne of Elohiym and of the Lamb" (22:1, CEPH). Aquarius represents the eternal state of the Redeemed, washed pure and filled with the water of life and the spirit of their God.

To summarize, the ages progress from the sign of God Almighty as Taurus, to the sign of the Lamb of God, to the sign of Israel's redemption, to the sign of the overflowing blessing of the Elect. The procession of the equinoxes paints the entire seven-millennium history of God's people using a third (33.3%) of the zodiacal signs.

Draco's Tail

One of the effects of axial precession is that the pole stars change over the course of the cycle. The true celestial (not magnetic) north pole currently points to a star named Polaris, in the constellation Ursa Minor, but it has pointed to other stars in the past. In 3000 BC, the north pole star was Thuban in Draco.

Draco, the constellation of the dragon, is wrapped around the center

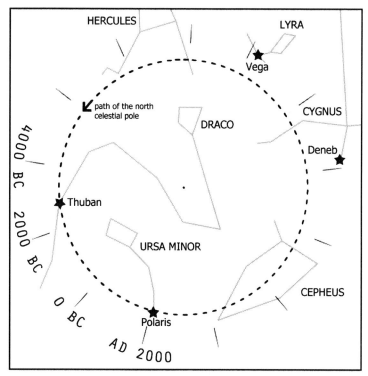

Figure 20–16. Axial precession causes the direction of the North Pole to trace a circle around Draco once every 26,000 years.

of the imaginary precessional circle above the north pole, and his tail intersects that circle. As the ages roll on and the pole traces the circle counterclockwise, the tail of Draco travels in the opposite direction, appearing to sweep the heavens. As revealed by author David Flynn in *Temple at the Center of Time*, the motion of Draco in the sky is not meaningless happenstance, but rather the unfolding of a biblical drama.[398] In Revelation 12, the apostle John witnesses wonders in heaven—a pregnant woman clothed with the sun, and the moon under her feet, and also a dragon. Of the latter John writes, "And another sign appeared in heaven: behold, a great red dragon, with seven heads and ten horns, and on his heads seven diadems" (v. 3). John does not tell us which heaven he was viewing. It could have been the second heaven, which is the cosmos, rather than the third heaven, where YHVH dwells. There is, after all, a dragon among the signs of the stars. John says about this dragon that "his **tail swept down a third of the stars** of heaven and cast them to the earth" (v. 4). As discussed in ch. 3 of this book, stars are linked to angels, so we are led to conclude that Satan convinced a third of the heavenly host to join him at the time of his rebellion. The "torso" of Draco occupies the northernmost portion of the celestial sphere, and that is where the cosmic Mount of Assembly is located (Isa. 14:13; cf. Job 26:7, 37:22; and Ezek. 1:4). David Flynn made an inspired connection between the fraction of the stars affected by the Dragon's tail, and the portion of the sky traversed by Draco's tail. The span of time from the rebellion of Satan until the final consummation of heaven and earth is one-third the length of the total precessional cycle.

One-third of the 25,920-year circuit of the precession is equal to 8,640 years. We know that Satan and his angels will be destroyed in the Lake of Fire at the end of the last millennium, and we know that the seventh and last millennium will begin soon (perhaps the 2060s); if we put the Great White Throne Judgment at ca. AD 3065 (2065 + 1000) and then subtract 8,640 years, we arrive at approximately 5575 BC. That date would mark the rebellion of the Dragon, but not the beginning of Creation Week, for Elohiym created the heavens before he created the light which marked the beginning of the first day. (We have no idea how long the heavenly host existed before the division of light from darkness in the material realm.) In 5575 BC, when Satan rebelled, the sun at vernal equinox was floating between the horns of Taurus. 8,640 years later, the sun will be entering into the water of Aquarius. The movement of Draco's tail in a sweeping motion across a third of the sky is a cosmic illustration of the exact length of time during which fallen angels are allowed to plague God's creatures.[a]

The Seed of the Virgin

Besides the Dragon, the other great wonder that John sees in the sky during his vision is a woman in labor. She is "clothed with the sun, with the moon under her feet, and on her head a crown of twelve stars" (Rev. 12:1). The Dragon waits to devour her child as soon as it is delivered. Most commentators agree that this is symbolic of Mary becoming pregnant by the Holy Spirit and giving birth to Yeshua, while Satan acts through King Herod in an attempt to kill the newborn boy. The twelve stars on the virgin's head are like those seen in a dream by Joseph (Gen. 37:9), and

---

[a] Satan will be imprisoned for a thousand of these years but will then be released to deceive the world again for a short time (Rev. 20).

they represent the twelve tribes of Israel. What went unnoticed until the dawn of the 21st century is that the image seen by John actually occurred in the sky in 3 BC.

Credit for the following discovery goes to Texas law professor Frederick A. Larson, creator of a well-known presentation about the Star of Bethlehem (see BethlehemStar.net). Mr. Larson's research is wholly convincing when it comes to identifying the celestial events that took place around the arrival of Yeshua.

In 3 BC, the king planet, Jupiter, moved through the constellation of the King of Kings, Leo. While passing through the breast of the lion, Jupiter moved directly over the star *Regulus*, whose name means "King." This conjunction was especially close but not unprecedented. But what Jupiter did next is very rare.

Because we observe their dance from a moving platform, the planets sometimes appear to slow and reverse course during their journeys, though in fact they are continuing forward in their orbits at the normal pace. This illusion is called *retrograde motion*. Jupiter entered this kind of motion after passing over Regulus. It stalled, turned around, and passed over the star a second time. Then it paused yet again, rejoined Regulus a third time, and continued on its original course—a triple conjunction. The king planet traced out a halo over the king star.

This is exciting enough, but what was happening simultaneously in the adjacent zodiacal sign is mind-blowing. On Yom Teruah, the Feast of Trumpets (Rosh Hashanah), in 3 BC, as Jupiter was beginning the coronation of Regulus, the constellation Virgo rose clothed in the sun, with the sliver of the new moon under her feet. The planet Mercury, the Messenger, hovered at Virgo's shoulder, just as the angel Gabriel acted as a messenger of God to Mary before the incarnation (Luke 1:16-33). This was the moment of Yeshua's conception, when the priests were blowing their shofars in holy proclamation.

Nine months later, in June of 2 BC, Jupiter gave us another sign. Larson explains that

> By the following June, Jupiter had finished crowning Regulus. The Planet of Kings traveled on through the star field toward another spectacular rendezvous, this time with Venus, the [Morning Star]. This conjunction was so close and so bright that it is today displayed in hundreds of planetaria around the world by scientists who may know nothing of Messiah. They do it because what Jupiter

did makes such a great planetarium show. Jupiter appeared to join Venus. The planets could not be distinguished with the naked eye. If our magus had had a telescope, he could have seen that the planets sat one atop the other, like a figure eight. Each contributed its full brightness to what became the most brilliant star our man had ever seen. Jupiter completed this step of the starry dance as it was setting in the west. That evening, our Babylonian magus would have seen the spectacle of his career while facing toward Judea. [399]

The magi had their signal; they grabbed their camels, loaded up their gear and gifts, and headed for Jerusalem. It was December by the time they completed the journey from Babylonia. They talked with Herod at the palace in Jerusalem and then headed south towards Bethlehem. On December 25 of 2 BC, Jupiter entered retrograde, making a full stop just above the town where the baby Yeshua and his family dwelt.

Take a moment to appreciate the wonder of this preordained light-show, because it demonstrates the awesome sovereignty and all-surpassing power of YHVH Elohiym.

Incidentally, the day of Messiah's delivery was not honored by God with an annual holiday, because that was not when Yeshua's earthly life began. The Feast of Trumpets foreshadowed—and now memorializes— the miraculous *conception* of our Lord. His birth was a joyous occasion, but it was not the moment when the course of history forever changed. *That* moment was when God the Father began to knit Yeshua together in his mother's womb. The winter festival that we call Christmas commemorates only the arrival of the Magi, whereas the late summer festival of Yom Teruah (Feast of Trumpets) has been heralding the arrival of the King for four thousand years.

A Grim Déjà Vu

Scott Clarke of *Eternal Rhythm Flow Ministries* has shown in one of his online videos that the sign of the virgin clothed in the sun, with the moon below her feet, will occur one more time in history. [400] John's vision as recorded in Revelation 12 is not only about the past, it is also about the future, for the virgin first gives birth to a child "who is to rule all the nations" and who is "caught up to God and to his throne," and then there is a war in heaven, and the woman is flown into the wilderness "where she is to be nourished for 1,260 days." The Dragon will try to destroy her but will fail due to the protection of God, after which the fallen Cherub will set out in a rage to make war on the rest of the saints. The snatching up of the child is a past event, but the rest is yet to come.

On September 23 of 2017, either the day of the Feast of Trumpets or the day after it, the sun will once again clothe Virgo while the moon passes under her feet. Jupiter will have come to a dead stop between the legs of the virgin. Mercury, Mars, Venus, Regulus, and the sun will lie in a straight line extending down from Leo, and when added to the eight remaining stars of that constellation, there will be precisely twelve stars over the head of Virgo.

Scott Clarke, one of the few to have identified this alignment, suspects that it heralds the Rapture and the start of Daniel's 70th week, but we have already established that a pre-Tribulation Rapture is highly unlikely, and besides, Clarke's find appears to be about gestation and delivery, not marriage. He notes that the king planet, Jupiter, will spend exactly the duration of an average pregnancy hovering inside Virgo and emerge nine months after first crossing into the constellation. This is the sign of a birth, not the ultimate consummation of Christ's betrothal. It's only wise to consider the hypothesis that this 2017 sign announces something very similar to the sign of 3 BC.

Is it a dark reflection of the sign that announced the arrival of the Messiah? Will this repeat of the heraldic imagery act as an announcement of the arrival of the False Messiah? Unfortunately, the answer is probably yes. It is my suspicion that the Seed of Satan—a fertilized egg made only from the reconstructed genetic material of Asshur—will be implanted in a virgin surrogate mother on the same holiday that Yeshua was conceived by the Holy Ghost. The public may have no clue that this has been done until decades later, when the child has matured and stepped into the public arena. Of course, it could be that the Antichrist is somehow resurrected as an adult, but I consider that the less likely of the possibilities, considering the gestational period of Jupiter in Virgo.

The Roman poet Virgil prophesied by the Muses in his *Eclogue IV*

(37 BC) that the "return of the virgin" would bring about the reign of Saturn, meaning darkness, cold, and chaos; but the reappearance of the maiden would also signal the arrival of "a new generation sent down from heaven" and the birth of a boy "in whom the golden race [shall] arise." That boy, says Virgil, will be Apollo, the sun god. Apollo is the shining destroyer to whom we previously linked Shiva and Osiris. Lines 15–17 of the poem indicate that the child will possess divinity, will see heroes mingled with gods (a reference to transhumanism or another fallen angel incursion?), and eventually rule over the world which his father brought to peace. Apollo's father was none other than Zeus, the god who was often portrayed as a serpent and whose altar Yeshua called "the seat of Satan."

Virgil was no prophet of YHVH, but if he was channeling devils who understood the signs in the heavens and the end-game of Satan, then the words he penned may be surprisingly accurate—except that, try as he might, Apollo/Asshur will not succeed in healing the earth and ushering in a lasting utopia. Only Yeshua will accomplish that.

TWENTY-ONE

Conclusion

Now the Spirit expressly says that in later times some will depart from the faith by devoting themselves to deceitful spirits and teachings of demons…

–1 Timothy 4:1–3

They perish because they refused to love the truth and so be saved. For this reason God sends them a powerful delusion so that they will believe the lie.

–2 Thessalonians 2:10–11, NIV

W e've covered a lot of ground to get here. Some readers may be overwhelmed by all that has been presented, so let's do a quick recap of this first volume to make sure that we have it all under our belts, and then we'll discuss the implications.

Synopsis

The preeminent created being, the Dragon, who is represented by the Ouroborous above and serpents below, and whose mascot and kingdom is Leviathan, corrupted his wisdom through pride and decided that he could run the cosmos better than YHVH. He convinced a third of the spirits to join him in what amounts to the first class-action lawsuit, accusing God of malpractice. He also convinced the first humans that God was withholding good things from them, things which they deserved, and that God was doing so to test whether or not they had the wisdom and will to elevate themselves to a higher station. It was the lie of auto-theism—the same lie that Satan has been selling the world every since. Adam and Eve believed the word of the *nacash* over the word of YHVH, and it led them to disobey the Creator and bring upon themselves a curse. Their spirits died that day, and every child descended from Adam has received a dead spirit from its father. Only Yeshua of Nazareth, who had no earthly father, was born alive to God.

During the days of Jared, the sixth patriarch from Adam, two hundred angels called Watchers took on the form of human men and descended from heaven to Mount Hermon. Their mission was to assist the burgeoning population of men to construct a proper society, but during their time on earth they became enamored of the women of that era, who were exceedingly fair. Obeying their unnatural inclinations, they swore an oath that they would collectively break the laws of heaven for the sake of pleasure and procreation. Taking whomever they pleased, the Watchers married the daughters of men and impregnated them. The results of these unnatural unions were children of gigantic size and acute immorality. They were the Nephiliym.

The giants mistreated normal human beings and animals terribly, and thrust the world into an era of deep distress. Seeing the state of affairs brought about by their rebellious brethren, the holy angels appealed to YHVH to intervene, and God agreed to do so. He ordered the abominable Nephiliym annihilated and their fathers cast into the Abyss.

Before being imprisoned, the Watchers had added to their initial transgression by proceeding to teach men the secrets of heaven, perhaps as appeasement for the crime of stealing their daughters. This led to an advanced but morally bankrupt society later known as Atlantis. Among the worst sins of Atlantis was the bio-engineering of creatures of mixed kinds. This included modifying humans, and eventually so many people were genetically corrupted that Moses had to specify in the Genesis account that the godly Noah was biologically unblemished.

God wiped the slate clean with a global flood, and for a short time there was peace. But the spirits of the Nephiliym wandered the earth and began to prey upon Noah's spiritually vulnerable grandchildren. Hearing of this, Noah called upon YHVH to imprison these spirits, and his request was granted save for ten percent of the ghouls, which portion Satan retained to execute his will. Holy angels were sent to the family of Noah to teach them which plants were useful for medicine that would heal the sicknesses caused by the remaining unclean spirits.

Although none of the angelic spirits inherited by the Nephiliym were present in Noah's family, Ham's wife was a carrier of the genetic code for gigantism, and their first child, Canaan, became the father of tribes of postdiluvian giants. Most of these tribes settled in the Levant in direct opposition to the results of a lottery by which the sons of Noah assigned regions of the earth to each family. These over-sized squatters were later destroyed from the Levant by God's authorization.

It didn't take long for the Adversary to lure Noah's descendants away from YHVH. Instead of spreading out and filling the earth as God had commanded, the majority of people in the first five or six generations after the Flood banded together and set about building a tower and a commonwealth in Shinar. The Tower, being most likely a ziggurat, was intended to allow transit between the material and spiritual dimensions, and this quest greatly concerned the members of the Divine Council. God took the threat seriously, stating that mankind would be able to accomplish anything if left to its own devices. The knowledge necessary to create a rift in the veil between dimensions was probably garnered from the Watcher's arcane wisdom that had been carved into the limestone of the Giza Plateau, where Osiris later went to learn magical secrets. According the Book of Jubilees, the secrets of the Watchers were first discovered by a man named Kainam in an area where there had once been cities, and he transcribed some or all of those secrets onto tablets that he could take with him. Evidently his illicit findings were then shared in part with others and applied to the building of Babel. God was forced to take drastic measures and disperse the families from Babel by dividing their languages.

During or soon after the time of Babel, Cush, son of Ham, developed the first postdiluvian pagan religion, basing it upon the worship of the primary triad of Sun, Moon, and Venus. He and his son, Nimrod, began to war with the inhabitants of southern Mesopotamia, and then to subjugate and assimilate them into their political-religious system. Nimrod began to become a *gibbor*, a giant, possibly through the use of arcane arts similar to the necromantic medicine of the Rephaiym giants. It is conceivable that Satan had a hand in this and may have also imparted special wisdom to Nimrod, for the son of Cush began to worship and serve Enki (the Sumerian name for Satan). He even demanded that the kingdom of Aratta send him building materials for the construction of a temple to Enki. The temple was built at Eridu, beside the river Euphrates, over a place known as the mouth of the Abyss.

Nimrod had a sister or half-sister who was a priestess in Aratta. She was known as Inanna, goddess of Venus, but her real name may have been Semiramis, and as high priestess of Inanna she was considered indwelt by the goddess. Nimrod wooed her away from the king of Aratta and made her high priestess of Uruk, one of the centers of his kingdom. They wed, and through hieros gamos (sacred marriage) the god Dumuzi/Tammuz became manifest in Nimrod. Possessed of occult knowledge, great physical power, and the support of the pagan religious system, Nimrod was able to subdue most of the clans of the ancient world and impose his flavor of morality and society upon them in the centuries following the Dispersion from Babel. The hubs of his world empire were in Sumer, Assyria, Lebanon, and Egypt, but his reach extended even further than that. Most men came to view Nimrod as a god, and he took on the name Asshur/Asar/Asari, which the Greeks changed to Osiris.

Upon Asshur's death—probably at the hands of the gigantic descendants of Canaan—he became the first mummy, and his efflux was preserved and buried in a well-hidden location under Giza. Asshur's empire dissolved, leaving the seventy Kosmokraters of the Divine Council free to fully exercise their reign as gods over the Gentile nations. The priests of Semiramis preserved the arcana of Nimrod and carried on with his mission of restoring humanity to an illumined state through the mastery of the natural world and the practice of autotheism. Their end goal is the construction of a utopia run by a handful of illuminated masters, foremost of whom will be the resurrected Asshur.

I know: it's a tough pill to swallow. I would hardly believe it myself if I hadn't done the research. Then again, many of the claims of the Bible, and of religions in general, are marvelously improbable. Faith of any sort, even faith in naturalism, becomes absurd when its core precepts are examined. Anyone who asks enough questions will inevitably find it hard to believe that matter and energy are self-existent and that ordered minds could arise from disorder. The theory of macroevolution is a tremendous stretch to say the least. So are claims that genetic codes emerged from nothing or that the many tiny components of living cells continually and selflessly carry out complex functions in an orderly manner apart from the intelligent intention of a transcendent conductor. Either everything is a miracle or nothing is a miracle, and the latter supposition is the most unbelievable of all.

When it comes to the supernatural, nothing can be proven in the strictest sense. Yet there is an abundance of evidence—more than I could fit into this volume—that gives credence to the unseen reality of the great battle between Good and Evil. There is a Grand Conspiracy being leveled against us by the adversary of our souls; a plot perpetrated for nearly six thousand years. It's all been leading up to the next few decades, when we will witness the final showdown. Will we trust the Word of YHVH and stand firm when everyone around us is caught up in the lie?

Leviathan's Ruse

We've come to the end of the first half of our study, and with any luck, we've become wise to Satan's agenda in a whole new way. Any reader that has reached this point is probably thoughtful enough to mull over the implications for themselves, but allow me to offer a brief analysis combined with a run-down of the topics that we have yet to consider.

There are six main components to Leviathan's ruse, and in this book we have covered the first in depth but also touched upon the second and third. The remainder of these components will be dealt with in vol. 2. Here are the six aspects of which we must take heed:

THE FIRST COMPONENT is confusion over end-times prophecies. The masses have been conditioned to expect a Rapture, but instead the world will be faced with the resurrection of an ancient king. Even those believers who don't subscribe to a pre-Trib Rapture doctrine will be caught off-guard by the literal return of Nimrod. Unless we collectively wise up, the consequence of this confusion will be incorrigible contempt from skeptics and detractors. The disbelief of the ungodly will be magnified, their hearts further hardened, because of the fact that we Christians didn't know what was coming. Of what value is Bible prophecy, they will ask, if it led you to expect an escape that never came but failed to inform you about the return of a Middle Eastern god?

THE SECOND COMPONENT is a one-two punch of occult knowledge and occult wonders. Nimrod/Asshur will bring back with him all of the expertise that he gained from Watcher secrets, for he will speak "great things" (Dan. 7:8) and understand "dark sentences" (Dan. 8:23), and he "will succeed in whatever he does" (Dan. 8:24, NIV). He may well use this expertise to pull the world out of chaos and build his Utopian global society. Whether or not that is the case, we know for certain that the Beast and his False Prophet will perform wonders in front of the masses, "even making fire come down from heaven to earth" (Rev. 13:13).

Yeshua told us that the latter days would be like the days of Noah, implying that Watcher secrets would be employed once again, and people would think nothing of it. Great power, whether it comes from angels or scientific progress, is deceptive: having a high degree of command over our world creates the illusion that we no longer need YHVH, making it easy to buy into the serpent's lie that we can become our own gods. Satan keeps killing us with this false promise. No matter how much advanced knowledge we procure, we will never match the Maker or cease to need his animating breath and ceaseless energy. Accepting that fact leads to a childlike trust, which is crucial because only the humble and obedient will dwell with the Creator forever. He is our Heavenly Father, not our Heavenly Colleague.

THE THIRD COMPONENT is materialism. Revelation 17 and 18 make it abundantly clear that the whole world will be enchanted by Inanna's luxuries: "For your merchants were the great ones of the earth, and **all nations were deceived** by your sorcery" (18:23). In his vision of the far future, John is told by an angel that "the inhabitants of the earth were intoxicated with the wine of her [Mystery Babylon's] adulteries" (Rev. 17:2, NIV). The angel also says that when this spiritual adulterous is destroyed, all the merchants of the earth will mourn because the source of their prosperity is no more (18:11–17).

The secular world has long been obsessed with the offerings of Babylon's economic system. Like godless Esau, they cry, "Give me some of that stew now! I can't survive without it," and so they sell their souls for that which doesn't last (Heb. 12:16). Yeshua said that it is easier for a camel to pass through the eye of a needle than it is for a rich man to enter the kingdom of heaven. Satan took this to heart and has used prosperity to undo mighty works of God in nations like America and Great Britain.

Even many true disciples of Yeshua are sorely tested by the abundance of creature comforts available in the civilized world, as well as the illusory safety of a big bank account. Our hearts go where our treasure resides, and if we treasure the things of the world, then our allegiance will be to the world. Satan has enticed many of us with worldly baubles in the same way that he enticed Eve with the pleasing fruit of the Tree of

Knowledge, and the result has been the same: separation from YHVH Elohiym. Spiritually dulled by our fanatical consumerism and perpetually distracted by endless entertainments, we lose the ability to discern the heart of God and are inevitably swept into alignment with the doctrines of the Adversary (this includes passive approval of ungodliness). The debt-based economic system called Mystery Babylon is making us all drunk on her wine, and those who fall under her spell rarely come to their senses. As Peter Goodgame says in his blog, "Beware of bourgeois Christianity, it is the disease of the Laodicean Church."[401]

As bad as Babylon's wealth-making engine has been in every age past, the situation will be even worse at the end of the age. Wealth will be consolidated in a single city as never before, and the worldly-wise will flock to it like moths to a flame. They will export Inanna's merchandise and obscene entertainments to every corner of the world so that her influence will wrap around God's green earth like filthy tentacles. The western world has already accomplished this to a large degree.

THE FOURTH COMPONENT is a unified religious system which champions tolerance in the sense of universal acceptance of deviant behaviors. Whereas tolerance used to mean "putting up with someone or something not liked," it has now come to mean "endorsing all lifestyles, beliefs, and activities except those which directly and obviously harm another." This spells bad news for Bible-believing Jews and Christians because the exclusivity of biblical doctrines means that we're automatically "intolerant" and worthy of contempt. As the spirit of Antichrist is (even now) sweeping the globe, that contempt is turning into murderous rage. By the mid-point of Daniel's 70th week, those who hold fast to Scripture will be hunted down and killed the world over (Rev. 13:7–10). Ironically, this will be done under the mantra that "Love is the answer."

The identification of Asshur and his Prophet as the enlightened ambassadors of universal Providence will go hand-in-hand with end-times pluralism. Put more simply, the Antichrist and False Prophet will be viewed as mouthpieces of the Christ Consciousness into which all men of good will may enter. This kind of thinking is already present in traditional religious circles, as demonstrated by the Roman Catholic Bishop of Portland, Maine, who says,

> Because all people are created in the image and likeness of God according to the pattern of Christ the New Adam, Christ has significance for

all times and places, all peoples and cultures, even for all religions, even when he is only implicitly recognized. The Council affirms that in some mysterious way, **all persons of good will are mysteriously related to Christ and his saving action**, even if that relation remains obscure for us who believe in him explicitly. [402]

In the same speech, the bishop quotes Pope John Paul II regarding the commonalities of all religious faiths: "instead of marveling at the fact that Providence allows such a great variety of religions, we should be amazed at the number of common elements found within them."[403] Like these Catholic leaders, the False Prophet will make much of the common ground between all faiths and downplay or explain away the contradictory elements. The people of the world will be expected to discard those "outdated" and "misguided" tenets of their faiths which are incompatible with the Gospel of Inclusivity. If we as a race are to survive, he will state confidently, then everyone must grow up spiritually and put an end to foolish divisions so that we can be of a singular mind.

The False Prophet will further explain that all of the demigods and religious leaders of old were shadows of the divine messianic archetype, each demonstrating different facets of the Supreme Being, but that Asshur is the culmination and final expression of the archetype—the Elect One who is fully anointed and sent by a loving God to pull the world out of darkness. Asshur will be billed as the Redeemer, but in the sense that he redeems the world from chaos and ignorance, not sin. He will mediate between God and men not as a substitute but as a spokesman and role model, convincing his flock that they can all expand their inherent divinity and become like God. The terrible disasters and supernatural plagues that YHVH will send in the last days, as detailed in Revelation, will be attributed to an evil, adversarial deity (Rev. 13:6) and not to the "true" Architect of the Universe who desires for men of every faith to evolve into enlightened masters.

The occult societies have been cheering for this scenario all along. Take this passage from the preface of early editions of the official Masonic *Kentucky Monitor*, which argues for the validity of all the great religions:

All believed in a future life... and in a Mediator or Redeemer, by whom the Evil Principle was to be overcome and the Supreme Deity reconciled to His creatures. The belief was general that he was to be born of a virgin and suffer a painful death. The Hindus called him Krishna; the Chinese, Kioun-tse; the Persians, Sosiosch; the Chaldeans, Dhouvanai; the Egyptians, Horus; Plato, Love; the Scandanavians, Balder; the Christians, Jesus; Masons, Hiram. (xiv–xv)

This statement has been expunged from current editions, no doubt because it didn't keep true Masonic philosophy secret enough.

THE FIFTH COMPONENT of Leviathan's ruse is antinomianism (against *nomos*, meaning "against law"), and it is closely linked to the fourth. However, this component is aimed specifically at YHVH's people. In 2 Thess. 2:1–9, Paul thrice calls the Antichrist "the lawless one" or "man of lawlessness," and he also states that the "mystery of lawlessness is **already at work**." We'll discuss just what that means in the next volume. The embrace of antinomianism is a prerequisite for the acceptance of a hyper-grace, ultra-inclusive approach to the Bible that leads to doctrinal compromise and the dissolution of everything that makes the Church sacred and set-apart. Once the foundations have crumbled, there is nothing to prevent mainstream Christianity from joining hands with the False Prophet and entering the ranks of Leviathan's universal religious system. Daniel tells us that the Lawless One will flatter those who violate YHVH's covenant, but those who know their God will be strong and do exploits (11:32). We must be of the latter, not the former.

THE SIXTH COMPONENT is the disclosure of the existence of supposedly sympathetic alien helpers. Upon reading that last sentence, I suspect that many of you screwed up your faces in looks of confusion and skepticism. This component will surprise a lot of readers because we haven't yet addressed the topic of so-called extraterrestrials, and on the surface it appears to have no relevance to Bible prophecy. But I assure you that it does, and we must be ready for the Disclosure.

Government officials will soon reveal that extraterrestrials are real and that they have been visiting us for centuries. We will be told that ETs are more evolved and enlightened than human beings, and have been trying to guide our spiritual development since pre-history. (They may even claim to have seeded life on earth.) These aliens, it shall be claimed, are the gods of old, and they desire for us to now elevate ourselves to godhood and join them as cosmic brothers.

In truth, so-called extraterrestrials *are* the pagan gods, which are fallen angels, and they are more appropriately labeled *extradimensionals*. In vol. 2 we will discuss why the UFO and abduction phenomena are real, and how encounters with so-called aliens prove that they are lying spirits with a satanic agenda.

Hijacking His Story

In closing, let's keep in mind that each of the world's major religious factions awaits a wise, mighty, and glorious figure who will dramatically change the geopolitical and religious landscapes.

In Hinduism, the Puranas foretell the arrival of Kalki, the Tenth Avatar of Vishnu, riding atop a white horse and wielding a blazing sword. He is expected to enlighten mankind, defy oppression, and destroy evil leaders. He will have a spiritual guru by his side.

Buddhists expect a new Buddha called Maitreya to appear during a time when moral conduct is at an all-time low. He will be a completely enlightened world ruler that unites his subjects under a way of higher truths.

A majority of Muslims believe that a man known as the Mahdi will show up during a time of chaos to convert the world to Islam and usher in an era of peace and justice. His arrival will coincide with the second coming of Jesus (Arabic: *Isa*), who will assist him in a fight against a false Messiah.

The Jews still await a Messiah, or Anointed One, who will be a political figure and military conqueror as well as a prophet. Blind to the fact that their Messiah visited them once before on a mission of mercy, the members of Israel's southern tribes are expecting a militarily powerful deliverer to come to their aid in the very near future. Hebrew oracles state that the prophet Elijah will herald the arrival of the Anointed One.

The amazingly similar beliefs just listed strongly testify that an immortal being with global influence has set the stage for the arrival of a very special potentate and his right-hand man.

Satan is not omniscient, and he does not know the future, but he does know what YHVH announces about the future. At the Fall of Man in the Garden of Eden, God declared that the Seed (masculine singular) of the woman would crush the head of the serpent. At that moment, Satan became aware that his foe would be a male human being, the offspring of one of the daughters of Eve. His only option is therefore to delude mankind with an imitation of the Seed *before* the true Messiah arrives in glory to take the throne. Nimrod/Asshur is that imitation.

We must remember that Satan is intimately acquainted with the redemptive story as set forth in the heavens. Add to this the knowledge inherent in understanding the character of YHVH and the laws of the heavens, as well as the information that could have been gleaned from the Messianic prophecies given to Enoch before the Flood, and it becomes apparent that the Dragon would have known basically how things would play out and what major themes would mark the Messiah's career. Satan acted upon this knowledge by preemptively debuting his own Messiah.

To put it another way, Satan beat YHVH to the punch. (At least it seems that way to those unacquainted with the history of mankind in its entirety.) Satan's Seed was on course to reunite the early people of the postdiluvian world and rebuild Atlantis with himself at the center, worshiped as God. The real Elohiym could not allow Nimrod to continue on that trajectory so early history, before the formation of the Chosen People and the introduction of the real Messiah, so he heeded the petitions of the Kosmokraters to have Nimrod brought down to Sheol. But now that the Son of God has been revealed, his work accomplished, and the mystery of the Gospel carried to the ends of the earth, Nimrod will be allowed to reprise his role as the imitation Messiah.

The hundreds of pages through which we've forged were a dose of medicine to inoculate us against the sermons and spells of the Imposter. When one is aware that a sovereign and omniscient God wrote the tale of the ages in the sky before a single cell yet stirred upon the earth, and that the angels were around to see that tale being composed, one can remain confident in the authenticity of the Bible's end-times prophecies, even if a Middle Eastern god returns from the grave claiming to be the second coming of the Messiah. There is nothing about the coming supernatural events that hasn't been addressed ahead-of-time in Holy Writ, therefore our worldview need not be shaken when things get weird. This is one of the reasons why the Book of Enoch says that it is written for the final generation. Things were nearly as strange and twisted in the beginning as they will be in the end, and the righteous God who put things aright in the days of Noah will surely do so again in the days to come.

Blessed be our Great God, YHVH Elohei Yisrael, the LORD God of Israel, for inoculating us against the venom of Leviathan. And blessed be you, Reader, for daring to go where many are reticent to tread. Share what you've learned with your brothers and sisters, and make the most of the days, for they are evil. Shalom.

REFERENCES

1. Booth, William, and Ruth Eglash. "Kerry's Nine-Month Quest for Middle East Peace Ends in Failure." Washington Post. April 29, 2014. https://www.washingtonpost.com/world/middle_east/kerrys-nine-month-quest-for-middle-east-peace-ends-in-failure/2014/04/29/56521cd6-cfd7-11e3-a714-be7e7f142085_story.html.

2. Hudson, John. "From Tel Aviv to Turtle Bay." Foreign Policy. March 18, 2015. http://foreignpolicy.com/2015/03/18/from-tel-aviv-to-turtle-bay-israel-palestinians-un-resolution/.

3. McTernan, John. "The People Whose God is Jehovah." Chapter 3 in As America Has Done to Israel, 3rd ed. New Kensington: Whitaker House, 2008.

4. World Net Daily. "Prophetic Twist to Sharon's Death." World Net Daily. November 11, 2014. http://www.wnd.com/2014/01/prophetic-twist-to-sharons-death/.

5. Goodgame, Peter. Red Moon Rising: The Rapture and the Timeline of the Apocalypse. United States: Xulon Press, 2005. 20.

6. Oskin, Becky. "Big Earthquakes Double in 2014, But They're Not Linked." Live Science. 27 Jul. 2014. http://www.livescience.com/46576-more-earthquakes-still-random-process.html.

7. D. Guha-Sapir, R. Below, Ph. Hoyois. "Natural Disasters Trends." EM-DAT: The OFDA/CRED International Disaster Database. Brussels: Université Catholique de Louvain. Accessed December 7, 2013. http://www.emdat.be/natural-disasters-trends.

8. "Mass Animal Deaths for 2013." End Times Prophecy. Last modified December 27, 2013. http://www.end-times-prophecy.org/animal-deaths-birds-fish-end-times.html.

9. Devereux, Stephen. "Famine Mortality." The Economist. Daily Chart, May 13, 2013. http://www.economist.com/blogs/graphicdetail/2013/05/daily-chart-10.

10. Ahmed, Nafeez. "Peak Soil: Industrial Civilisation Is on the Verge of Eating Itself." TheGuardian.com. June 7, 2013. http://www.theguardian.com/environment/earth-insight/2013/jun/07/peak-soil-industrial-civilisation-eating-itself.

11. North American Pollinator Protection Campaign. Honey Bee Disappearance (CCD) and What You Can Do. San Francisco, 2007. http://www.pollinator.org/Resources/CCD%20Response%20FINAL.pdf.

12. Noah, Don, and George Fidas. The Global Infectious Disease Threat and Its Implications for the United States. Washington, DC: National Intelligence Council, 2000. http://www.dtic.mil/dtic/tr/fulltext/u2/a502015.pdf.

13. Snyder, Michael. "What is Causing the Strange Noises in the Sky that Are Being Heard All Over the World?" Infowars. March 23, 2012. http://www.infowars.com/what-is-causing-the-strange-noises-in-the-sky-that-are-being-heard

-all-over-the-world/.

14. Kovacs, Joe. "Are Mystery 'Trumpet Blasts' in Sky From God?" World Net Daily. May 18, 2015. http://www.wnd.com/2015/05/whats-causing-mystery-trumpet-blasts-in-sky/.

15. MacArthur, John. *Reckless Faith*. Wheaton, IL: Crossway Books, 1994. N.p.

16. Huxley, Aldous. *Ends and Means: An Inquiry into the Nature of Ideals and into the Methods Employed for Their Realization*. New York: Harper & Brothers Publishers, 1937. 270-272.

17. Gellman, Barton. "Edward Snowden, after months of NSA revelations, says his mission's accomplished." The Washington Post. December 23, 2013. Web.

18. Gennet, Robbie. "Donald Rumsfeld and the Strange History of Aspartame." The Huffington Post Online. May 25, 2011. http://www.huffingtonpost.com/robbie-gennet/donald-rumsfeld-and-the-s_b_805581.html; Sife, Charles. "Are Your Medications Safe?" Slate. February 9, 2015. http://www.slate.com/articles/health_and_science/science/2015/02/fda_inspections_fraud_fabrication_and_scientific_misconduct_are_hidden_from.html.

19. Steiger, Brad, and Sherry Steiger. *Conspiracies and Secret Societies: The Complete Dossier*. Canton, MI: Visible Ink Press, 2013. 370.

20. Thomson, Keith Stewart. "Piltdown Man: The Great English Mystery Story." American Scientist (May-June 1991). http://www.clarku.edu/~piltdown/map_prim_suspects/ABBOTT/Abbot_defense/piltman_englishmystery.html.

21. Pickrell, John. "How Fake Fossils Pervert Paleontology [Excerpt]." Scientific American Online. November 15, 2014. http://www.scientificamerican.com/article/how-fake-fossils-pervert-paleontology-excerpt/.

22. Miller, Michele A. "A Hoax in Japan." Athena Review: Journal of Archaeology, History, and Exploration 3(2) (2002): N.p. http://www.athenapub.com/japhoax.htm.

23. Adam, David. "History of modern man unravels as German scholar is exposed as fraud." The Guardian Online. February 18, 2005. http://www.theguardian.com/science/2005/feb/19/science.sciencenews.

24. Quilliam, Rebecca. "Historians rubbish claims of academic conspiracy." The New Zealand Herald Online. December 27, 2012. http://www.nzherald.co.nz/nz/news/article.cfm?c_id=1&objectid=10856261.

25. Butler, Alan, and Christopher Knight. *Before the Pyramids: Cracking Archaeology's Greatest Mystery*. London: Watkins Publishing, 2009. 10.

26. Jagel, Katie. "Poll Results: Exorcism," YouGov America. Accessed December 15, 2013. http://today.yougov.com/news/2013/09/17/poll-results-exorcism/.

27. Sagan, Carl. *The Demon-Haunted World: Science as a Candle in the Dark*. New York: Ballantine Books, 1996.

28. Ten Boom, Cornelia J. A. "Prepared for the Coming Tribulation." Written 1974. Accessed May 3, 2015. http://first-commandment.com/w/pdf/studies/Corrie_Ten_Boom_Rapture.pdf.

29. Hoekema, Anthony. *The Bible and the Future*. Grand Rapids, Michi-

gan: Wm. B. Eerdmans Publishing Co., 1979. 148.

30. Parsons, John J. "Yom Kippur--The Day of Atonement." Hebrew-4Christians. Accessed December 30, 2013. http://www.hebrew4christians.com/ Holidays/Fall_Holidays/Yom_Kippur/yom_kippur.html.

31. Satlow, Michael L. *Jewsih Marriage in Antiquity*. Princeton, NJ: Princeton University Press, 2001. 165.

32. Booker, Richard. *Here Comes the Bride: Jewish Wedding Customs and The Messiah*. Houston: Sounds of the Trumpet, 1995. 5.

33. Kasdan, Barney. God's Appointed Customs. Clarksville, MD: Lederer Books, 1996. 51.

34. Satlow, 175.

35. Levitt, Zola. *A Christian Love Story*. Dallas, TX: Great Impressions Printing, 1978. 4.

36. Booker. Here Comes the Bride. 9.

37. Schneid, Hayyim. Marriage. Philadephia, PA: Jewish Publication Society, 1973. 38.

38. Robison, Blaine. "Marriage in Ancient Israel." BlaineRobison.com. July 16, 2012; Revised December 19, 2014. http://www.blainerobison.com/ hebroots/marriage-israel.htm.

39. Greenberg, Irving. *The Jewish Way: Living the Holidays*. New York: Simon & Schuster, 1988. 115.

40. Enns, Paul. *The Moody Handbook of Theology*. Chicago: Moody, 1989. 392.

41. Saint Clement of Rome. "Epistle to the Corinthians," XXXIV, *The Early Christian Fathers*. Edited and translated by Hentry Bettenson and Geoffrey Cumberledge. Oxford: Oxford University Press, 1956. 47.

42. Keathley, III, J. Hampton. "Angelology: The Doctrine of Angels." Bible.org. 2004. https://bible.org/article/angelology-doctrine-angels.

43. Cohen, Andrew C. *Death Rituals, Ideology, and the Development of Early Mesopotamian Kingship: Toward a New Understanding of Iraq's Royal Cemetery of Ur*. Leiden, The Netherlands: Koninklijke Brill NV, 2005. 99.

44. Trachtenberg, Joshua. *Jewish Magic and Superstition: A Study in Folk Religion*. New York: Behrman's Jewish Book House, 1939. 98.

45. Noll, K. L. "Canaanite Religion." Religion Compass 1(1) (2007): 61-92. http://people.brandonu.ca/nollk/canaanite-religion/.

46. Camus, Albert. *The Rebel*. London: Hamish Hamilton, 1953. 20-21.

47. Frankfort, Henri. *Kingship and the Gods: A Study of Ancient Near Eastern Religion as the Integration of Society and Nature*. Chicago: University of Chicago Press, 1948. 107-108.

48. "The Fiery Flying Serpent." Creation Research Society Quarterly vol. 42, no. 4 (March 2006): 241-251. http://www.genesispark.com/essays/ fiery-serpent/.

49. Ibid.

50. Kramer, Samuel Noah. *Sumerian Mythology*. Philadelphia: University of Pennsylvania Press, 1972. 65.

51. Dalley, Stephanie. *The Legacy of Mesopotamia*. Oxford: Oxford University Press, 1998. 65.

52. Reitzenstein, Richard. *Das iranische Erlösungsmysterium: Religionsgeschichtliche Untersuchugen*. Marchus et Weber, 1921. 77.

53. Moorton, Jr., Richard F. "Hesiod as Precursor to the Presocratic Philosophers: A Voeglinian View." *Eric Voegelin Society Meeting 2001*. Baton Rouge, LA: Louisiana State University, 2001. http://www.lsu.edu/artsci/groups/voegelin/society/2001%20Papers/Panel42001.shtml.

54. Stromer, Richard. "The Good and the Terrible: Exploring the Two Faces of the Great Mother." SoulMyths.com. http://www.soulmyths.com/goodterrible.pdf.

55. Fox, Robin Lane. "A Travelling Mountain." In *Traveling Heroes in the Epic Age of Homer*, 243-58. New York: Knopf, 2009.

56. Schroeder, Gerald L. *The Science of God: The Convergence of Scientific and Biblical Wisdom*. New York: The Free Press, 1997. 57.

57. Wikipedia, s.v. "Chronology of the Universe." Accessed May 12, 2015. http://en.wikipedia.org/wiki/Chronology_of_the_universe.

58. Barnes, Albert, and James Murphy. "Commentary on Isaiah 14:12." *Barnes' Notes on the Old and New Testaments*. 1870. http://www.studylight.org/commentaries/bnb/view.cgi?bk=22&ch=14.

59. Pritchard, James. *Ancient Near Eastern Texts: Relating to the Old Testament*. 3rd ed. Princeton: Princeton University Press, 1969. 384.

60. *The Complete Jewish Bible: With Rashi Commentary*, s.v. "Yeshayahu-Isaiah-Chapter 14." http://www.chabad.org/library/bible_cdo/aid/15945#v=12&showrashi=true.

61. Jacobsen, Thorkild. *The Harps that Once--: Sumerian Poetry in Translation*. Binghamton, NY: Vail-Ballou Press, 1987. 117.

62. Kramer, Samuel Noah. *The Sumerians: Their History, Culture, and Character*. Chicago: University of Chicago Press, 1963. 21.

63. Haleem, Asia. "The Venus Cycle and Venus Worship in the Ancient Near East." Layish. 2013. http://www.layish.co.uk/venusworship.pdf.

64. Ibid.

65. Burger, Michael. *The Shaping of Wester Civilization: From Antiquity to the Enlightenment*. Toronto: University of Toronto Press, 2008. 31.

66. Wolkstein, Diane, and Samuel Noah Kramer. *Inanna, Queen of Heaven and Earth: Her Stories and Hymns From Sumer*. New York: Harper Collins, 1983. 101.

67. Langdon, Stephen Herbert. *The Mythology of All Races, Volume V*. New York: Cooper Square Publishers, 1964. 25.

68. Jacobsen, Thorkild. *The Harps that Once...: Sumerian Poetry in Translation*. New Haven, CT: Yale University Press, 1997. 112.

69. The Electronic Text Corpus of Sumerian Literature, s.v. "A hymn to Inana (Inana C)." Accessed May 14, 2015. http://etcsl.orinst.ox.ac.uk/cgi-bin/etcsl.cgi?text=t.4.07.3#; Meador, Betty De Shong. *Inanna, Lady of Largest Heart: Poems of the Sumerian High Priestess Enheduanna*. Austin: University of Texas

Press, 2000. 171.

70. Ancient History Encyclopedia, s.v. "Inanna," by Joshua Mark. Accessed February 9, 2014. http://www.ancient.eu.com/Inanna/.

71. Ball, Warwick. *Rome in the East: The Transformation of an Empire.* London and New York: Routledge, 2000. 89.

72. *New Larousse Encyclopedia of Mythology*, s.v. "Assyro-Babylonian Mythology," edited by Felix Guirand. Translated by Richard Aldington and Delano Ames. London: Hamlyn, 1968. 49-72.

73. *A Dictionary of Greek and Roman Antiquities*, s.v. "Apex," edited by William Smith. Boston: Little, Brown, and Company, 1859. 102.

74. "Headshaping." Australian Museum. Last updated 26 October 2010. http://australianmuseum.net.au/headshaping.

75. Murie, James R. *Ceremonies of the Pawnee.* Lincoln, NE: University of Nebraska Press, 1981. 39.

76. Budge, E. A. Wallis. "The Legend of Ra and Isis." Chap. 8 in *Legends of the Gods.* Sunnyvale, CA: Netlancers, 2014.

77. Cotterell, Arthur. *A Dictionary of World Mythology.* Oxford: Oxford University Press, 1986. 135.

78. Addison, Joseph. "The Spacious Firmament on high." In *Spectator*, No. 463. 1712.

79. Pike, Albert. *Morals and Dogma of the Ancient and Accepted Scottish Rite of Freemasonry.* Charleston, 1871. 77.

80. Charles, R. H. "The Book of Jubilees." Wesley Center online. From *The Apocrypha and Pseudepigrapha of the Old Testament.* Oxford: Clarendon Press, 1913. http://wesley.nnu.edu/sermons-essays-books/noncanonical-literature/noncanonical-literature-ot-pseudepigrapha/the-book-of-jubilees/.

81. *The Book of Jubilees, or The Little Genesis.* Translated by R. H. Charles. New York: The MacMillan Company, 1917. 79-81.

82. Ibid, 81-82.

83. Budge, E. A. Wallis. "The Seven Tablets of Creation. Description of Their Contents." In *The Babylonian Legends of the Creation and the Fight Between Bel and the Dragon.* London: Harrison and Sons, 1921. http://www.sacred-texts.com/ane/blc/blc07.htm.

84. Olcott, William Tyler. *Sun Lore of All Ages.* New York: G.P. Putnam's Sons, 1914. 35-36.

85. Kramer, Samuel Noah. *Myths of Enki, the Crafty God.* New York: Oxford University Press, 1989. 88-89.

86. Sitchin, Zecharia. Chapter 6 in *The Anunnaki Chronicles: A Zecharia Sitchin Reader.* N.l.: Inner Traditions / Bear & Co, 2015. Electronic version.

87. Litke, R.L. *A Reconstruction of the Assyro-Babylonian God-Lists, An: dA-nu-um and An: Anu šá amēli.* Bethesda: CDL Press, 1998.

88. Black, Jeremy A. et al. *The Literature of Ancient Sumer.* Oxford: Oxford University Press, 2004. 147.

89. The Electronic Text Corpus of Sumerian Literature, s.v. "Enki and the world order: translation." Accessed May 17, 2015. http://etcsl.orinst.ox.ac.uk/

section1/tr113.htm.

90. Karahashi, Fumi. "Fighting the Mountain: Some Observations on the Sumerian Myths of Inanna and Ninurta." *Journal of Near Eastern Studies* 63, no. 2 (April 2004): 111-8. http://www.jstor.org/stable/10.1086/422302.

91. The Electronic Text Corpus of Sumerian Literature, s.v. "Inana and An." Accessed May 17, 2015. http://etcsl.orinst.ox.ac.uk/cgi-bin/etcsl.cgi?text=t.1.3.5#.

92. Ibid, s.v. "Ninurta's exploits: a šir-sud (?) to Ninurta." Accessed May 17, 2015. Line 310. http://etcsl.orinst.ox.ac.uk/cgi-bin/etcsl.cgi?text=t.1.6.2#.

93. *The Epic of Gilgamesh.* Translated by Maureen G. Kovacs. Stanford, CA: Stanford University Press, 1989. Tablet 1, lines 28-67.

94. Sandars, Nancy K. *Poems of Heaven and Hell from Ancient Mesopotamia.* London: Penguin, 1971. 160-165.

95. Cochrane, Ev. "Aphrodite, from: The Many Faces of Venus." Maverick Science. Accessed March 13, 2016. http://www.maverickscience.com/venus-aphrodite.htm.

96. Eilers, Wilhelm. "Iran and Mesopotamia." Edited by E. Yarshater. *The Cambridge History of Iran* 3. Cambridge: Cambridge University Press, 1983.

97. The Electronic Text Corpus of Sumerian Literature, s.v. "Enmerkar and the lord of Aratta: translation." Accessed May 17, 2015. Lines 25-64. http://etcsl.orinst.ox.ac.uk/section1/tr1823.htm.

98. Jacobsen, Thorkild. *The Sumerian King List.* Chicago: University of Chicago Press, 1939. 87.

99. López, Raúl Erlando. "The Antediluvian Patriarchs and the Sumerian King List." *CEN Technical Journal* 12(3) (1998): 347-57.

100. Penglase, Charles. *Greek Myths and Mesopotamia: Parallels and Influence in the Homeric Hymns and Hesiod.* London: Routledge, 1994. 76-125.

101. Heimpel, Wolfgang. "A Catalog of Near Eastern Venus Deities." *Syro-Mesopotamian Studies* 4(3) (1982). 12.

102. Mundkur, Balaji. *The Cult of the Serpent: An Interdisciplinary Survey of Its Manifestations and Origins.* Albany, NY: State University of New York Press, 1983. 187.

103. Goodgame, Peter. *The Second Coming of the Antichrist.* Crane, MO: Defense, 2012. 62.

104. The Electronic Text Corpus of Sumerian Literature, s.v. "The Sumerian king list." Accessed May 17, 2015. Lines 93-101. http://etcsl.orinst.ox.ac.uk/cgi-bin/etcsl.cgi?text=t.2.1.1#.

105. Goodgame. *Second Coming.* 75-76.

106. Diodorus Siculus. *Bibliotheca historia.* 1.27.28.

107. "Hammurabi's Code of Laws." Translated by L. W. King. Exploring Ancient World Cultures. http://eawc.evansville.edu/anthology/hammurabi.htm.

108. Dalley, Stephanie. "Babylon as a Name for Other Cities Including Nineveh." *Proceedings of the 51st Rencontre Assyriologique Internationale, Held at the Oriental Institute of the University of Chicago, July 18–22, 2005* (62). 25-33.

109. Leick, Gwendolyn. "Eridu." Chap. 1 in *Mesopotamia: The Invention of the City*. London: Penguin, 2002.

110. *Encyclopaedia Britannica* online, s.v. "Babylon," by Henry W. F. Saggs. Accessed May 10, 2015. http://www.britannica.com/EBchecked/topic/47575/Babylon/529/The-ancient-city.

111. Fu'ād Safar, Muhammad 'Alī Muşţafá, Seton Lloyd. *Eridu*. Baghdad: Republic of Iraq, Ministry of Culture and Information, State Organization of Antiquities and Heritage, 1981. 46.

112. The Pennsylvania Sumerian Dictionary Project, s.v. "abzu." University of Pennsylvania Museum of Anthropology and Archaeology. http://psd.museum.upenn.edu/epsd/epsd/e114.html.

113. Leick, Gwendolyn. *Sex and Eroticism in Mesopotamian Literature*. London: Routledge, 1994. 12.

114. Parpola, Simo. "Monotheism in Ancient Assyria." *One God or Many? Concepts of Divinity in the Ancient World: Essays on the concept of monotheism/polytheism in ancient Assyria, Egypt, Greece, and Israel*. Edited by Barbara Nevling Porter. Casco Bay, ME: Casco Bay Assyriological Institute, 2000. 176.

115. Pouysségu, Patrick. "Stele of Vultures." *Louvre* online. Accessed April 25, 2015. http://www.louvre.fr/en/oeuvre-notices/stele-vultures.

116. The Electronic Text Corpus of Sumerian Literature, s.v. "Gilgameš and Aga." Accessed May 17, 2015. Lines 40-47. http://etcsl.orinst.ox.ac.uk/cgi-bin/etcsl.cgi?text=t.1.8.1.1#.

117. Eusebius. "From the Summary of Castor, on the kingdom of the Assyrians." *Chronicle*. http://rbedrosian.com/euseb3.htm.

118. Ovid. *Fasti*. Translated by James George Frazer. *Loeb Classical Library Volume*. Cambridge, MA: Harvard University Press; London: William Heinemann Ltd., 1931. Verse 104.

119. Hislop, Alexander. *The Two Babylons or The Papal Worship Proved to be the Worship of Nimrod and His Wife*. 5th ed. London: S. W. Partridge and Co, 1873. 43.

120. Ibid. 44-45.

121. Budge, E. A. Wallis. *The Papyrus of Ani: A Reproduction in Facsimile, Edited, with Hieroglyphic Transcript, Translation, and Introduction, Vol. 2*. London: Philip Lee Warner, 1913. 444.

122. Rohl, David. *Legend: The Genesis of Civilisation*. Post Falls, ID: Century Publishing, 1998. 304-5.

123. Smith, W. Robertson. "Ctesias and the Semiramis Legend." *English Historical Review* (1887) II(VI). 304. doi:10.1093/ehr/II.VI.303.

124. Marcus Junianus Justinus. *Epitome of the Philippic History of Pompeius Trogus*. Translated by John Selby Watson. London: Henry G. Bohn, 1853. 1.

125. Nichols, Andrew. *The Complete Fragments of Ctesias of Cnidus: Translation and Commentary with an Introduction*. University of Florida, 2008. 18-19. http://etd.fcla.edu/UF/UFE0022521/nichols_a.pdf.

126. Ibid. 59.

127. Muller, Theodor, ed. Vol. 1 of *Fragmenta historicorum graeco-*

rum...: Apollodori bibliotheca cum fragmentis auxerunt. Fragment 68. 440.

128. Gerig, Bruce L. "Eunuchs In the OT, Part 2: Castration in Ancient Assyria, Babylonia, and Persia." The Epistle. 2010. http://epistle.us/hbarticles/eunuchs2.html.

129. Ibid.

130. Smith, W. Robertson. "The Semiramis Legend." *The English Historical Review 2* (1887): 303-17.

131. Gmirkin, Russell E. *Berossus and Genesis, Manetho and Exodus: Hellenistic Histories and the Date of the Pentateuch.* New York: T & T Clark International, 2006. 116.

132. Diodorus Siculus. *Library of History* (2.8.6.). http://penelope.uchicago.edu/Thayer/E/Roman/Texts/Diodorus_Siculus/2A*.html.

133. Langdon, Stephen Herbert. *Semitic.* Vol. 5 of *The Mythology of All Races.* New York: Cooper Square Publishers, Inc., 1964. 12-15.

134. Wikipedia, s.v. "Gesta Hungarorum." Accessed April 10, 2015.

135. Shearer, Tony. Lord of the dawn: Quetzalcoatl, the plumed serpent of Mexico. N.l.: Naturegraph, 1971. 4.

136. Ke, Yuan. *Dragons and Dynasties: An Introduction to Chinese Mythology.* Translated and edited by Nie Zhixiong. London: Penguin, 1993. 32.

137. Grinnell, George B. *Blackfoot Lodge Tales: The Story of a Prarie People.* New York: n.p., 1912. 98.

138. Harris, Rivkah. *Gender and Aging in Mesopotamia: The Gilgamesh Epic and Other Ancient Literature.* Norman, OK: University of Oklahoma Press, 2000. 163.

139. Stuckey, Johanna. Edited by Patricia Monaghan. *Goddesses in World Culture, Volume 1: Asia and Africa.* Santa Barbara: Praeger, 2011. 27.

140. Dietrich, Thomas Karl. *The Culture of Astronomy: Origin of Number, Geometry, Science, Law, and Religion.* Minneapolis, MN: Bascom Hill Publishing Group, 2011. 421.

141. Hall, Manly P. *The Secret Destiny of America.* NY: Penguin, 2008. 19.

142. Haywood, H. L. *The Great Teachings of Masonry.* New York: George H. Doran Company, 1923. 33.

143. Murphy, Todd. "The God Helmet." Inner Worlds. 2015. http://www.innerworlds.50megs.com/God_Helmet/god_helmet.htm.

144. Heindel, Max. *The Rosicrucian Cosmo-Conception, or Mystic Christianity.* 6th ed. London: L. N. Fowler, 1911. 179.

145. Waite, Arthur Edward. *The Mysteries of Magic: A Digest of the Writings of Éliphas Lévi.* 2nd ed. London: Kegan Paul, Trubner & Co., 1897. 428.

146. Ibid. 121.

147. Pike, Albert. Instructions to the 23 Supreme Councils of the World. July 14, 1889. Recorded by A.C. De La Rive in *La Femme et l'Enfant dans la FrancMaconnerie Universelle* (1894). 588

148. Wasserman, James. *The Secrets of Masonic Washington: a guidebook to signs, symbols, and ceremonies at the origin of America's capital.* Rochester, VT: Destiny Books, 2008. 42.

149. *Encyclopaedia Iranica* online, s.v. "Yazidis." Accessed February 20, 2015. http://www.iranicaonline.org/articles/yazidis-i-general-1.

150. Walsch, Neale Donald. *Conversations with God, Book 1*. NY: G.P. Putnam's Sons, 1995. 75.

151. Waite. *Mysteries*. 85.

152. Martinez, Juan. "New Age Pragmatism." *Publishers Weekly*. September 22, 2008. http://www.publishersweekly.com/pw/print/20080922/10447-new-age -pragmatism.html.

153. Groothuis, Douglas R. *Unmasking the New Age*. Downers Grove, IL: InterVarsity Press, 1986. 28.

154. Flynn, Ted. *Hope of the Wicked: The Master Plan to Rule the World*. Sterling, VA: MaxKol Communications, Inc., 2000. 7.

155. UNESCO pamphlet. *Toward World Understanding, Vol. 1: Some Suggestions on Teaching about the United Nations and its Specialized Agencies*. France: 1948. 18.

156. "Global Consciousness." UNESCO. 2014. http://www.unesco.org/ new/en/bureau-of-strategic-planning/themes/culture-of-peace-and-non-violence/ flagship-programmes/global-consciousness/.

157. Ibid.

158. Jasper, William F. "UNESCO's Rotten Track Record." The New American. May 19, 2003. http://www.thenewamerican.com/world-news/ item/13845-unesco%E2%80%99s-rotten-track-record.

159. Teichrib, Carl. *Lucifer Rising Part 3: Educating for the New Age*. 2002. http://www.crossroad.to/articles2/2002/carl-teichrib/lucifer3.htm.

160. Sharma, Monica. "Personal to Planetary Transformation." *Kosmos Journal*. Fall/Winter 2007. http://www.kosmosjournal.org/article/ personal-to-planetary-transformation/.

161. Ibid.

162. Huxley, Julian. *UNESCO: Its Purpose and Its Philosophy*. Oakland, CA: Public Affairs Press, 1947. 41.

163. "Acceptance Speech by Robert Muller." In *UNESCO Prize 1989 for Peace Education*. Paris: Unesco, 1990. 29-31.

164. Muller, Robert and Southern Association of Colleges and Schools. *The Robert Muller World Core Curriculum Manual*. Arlington, TX: Robert Muller School, 1986. Preface.

165. Blavatsky, Helena P. "What is Theosophy?" *The Theosophist, Vol. 1, No. 1*. Theosophical University Press electronic version. Originally published in Bombay, 1879. 3. http://www.theosociety.org/pasadena/theosoph/theos1a.htm.

166. Blavatsky, Helena P. The Secret Doctrine: *The Synthesis of Science, Religion, and Philosophy, Vol. 1*. 3rd ed. London: The Theosophical Publishing Society, 1893. 446.

167. Ibid. 100.

168. Monteith, Stanley. Brotherhood of Darkness. Oklahoma City, OK: Hearthstone Publishing, 2000. 81.

169. Blavatsky, Helena P. *The Secret Doctrine: The Synthesis of Science, Re-*

ligion, and Philosophy, Vol. 2. London: The Theosophical Publishing Company, 1888. 513.

170. "Mars and Beyond." *Disneyland*. TV episode. Directed by Ward Kimball. Aired Wednesday, December 4, 1957 on ABC.

171. King, Francis and Isabel Sutherland. *The Rebirth of Magic*. London: Corgi Books, 1982. 182.

172. Flynn, David. *The David Flynn Collection*. Crane, MO: Defense Publishing, 2012. 464.

173. Parsons, John Whiteside. *Freedom is a Two-Edged Sword*. Edited by C. R. Runyon. 1976. Las Vegas, NV: New Falcon Publications, 1990. http://www. bibliotecapleyades.net/bb/babalon210.htm.

174. Livergood, Norman D. "The Higher Mysteries." The New Enlightenment. 2004. http://www.hermes-press.com/high_myst.htm.

175. Morgan, Giles. *Freemasonry*. Edison, NJ: Chartwell Books, Inc., 2007. 33.

176. Booth, Mark. *The Secret History of the World As Laid Down by the Secret Societies*. Woodstock & New York, NY: The Overlook Press, 2008. 193.

177. Angus, Samuel. *The Mystery-Religions and Christianity*. 2nd ed. New York: Charles Scribner's Sons, 1928. 96-7.

178. Hamilton, Edith. *The Greek Way*. New York: W. W. Norton & Company, 1993. 223.

179. Buck, J. D. *Mystic Masonry; Or, The Symbols of Freemasonry and the Greater Mysteries of Antiquity*. 2nd ed. Cincinnati, OH: The Robert Clarke Company, 1897. 130.

180. Stace, Walter Terence. *Mysticism and Philosophy*. Philadelphia: J. B. Lippincott, 1960. 309.

181. Hall. *Secret Destiny*. 34.

182. Spangler, David. *Reflections on the Christ*. Forres, Scotland: Findhorn Press, 1981. 45.

183. Lazarus, M. Edgeworth. *The Zend-Avesta, and Solar Religions: An Historical Compilation; with Notes and Additions*. New York: Fowlers & Wells, 1852. 63.

184. Budge, E. A. Wallis. *The Book of the Dead: The Chapters of Coming Forth by Day; An English Translation with Introduction, Notes, Etc.* London: Kegan Paul, Trench, Trübner & Company, Ltd., 1898. 81-2.

185. Doxey, Denise. "Priesthood." *The Oxford Encyclopedia of Ancient Egypt, Vol. 3*. Edited by Donald B. Redford. Oxford: Oxford University Press, 2001. 69-70.

186. Dollinger, Andre. "Heka: The magic of ancient Egypt." Kibbutz Reshafim. Last updated August 2008. http://www.reshafim.org.il/ad/egypt/religion/magic.htm.

187. Chassinat, Emile. *Le Mystère d'Osiris au mois de Khoiak*. Cairo: Imprimerie de l'Institut Français d'Archéologie Orientale, 1966. 11-12.

188. Knight, Richard Payne. *The Symbolical Language of Ancient Art and Mythology: An Inquiry*. 2nd ed. New York: J. W. Houton, 1876. 4.

189. Murray, Margaret A., J. Grafton Milne and W. E. Crum. *The Osireion at Abydos*. London: Bernard Quaritch, 1904. 25.

190. Ibid.

191. Plutarch. *Isis and Osiris*. 13. http://www.osirisnet.net/dieux/osiris/e_osiris_mathieu.htm#_ednref13.

192. Hall, Manly P. *Freemasonry of the Ancient Egyptians*. In *The Lost Keys of Freemasonry*, 2nd ed. New York: Tarcher, 2006. 145.

193. Ibid. 147.

194. Bauval, Robert. *Secret Chamber: The Quest for the Hall of Records*. London: Century, 1999. 95–96.

195. "About this Order's Teachings." Ancient Mystery Teachings. Last modified May 14, 2015. http://www.ancientmysteryteachings.org/.

196. Josephus. *Jewish Antiquities, Books I-IV*, with an English Translation, vol. 4 (Loeb Classical Library). Translated by H. S. J. Thackeray. New York: G. P. Putnam's Sons, 1930. 4.33.

197. Austin, Allen. *The Messianic Temple*. N.l.: Xulon Press, 2011. 59.

198. Flynn, David. *Collection*. 336.

199. Lewis, Harvey Spencer. *The Symbolic Prophecy of the Great Pyramid*. San Jose, CA: Supreme Grand Lodge of AMORC, 1936. 95.

200. Skiba, Rob. "The Great Pyramid, Part 3: Why Giza?" Babylon Rising blog. Accessed June 2, 2015. http://www.babylonrisingblog.com/GreatPyramid3.html.

201. Skiba, Rob. "The Great Pyramid, Part 1: Who Done it?" Babylon Rising blog. Acessed June 2, 2015. http://www.babylonrisingblog.com/GreatPyramid1.html.

202. Hall, Manly P. *The Secret Destiny of America*. Los Angeles: Philosophical Research Society Inc., 1988. 91.

203. Horn, Thomas. *Zenith 2016: The Revised and Expanded Edition of Apollyon Rising 2012*. Crane, MO: Defender, 2013. 128.

204. MacArthur, John D. "Third Great Seal Committee--May 1782." Great Seal. Accessed May 27, 2015. http://www.greatseal.com/committees/thirdcomm/index.html.

205. Clark, Robert Thomas Rundle. *Myth and Symbol in Ancient Egypt*. New impression ed. London: Thames & Hudson Ltd, 1978. 246-9.

206. Bauval. *Secret Chamber*. 92-93.

207. Al Masudi. *The Meadows of Gold*. Translated by Barbier de Meynard and Pavet de Courteille. Quoted in Budge, E. A. Wallis. *The Mummy: A Handbook of Egyptian Funerary Archaeology*. Revised and enlarged ed. New York: Cosimo, Inc, 2011. 409n2.

208. Al-Maqrizi. Chapter 40 in *Al-Khitat*. Translated by Jason Colavito from the 1895 French edition. "Al-Maqrizi on the Pyramids of Egypt." Jason-Colavito.com. Accessed June 2, 2015.

209. Flynn, Mark A. *Forbidden Secrets of the Labyrinth: The Awakened Ones, the Hidden Destiny of America, and the Day After Tomorrow*. Crane, MO: Defender, 2014. 189.

210. "The Great Work in Speculative Masonry." *The Dormer Masonic Study Circle #47*. Accessed May 27, 2015. http://www.mt.net/~watcher/greatwork.html.

211. Hall. *Secret Destiny*. 58.

212. Benderitter, Thierry. "Re." Translated by Jon J. Hirst. Osiris Net. 2003. http://www.osirisnet.net/dieux/re/e_re.htm.

213. Rose, Sharron. "Isis and the Tree of Life." Accessed January 25, 2015. http://www.sharronrose.com/IsisTreeLife.htm.

214. "The Book of Thoth." Edited by April McDevitt. Ancient Egypt: the Mythology. Last updated August 17, 2014. http://www.egyptianmyths.net/mythbookthoth.htm.

215. Hall, Manly P. *The Lost Keys of Freemasonry*. Chelmsford, MA: Courier Corporation, 2012. 9.

216. Buck. *Mystic Masonry*. 133-134.

217. Campbell, Joseph. *The Hero with a Thousand Faces*. 3rd ed. Novato, CA: New World Library, 2008. 321.

218. Plutarch. *Prolegomena*. Edited by G. R. S. Mead. Vol. 1 of *Thrice-Greatest Hermes: Studies in Hellenistic Theosophy and Gnosis*, edited by G. R. S. Mead. London and Benares: The Theosophical Publishing Society, 1906. 317.

219. Frazer, James G. *The Golden Bough: A Study in Magic and Religion*. 3rd ed. London: MacMillan and Company, 1922. 39.2.6.

220. Cooper, William. "Hour 4: Osiris and Isis, Part 1." In "Mystery Babylon Series: The history, the dogma, and the identity of Mystery Babylon." *The Hour of the Time* radio broadcast. Aired February 17, 1993.

221. Frazer. *Golden Bough*. 29.1.4.

222. Jackson, Samuel Macauley, ed. *The New Schaff-Herzog Encyclopedia of Religious Knowledge*. Vol. 11, *Son of Man--Tremellius*. New York and London: Funk and Wagnalls Company, 1911. 264; MacKenzie, Donald A. *Myths of Babylonia and Assyria*. London: The Gresham Publishing Company, 1915. 82.

223. Morgenstern, Julian. "The King-God among the Western Semites and the Meaning of Epiphanes." *Vetus Testamentum* 10, Fasc. 2 (April 1960): 140. http://www.jstor.org/stable/1516133.

224. Langdon, Stephen H. *Tammuz and Ishtar: A Monograph Upon Babylonian Religion and Theology, Containing Extensive Extracts from the Tammuz Liturgies and All of the Arbela Oracles*. Oxford: Clarendon Press, 1914. 53.

225. Margolis, Max L., Henry T. Fowler, and Frank C. Porter, eds. *Journal of Biblical Literature* 36 (March 1917): 108.

226. Frazer. *Golden Bough*. 29.1.6.

227. Margolis. *Biblical Literature*. 106.

228. Wolkstein, Diane, and Samuel Noah Kramer. *Inanna, Queen of Heaven and Earth: her stories and hymns from Sumer*. New York: Harper & Row, 1983. 76.

229. Wolkstein, Diane, and Samuel Noah Kramer, translators. *The Courtship of Inanna and Dumuzi*. Accessed May 28, 2015. http://academic.brooklyn.cuny.edu/classics/jvsickle/mpinacrt.pdf.

230. Darnell, John. "Opet Festival." *UCLA Encyclopedia of Egyptology* 1(1) (December 2010): 4-5. Department of Near Eastern Languages and Cultures. nelc_uee_7964. https://escholarship.org/uc/item/4739r3fr#.

231. Horn. *Zenith*. 340.

232. Ibid. 343-4.

233. Mansfield, Stephen. *The Faith of George W. Bush*. Lake Mary, FL: Charisma House, 2003. 49.

234. US Government Printing Office. *George W. Bush, Book 1: January 1 to June 30, 2005*. Washington, DC: Government Printing Office, 2009. 69.

235. Goodgame, Peter. "The Giza Discovery." Red Moon Rising blog. February 18, 2006. http://www.redmoonrising.com/Giza/SavDest7.htm.

236. See "A Short Biography of Osiris," Ch. 8.

237. Christian, Paul. *The History and Practice of Magic*. Vol. 2. Secaucus, NJ: University Books, 1979. 304.

238. "NASA's Cassini Spacecraft Obtains Best Views of Saturn Hexagon." *Jet Propulsion Laboratory*. December 4, 2013. http://www.jpl.nasa.gov/news/news.php?release=2013-350.

239. Morgenstern. *King-God*. 145.

240. McCaffrey, Kathleen. Edited by Harriet Crawford. "The Sumerian Sacred Marriage: Texts and Images." *The Sumerian World*. New York: Routledge, 2013. 240.

241. Goodgame, Peter. "The Giza Discovery, Part Nine: The Mighty One." Red Moon Rising blog. May 28, 2007. http://www.redmoonrising.com/Giza/Asshur9.htm.

242. Steiner, Rudolf. *Egyptian Myths and Mysteries*. Norman Macbeth, trans. New York: Steiner Books, 1990. 100. Quoted in foreword to *The Second Coming of the Antichrist*, by Peter Goodgame, x. Crane, MO: Defense, 2012.

243. Smith, William Robertson. "Ctesias and the Semiramis Legend." In *The English Historical Review 2*. Edited by Mandell Creighton. London: Longmans, Green, and Co, 1887. 307.

244. Campbell, Joseph. *The Hero with a Thousand Faces*. Princeton, NJ: Princeton University Press, 1972. 342.

245. Hislop, Alexander. *The Two Babylons; Or, The Papal Worship Proved to be the Worship of Nimrod and His Wife*. Neptune, NJ: Loizeaux Brothers, 1916. 19.

246. Ostling, Richard N. "Mary: Handmaid Or Feminist?" *Time Magazine*. December 1991. 62-66.

247. Lemesurier, Peter. *The Armaggedon Script*. Rockport, MA: Element Books Ltd., 1993. 245-46.

248. Banko, Stephen. *The Virgin Goddess: Studies in the Pagan and Christian Roots of Mariology*. Leiden, The Netherlands: E. J. Brill, 1993. 18.

249. Hall. *Secret Teachings*. 44.

250. Hall. *Lost Keys*. 155.

251. The Electronic Text Corpus of Sumerian Literature, s.v. "The temple hymns: translation." Accessed June 14, 2015. http://etcsl.orinst.ox.ac.uk/section4/tr4801.htm.

252. Morgenstern. *King-God.* 152-3.

253. *Jewish Encyclopedia* online, s.v. "Antiochus IV., Epiphanes." Accessed May 31, 2015. http://jewishencyclopedia.com/articles/1589-antiochus-iv-epiphanes.

254. Bonfante, Larissa, ed. *Etruscan Life and Afterlife: A Handbook of Etruscan Studies.* Detroit, MI: Wayne State University Press, 1986. 228.

255. Goodgame. *Second Coming.* 180.

256. Goodgame, Peter. "Isaiah 9:10 and the Tower of Babel." Red Moon Rising blog. August 16, 2012. http://www.redmoonrising.com/IsaiahBabel.htm.

257. Horowitz, Wayne. *Mesopotamian Cosmic Geography.* Winona Lake, IN: Eisenbrauns, 1998. 318.

258. Alouf, Michael M. *History of Baalbek.* Escondido, CA: Book Tree, 1999. 29.

259. Griffiths, John G. *The Origins of Osiris and His Cult.* Leiden, the Netherlands: E. J. Brill, 1980. 90–95.

260. Andrews, Carol. *Amulets of ancient Egypt.* Austin: University of Texas Press, 1994. 75.

261. Redford, Donald B., ed. "Contendings of Horus and Seth." *The Oxford Encyclopedia of Ancient Egypt.* Online Version ed. Oxford UP, 2005.

262. Bauval. *Secret Chamber.* 92-94.

263. Eusedbius of Caesarea. *Chronicle,* Book 1, s.v. "How the Hebrews chronicled [their history]." Translated by Robert Bedrosian. 2008. http://www.tertullian.org/fathers/eusebius_chronicon_02_text.htm.

264. Abbas, Abbas Mohamed, EI-said A. El-Sayed, Fathy A. Shaaban and Tarek Abdel-Hafez, "Uncovering the Pyramids Plateau–Giza Plateau–in a Search for Archaeological Relics by Utilizing Ground Penetrating Radar." *NRIAG Journal of Geophysics, 2006 Special Issue.* 2, 12.

265. Hawass, Zahi. Statement to the Egyptian Press. April 14, 1996.

266. Bauval, Robert. *Secret Chamber Revisited: The Quest for the Lost Knowledge of Ancient Egypt.* Rochester, VT: Bear & Company, 2014. 123-24.

267. Ibid. 132.

268. Al Qodai, Al Masudi, and Al Maqrizi. Cited in Jochmans, Joseph (Jalandris). *The Hall of Records: Hidden Secrets of the Pyramid and Sphinx.* 2nd rev. ed. N.l.: Holistic Life Travels, 1980. 210.

269. Diodorus. *Library* (2.7.1).

270. Zimmer, Carl. "Bringing Them Back to Life." *National Geographic* online. April 2013. http://ngm.nationalgeographic.com/2013/04/125-species-revival/zimmer-text?source=hp_dl2_ngm_reviving_species_2130325.

271. "Fascist stain: Italian poet's DNA reconstructed from 100yo sperm." RT.com. March 13, 2015. http://rt.com/news/240337-italy-fascist-dna-reconstructed/.

272. Hall, Manly P. *The Secret Teachings of All Ages: An Encyclopedic Outline of Masonic, Hermetic, Qabbalistic and Rosicrucian Symbolical Philosophy*. San Francisco: H. S. Crocker Company, Inc., 1928. 37.

273. Shimura, Gonz. "GRAVITY FALLS 'Not What He Seems' EXPOSED." YouTube video. March 11, 2015. https://youtu.be/LBSEAUyPH0o.

274. Orwig, Jessica. "The crazy phenomena that caused 2 men to sue the machine that brought us the Higgs boson." *Business Insider* online. April 6, 2015. http://www.businessinsider.com/will-the-lhc-produce-black-holes-2015-4.

275. Ovason, David. *The Secret Architecture of Our Nation's Capital: The Masons and the Building of Washington, D.C.* Perennial, 2002. 349.

276. Horn. *Zenith*. 343.

277. Gollner, Adam Leith. *The Book of Immortality*. New York: Scribner, 2013. 378.

278. Huxley, Aldous. *Brave New World Revisited*. Electronic ed. New York: RosettaBooks LLC, 2010. 27.

279. McKenney, Tom C. *Please Tell Me...: Questions People Ask About Freemasonry--And the Answers*. Lafayette, LA: Huntington House Publishers, 1994. 61-72.

280. White, Chris. "Daniel 7 - The Contemporaneous Beast View - A Blueprint To Identify The Antichrist." YouTube video, 34:04-16. May 21, 2013. https://www.youtube.com/watch?v=3qTdx2B0NT4.

281. Ibid. 11:10-40.

282. Barret, C. E. "Was dust their food and clay their bread? Grave goods, the Mesopotamian afterlife, and the liminal role of Inana/Ištar." *Journal of Ancient Near Eastern Religions* 7 (2007): 7-65.

283. Hunt, Dave. *A Woman Rides the Beast*. Eugene, OR: Harvest House Publishers, 1994. 43.

284. Harris, Rivkah. *Gender and Aging*. 166.

285. Ibid. 167.

286. Meador, Betty De Shong. *Inanna, Lady of the Largest Heart: Poems of the Sumerian High Priestess Enheduanna*. Austin, TX: University of Texas Press, 2000. 52.

287. Tertullian. "Concerning the Genuineness of 'The Prophecy of Enoch.'" Ante-Nicene Fathers. Vol. IV. Tertullian, Book 1. The Tertullian Project. Last updated January 20, 2016. http://www.tertullian.org/anf/anf04/anf04-06.htm.

288. Fitzmyer, Joseph A. "Implications of the New Enoch Literature from Qumran." *Theological Studies* 38(2) (1977): 332.

289. Beckwith, Roger T. *Calendar, Chronology And Worship: Studies in Ancient Judaism And Early Christianity*. Leiden, The Netherlands: Koninklijke Brill NV, 2005. 17.

290. Suter, David W. *Enoch in Sheol: Updating the Dating of the Book of Parables*. Grand Rapids, MI: Wm. B. Eerdmans Publishing Company, 2007. 423.

291. Abbott, Lyman. Introduction to *The Book of Enoch the Prophet: An Apocryphal Production, Supposed for Ages to Have Been Lost : But Discovered*

at the Close of the Last Century in Abyssinia, 3rd ed, by Richard Laurence, tr., lx-lxi. Oxford: Oxford University Press, 1883.

292. Laurence, Richard: quoted in Butt, John Marten. *The Genuineness of the Book of Enoch Investigated*. London: L. B. Seeley and Son, 1827. 16.

293. Martyr, Justin. *Dialogue with Trypho* (79). Translated by Marcus Dods and George Reith. From *Ante-Nicene Fathers*. Vol. 1. Edited by Alexander Roberts, James Donaldson, and A. Cleveland Coxe. Buffalo, NY: Christian Literature Publishing Co., 1885. Revised and edited by Kevin Knight for New Advent website. http://www.newadvent.org/fathers/01286.htm.

294. Milik, J. T., and Matthew Black. *The Books of Enoch: Aramaic Fragments of Qumran Cave 4*. Oxford: Clarendon Press, 1976. 7.

295. Ibid. 31.

296. Chysostom, Jean. "Homelies sur la Genèse." *Saint Jean Chrysostome Ouevres Complètes*. Vol 5. Translated by M. Jeannin. Edited by L. Guerin. Paris, 1865. 136-7.

297. Heiser, Michael. *The Myth That is True*. Unpublished manuscript, 2012. 75. Forthcoming in revised and expanded form as *The Unseen Realm*.

298. "Defense Advanced Research Projects Agency Justification Book Volume 1: Research, Development, Test & Evaluation, Defense-Wide." *Department of Defense Fiscal Year (FY) 2013 President's Budget Submission*. 2012. 47. http://www.darpa.mil/newsevents/budget.aspx; "Darpa to Genetically Engineer Humans by Adding a 47th Chromosome." TIP News. July 31, 2013. http://topinfopost.com/2013/07/31/darpa-to-genetically-engineer-humans-by-adding-a-47th-chromosome.

299. Fox, Maggie. "Genetically Modified Cattle With Human DNA Might Hold Ebola Cure." *NBC News* online. January 19, 2015. http://www.nbcnews.com/storyline/ebola-virus-outbreak/genetically-modified-cattle-human-dna-might-hold-ebola-cure-n287796.

300. Genesis Park. "Update of the Mysterious Bell Found in Coal." *Creation Matters*. Vol. 18, no. 6 (November/December 2013). http://www.genesispark.com/essays/update-on-the-mysterious-bell-found-in-coal/.

301. Jochmans, J. R. *Strange Relics from the Depths of the Earth*. Lincoln, NE: Forgotten Ages Research Society, 1979. 8-9.

302. Vintini, Leonardo. "The Russian Rock from Outer Space." *The Epoch Times* online. Last updated September 14, 2012. http://www.theepochtimes.com/n2/science/rock-screw-russia-china-mazong-mountains-prehistoric-zhilin-wang-11273.html.

303. Delitzsch, Franz. *Biblical Commentary on the Book of Job*. Vol. 2. Translated by Francis Bolton. Edinburgh: T. & T. Clark, 1866. 324.

304. Smith, George. *The Chaldean Account of Genesis*. London: Thomas Scott, 1876. 69.

305. Wikipedia, s.v. "Babylonian star catalogues." Accessed May 31, 2015.

306. Bonnet-Bidaud, Jean-Marc. "The Oldest Extant Star Chart." Institut de recherche sur les lois fondamentales de l'Univers. September 23, 2011. http://irfu.cea.fr/Sap/Phocea/Vie_des_labos/Ast/ast.php?t=actu&id_ast=2615.

307. Cody, William F. Chapter 6 in *An Autobiography of Buffalo Bill (Colonel W. F. Cody)*. Rahway, NJ: Quinn & Boden Co., 1920. E-book #12740 by *The Project Gutenberg*. Produced by Kevin O'Hare, Beth Trapaga, and the Online Distributed Proofreading Team. June 25, 2004. http://www.gutenberg.org/files/12740/12740-h/12740-h.htm.

308. Lincoln, Abraham. "Fragment: Niagara Falls." *Collected Works of Abraham Lincoln*. The Abraham Lincoln Association. Last update September 11, 2008. http://quod.lib.umich.edu/l/lincoln/lincoln2/1:6?rgn=div1;view=fulltext.

309. Mesic, Charles T. "Truth Is Sometimes Stranger Than Fiction." Chapter 1 in *Doctrines of Devils and the Coming Delusion*. N.l.: Xulon Press, 2013.

310. *Encyclopedia of Human Evolution and Prehistory: Second Edition*, s.v. "Meganthropus." Edited by Eric Delson, Ian Tattersall, John A. Van Couvering, and Alison S. Brooks. London: Routledge, 2004. 405-6.

311. University of Oxford. "Giant Stone-age Axes Found in African Lake Basin." ScienceDaily. September 14, 2009. http://www.sciencedaily.com/releases/2009/09/090911134624.htm.

312. Fenton, Bruce. "'Lost City of Giants' Could Be Hidden in the Jungle—Can These Extremely Large Ancient Tools Shed More Light on the Mystery?" MessageToEagle.com. March 11, 2014. http://www.messagetoeagle.com/lostcitygiants.php.

313. "Giants in South Africa - by Michael Tellinger." YouTube. November 17, 2013. https://youtu.be/SnAgOagVO2c.

314. Bousfield, Jonathan, and Rob Humphreys. *The Rough Guide to Austria*. 2nd ed. London: Rough Guides Ltd, 2001. 471.

315. Keyssler, Johann Georg. *Travels Through Germany, Italy, Switzerland, Italy, and Lorrain: Giving a True and Just Description of the Present State of Those Countries*. Vol. 1. 3rd ed. Translated from German. London: G. Keith, 1760. 52.

316. "Ancient American Giants." *Scientific American*. August 14, 1880. 106. http://www.unacknowledged.info/wp-content/uploads/2013/07/scientific-american-v43-n07-1880-08-14-small.pdf.

317. Barnes, Ethne. "Polydactyly in the Southwest." *Kiva* 59, no. 4 (Summer, 1994): 419. http://www.jstor.org/stable/30246141.

318. Legner, E. Fred. "European Bronze Age Visitors in America." Discoveries in Natural History & Exploration. Accessed June 4, 2015. http://www.faculty.ucr.edu/~legneref/bronze/bronze.htm.

319. Williamson, Roger L. "Turning Right at the Burning Bush: Reflections on a National Treasure from Ancient America." Ancient Hebrew Research Center. Accessed June 4, 2015. http://www.ancient-hebrew.org/15_williamson.html.

320. Chapman, Glen W. "Bearded Faces in Ancient America." Chapman Research Group. Last updated February 1998. http://chapmanresearch.org/PDF/Bearded%20Faces%20%20in%20%20Ancient%20America.pdf.

321. Johnston, Philip. *Shades of Sheol: Death and Afterlife in the Old Testament*. Downers Grove, IL: InterVarsity Press, 2002. 129.

322. Harner, Michael. *Cave and Cosmos: Shamanic Encounters with Another Reality*. Berkeley, CA: North Atlantic Books, 2013. 26-7.

323. Kolata, Gina. "Study Finds How Genes That Cause Illness Work." *The New York Times* online. January 20, 2013. http://www.nytimes.com/2013/01/21/health/study-pinpoints-what-activates-disease-causing-genes.html?_r=1.

324. Ibid.

325. Coppens, Philip. "Maize: food from the Gods?" PhilipCoppens.com. Accessed June 7, 2015. http://www.philipcoppens.com/maize.html.

326. "DNA Testing Summary." Starchild Project. Last updated 2012. http://www.starchildproject.com/dna-testing-the-evidence-to-date/dna-testing-summary#.

327. Hall. *Secret Destiny*. 250.

328. Hijiya, James A. "The Gita of Robert Oppenheimer." *Proceedings of the American Philosophical Society* 144(2). PDF. http://www.amphilsoc.org/sites/default/files/proceedings/Hijiya.pdf.

329. Heron, Patrick. *The Nephilim and the Pyramid of the Apocalypse*. New York: Kensington Publishing Corp, 2004. 208-9.

330. Ibid. 210.

331. Bautch, Kelley Coblentz. *A Study of the Geography of 1 Enoch 17-19: 'No One Has Seen What I Have Seen.'* Leiden, The Netherlands: Koninklijke Brill, 2003. 62.

332. *Encyclopaedia Britannica* online, s.v. "Cuzco, Peru." Accessed June 9, 2015. http://www.britannica.com/EBchecked/topic/147674/Cuzco.

333. Coppens, Philip. *The Lost Civilization Enigma*. Pompton Plains, NJ: Career Press, Inc, 2013. 261.

334. Rossi, Corinna. *Architecture and Mathematics in Ancient Egypt*. Cambridge: Cambridge University Press, 2004. 182.

335. "Tetradrachm with Antiochus 1." The J. Paul Getty Museum (Los Angeles). Donated by Chester B. Franz, 1980. Accessed June 10, 2015. http://www.getty.edu/art/collection/objects/19483/unknown-maker-tetradrachm-with-antiochus-i-greek-seleucid-about-281-261-bc/.

336. Knab, Timothy J., ed. *A Scattering of Jades: Stories, Poems, and Prayers of the Aztecs*. Translated by Thelma D. Sullivan. Tucson, AZ: University of Arizona Press, 2003. 99.

337. Rocca, Julius. *Galen on the Brain: Anatomical Knowlede and Physiological Speculation in the Second Century AD*. Leiden, The Netherlands: Brill, 2003. N.p.

338. Hall. *Secret Teachings*. 79.

339. Mackey, Albert G. *Encyclopedia of Freemasonry and its Kindred Sciences: Comprising the Whole Range of Arts, Sciences, and Literature as Connected with the Institution*. Philadelphia: McClure Publishing Company, 1917. 601.

340. Frazer. *The Golden Bough*. 40.2.1.

341. *The Book of the Dead*. Spell 53. Translated by Normandi Ellis in *Awakening Osiris: A New Translation of the Egyptian Book of the Dead*. Boston: Phanes Press, 2009. N.p. https://books.google.com/books?id=cAI_OKe4DkUC&dq.

342. Steiner, Rudolf. *An Outline of Occult Science*. 4th ed. New York: AnthropoSophic Press, 1922. 4.

343. Patterson, William Patrick. *The Life & Teachings of Carlos Castaneda*. Fairfax, CA: Arete Communications, 2008. 244-6.

344. Ibid. 248.

345. Emboden, William A. "The Sacred Narcotic Lily of the Nile: Nymphaea Caerulea." *Economic Botany* 32(4) (1979): 395-407.

346. Rätsch, Christian. *The Encyclopedia of Psychoactive Plants: Ethnopharmacology and Its Applications*. Rochester, VT: Inner Traditions/Bear & Company, 2005. N.p. https://books.google.com/books?id=Rs5rAwAAQBAJ&dq.

347. Booth, Martin. *Cannabis: A History*. New York: Picador, 2003. 29-30.

348. Rosenbaum, Ron. "At Skull and Bones, Bush's Secret Club Initiates Ream Gore." *Observer*. April 23, 2001. http://observer.com/2001/04/at-skull-and-bones-bushs-secret-club-initiates-ream-gore-2/.

349. Neihardt, John G. *Black Elk Speaks: Being the Life Story of a Holy Man of the Oglala Sioux*. Lincoln, NE: University of Nebraska Press, 1961. Preface, ix.

350. Lummis, Charles F. *Some Strange Corners of Our Country: The Wonderland of the Southwest*. New York: The Century Co., 1898. 83.

351. Ibid. 84, 89.

352. Salak, K. "Ayahuasca." *National Geographic* online. March 1, 2006. http://www.nationalgeographic.com/adventure/0603/features/peru.html.

353. Booth. *Secret History*. 237-38.

354. Acosta, José de. *Natural and Moral History of the Indies*. Vol. 5, Ch. 26. Translated by Frances López-Morillas. Durham, NC: Duke University Press, 2002. 310.

355. Puthoff, Hal E. "CIA-Initiated Remote Viewing At Stanford Research Institute." *Journal of Scientific Exploration* 10(1) (March 1996): 63-76. http://www.biomindsuperpowers.com/Pages/CIA-InitiatedRV.html.

356. Sugrue, Thomas. *There is a River: The Story of Edgar Cayce*. Virginia Beach, VA: A.R.E. Press, 1994. 305.

357. Horn. *Zenith*. 177.

358. Booth. *Secret History*. 18.

359. Ibid. 42.

360. Hall. *Secret Teachings*. 101.

361. Ibid.

362. Chinmoy, Sri. *The Supernatural and the Beyond*. Jamaica, NY: Agni Press, 1973. 62.

363. Ankerberg, John and John Weldon. "What Eastern Gurus Say About Occult Practices." In Plain Site. February 23, 2014. http://www.inplainsite.org/html/eastern_gurus_say.html.

364. Hartmann, Franz. "The Dangers of Occultism." *Quest* (Jan-Feb 2006): 7-10.

365. Harner. *Cave and Cosmos.* 26.

366. Calvin, John. Edited by John T. McNeill. *Calvin: Institutes of the Christian Religion, Volume 1.* Louisville, KY: Westminster John Knox Press, 2006. 17.

367. Jones, David. *Sid Roth's It's Supernatural!* January 20, 2014. Online broadcast archive. http://sidroth.org/television/tv-archives/david-jones-0.

368. Ibid.

369. Rolleston, Frances. *Mazzaroth; or, The Constellations.* London: Gilbert and Rivington, 1862. 1:18.

370. Olcott, William Tyler. *Star Lore of All Ages: A Collection of Myths, Legends, and Facts Concerning the Constellations of the Northern Hemisphere.* New York and London: G. P. Putnam's Sons, 1911. 236-7.

371. Bullinger, E. W. *The Witness of the Stars.* New York: Cosimo Inc, 2007. 151.

372. Opsopaus, Ioannes Apollonius. "Sol - Helios - Sun." Chapter 18 in *The Pythagorean Tarot An Interpretation of the Major and Minor Arcana on Pythagorean and Alchemical Principles.* Woodbury, MN: Llewellyn, 1996. Reproduced online. Last updated February 10, 2005. http://web.eecs.utk.edu/~mclennan/BA/PT/M18.html.

373. *New Standard Encyclopedia.* Vol. 6. Chicago: Standard Educational, 1991. E-25-27.

374. Carnell, Simon. *Hare.* London: Reaktion Books, 2010. 71-3.

375. Deora, Eadha. "Hares and the Spring Equinox." Druidic Dawn. March 20, 2009. http://www.druidicdawn.org/node/1490.

376. Iles, Linda. "Wenet The Swift One: Unnut, Lady of Unu." Mirror of Isis. Accessed June 11, 2015. http://mirrorofisis.freeyellow.com/id599.html.

377. Bonwick, James. *Egyptian Belief and Modern Thought.* London: C. Kegan Paul & Company, 1878. 229-30.

378. Evans, George Ewart and David Thomson. *The Leaping Hare.* London: Faber & Faber, 2001. Electronic edition. N.p.

379. Day, Alfred Ely. *International Standard Bible Encyclopedia,* s.v. "Wolf." Online. Accessed June 11, 2015. http://www.internationalstandardbible.com/W/wolf.html.

380. Didorus Siculus. *The Historical Library of Diodorus the Sicilian: In Fifteen Books. To which are Added the Fragments of Diodorus, and Those Published by H. Valesius, I. Rhodomannus, and F. Ursinus.* Vol. 1. Translated by G. Booth. London: W. M'Dowall, 1814. 24.

381. *Chronicon Paschale.* Vol. 1. Bonn ed. 1832. 64; Layard, Austen Henry citing Birch. *Nineveh and Its Remains: With an Account of a Visit to the Chaldaean Christians of Kurdistan, and the Yezidis, Or Devil-worshippers, and an Enquiry Into the Manners and Arts of the Ancient Assyrians.* Vol. 2. London: John Murray, 1849. 440.

382. Kacsoh, Balint. "Books about the Origins of Hungarians." *Hungarian Studies Review* 40(2) (Fall 2013): 203.

383. Bauval, Robert. "The Giza Pyramids as a Stellar Representation of Orion's Belt." Robert Bauval's website. 2000. http://robertbauval.co.uk/articles/articles/gizaorion.html.

384. Bayer, Johann. *Uranometria: omnium asterismorum continens schemata, nova methodo delineata, aereis laminis expressa.* Augsburg: Christoph Mang, 1603. N.p. Reproduced by Linda Hall Library Digital Collections. Call number QB41.B293 1603. Accessed June 12, 2015. http://lhldigital.lindahall.org/cdm/ref/collection/astro_images/id/1805.

385. *Behind the Name*, s.v. "Medusa." Accessed June 14, 2015. http://www.behindthename.com/name/medusa.

386. Lanman, Charles Rockwell. *A Sanskrit Reader: With Vocabulary and Notes.* Boston: Ginn and Company, 1888. 220; Dolmage, Jay. "Metis, Mêêtis, Mestiza, Medusa: Rhetorical Bodiesacross Rhetorical Traditions." *Rhetoric Review* 28(1) (January 2009): 1-28. doi: 10.1080/07350190802540690.

387. Seiss, Joseph A. *The Gospel in the Stars.* Grand Rapids, MI: Kregel Publications, 1972. 74.

388. "Who are the Nicolaitans?" BibleStudy.org. Accessed June 12, 2015. http://www.biblestudy.org/basicart/why-does-god-hate-practices-of-the-nicolaitans.html.

389. Flynn, David. *Collection.* 231.

390. Liddell, Henry George and Robert Scott. *A Greek-English Lexicon*, s.v. "Ἐγγόνασιν." Oxford: Clarendon Press, 1940.

391. Chartrand, Mark R. and Helmut K. Wimmer. *Skyguide: A Field Guide for Amateur Astronomers.* New York: Golden Press, 1982. 160.

392. Allen, Richard Hinckley. *Star-names and Their Meanings.* New York and London: G. E. Stechert, 1899. 278.

393. Koch-Westenholz, Ulla Susanne. *Mesopotamian Astrology: An Introduction to Babylonian and Assyrian Celestial Divination.* Copenhagen: Museum Tusculanum Press, 1995. 207.

394. Dictionary.com, s.v. "Sphinx." Accessed June 14, 2015. http://dictionary.reference.com/browse/sphinx.

395. Bullinger. *Witness.* 35.

396. Rolleston. *Mazzaroth.* 2:17.

397. St. Clair, George. "The Atlas Legend." *The Westminster Review* 150 (1898): 648n2.

398. Flynn, David. *Collection.* 141-145.

399. Larson, Frederick A. "The Starry Dance." The Star of Bethlehem. Accessed December 21, 2002. http://www.bethlehemstar.net/dance/dance.htm.

400. Clarke, Scott. "Astonishing! | The KING Is Born in 2017!" YouTube. August 19, 2013. https://youtu.be/v5dyEnZFu0w.

401. Goodgame, Peter. "Global Capitalism: Mankind's great end-times Maximum Temptation Delivery System." Red Moon Rising blog. Accessed August 7, 2015. http://redmoonrising.com/capitalism.html.

402. Gerry, Joseph J. "Religious Toleration from the Christian Perspective." From an address presented to the Masonic Research Lodge of Maine on

November 22, 1997. The Maine Lodge of Research. http://www.mainemason.org/
mlr/gerry.htm.

403. Pope John Paul II and Vittorio Messori. *Crossing the Threshold of
Hope*. New York: Alfred A. Knopf, 2005. 82.

CPSIA information can be obtained
at www.ICGtesting.com
Printed in the USA
LVOW12s0033200117

521611LV00002B/115/P